A Brief History of Analytic Philosophy

A Brief History of Analytic Philosophy

From Russell to Rawls

By Stephen P. Schwartz

WILEY-BLACKWELL

A John Wiley & Sons, Ltd., Publication

Wiley-Blackwell is an imprint of John Wiley & Sons, formed by the merger of Wiley's global Scientific, Technical and Medical business with Blackwell Publishing.

Registered Office
John Wiley & Sons Ltd, The Atrium, Southern Gate, Chichester, West Sussex, PO19 8SQ, UK

Editorial Offices
350 Main Street, Malden, MA 02148-5020, USA
9600 Garsington Road, Oxford, OX4 2DQ, UK
The Atrium, Southern Gate, Chichester, West Sussex, PO19 8SQ, UK

For details of our global editorial offices, for customer services, and for information about how to apply for permission to reuse the copyright material in this book please see our website at www.wiley.com/wiley-blackwell.

Library of Congress Cataloging-in-Publication Data

Schwartz, Stephen P., 1944–
 A brief history of analytic philosophy: from Russell to Rawls / by Stephen P. Schwartz.
 pages   cm
 Includes bibliographical references and index.
 ISBN 978-0-470-67207-5 (hardback) – ISBN 978-0-470-67208-2 (paperback)
 1. Analysis (Philosophy)–History. I. Title.
 B808.5.S39 2013
 146′.409–dc23
                                                              2011050471

A catalogue record for this book is available from the British Library.

Typeset in 10/12pt Palatino by Laserwords Private Limited, Chennai, India.

1   2012

To my wife, Diane

Contents

Contents

Contents

Preface

Analytic philosophy was the dominant Anglo-American philosophical movement of the twentieth century, and remains dominant today. Enough time has now passed that we are able to have historical perspective on this vital philosophical tradition. My aim with this book is to provide a general overview of the leading philosophers, theories, movements, and controversies of analytic philosophy, as well as some idea of its cultural, political, and social setting.

The Anglo-American analytic tradition starts with Bertrand Russell and G. E. Moore at the beginning of the twentieth century. The most recent works that I focus on are from the 1970s. The Epilogue is a brief discussion of the development of analytic philosophy from 1980 to the present day, and a look to the future.

I have not assumed that the reader has any formal background in philosophy. Analytic philosophy is technical, however. It grew out of developments in logic and the foundations of mathematics. Leaving out all technicalities would mean leaving out many interesting and central aspects of analytic philosophy. Rather than clutter the text with explanations of terms and issues that would be familiar to those readers who have studied philosophy, I have provided background snippets at the end of each chapter. These are indicated in the text as [*Background n.m* – Subject]. Those who would find the background helpful can flip to the end of the chapter. Others can skip them. The use of symbolic logic at places in the text is unavoidable. At the end of Chapter 1 I have provided a background on basic symbolism for those unfamiliar with symbolic logic. At the end of each chapter I have appended an annotated list of further readings for those interested in pursuing topics in more depth or following out other tentacles.

For each philosopher that I discuss I have given relevant and representative quotes to illustrate my expositions. I want the philosophers to have a chance to speak for themselves, and to give a sense of how they sound in their own voices. I hope to inspire readers to seek out the original sources and pursue them on their own. But for many, I realize, this book will be their only chance to engage with many of these texts. For each quote I give the source including page number. Often I give two publication dates. Many of the works I cite are classics that have been reprinted. Thus I may quote from a 1978 reprint of an article that was originally published in 1912. I indicate this by (Author's name 1978/1912, p. *nn*). Refer to the bibliography. I transcribe these quotes exactly as they appear in the original texts. I have not edited them for consistency of spelling and punctuation. I have usually not included the works cited in the text in the suggested further readings, since they are obvious choices for further reading and study.

I have given standard, accepted interpretations when they square with my understanding of the original texts. I have not engaged in historical disputes or attempted to adjudicate among various interpretations of the philosophers' ideas. This history is meant to be a start, not the final word. It would be an appropriate text in courses such as Analytic Philosophy, Twentieth-Century Philosophy, and Contemporary Philosophy.

The structure of the book is basically chronological beginning about 1905 and extending into the 1970s. The history of analytic philosophy is not, however, a direct chronological development. Some strands that differ markedly are simultaneous. Within the tradition of analytic philosophy, criticizing, rethinking, and reworking former notions is crucial. Major figures such as Bertrand Russell and Ludwig Wittgenstein changed their views, attacking their earlier selves. The story of analytic philosophy is the story of analytic philosophers struggling with and against themselves, and each other; struggling with and against its origins, and former movements and doctrines. Later parts of the story can only be understood as reactions to earlier parts. The reader will not find discussion of major thinkers limited to single chapters. Rather, the philosophical stories of Russell, Wittgenstein, Carnap, Quine, and others weave through several chapters. I have provided a useable index for those who want to trace a particular thinker or issue through the history. I have included a list of the leading analytic philosophers at the end of the introduction. No doubt others would have made somewhat different lists, but anybody familiar with the history of analytic philosophy will recognize that the list I give suffers, if at all, only by omission.

I devote a single chapter to ethics in the analytic tradition (Chapter 8). After G. E. Moore's *Principia Ethica* of 1903, ethics was out of the mainstream of analytic philosophy until the 1960s. None of the major figures of analytic philosophy before 1950 (with the exception of early Moore) did much work on ethics, because they thought that it was outside the province of philosophy. Ethical issues and questions about the analysis of ethical language come up only briefly in earlier chapters. Starting in the 1950s and continuing today a great expansion of interest and work in ethics and value theory has occurred for reasons that I explain in the text. My main focus has been on logic, philosophy of language, metaphysics, and epistemology as was the main focus of analytic philosophy from 1905 to the 1950s and 1960s. I provide only a brief discussion of analytic philosophy since the 1970s for several reasons (Epilogue). For one thing, it is current events, not history. We are too close to have a historical view on the last 30 years of philosophy. For another, work in analytic philosophy has become so specialized and technical that the text would be little more than a collection of technical explanations. Lastly, the volume of publications due to the computer, the Internet, and the consequent increased communications has expanded beyond the point where any overview is possible.

Vincent van Gogh wrote: "I exaggerate, I sometimes make changes to the subject, but still I don't invent the whole of the painting; on the contrary, I find it readymade – but to be untangled – in the real world." This is a good description of history writing, and of philosophy itself. We find the subject in the real world to be untangled. I have tried to untangle the story of analytic philosophy, without too much exaggeration and invention, I hope. But I am an analytic philosopher. I have taught philosophy since the mid-1960s and made my own modest contributions in print. I cannot keep my personal feelings out of the story entirely. I have known, listened to, studied with, talked to, or at least met many of the leading analytic philosophers. I am a participant, not an observer. At places I express my opinions and try to support them briefly. I am personally and passionately involved in the enlightening and edifying enterprise of analytic philosophy.

I would like to thank the following for their help: My colleagues in the Ithaca College Department of Philosophy and Religion, Frederik Kaufman and Craig Duncan, read and made valuable suggestions on parts of the manuscript. John Rosenthal of the Ithaca College Department of Mathematics patiently and kindly helped me with difficult parts of the text. Gerald Hull read much of the manuscript and made many helpful comments, as did Steven Lee on an earlier version. I would also like to thank Eric Lerner for helpful suggestions. My wife, Diane Schwartz, read the entire manuscript as I was writing and gave me valuable suggestions from a non-philosophical perspective. I would also like to thank John Heil and Peter Singer for reading parts of the manuscript and for their useful comments and suggestions. Two anonymous reviewers for Wiley-Blackwell made extensive and very helpful comments on the entire manuscript. I owe them a special debt of gratitude. I would also like to thank Sheryl Englund for generous help with practical aspects of my project and Jeff Dean of Wiley-Blackwell for encouragement and guidance. I, of course, am solely and entirely responsible for the contents of this book including any errors it may contain.

Stephen P. Schwartz
Ithaca 2012

Acknowledgments

The photo of Pembroke Lodge was made available by the kind permission of Sian Davies. I would also like to acknowledge and thank the photographer, Paul Fairbairn-Tennant.

The Checker Shadow Illusion ©1995, Edward H. Adelson.

The picture of the Wittgenstein House in Vienna is due to Robert Schediwy and is made available under the terms of Creative Commons: http://creativecommons.org/licenses/by-sa/3.0/deed.en.

The cartoon on p. 314 is due to Brian K. Johnson.

Introduction: What is Analytic Philosophy?

> *Modern analytical empiricism, of which I have been giving an outline,*
> *differs from that of Locke, Berkeley, and Hume by its incorporation of*
> *mathematics and its development of a powerful logical technique. (Russell*
> *1945, p. 834)*

I have before me on my desk a famous book entitled *What is Mathematics?* In it you will find basic descriptions of number theory, algebra, geometry, topology, and so on. What you will not find is a definition or explanation of what mathematics is, even though the first section of the book is also titled "What is Mathematics?" The final answer: "For scholars and layman alike it is not philosophy but active experience in mathematics itself that alone can answer the question: What is mathematics?" (Courant and Robbins, 1941, no page number) In the same spirit, my answer to the question "What is analytic philosophy?" is – the rest of this book starting with Chapter 1. Analytic philosophy is what the philosophers on the list "Leading Analytic Philosophers" (located at the end of this chapter) did philosophically.

If a historian had to give an exact definition in terms of necessary and sufficient conditions of his subject, no histories would get written. I have another book before me on my desk. It is also a classic: *A Brief History of Science* by A. Rupert Hall and Marie Boas Hall (1964). This is a wonderful overview of the development of science from the ancient world to today, but the book contains no definition of "science, " no discussion of what science is, or what distinguishes science from other endeavors. If the Halls had to answer these questions first, they would still be working on them and their history would never have been

A Brief History of Analytic Philosophy: From Russell to Rawls, First Edition. Stephen P. Schwartz.
© 2012 John Wiley & Sons, Inc. Published 2012 by John Wiley & Sons, Inc.

written. Philosophers of science, even now, do not have settled answers to these questions. The Halls prudently begin their book with the history of the origins of science in the ancient world. They do not worry about the demarcation problem: the problem of how to distinguish science, the subject of their brief history, from other pursuits. It would also be prudent of me to avoid the vexed question of the demarcation of analytic philosophy from other philosophical traditions.

Yet, we have a sense that an overview of mathematics or a history of science does deal with a delimited subject matter. A history of science is not the same as a history of the English novel or a history of modern art. I, along with my philosophical colleagues, recognize that analytic philosophy is a distinct tradition even if we are not quite prepared to draw the exact borders of it. A history of analytic philosophy is not the same as a history of twentieth-century Catholic philosophy, or Marxist philosophy, or twentieth-century Continental philosophy, or twentieth-century American philosophy.

So, so much for prudence. I'll try to say something useful in answer to the question "What is analytic philosophy?" (Without having any pretense to being able to give necessary and sufficient conditions for demarcating the tradition.)

Analytic philosophy begins in the first years of the twentieth century and is the dominant tradition in philosophy today. Of course, analytic philosophy is not the same as it was in its early days. Like any movement or tradition, it evolved due to catastrophic political events, advances in technology, the influence of other subjects and disciplines, and its own searching self-scrutiny and criticism.

Analytic philosophy developed out of many sources. Among them were the British tradition of empiricism, mentioned in the leading quote by Bertrand Russell, and developments in the natural sciences in the late nineteenth and early twentieth centuries, especially physics. But the chief impetus was the revolutionary advances in logic, set theory, and the foundations of mathematics in the late nineteenth and very early twentieth centuries. For philosophy the most important of these innovations was the development of symbolic logic, which became the indispensable tool and source of ideas for analytic philosophers. Analytic philosophers got their inspiration, ideas, problems, and methods from British empiricism, formal logic, mathematics, and natural science. (For a definition of empiricism see *Background 1.1* – Epistemology: empiricism versus rationalism, p. 39. For symbolic logic see *Background 1.3* – Mathematical logic of *PM* versus traditional Aristotelian logic and note on symbolism, p. 40.)

How did analytic philosophy evolve and mature? Toward the middle of the twentieth century many analytic philosophers were able to adopt a more distanced and critical attitude to empiricism, science, and mathematics than its earlier practitioners had embraced. This allowed an expansion of analytic ethics, renewed interest in metaphysics, and increased attention to and appreciation of philosophers of the past, starting with the ancient Greeks. Ethicists, metaphysicians, and historians of philosophy brought to their subject the methods of analytic philosophy: clarity of expression, logical argumentation, direct and extensive dialectical interchange among philosophers, and a piecemeal scientific approach to problems, but they left behind the more doctrinaire aspects of the early movement. (All of this is described in detail in the following chapters.)

The name "analytic philosophy" refers more to the methods of analytic philosophy than to any particular doctrine that analytic philosophers have all shared.[1] An analytic philosopher analyzes problems, concepts, issues, and arguments. She breaks them down into their parts, dissects them, to find their important features. Insight comes from seeing how things are put together and how they can be prized apart; how they are constructed and how they can be reconstructed. Symbolic logic was and remains the most distinctive tool of analytic philosophers.

Analytic philosophers have always struggled with themselves and each other, their tradition, its origins and ideas. No feature of analytic philosophy has gone unchallenged by other analytic philosophers. After World War II many analytic philosophers in Great Britain reacted against the overreliance, as they saw it, on symbolic logic, natural science, and formal analysis. American philosophers around the same time attacked what they claimed were the unjustified dogmas of analytic philosophy. One of the perennial issues that analytic philosophers focus on is method, including such questions as: How much should we rely on formal logic? Is natural science the only source of reliable knowledge? Should philosophy attempt to be scientific? Analytic philosophy, its methods and doctrines, is one of analytic philosophers' favorite subjects to ponder.

Analytic philosophy is a dialectical enterprise that is always struggling with itself. This is why defining analytic philosophy is so difficult. It is not a unified movement or school. It is loosely organized around a set of problems, methods, and issues but no party line on these has

---

[1] The word "analytic" in "analytic philosophy" does not mean the same as the term used in "the analytic/synthetic distinction." That is a different, but distantly related, concept. (See *Background 1.2* – A priori, analytic, necessary, p. 40.)

ever defined analytic philosophy. Analytic philosophers look to Frege, Russell, Wittgenstein, and Moore as the patriarchs of our large extended and argumentative family.

Geographically, analytic philosophy began almost simultaneously in the very early twentieth century in England and in German-speaking countries. With the rise of the Nazis in the 1930s, most analytic philosophers in Austria and Germany emigrated to Britain or North America. Despite the stresses of World War II, this influx of brilliant minds produced tremendous renewed energy and optimism for analytic philosophy in England and the United States. Today almost all philosophy departments in English-speaking countries would self-describe their orientation as analytic. Interest and participation in analytic philosophy has increased dramatically in Continental Europe and Scandinavia in the past few decades.

As a cultural phenomenon analytic philosophy was an expression of modernism in philosophy.[2] As a loose movement in visual art, literature, and music, modernism began in the nineteenth century but gained cultural dominance after the catastrophic Great War of 1914-18. Like analytic philosophy, modernism cannot be precisely defined. Modernism is characterized by rejection of past traditions; experimentation with new forms that can be shocking and disturbing, reflecting the cultural disillusionment of the post-World War I era; attention to language and method, or surface in the case of painting; anxiety about technology and science, but also utilization of new developments.

In literature the best representative of modernism is James Joyce's *Ulysses*. We also think of such authors as William Faulkner and Virginia Woolf as being paradigmatically modernist. Modernist authors reject the traditional expectation that a novel will comprise a sequential storyline, with plot, character development, and so on. Instead the modernist novel is characterized by fractured time, no identifiable story or plot, stream of consciousness, experimentation with language. In music modernist composers moved away from tunes, harmony, and key structure. Such composers as Stravinsky intentionally made their music dissonant and discordant. Twelve tone composers such as Schoenberg used a new formal system that abandoned traditions of classical Western music. Modernism in painting begins with the impressionists and characterizes the entire development of modern art. Especially beginning with Cezanne, artists more and more got away

---

[2] Modernism is not to be confused with modern. "Modern" means different things in different contexts. Modern philosophy is usually considered to start with Descartes about 1640. Modern art starts with the impressionists around 1870.

from depicting recognizable objects. They rejected the "old master" traditions of pictorial art. Picasso and then others eventually moved toward abstract art. Modernist painters were more interested in the surfaces of their paintings as objects than in other objects which their painting would depict as a mirror or through a window.

The basic aspects of modernism – rejection of past traditions, experimentation with new methods and forms; fascination with and anxiety about technology and use of new technical methods; focusing on method, surface, expression, and language – all characterize analytic philosophy. Analytic philosophy was born from new technical developments in logic and the foundations of mathematics. Analytic philosophers saw themselves, initially, as revolutionary, breaking with the past traditions of Western philosophy. They saw their work as freeing philosophy and even society, from its past forms and obsessions. Analytic philosophers, especially Wittgenstein and those influenced by him, experimented with new ways of expressing their views. Wittgenstein, as you will see in Chapter 2, did not express his philosophy in sequential arguments as did traditional philosophers, nor did several other analytic philosophers. Early analytic philosophers rejected virtually all of past philosophy and would only rely on science to provide knowledge. Analytic philosophers with a formalist bent filled their pages with arcane symbols. The evolution of analytic philosophy exhibits the conflict between formalism and expressionism that we see in modern art. I am thinking of the contrast between the cubists and some abstract painters such as Mondrian on the one hand and van Gogh and the German expressionists on the other. Modernism is reflected in both an extreme formalism and an ardent expressionism. Analytic philosophy went through this internal struggle most stridently just after World War II, but it is present throughout its history. See especially Chapter 4.

Modernism is a point of contact between analytic philosophy and Continental philosophy. Among Continental philosophers, Nietzsche and Kierkegaard can be seen as anticipating or inspiring modernist forms of philosophical activity. Among later Continental philosophers, Heidegger, the French existentialists Camus and Sartre, and later deconstructionist and post-modernist philosophers (despite the title) embody modernism. Viewed as cultural phenomena of the twentieth century, Continental philosophy and analytic philosophy are brothers in arms.

Analytic philosophy, as a cultural phenomenon, was never as obsessively modernist as painting and music in the twentieth century (nor as obsessively modernist as some Continental philosophers such as Heidegger), and always retained a commitment to the essence of philosophy – reasoned argumentation – although with Wittgenstein and some ordinary language philosophers this is difficult to see through the mists. Analytic philosophers rejected the pretensions of the Enlightenment philosophers but not their commitment to reason. Analytic philosophers aimed to replace what they considered to be the outmoded ways of traditional philosophy with their new techniques based on symbolic logic, the analysis of language, and scientific methods.

This is the story that will unfold in the chapters that follow.

Leading Analytic Philosophers

*Gottlob Frege 1848–1925 German
Bertrand Russell 1872–1970 British
George Edward Moore 1873–1958 British (known as G. E. Moore)
Otto Neurath 1882–1945 Austrian
Moritz Schlick 1882–1936 German
Ludwig Wittgenstein 1889–1951 Austrian/British
Rudolf Carnap 1891–1970 German/American
Hans Reichenbach 1891–1953 German/American
Gilbert Ryle 1900–1976 British
Karl Popper 1902–1994 Austrian/British
*Alfred Tarski 1902–1983 Polish/American
Carl Hempel 1905–1997 German/American
*Kurt Gödel 1906–1978 Austrian/American
Nelson Goodman 1906–1998 American
Willard Van Orman Quine 1908–2000 American (W. V. Quine or W. V. O. Quine)
Charles Leslie Stevenson 1908–1979 American (Charles L. Stevenson or C. L. Stevenson)
Max Black 1909–1988 Russian/British/American
Alfred Jules Ayer 1910–1989 British (A. J. Ayer)
John Austin 1911–1960 British (J. L. Austin)
Norman Malcolm 1911–1990 American
Wilfrid Sellars 1912–1989 American
*Alan Turing 1912–1954 British
Herbert Paul Grice 1913–1988 British (Paul Grice)
Roderick Chisholm 1916–1999 American
Donald Davidson 1917–2003 American
Gertrude Elizabeth Margaret Anscombe 1919–2001 British (Elizabeth Anscombe or G. E. M. Anscombe)
Richard Mervyn Hare 1919–2002 British (R. M. Hare)
Peter Frederick Strawson 1919–2006 British (Peter Strawson or P.F. Strawson)

John Jamieson Carswell Smart 1920 Australian (J. J. C. Smart)
Philippa Foot 1920–2010 British
Ruth Barcan Marcus 1921 American
John Rawls 1921–2002 American
Thomas Kuhn 1922–1996 American
Michael Dummett 1925 British
David Malet Armstrong 1926 Australian (D. M. Armstrong)
Stanley Cavell 1926 American
Hilary Putnam 1926 American
*Noam Chomsky 1928 American
Keith Donnellan 1931 American
Richard Rorty 1931–2007 American
Alvin Plantinga 1932 American
John Searle 1932 American
Jaegwon Kim 1934 Korean/American
Thomas Nagel 1937 American
Robert Nozick 1938–2002 American
Saul Kripke 1940 American
Robert Stalnaker 1940 American
David Lewis 1941–2001 American
Peter Singer 1946 Australian

*See *Background 5.1* – Are Frege, Gödel, Tarski, Turing, and Chomsky analytic philosophers? (p. 196). Although I include Frege, Gödel, Tarski, Turing, and Chomsky on this list because of their influence, I do not consider them to be analytic philosophers.

Further Reading

Philosophical Analysis in the Twentieth Century by Scott Soames (Princeton University Press 2003) is a tendentious and controversial two volume history of analytic philosophy. His approach is selective and technical, but useful on the topics he discusses.

Two works on the history and nature of analytic philosophy are *Twentieth-Century Analytic Philosophy* by Avrum Stroll (Columbia University Press 2000) and *What is Analytic Philosophy* Hans-Johann Glock (Cambridge University Press 2008). Glock is generally reliable, but like Soames selective. Stroll is uneven. His extensive discussion of the material I cover in Chapter 7 (the new theory of reference) is unreliable.

A good place to go for individual essays on many of the leading analytic philosophers is *A Companion to Analytic Philosophy* edited by A. P. Martinich and E. David Sosa (Wiley-Blackwell 2005). In this impressive collection each of the 40 articles is written by a different leading scholar.

1

Russell and Moore

The question which Kant put at the beginning of his philosophy, namely "How is pure mathematics possible?" is an interesting and difficult one, to which every philosophy which is not purely sceptical must find some answer. (Russell 1959a/1912, p. 84)

Empiricism, Mathematics, and Symbolic Logic

Bertrand Russell – aristocrat (3rd Earl Russell), anti-war activist, prolific writer, and brilliant philosopher and mathematician – is the father of Anglo-American analytic philosophy. Russell did the hard work of expounding and promulgating the new symbolic logic that was to revolutionize the method of philosophy. Equally important for analytic philosophy, he introduced others to the works of Gottlob Frege and Ludwig Wittgenstein, who might otherwise have languished unappreciated. Russell proposed and energetically pursued philosophical issues that were keenly examined by philosophers throughout the twentieth century. Without Bertrand Russell's work, especially the work he produced early in his career in logic and the philosophy of language, there would have been no Anglo-American analytic philosophy.

Russell says that Frege was the pioneer and no doubt this is true. "Many matters which, when I was young, baffled me by the vagueness of all that had been said about them, are now amenable to an exact technique, which makes possible the kind of progress that is customary in science. . . . [T]he pioneer was Frege, but he remained solitary until his old age"(Russell 1963/1944, p. 20).[1] Russell's optimism about

---

[1] Citations here and throughout are indicated as (Name date/original publication date if significantly different, page)

A Brief History of Analytic Philosophy: From Russell to Rawls, First Edition. Stephen P. Schwartz.
© 2012 John Wiley & Sons, Inc. Published 2012 by John Wiley & Sons, Inc.

philosophical progress may seem overstated, but not his judgment of Frege. Frege did revolutionary work on the foundations of mathematics and was the first to clarify and investigate issues in the philosophy of language that were central to twentieth-century philosophy and are still central today. Indeed Gottlob Frege *was* the pioneer of the techniques that gave life to analytic philosophy, but he would not have had an impact without Russell's influence. Frege would have remained solitary. Russell brought Frege to the attention of other philosophers and mathematicians, especially in the English-speaking world, and developed and improved Frege's pioneering ideas.

Russell's greatest contribution to logic, philosophy, and mathematics was his publication of *Principia Mathematica* with Alfred North Whitehead (published in three volumes, 1910–13). Based on ideas originally articulated by Frege in the late nineteenth century, Russell developed and founded the field of symbolic logic. Symbolic logic today is central not only to philosophy but to many other areas including mathematics and computer science.[2] In addition to *Principia Mathematica* (often referred to simply as *PM*), Russell expounded the ideas and methods of the new symbolic logic energetically in his *Principles of Mathematics* and many other influential publications early in the twentieth century. The influence, importance, and central role of *PM* cannot be overemphasized. For example, Kurt Gödel titled his historic paper "On formally undecidable propositions of *Principia Mathematica* and related systems." (More on this influential mathematical paper below (see pp. 162–4).)

The methodology that gives analytic philosophy its strength and structure is the logic and philosophy of language generated by the original work of Frege, Russell, and Whitehead.

Their results in logic and the philosophy of language have also had major impacts in other areas of philosophy. The revolution in logic in the early years of the twentieth century gave analytic philosophers the tools to articulate and defend a sophisticated form of empiricism. [*Background 1.1* – Epistemology: empiricism versus rationalism (The background snippets are found at the end of the chapter.)] With the new tools in logic and philosophy of language, philosophers were able to repair the flaws and gaps in thinking of the classical British empiricists. The major gap was the lack of an explanation of how pure mathematics is possible. Modern logic as developed by Frege, Russell, and Whitehead yielded definite results in the foundations of mathematics and the philosophy of language that, though technical

---

[2] *Principia Mathematica* was voted number 23 of the 100 most important nonfiction books of the twentieth century – the highest rated philosophy book. (http://www.infoplease.com/ipea/A0777310.html)

and expounded in daunting detail, went to the heart of epistemological issues. Empiricists could claim to have solved the outstanding problems plaguing their theory – namely our knowledge of mathematics – by using the techniques of mathematical logic. (This is explained in the next section.)

Although Russell was uneasy with empiricism, his sympathy was with the classical British empiricists. Virtually all analytic philosophers have shared this sympathy while at the same time becoming increasingly uneasy with the details and presuppositions of classical empiricism. Russell could not accept "pure empiricism" – the view that all knowledge is derived from immediate sensory experience – but sought to move only as far from it as was absolutely necessary. Speaking of his very early views Russell says: "it seemed to me that pure empiricism (which I was disposed to accept) must lead to skepticism . . . "(Russell 1959b/1924, p. 31). Even worse than skepticism, Russell came to believe that pure empiricism led to solipsism and could not account for our knowledge of scientific laws or our beliefs about the future. Still, Russell always seemed to feel that these were problems for empiricism, not reasons to discard it outright.

Despite his sympathy with empiricism, in places Russell sounds like an unabashed rationalist: "It is, then, possible to make assertions, not only about cases which we have been able to observe, but about all actual or possible cases. The existence of assertions of this kind and their necessity for almost all pieces of knowledge which are said to be founded on experience shows that traditional empiricism is in error and that there is *a priori* and universal knowledge" (Russell 1973, p. 292. From a lecture given in 1911). [*Background 1.2* – A priori, analytic, necessary]

Despite his wavering philosophical sympathies, Russell's mathematical logic gave later empiricists the tools to respond to the troubling difficulties with their position that Russell was pointing out. Mathematics is *a priori* and universal, so how can it be empirical? Twentieth-century analytic philosophy got its first shot of energy from a plausible answer to this question – an answer offered by the logical investigations of Frege and Russell.[3]

Frege and Russell were able to use symbolic logic to reconceptualize the very nature of mathematics and our mathematical knowledge (Figure 1.1). I must emphasize that symbolic logic as developed in

---

[3] Whitehead, also a brilliant philosopher, logician, and mathematician did much of the technical work of developing symbolic logic but did not play the kind of role that Russell did in publishing it, publicizing it, and making it accessible to fellow philosophers, and showing how fruitful and valuable a tool it was.

$*11 \cdot 401.$ $\vdash :: (x, y) : \phi(x, y) . \equiv . \psi(x, y) : \supset :.$

$\qquad (x, y) : \phi(x, y) . \chi(x, y) . \equiv . \psi(x, y) . \chi(x, y)$ $\left[*11 \cdot 4 \frac{\chi}{\theta} . \text{Id} \right]$

$*11 \cdot 41.$ $\vdash :. (\exists x, y) . \phi(x, y) . \mathbf{v} : (\exists x, y) . \psi(x, y) :$

$\qquad \equiv : (\exists x, y) : \phi(x, y) . \mathbf{v} . \psi(x, y)$ $[*10 \cdot 42 \cdot 281]$

$*11 \cdot 42.$ $\vdash :. (\exists x, y) . \phi(x, y) . \psi(x, y) . \supset : (\exists x, y) . \phi(x, y) : (\exists x, y) . \psi(x, y)$ $[*10 \cdot 5]$

$*11 \cdot 421.$ $\vdash :. (x, y) . \phi(x, y) . \mathbf{v} . (x, y) . \psi(x, y) : \supset : (x, y) : \phi(x, y) . \mathbf{v} . \psi(x, y)$

$\qquad \left[*11 \cdot 42 \frac{\sim\phi, \sim\psi}{\phi, \psi} . \text{Transp} . *4 \cdot 56 \right]$

$*11 \cdot 43.$ $\vdash :. (\exists x, y) : \phi(x, y) . \supset . p : \equiv : (x, y) . \phi(x, y) . \supset . p$ $[*10 \cdot 34 \cdot 281]$

$*11 \cdot 44.$ $\vdash :. (x, y) : \phi(x, y) . \mathbf{v} . p : \equiv : (x, y) . \phi(x, y) . \mathbf{v} . p$ $[*10 \cdot 2 \cdot 271]$

$*11 \cdot 45.$ $\vdash :. (\exists x, y) : p . \phi(x, y) : \equiv : p : (\exists x, y) . \phi(x, y)$ $[*10 \cdot 35 \cdot 281]$

$*11 \cdot 46.$ $\vdash :. (\exists x, y) : p . \supset . \phi(x, y) : \equiv : p . \supset . (\exists x, y) . \phi(x, y)$ $[*10 \cdot 37 \cdot 281]$

$*11 \cdot 47.$ $\vdash :. (x, y) : p . \phi(x, y) : \equiv : p : (x, y) . \phi(x, y)$ $[*10 \cdot 33 \cdot 271]$

$*11 \cdot 5.$ $\vdash :. (\exists x) : \sim \{(y) . \phi(x, y)\} : \equiv : \sim \{(x, y) . \phi(x, y)\} : \equiv : (\exists x, y) . \sim \phi(x, y)$

Dem.

$\qquad \vdash . *10 \cdot 253 . \supset \vdash :. (\exists x) : \sim \{(y) : \phi(x, y)\} : \equiv : \sim \{(x) : (y) . \phi(x, y)\} :$

$\qquad [(*11 \cdot 01)] \qquad\qquad\qquad \equiv : \sim \{(x, y) . \phi(x, y)\}$ (1)

$\qquad \vdash . *10 \cdot 253 . \supset \vdash : \sim \{(y) . \phi(x, y)\} . \qquad \equiv . (\exists y) . \sim \phi(x, y) :$

$\qquad [*10 \cdot 11 \cdot 281] \supset \vdash :. (\exists x) : \sim \{(y) . \phi(x, y)\} : \equiv : (\exists x) : (\exists y) . \sim \phi(x, y) :$

$\qquad [(*11 \cdot 03)] \qquad\qquad\qquad \equiv : (\exists x, y) . \sim \phi(x, y)$ (2)

$\qquad \vdash . (1) . (2) . \supset \vdash . \text{Prop}$

$*11 \cdot 51.$ $\vdash :. (\exists x) : (y) . \phi(x, y) : \equiv : \sim \{(x) : (\exists y) . \sim \phi(x, y)\}$

Dem.

$\qquad \vdash . *10 \cdot 252 . \text{Transp} . \supset \vdash :. (\exists x) : (y) . \phi(x, y) : \equiv : \sim [(x) : \sim (y) . \phi(x, y)]$ (1)

$\qquad \vdash . *10 \cdot 253 . \supset \vdash :. \sim (y) . \phi(x, y) . \qquad \equiv : (\exists y) . \sim \phi(x, y) :.$

$\qquad [*10 \cdot 11 \cdot 271] \supset \vdash :. (x) : \sim (y) . \phi(x, y) : \qquad \equiv : (x) : (\exists y) . \sim \phi(x, y) :.$

$\qquad [\text{Transp}] \qquad \supset \vdash :. \sim [(x) : \sim \{(y) . \phi(x, y)\}] . \qquad \equiv : \sim [(x) : (\exists y) . \sim \phi(x, y)]$ (2)

$\qquad \vdash . (1) . (2) . \supset \vdash . \text{Prop}$

$*11 \cdot 52.$ $\vdash :. (\exists x, y) . \phi(x, y) . \psi(x, y) . \equiv . \sim [(x, y) : \phi(x, y) . \supset . \sim \psi(x, y)]$

Dem.

$\qquad \vdash . *4 \cdot 51 \cdot 62 . \supset$

$\qquad \vdash :. \sim \{\phi(x, y) . \psi(x, y)\} . \qquad \equiv : \phi(x, y) . \supset . \sim \psi(x, y)$ (1)

$\qquad \vdash . (1) . *11 \cdot 11 \cdot 33 . \supset$

$\qquad \vdash :. (x, y) . \sim \{\phi(x, y) . \psi(x, y)\} : \equiv : (x, y) : \phi(x, y) . \supset . \sim \psi(x, y)$ (2)

$\qquad \vdash : (2) . \text{Transp} . *11 \cdot 22 . \supset \vdash . \text{Prop}$

$*11 \cdot 521.$ $\vdash :. \sim (\exists x, y) . \phi(x, y) . \sim \psi(x, y) . \equiv : (x, y) : \phi(x, y) . \supset . \psi(x, y)$

$\qquad \left[*11 \cdot 52 . \text{Transp} . \frac{\sim \psi(x, y)}{\psi(x, y)} \right]$

Figure 1.1 This is a page chosen at random from *Principia Mathematica*. *PM* is extremely daunting and is today studied only by specialists, although it has an accessible introduction that is a brief overview of symbolic logic.

PM was not just the use of symbols – so that for example we use "∨" instead of the word "or" and "(∃x)" for "some." That would be impressive perhaps and simplifying in some ways, but not revolutionary. The revolution in logic, pioneered by Frege, and expounded by *PM* was based on the concept of treating logic mathematically, and then treating mathematics as a form of logic. This is Frege's and Russell's logicism.[4] [*Background 1.3* – Mathematical logic of *PM* versus traditional Aristotelian logic and a note on symbolism]

Symbolic logic is not only of technical interest for those concerned about the foundations of mathematics. Virtually every philosophy major in every college and university in the United States and elsewhere is required to pass a course in symbolic logic. Not only philosophy majors, but other students as well – computer science majors, mathematics majors, not to mention English majors – take symbolic logic courses. Symbolic logic has also been central to the development of computers, and it is now a branch of mathematics, and is an indispensable tool for theoretical linguistics and virtually anyone working in technical areas of the study of language.

Symbolic logic has been the central motivating force for much of analytic philosophy. Besides giving philosophers the tools to solve problems that have concerned thinkers since the Greeks, the notion that mathematics is logic points to an answer to the question posed by Kant in the quote that opens this chapter. "How is pure mathematics possible?" This is an answer that removes mathematics as an obstacle to empiricism. Mathematics is possible because it is analytic.

Logicism

Whitehead and Russell's *PM* was an elaborate argument for logicism, which in turn was based on earlier work by Frege. The logicist program is succinctly stated by Russell and attributed to Frege: "Frege showed in detail how arithmetic can be deduced from pure logic, without the need of any fresh ideas or axioms, thus disproving Kant's assertion that '7 + 5 = 12' is synthetic" (Russell 1959b, p. 32).

Logicism was one of several responses to difficulties that emerged in the foundations of mathematics toward the end of the nineteenth century. These difficulties perplexed Russell and many others. We can skip over the technicalities for now, and keep in mind that none of the difficulties that troubled Russell would matter for any practical applications of mathematics or arithmetic. You could still balance your checkbook even if the foundations of mathematics had not been put on a firm footing. Nevertheless, to a philosopher of Russell's uncompromising character these difficulties were intellectually troubling. The results of his investigations have thrilled and baffled philosophers ever

---

[4] As opposed, e.g., to psychologism, the view that mathematics is derived from human psychology. Frege was deeply opposed to psychologism.

since and tormented and fascinated (at least a few) students taking Symbolic Logic.

The nature of mathematics and arithmetic is a central problem for philosophers, especially in the area of epistemology. In the argument between the empiricists and rationalists, the question of our knowledge of mathematical facts plays a key role. Even an impure (i.e., moderate) empiricist must answer the question how we know that $7 + 5 = 12$, that the interior angles of a triangle equal $180°$, that there are infinitely many prime numbers, and so on. "Of course, we know them because we were told them in school and read them in the textbook." This answer, while having an appealing simplicity, would disappoint both the rationalist and the empiricist and is abjectly unphilosophical. We know those mathematical facts because we can figure them out, "see the truth of them," especially when we've been shown the proofs or done the calculations. [*Background 1.4* – Proofs that the sum of the interior angles of a triangle is $180°$ and that there are infinitely many prime numbers] And the marvelous thing is, not only that we "see" the truths, but also understand that they must be so, could not be otherwise, and are necessary and absolute. No experience could impart such certainty. Mathematical knowledge dooms the empiricist claim that all knowledge is based on experience.

Russell's assertions about geometry in the following quote apply to all of mathematics. (When he uses the term "idealists" his description applies to rationalists.)

> Geometry, throughout the 17th and 18th centuries, remained, in the war against empiricism, an impregnable fortress of the idealists. Those who held – as was generally held on the Continent – that certain knowledge, independent of experience, was possible about the real world, had only to point to Geometry: none but a madman, they said, would throw doubt on its validity, and none but a fool would deny its objective reference. The English Empiricists, in this matter, had, therefore, a somewhat difficult task; either they had to ignore the problem, or if, like Hume and Mill, they ventured on the assault, they were driven into the apparently paradoxical assertion that Geometry, at bottom, had no certainty of a different kind from that of Mechanics... (Russell 1897, p. 1)[5]

The problem that empiricism has with mathematics is worth pondering. Even if "$7 + 5 = 12$" and "the interior angles of a triangle equal

---

[5] Infamously, John Stuart Mill claimed that mathematical truths were based on experience. Few empiricists have agreed with Mill's view. Russell could not accept it and surely Russell is right.

180°'' are derived in some way from experiences of counting and measuring angles, it is impossible that, e.g., our knowledge of the infinitude of primes comes from experience. Although perhaps the idea could be led back by many steps to experiences with counting and dividing and so on, I do not see how any experience or observation (other than "seeing" the proof) could get one to know with certainty that there are infinitely many prime numbers. Using a computer to generate prime numbers wouldn't help. It would just keep calculating primes, but how could we know it would never get to the last one? There is no possible empirical test that would establish that there are infinitely many primes. Yet the proof is so simple and obvious that there can be no doubt. If you are troubled by the indirect nature of the proof, be assured there are direct proofs. In any case, Euclid's proof assures us there is a larger prime given any series of primes.

Empirical evidence and observations even if pervasive and universal cannot explain the certainty and necessity of mathematical propositions. In the case of a mathematical proposition such as "$7 + 5 = 12$," empirical observations are not evidence or support. If a proposition is based on observational evidence, then there must be possible observations that one could describe that would refute the proposition. No possible observations would refute "$7 + 5 = 12$." If every possible observation, test, and experiment is compatible with the truth of the proposition, then observation, test, and experiment is irrelevant to the proposition. This is the case with the true mathematical propositions that I cited. A simple example should suffice: If I put 7 sheep in the pen, and then 5 more and counted all the sheep and kept getting 11, I would assume that one of the sheep was stolen, escaped, or had been kidnapped by aliens. The last thing I would ever judge is that $7 + 5$ does not equal 12. Indeed, I would never judge that unless I had lost all sense of reason. To repeat, if no possible experience or observation would lead us to give up a proposition, then it is not based on experience or observation. In mathematics we have decisive counterexamples to empiricism: propositions that are true, that we know to be true and in fact are absolutely certain but are not based on observation, test, experiment, or experience.

This much was accepted by Russell and empiricists (other than Mill) and has been accepted by most philosophers since. Our mathematical statements and ones like them are necessarily true and are not based on sensory experience in that they are not empirical scientific results established in the lab or field by the scientific method and observation. The only alternative source seems to be pure reason. The victory cheers of the rationalists are ringing through the ages. Here are clear examples of important, useful, evident items of knowledge based on and derivable from pure reason. There's an old saying that goes something like this: "If the camel once gets his nose in the tent, his body will soon follow." If we once grant that mathematical knowledge is non-empirical and based on pure reason as the rationalist claims, then there will be no stopping the rest of the body getting into the tent: metaphysics, religion, ontology, cosmology, ethics, aesthetics, etc. all will follow. Empiricism will be bankrupt.

The most influential modern version of the rationalist claim is Kant's view that, e.g., "$7 + 5 = 12$" is synthetic *a priori*. The empiricist response to this apparently devastating claim, a response based on the logical system of Frege and Russell, forms a main current of analytic philosophy. One central tenet of the logical positivists (see Chapter 2) – often called logical empiricists – is that there are no synthetic *a priori* propositions. Russell (and Whitehead) following Frege made the first key step in the empiricist response. This step is their logicism.[6]

> From Frege's work it followed that arithmetic, and pure mathematics generally, is nothing but a prolongation of deductive logic. This disproved Kant's theory that arithmetical propositions are "synthetic" and involve a reference to time. The development of pure mathematics from logic was set forth in detail in *Principia Mathematica* by Whitehead and myself. (Russell 1945, p. 830)

Kant's views on mathematics were outmoded in any case and ready to be replaced by more modern ones. For example, many developments in nineteenth-century mathematics such as non-Euclidean geometry cast suspicion on Kant's method of arguing for his synthetic *a priori*.

Frege attempted to demonstrate that all of mathematics could be derived from pure logic – thus logicism. The derivation of mathematics from logic was a complex and stepwise procedure. Many previous mathematical results were required. By the end of the nineteenth century, mathematicians believed they had shown how all statements of traditional mathematics could be expressed as statements about the natural numbers, so all statements of mathematics could be reformulated as statements about the natural numbers. And furthermore, all theorems about the natural numbers could be derived from Peano's five axioms.[7] So it was believed that all of traditional mathematics could be derived from the Peano postulates. This made the plans of

---

[6] Neither Russell, Whitehead, nor Frege ever used the term "logicism." The term was coined by Rudolf Carnap, one of the foremost logical empiricists, in the 1930s.
[7] Named after Giuseppe Peano (1858–1932), an Italian mathematician who developed the postulates and influenced Russell's view of mathematics.

Russell, following upon the work of Frege, vastly simpler. Instead of focusing on all of the vastness of mathematics, he could focus just on the Peano postulates. Russell discovered a fatal flaw in Frege's work (described below) and working with Whitehead attempted to overcome this flaw and thus successfully complete the work begun by Frege.

If this logicist program could be neatly carried out, it would solve both the problems with the synthetic *a priori* and the view that mathematical knowledge is based on observation. The point is that logic is analytic, so if the Peano postulates could be shown to be purely logical in nature, this would demonstrate that the postulates are analytic – and thus that anything that followed from them by pure logic would also be analytic. We could see, then, exactly why and how "$7 + 5 = 12$" is not synthetic *a priori*. It is analytic, and thus *a priori* at least in the special sense that it could be justified without appeal to observation or experience – justified simply by its form once the meanings of its constituent terms are fully spelled out.

Although Frege and Russell had determined that mathematics is reducible to logic – that mathematics and logic are one – they had not fully realized the extent to which this trivialized mathematics. Russell was reluctantly driven to the view that mathematics is all tautological. "I thought of mathematics with reverence, and suffered when Wittgenstein led me to regard it as nothing but tautologies" (Russell 1963/1944, p. 19). (In the next chapter we will see how Wittgenstein developed this idea.) The view that mathematics consists of nothing but tautologies disappointed Russell but energized the empiricist philosophers who followed Frege, Russell, and Wittgenstein. It answers Mill and at once appeals to the empiricists, because it demystifies mathematics – gets the camel's nose out of the tent. Neither the rationalists nor anybody else would be happy to say that the truths of religion, metaphysics, ethics, etc. are tautologies like the truths of mathematics. The empiricists now had a simple, clear explanation of how we know and how we can justify mathematical knowledge without Kant's synthetic *a priori* or any other form of knowledge that would give support to rationalism.

The logicist program consists of several steps. First mathematics is reduced to a relatively simple base such as the Peano postulates. Then the base is shown to be translatable into terms solely from pure logic. Then the axioms are shown to be truths of logic. The final step due to Wittgenstein is the claim that the truths of logic are tautological. This explains how mathematical knowledge can be *a priori*, but the rationalist can no longer use mathematics as a weapon against the empiricist. The rationalist is left holding an empty bag. Granted, mathematical propositions are not based on experience or observation, but they are not the results of pure rational insight into the ultimate nature of reality either. They are based on a clear process that involves no rationalist mystification and involves only epistemic procedures that are acceptable to the empiricists. We know mathematical propositions in the way that we know that "All grandmothers are mothers" or that "Either all insects have eight legs or it is not the case that all insects have eight legs."

> The further property needed to make a proposition one of mathematics or logic...is the property traditionally expressed by saying that the propositions concerned are 'analytic' or 'logically necessary'. Or we may say that the propositions of logic or mathematics are 'true in virtue of their form'. If I say 'Socrates was wise', I say something substantial, which is known from history and cannot be known otherwise. But if I say 'Socrates was wise or not wise', I say something which requires no knowledge of history; its truth follows from the meanings of the words. (Russell 1973, p. 303)

If we spin out more and more complex versions of these analytic propositions, things can get very hairy and even surprising, but there is nothing mysterious or epistemically wonderful about the process.

Alas, the work of Russell and Whitehead did not result immediately in the smooth resolution of foundational issues that Russell had hoped for.

> In June 1901, this period of honeymoon delight came to an end. Cantor had a proof that there is no greatest cardinal; in applying this proof to the universal class, I was led to the contradiction about classes that are not members of themselves. It soon became clear that this is only one of an infinite class of contradictions. I wrote to Frege, who replied with the utmost gravity that *"die Arithmetik ist ins Schwanken geraten."* At first, I hoped the matter was trivial and could be easily cleared up; but early hopes were succeeded by something very near to despair. (Russell 1963/1944, p. 13)

The problems Russell had found with Frege's program had to do with self-reference and self-containment of sets. The axiom that caused the problems was the comprehension axiom that said that any formula of the form "x is Φ" yields a set of x's that satisfies Φ. E.g., "x is red" yields the set of things that are red. Since there is always the empty set, how could the comprehension axiom cause problems? If Φ was screwy enough or did not apply to anything, then the set of x's that satisfied Φ would be the empty set. Oddly enough and to Frege's despair and Russell's chagrin there are Φ that do not and cannot yield any set, not even the empty set, thus the unrestricted comprehension axiom despite its obviousness had to be revised. [*Background 1.5* – Technical explanation of Russell's paradox and other problems and a brief tour through Cantorian set theory]

Russell considered many ways of dealing with the problems created by his eponymous paradox. Ultimately, work on resolving the paradoxes led to the full complexities of *Principia Mathematica*. The problems were solved by Russell and Whitehead by introducing the theory of types. The idea of Russell and Whitehead's theory of types[8] was that propositions were not allowed to apply to themselves and sets were not allowed to contain themselves. The technical details need not detain us, but they never fully resolved the problems in a satisfactory manner. Avoiding problems of self-reference seems simple enough in theory, but becomes very complex in practice when one is trying to generate all of mathematics. How can one be sure that a proposition does not apply to itself? There is no easy way to be certain that self-reference has not crept in somewhere.[9]

To the ordinary chap perhaps such apparently minor problems as self-reference do not seem worthy of the years of agonizing work of Russell and Whitehead. As Desdemona (*Othello* act 2, scene 1) says: "These are old fond paradoxes to make fools laugh i' th' alehouse." Well in a sense they were old paradoxes, because they were based on the liar's paradox well known to the ancients and mentioned in the Bible, but Russell and Whitehead were not fools and they weren't laughing. (I don't know how much time they spent in the alehouse – probably not much given all the work they had to do generating *PM*.) Keep in mind that Russell mentions in his autobiography that at age 11 he was troubled by the lack of proof for Euclid's axioms. Since Frege, Whitehead, and Russell were concerned to establish firm foundations for mathematics because of technical problems that emerged in the nineteenth century, they could hardly ignore technical problems of their own. Russell would be the last person to do that.

No one worried that these paradoxes would cause any difficulties for practicing mathematicians. The problems that Russell was confronting were and are philosophical problems. They would be of concern to someone who craved an account of the human capacity for knowledge of mathematics. Unfortunately, as Russell's logical system became more

---

[8] Usually just called "Russell's Theory of Types."

[9] In Chapter 5 we will see that Gödel's famous proof, which helped to undermine logicism, is based on a form of self-reference.

and more complex in order to avoid the paradoxes it was no longer able to generate all of classical mathematics without the addition of more axioms that did not seem to be purely logical. For example, Russell needed to add the axiom of infinity – that there are infinitely many items available. This does not look to be analytic nor logically necessary. Other such axioms were also required. Russell and Whitehead were able to show that all of classical mathematics was derivable with the addition of these non-logical axioms. Although this in itself was a great achievement, they could no longer plausibly claim that mathematics was reducible to pure logic – that it was all analytic. So much for logicism. Today the consensus is that an astonishing amount of classical mathematics can be derived from pure logic and set theory (suitably complicated to avoid paradoxes). All notions of classical mathematics can be defined using only logical notions such as "or," "if . . . , then . . . ," "all . . . " and "∈" of set theory.

Despite the logicist program's failure, twentieth century set theory, model theory, and proof theory – the core of foundations of mathematics – would not have existed without *PM*. *PM* is the great source of what comes later, even if it did not succeed in its purpose. And logicism did not die a quiet, peaceful death. The claim that mathematics and geometry are analytic is too appealing to give up without a fight, because it offers a neat explanation of the certainty of mathematics, the necessity of mathematical truths, and why they are *a priori*. It solves one of the philosophical riddles of the ages – how is pure mathematics possible? Such a wonderful thing should not be given up lightly. The logical positivists (see Chapter 2) needed logicism, and were unwilling to abandon it. Logical positivists continued to claim that mathematics was derivable from pure logic and that it was analytic well into the 1950s. The modern empiricists made many attempts to refine and defend logicism, and these attempts still continue today.

Particularly frustrating to Russell and the logical positivists was that the technical program of logicism was so close to being successfully completed. To the outside observer, even to the philosopher not steeped in these issues, the problems that defeated Russell and Whitehead seem like the tiniest little flyspecks. To give up a program that accomplished so much, and that promises the solution to such deep and troubling problems on the basis of a few technical difficulties that could just be ignored seems like extreme intellectual fastidiousness. It is also forthright honesty and commitment to seeking the truth that would have made Socrates proud. This is the essence of philosophy.

Russell on Definite Descriptions

Russell's 1905 article "On Denoting," published in the leading British philosophy journal *Mind*, is considered by philosophers of language to be the most seminal article in twentieth-century philosophy of language. Philosophy of language, along with logic, has been central to the development of analytic philosophy. "On Denoting" was a key source of this analytic revolution. The results that Russell propounded in "On Denoting" are based on his symbolic logic and his work on the foundations of mathematics.

The question Russell is attempting to answer is how to properly interpret what he calls "definite descriptions." A definite description is a phrase that is meant to pick out one object; for example, "the first president of the United States," or "the computer on which I composed this text." Definite descriptions are distinguished from names such as "George Washington" and general descriptive phrases such as "a computer." A definite description picks out its object by the descriptions involved, whereas a name just tags an object without its fitting any specific description. One notoriously troubling problem is how to understand definite descriptions that seem to pick out something non-existent, for example "the king of the United States in 2008." Russell famously concentrated his attention in 1905 on the definite description "the present king of France." The question is how to understand the statement "The present king of France is bald." Is this true or false? Or perhaps it has no truth-value.

Before we consider Russell's answers to these questions, we need to address more general issues about the philosophy of language. Put bluntly: Why is philosophy of language an interesting, valuable, and worthwhile pursuit for otherwise busy and intelligent adults? We all know how to talk, read, and write. While no doubt most of us could use some improvement in these skills, the results in philosophy of language are not going to help with our language skills. In some ways, philosophy of language is like philosophy of mathematics. Mathematicians do not need philosophy of mathematics, and language users do not need philosophy of language. We will get along talking and writing just fine without it.

So then, what is the value of philosophy of language? It is not just satisfying an idle curiosity and a fascination with puzzles, although having an interest in puzzle solving helps add a bit of spice to an admittedly dry subject. As a preliminary point, no one should be deceived that issues in the philosophy of language are simple and pellucid just because it is oh so easy to talk. Just because we can all use language competently does not mean we understand how it works. We are all able to walk just fine, or at least most of us are who are temporarily abled, but walking is an amazingly complex process that involves difficult and continuous feats of balance. The physics and physiology of walking are dauntingly complex. Likewise, the problems in the philosophy of language, while easy to ask, are anything but easy to answer satisfactorily.

The value and importance of philosophy of language stems from various applications. 1) Much that goes under the heading of philosophy of language is actually logic or informal logic. Logic is the science of reasoning and drawing inferences. Reasoning can be difficult, and always could use careful, even meticulous attention. People are subject to screw-ups when reasoning. 2) More directly relevant to our topics here, results in the philosophy of language are relevant to epistemology, metaphysics, and ethics and these areas do have practical and theoretical importance. People claim to know things that they do not know, and vice versa. The entire question of how humans should best pursue knowledge is difficult and conflicted, and of obvious practical importance. While the practical value of metaphysics is not as obvious as epistemology and ethics, one's view of the cosmos and one's place in it affects one's religious views and one's attitude to life's activities. Twentieth-century philosophers have found that apparently small and technical issues in the philosophy of language have had deep implications in these other more exciting realms. In fact, the study of linguistic issues has proven so rich in philosophical insights that twentieth-century philosophers have tended to start with philosophy of language as a way into other areas of philosophy. Methods and tools developed in the philosophy of language throughout the twentieth century have been applied fruitfully to these other areas.

Before examining Russell's "On Denoting," I should emphasize that my writing of "results" in the philosophy of language is a bit disingenuous. To the extent that issues in philosophy of language are actually part of logic we can speak of results, but there are no, or few, results in philosophy outside of logic. Russell's theory of definite descriptions while widely admired by philosophers is not universally accepted as a result in the sense in which there are results in mathematics or natural science. There are alternative views, as we shall see (Chapter 4), and the issue of how to interpret definite descriptions is still being energetically examined by philosophers. Nevertheless, Russell's theory of definite descriptions is considered by analytic philosophers to be a paradigm of philosophy and to represent real progress in the philosophy of language and linguistics.

The question is "How do definite descriptions work?" Here's a simple answer: The description mentions certain features and whichever is the unique object that has the features is the object denoted (i.e., picked out) by the description. So "the first president of the United States of America" denotes George Washington, because he uniquely fits that description. Alas, what seems obvious, easy, and commonsensical, so often won't work when we get to puzzle cases. Certainly George Washington fits that description, and uniquely, but the claim that this explains why the description denotes him is uncomfortable. If we just considered George Washington our discomfort might be minimal, but we want a uniform treatment of definite descriptions. Our mechanism for explaining the denoting of "the first president of the United States of America" does not comfortably work across the board. There are too many puzzle cases left. Even with George Washington there is a bit of a puzzle, since he himself is no longer around to be denoted. Note that this problem will also arise with proper names. How can we use a name to talk about a man who does not now exist? Let's leave names and this puzzle aside for the moment. (We will see in Chapter 7 that Kripke and Putnam have an answer.)

Puzzles arise about definite descriptions when there is no single object that fits the description or when nothing fits the description. How does one decide if an assertion that contains such a description is true or false? If I assert "The only prime number between 10 and 15 is larger than 2×6," is what I've said true, false, or neither? The trouble is we do not know what "the only prime number between 10 and 15" denotes if anything. Does it denote 11, or 13, both, or neither? Our simple theory that handled "the first president of the United States of America" will not handle this example. Even more troubling difficulties arise with definite descriptions which nothing fits – Russell's famous example "the present king of France" or for another example "The president of Canada." How are we to respond if someone said "The president of Canada is a woman"? We would naturally respond "Canada doesn't have a president." So is the statement true, false, or neither? There are good reasons in favor of each of these answers and eminent philosophers have argued for each of them. For example, since the *head of state* of Canada is a woman, we might suppose that "the president of Canada" must denote Elizabeth II and so the statement is true. But maybe the speaker wasn't thinking of Elizabeth II, and was just simply mistaken about Canada's political system. What are we to say then? Annoyingly, reasons in favor of one answer are also reasons against the other two and there are plenty of reasons pro and con to go around.

One answer that Russell particularly disliked, but that was popular in the period before his article appeared in 1905, was that there are objects that have being but do not exist. This view has come to be called Meinongianism after Alexius Meinong who propounded it in the late nineteenth century. Meinongianism is a result of taking our simple common sense theory of definite descriptions very seriously. So according to this view there is a present king of France and even a president of Canada (not head of state, president). They are not real physical people; they would be counted in no census. These abstract beings are the entities that are denoted by the phrases "the present king of France" and "the president of Canada." If the proposition "The president of Canada is a woman" is meaningful as it appears to be, then there must be an object denoted by "the president of Canada," and that object either is or is not a woman. Since no real person is the president of Canada, the object denoted must be a nonexistent being. Now other problems begin to swarm. No such nonexistent objects are observable or even members of our physical universe. Worse still, there are too many of them – one for each possible description thought of or not. This is a felonious violation of Occam's Rule – "Don't multiply entities when you don't need to" – in other words don't make things more complex than they absolutely have to be, "Keep it simple!" The simple, common sense theory of definite descriptions is simple, but in order to make it work we need this swarm of nonexistent entities. These entities are not subject to empirical scientific investigation and they aren't well behaved like mathematical objects. Unlike numbers and sets, there are no clear criteria of identity or individuation for unreal entities. Is the president of Canada the same or different from the present king of Canada? Is the nonexistent president of Canada a woman? Can a nonexistent woman be a king? Why not? Do these questions even make sense? None of these problems is insurmountable. There are Meinongians today in philosophy, fortunately only a very few, and they are by no means considered to be kooks.

Nevertheless, the problems with Meinongianism were severe enough in Russell's view to demand an alternative. Russell's theory of definite descriptions offers that alternative. Russell was engaged in reducing, that is eliminating, the need for postulating mathematical entities, so he would hardly abide other ethereal objects. Of course, if there is no alternative, then no matter how complex and no matter how much we dislike a theory, we must accept it. If there is an alternative, then we can in good conscience turn away from that bad old overly complex theory. One of the reasons that Russell's theory of definite descriptions was so joyfully received by philosophers is that many could not see an alternative to Meinongianism. To those of us who are empirically-minded and favor demystification, Russell's theory was like finding a working flashlight when you are stumbling in the dark.

Russell's method of dealing with definite descriptions, which he also applied to many other types of expressions, is to deny they have a denotation in isolation. The key confusion according to Russell is the assumption that "the present king of France" or "the president of Canada" are denoting expressions. In fact when properly analyzed using his and Frege's methods of logic the expressions disappear entirely. Definite descriptions are not denoting expressions by themselves. So "the president of Canada" does not occur in the analysis of the statement "The president of Canada is a woman." According to Russell the statement "The president of Canada is a woman" is a somewhat incorrect and shorthand way of saying "There is one and only one president of Canada and that one is a woman." The latter is the real statement, the former is a misleading but natural of way of saying it.

We now have a clear and uniform answer to the question about truth and falsity. It is false that there is one and only one president of Canada and that one is a woman, because this implies that there is a president of Canada, which there is not. In cases where more than one thing fits the description, the statement is false because the statement logically implies that there is only one. When one and only one thing fits the description, such as "the first president of the United States," then the statement is true if the predicate is true of that thing and false otherwise. So the statement "The first president of the United States was born in Virginia" is true. There is one and only one first president of the United States and he was born in Virginia. Here it is in contemporary symbolic logic: $\exists x\{[Fx \ \& \ \forall y(Fy \supset x = y)] \ \& \ Vx\}$. The first part says there is at least one thing that is the first president of the United States (there is a first president of the United States), the next part is impossible to put into plain English from the symbols but says in effect that there is at most one, and the last part says that that unique president was born in Virginia. Voila!

Although the symbolic form of the statement is not strictly necessary to understand the analysis, the analysis would not have occurred to Russell or appealed so much to others if it had not been so readily symbolized. Russell's use of logical symbols does not just come from a relish for technical and mathematical symbolization. According to the old way of symbolizing, our statement about the president of Canada would look like this: "Wa" where "W" stands for "is a woman" and "a" stands for the non-existent object "the president of Canada." When we look at the Russellian symbolization we see how profoundly different his analysis is: "∃x{[Hx & ∀y(Hy ⊃ x = y)] & Wx}." Note that in the fully analyzed expression there is no "a" or any other term that denotes an individual. In fact, this is a statement not about an individual but about the universe as a whole – it is a general statement. It says that among things that exist in the universe there is an object that is president of Canada – has the property of being the president of Canada – that there is only one such object and that object is a woman. What it says is, of course, false. Such an analysis has the effect of shedding light on mysteries, solving puzzles, and making progress by giving clear defendable answers.

Philosophers inspired by Russell have used symbolic logic since 1905 to attempt to solve their own philosophical problems, often with less success but no less energy.

Russell developed a metaphysics and philosophy of language based on his symbolic logic. He called it "logical atomism." The name is revealing. The metaphysics of logical atomism can be understood on analogy with physics and chemistry. Larger objects are built up out of smaller atomic ones. Russell held that language when fully analyzed consists of atomic propositions and molecular ones constructed out of them by the logical functions – not, or, and, if . . . , then . . . . In this fashion, all of language and thought could be constructed out of the simplest atomic elements.

Although developments in physics influenced Russell, the prime motivation for his logical atomism came from his work on the foundations of mathematics. Since mathematics could be "rebuilt" firmly on the basis of the most simple elements and operations, Russell embraced the idea that every organized area of knowledge could be so treated. First analyze a body of knowledge – say, for example, physics – into the simplest basic elements and then rebuild it step by step from those simple elements. The rebuilt theory or body of knowledge would be vastly improved over the old vague and disordered one, but still contain all its truths. The rebuilding process would exhibit clearly the essential structure of the area of knowledge. Note, however, that the basic elements of physics, according to Russell, would not be atoms. Atoms are already highly derived.

> If your atom is going to serve purposes in physics, as it undoubtedly does, your atom has got to turn out to be a construction, and your atom will in fact turn out to be a series of classes of particulars. The same process which one applies to physics, one will also apply elsewhere. (Russell 1971/1918, p. 274)

The classes of particulars Russell is here talking about are not such things as space/time points or energy packets. They are classes of metaphysical simples discovered by philosophical analysis. Russell here is concerned with the logical structure of an area of knowledge, not the material structure it describes.

Russell analyzes our knowledge of the external world: that is, our common sense knowledge of tables, chairs, other people, and our own bodies along these lines. The world is built of logical atoms.

> Our purpose that has run through all that I have said, has been the justification of analysis, i.e., the justification of the logical atomism, of the view that you can get down in theory, if not in practice, to ultimate simples, out of which the world is built, and that those simples have a kind of reality not belonging to anything else. (Russell 1971/1918, p. 270)

Russell does not explain what the simples are, just that they are metaphysically necessary for the construction of reality. Sometimes they are taken to be particular instantaneous sense impressions, and they can also be qualities or relations.

> The reason that I call my doctrine *logical* atomism is because the atoms I wish to arrive at as the sort of last residue in analysis are logical atoms. Some of them will be what I call 'particulars' – such things as little patches of colour or sounds, momentary things – and some of them will be predicates or relations and so on. The point is that the atom I wish to arrive at is the atom of logical analysis, not the atom of physical analysis. (Russell 1971/1918, p. 178)

Atomic facts are built of simples. Molecular facts are built of atomic facts. Language when suitably reconstructed will consist of atomic propositions representing atomic facts, and molecular propositions. The molecular propositions are built up out of the atomic ones by logical functions: not, or, and, if..., then. The common structure of language and the world is represented by symbolic logic. The structure of language is also the structure of thought (when suitably analyzed).

Russell's vision of logical analysis has been amazingly influential given its highly theoretical nature. As we will see in the next chapter Wittgenstein's *Tractatus Logico-Philosophicus*, which influenced the logical positivists and others, was based on Russell's views and is a version of logical atomism. A great deal of analytic philosophy, such as Oxford ordinary language philosophy (see Chapter 4), is a reaction against logical atomism.

G. E. Moore's Philosophy of Common Sense

While Frege influenced Russell's development of symbolic logic and logicism, Russell's wider outlook was shaped by his contact with G. E. Moore – a philosopher only slightly less significant in creating analytic philosophy than Russell himself. As young men at Cambridge University both Russell and Moore embraced versions of Hegelian philosophy filtered through the British Hegelians, F. H. Bradley and J. M. E. McTaggart, philosophers hardly known or read today (although see mention of McTaggart in the Epilogue). Bradley denied that there are any individual things, and argued that reality consists of a single purely spiritual Absolute. McTaggart's most famous book is titled *The Unreality of Time.*

German philosophy after Kant, represented especially by Fichte, Schelling, and Hegel, has come to be called "German idealism." [*Background 1.6* – German idealism and Bradley and McTaggart] In many ways, German idealism and its most ardent and well-known proponent G. W. F. Hegel represents an extreme form of metaphysical speculation. This is the kind of philosophy the logical positivists and other analytic philosophers were reacting against. The logical positivists embraced the term "positivism" to emphasize their resistance to German idealism with its emphasis and use and overuse of dialectical negation. Negation in one way or another is at the heart of German idealism. Hegel and the Hegelians are always going on about the "negation of the negation" and such things. This sort of metaphysical mystification is anathema to empiricists. The empiricists are "positivists," as opposed to those obscurantist metaphysical "negationists."[10] The term "metaphysical" came to mean anything even loosely associated with negative Hegelian dialectic and by extension anything other than "scientific," "clear-headed," and "straightforward." To empiricist-minded philosophers "metaphysical" meant anything obscure, unscientific, tending to mystification.[11]

---

[10] This distinction is still alive today. For example, Harold Bloom, not a philosopher but a literary critic associated with Continental philosophy, said in a 1983 interview "What I think I have in common with the school of deconstruction [a major Continental movement] is the mode of negative thinking or negative awareness, in the technical, philosophical sense of the negative, but which comes to me through negative theology" (Bloom internet reference).

[11] Abetting this demotion of metaphysics from "The Queen of Sciences," we find that in popular culture today "metaphysics" is used to mean "occult," "supernatural," "mystical."

The rebellion against Hegelianism and German idealism began with G. E. Moore, and quickly spread to Russell.

But these motives [dissatisfaction with Hegel's logic and philosophy of mathematics] would have operated more slowly than they did, but for the influence of G. E. Moore. He also had had a Hegelian period, but it was briefer than mine. He took the lead in rebellion, and I followed, with a sense of emancipation. Bradley argued that everything common sense believes in is mere appearance; we reverted to the opposite extreme, and thought that *everything* is real that common sense, uninfluenced by philosophy or theology, supposes real. With a sense of escaping from prison, we allowed ourselves to think that grass is green, that the sun and stars would exist if no one was aware of them, and also that there is a pluralistic timeless world of Platonic ideas. The world, which had been thin and logical, suddenly became rich and varied and solid. Mathematics could be *quite* true, and not merely a stage in dialectic.[12] (Russell 1963/1944, p. 12)

Moore had a profound influence on Russell, but apparently the influence did not go the other way. Moore never seemed to use symbolic logic or very much technical vocabulary at all, nor was he interested in science, mathematics, or anything but pure philosophical reasoning. He has a unique style that is at once daunting in its detail and disarming in its simplicity. Russell in his autobiography writes of Moore:

In my third year [as a student at Cambridge], however, I met G. E. Moore, who was then a freshman, and for some years he fulfilled my ideal of genius. He was in those days beautiful and slim, with a look almost of inspiration, and with an intellect as deeply passionate as Spinoza's. He had a kind of exquisite purity. I have never but once succeeded in making him tell a lie, and that was by a subterfuge. "Moore," I said, "do you *always* speak the truth?" "No," he replied. I believe this to be the only lie he had ever told. (Russell 1968, p. 77)

(Russell's love of paradox comes out even in this brief passage.) Moore must have been very personally compelling, because his writing and style of argumentation is convoluted, humorless, and so often

---

[12] Although freed of Hegelianism, we can see that Russell was still struggling to emerge from metaphysical intoxication. The "Platonic ideas" that Russell mentions do not fit well with an empiricist philosophy. Russell felt that empiricism left out too much. Platonic ideas – eternal, perfect, abstract, and not perceptible by the senses – do not sit well with a "grass is green" common sense philosophy. Hard-core empiricists would have trouble seeing much difference between Plato's forms and Bradley's Absolute. Once one is intoxicated with the idea of non-physical entities existing outside of time, one might as well go all the way to the timeless Absolute of the British Hegelians.

unconvincing that I doubt his writings alone would have had the kind of influence that he has had on philosophy.

The two most famous expressions of Moore's reaction against idealism and Hegelianism are his classical articles "The Refutation of Idealism" (Moore 1959), originally published in *Mind* in 1903 and "A Defence of Common Sense"(Moore 1993), published in 1925. Today, among his heirs, Moore is best known, remembered, and loved for these two articles despite their obscurity of style.[13] Although Moore is defending common sense and attacking German philosophical mystification, his argumentation is not available to common sense. One must bring a dedicated close attention to minute detail when studying Moore's articles. Moore has other annoying habits. In "A Defence of Common Sense" he attributes numerous views to other philosophers, views that he is claiming to demolish, but only once mentions another thinker – Berkeley. Moore cannot be bothered with citations, quotes, and footnotes – the standard forms of scholarly apparatus.

The charm of Moore's common sense appeal is its simplicity, its air of boldly clearing away the crusty adhesions of generations of philosophy without adding new and doubtful complications of its own. From the time of ancient Greek philosophy to the present day, there have been philosophers, such as Hegel and Bradley, who for one reason or another have denied the ultimate reality of the objects of the common sense world of sense perception. This is the target of Moore's common sense thrust. Moore's claim is that he is more certain of specific facts of common sense, such as that he has two hands, that there are other people, and that the world existed before he was born, than he is of any of the steps of the abstruse or involved philosophical arguments offered by Platonists, Kantians, idealists, Hegelians, skeptics, or even by some of his fellow analytic philosophers, such as Russell. So any philosopher who denies or doubts or questions those facts of common sense must be in the grip of a delusion – he is deluded, or perhaps we should say "enchanted," by his apparently clever arguments. In any case, according to Moore, even if we are not at present able to dissect them, those sophisticated philosophers' arguments that deny or question the facts of common sense cannot be correct.

---

[13] Moore is also well known for his work in ethics and in particular for his discussion of the so-called naturalistic fallacy. Moore introduced the naturalistic fallacy in his influential work *Principia Ethica* (they had to flaunt that Latin they learned at those English "public" schools even if they couldn't get away with writing their books in Latin). Unlike Russell who never devoted much attention to ethics as a branch of philosophy, Moore wrote his only full-length treatise on theoretical ethics. The development and history of twentieth-century ethics is the topic of a separate chapter (Chapter 8), and Moore's work in ethics features prominently there.

Unfortunately, Moore's approach fails to satisfy the philosophical yearning for substance. His common sense argument is too thin, and has failed to triumph even though Oxford ordinary language philosophers and Wittgenstein later tried to keep it alive (see Chapter 4). Moore's common sense philosophy brings to mind those who denied the discoveries of Galileo by claiming that they were more certain that the earth stood still than they could be of his theories and observations using lenses trained on the moon and spots of light in the sky. Isn't the earth's standing still an evident fact of ordinary perception and common sense? It certainly was before Copernicus and Galileo. Common sense does not simply trump the skeptics' and idealists' arguments any more than the common sense of the time trumped modern astronomy.

Moore and Russell on Sense Data

What seemed to be obvious and commonsensical to Moore was often not so to other philosophers. Moore did more than any other thinker to focus attention on the idea of sense data. "Sense data" was a term coined by Russell, but Moore put the concept to work in his philosophy and gave it heavy burdens to shoulder. A sense datum is a present sensation of one sense that is private to an individual. Thus a present smell and a colored patch of my visual field are sense data. Sense data are not public objects, although at times Moore states that sense data are on the surfaces of objects. As we will see later in Chapter 4, sense data are introduced primarily by the argument from illusion. For example, a straight stick looks bent when partly in water, and there are optical illusions such as the Checker Shadow illusion (Figure 1.2). The idea is that we do see *something* even if we do not see the object as it is. What do we see? We see or have sense data, supposedly.

Moore argued, or rather claimed, that the existence of sense data is as evident as anything could be.

> "This is a hand," "That is the sun," "This is a dog," etc. etc. etc.
>
> Two things only seem to me to be quite certain about the analysis of such propositions (and even with regard to these I am afraid some philosophers would differ from me) namely that whenever I know, or judge, such a proposition to be true, (1) there is always some *sense-datum* about which the proposition in question is a proposition – some sense-datum which is *a* subject (and, in a certain sense, the principal or ultimate subject) of the proposition in question, and (2) that, nevertheless, *what* I am knowing or

Figure 1.2   Areas A and B are the same shade of gray. This seems incredible but is true. However something is different in our perceptions of A and B. What is it that is different? Copyright Edward H. Adelson.

judging to be true about this sense-datum is not (in general) that it is *itself* a hand, or a dog, or the sun, etc. etc., as the case may be.... But there is no doubt at all that there are sense-data, in the sense in which I am now using that term. I am at present seeing a great number of them, and feeling others. And in order to point out to the reader what sort of things I mean by sense-data, I need only ask him to look at his own right hand. (Moore 1993/1925, p. 128)

Here Moore has ventured far from common sense. Hands, the sun, a dog are all good objects well-known to common sense, but common sense knows no sense data; and note how different the meanings of "sense" are in the two uses – common sense and sense data.

Moore's love of common sense was never embraced by later analytic philosophers. The logical positivists who were in sympathy with Moore and Russell in many ways, and were especially influenced by Russell, never adopted common sense as a philosophical source of truth. The logical positivists were more inclined to look to natural science and especially physics for guidance. Later in the twentieth century, Oxford philosophers famously employed ordinary language as a source of argument and insight, but they would not have equated this with common sense. Recently intuition has again been prominent in philosophical research, but this reliance on intuition would not render the sort of results that Moore thought common sense could. Philosophical intuition as it has been used recently is closer to Russell's logical self-evidence than it is to Moore's common sense. Indeed some of the claims that Moore found to be "quite certain," others would find to be counter-intuitive.

Some members of the logical positivist movement, with their empiricist leanings, focused on the subject of sense data. They shared Moore's view that sense data are fundamental to our empirical knowledge, but unlike Moore and Russell, the logical positivists were troubled by the somewhat unscientific and subjective nature of sense data. Other philosophers, such as the Oxford philosopher J. L. Austin raised questions about the very existence of sense data. Even Wittgenstein and his followers seemed dubious about sense data; if not about their existence and our direct awareness of them, then about whether they can carry any epistemological weight. The nature, function, and even existence of sense data have continued to be issues of intense scrutiny. Sense data remained a central topic in epistemology in analytic circles for most of the twentieth century.

Like Moore, Russell relies on sense data in order to explain the foundations of our knowledge. Russell distinguishes between knowledge by acquaintance and knowledge by description. According to Russell, we are directly acquainted with our sense data.

> All our knowledge, both knowledge of things and knowledge of truths, rests upon acquaintance as its foundation..... Sense data...are among the things with which we are acquainted; in fact, they supply the most obvious and striking example of knowledge by acquaintance. (Russell 1959a/1912, p. 48)

Thus, according to Russell, we have direct knowledge by acquaintance of sense data that make up the appearance of the table, but I only indirectly know the physical table by description. According to Russell, we are only acquainted with our sense data, our memories, our present mental states that are available to introspection, and universals such as *whiteness, diversity,* and *brotherhood.* These are the metaphysical atoms of the world that he invoked in his logical atomism. We are not directly acquainted with any physical objects. How far we've strayed from common sense!

An empiricist would gladly follow Russell in agreeing that we are directly acquainted with sense data, and memories, and our present introspectable mental states, but would balk at direct knowledge by acquaintance of metaphysical universals. The classical empiricist John Locke, for example, argued that we create universal ideas as our own mental concepts by abstraction from individual experiences. Russell cannot quite tear himself away from this tradition even though in the same place he claims to espouse platonism. "Awareness of universals is called *conceiving,* and a universal of which we are aware is called a *concept"* (Russell 1959a/1912, p. 52).

Moore's and Russell's Anti-Hegelianism

As we have seen, both Moore and Russell rebelled against the German idealist tradition that culminates with Hegel. Any reader not already entranced by Hegelianism need only spend some time trying to fathom Hegel's writings to appreciate the kind of scorn they provoke. His writings are like a word salad and the reasoning when it apparently can be understood is abstruse. Nevertheless, neither Moore nor Russell ever claimed to be able to refute idealism or Hegelian philosophy. Moore, in particular, is very modest in his claims. Although his article is titled "The Refutation of Idealism," he explicitly denies that anything in the article is a refutation of idealism:

> I say this lest it should be thought that any of the arguments which will be advanced in this paper would be sufficient to disprove, or any refutation of them sufficient to prove, the truly interesting and important proposition that reality is spiritual. For my own part I wish it to be clearly understood that I do not suppose that anything I shall say has the smallest tendency to prove that reality is not spiritual. (Moore 1959/1903, p. 2)

Although Moore does not claim to refute idealism he does argue cogently that no one has any intellectual reason to embrace idealism. In that article Moore also argues, in a way that anticipates Wittgenstein and especially Austin (see Chapter 4), that we directly perceive tables, chairs, and other people. He later repudiated that view.

Moore and Russell may have had other than purely intellectual reasons for rejecting Hegelianism. Here we see Moore and Russell ridiculing Hegel in their famous articles. First Moore from his 1903 "The Refutation of Idealism":

> Many philosophers, therefore, when they admit a distinction, yet (following the lead of Hegel) boldly assert their right, in a slightly more obscure form of words, *also* to deny it. The principle of organic unities, like that of combined analysis and synthesis, is mainly used to defend the practice of holding *both* of two contradictory propositions, wherever this may seem convenient. In this, as in other matters, Hegel's main service to philosophy has consisted in giving a name to and erecting into a principle, a type of fallacy to which experience had shown philosophers, along with the rest of mankind, to be addicted. No wonder that he has followers and admirers. (Moore 1959/1903, p. 14)

I note in passing that analytic philosophers have felt that their Continental brothers and sisters were addicted to this fallacy, just as Moore claims. Russell, being Russell, is more sprightly and humorous:

> By the law of excluded middle, either 'A is B' or 'A is not B' must be true. Hence either 'the present King of France is bald' or 'the present King of France is not bald' must be true. Yet if we enumerated the things that are bald, and then the things that are not bald, we should not find the present King of France in either list. Hegelians, who love a synthesis, will probably conclude that he wears a wig. (Russell 1973/1903, p. 110)

The turning away from Hegel was accompanied by a turning toward the British empiricists – John Locke, David Hume, George Berkeley, and John Stuart Mill. Although neither Russell nor Moore were fully committed to the British empiricist tradition in philosophy, they moved now in its spirit, gave it new respect, and were no longer put off by its supposed crudity. They came to view this "crudity" as a forthrightness and clarity, a groundedness in reality, that was notably lacking in the ethereal, incomprehensible mystifications of the philosophies of Kant, Hegel, Bradley, and their followers. Analytic philosophers continued to view Continental philosophers as unable and unwilling to shed Hegelianism. And analytic philosophers continued to adopt Russell's and Moore's attitude. Analytic philosophers proudly contrast the clarity, technical proficiency, and respect for natural science of analytic philosophy versus the ultra-sophistication, contrived jargon, and mystification of Continental philosophy. (But as I noted in the Introduction, both the analytic and Continental philosophical traditions have more in common than they may like to recognize in that they are both manifestations of modernism.)

Sociological and cultural reasons also played a role in Moore's and Russell's turning away from Hegelianism and Kantianism and toward British empiricism, and perhaps these sociological and cultural reasons had more influence than either Moore or Russell would like to admit. At the time of the key essays "On Denoting" and "A Refutation of Idealism," England was in a period of high tension with Germany and especially Prussia. Both Kant and Hegel were north Germans – Kant spent his life in the Prussian capital Königsberg, and Hegel was at Jena and then Berlin.

When the lines in the above anti-Hegelian quotes from Moore and Russell were being written, Germany was a chief rival and threat to Britain; and in ten years the two nations would be engulfed as opponents in the catastrophe of World War I. In the 1890s and early 1900s Germany was emerging as a naval power to threaten Britain.

According to the Tirpitz Plan, Germany was to force Britain to submit to German hegemony in the international arena. Germany was building a fleet of mighty ships that would cow the Royal Navy. German intentions, which eventually led to World War I, naturally led to a fearful and scornful attitude toward Prussia and the Kaiser among the British. This was occurring when Moore and Russell were turning away from Hegelianism.

Russell (but not Moore), of course, was influenced by and respected Frege, a north German mathematician, and he and Moore were close friends with the Viennese Ludwig Wittgenstein, but Hegelianism represented a different cultural milieu. Hegelianism was something like the official philosophy of Germany, and especially Prussia. Hegel seemed to suggest in his philosophy of history that contemporary Prussia was the culmination of the march of historical change – that there was a destiny to Prussian hegemony. These ideas were perhaps not so baldly stated in Hegel's writings, but his followers saw them there, and this is part of what Hegelianism meant. Later, Hegel was also to be, most unfairly, a source of inspiration to the Nazis as well. Hegel was also a key source of Marx's theories and was closely studied by early communists. The fact that Hegel could be claimed by two such ardently opposed camps as Nazism and Marxism is a tribute to his obscurity.

Anti-German sentiment was "in the air" in England in the early 1900s and young men could not help but be influenced by it. This anti-German sentiment would naturally attach to German idealism, if not to specific German friends such as Wittgenstein, or Germans working in very restricted technical fields such as Frege and Cantor.

By no means was Russell simply anti-German and an English chauvinist – Russell was not simply anything. His views and ideas were always conflicted and changing, just like his attitude to empiricism. As World War I was approaching, Russell became a pacifist, or as he later described his position a "relative pacifist" – a convenient way to dignify his always conflicted attitude to war and other things. I suppose we could also say that Russell was a relative empiricist,[14] a relative platonist, and so on. In any case, Russell as an opponent of British involvement in World War I courageously refused to follow the multitude to slaughter. As a result of his opposition to the British war effort, he was dismissed from his position at Trinity College, Cambridge, was fined and imprisoned for six months. Russell claimed that his pacifism was the only thing that claimed his true and deep commitment. It replaced mathematical logic. The upheaval of World War I and

---

[14] We will see in Chapter 3 that Quine uses the term "relative empiricism" in *Roots of Reference* in exactly this sense.

its effect on Russell partly explains his moving away from technical philosophy for the rest of his life. About three years after finishing *PM* Russell was still working on mathematical logic . . .

> Then came the war [WW I], and I knew without the faintest shadow of doubt what I had to do. I have never been so whole-hearted or so little troubled with hesitation in any work as in the pacifist work that I did during the war. For the first time I found something to do which involved my whole nature. (Russell 1933, p. 12)

He understandably felt "a great indignation at the spectacle of the young men of Europe being deceived and butchered in order to gratify the evil passions of their elders" (Russell 1933, p. 13). Russell's vision was so clear and so courageous, and almost solitary at the time of war fervor, that I marvel in admiration.[15] Alas, he had no effect on the carnage.

Russell came from a distinguished and aristocratic political family. Russell became 3rd Earl Russell on the death of his father – both his parents died when he was quite young. Russell's parents were scandalously liberal for the era, supporting birth control and women's rights. Russell's father was an open atheist and had appointed two "free thinkers," as Russell describes them, to be the guardians of him and his brother. The court overturned his father's will and Russell was brought up almost entirely by his puritanical grandmother at Pembroke Lodge in Richmond Park, London.

Although quite different from his parents and other ancestors, Russell's grandmother had a lasting impact if not on his views, at least on his courage to defend his views, which were often at odds with most of society.

> On my twelfth birthday she gave me a Bible (which I still possess), and wrote her favourite texts on the fly-leaf. One of them was "Thou shalt not follow a multitude to do evil;" another, "Be strong, and of a good courage; be not afraid, neither be Thou dismayed; for the Lord Thy God is with thee whithersoever thou goest." These texts have profoundly influenced my life, and still seemed to retain some meaning after I had ceased to believe in God. (Russell 1963/1944, p. 5)

Russell's pacifism, or rather "relative pacifism," guided him throughout his life. He supported the war against the Nazis, but agitated for nuclear disarmament and, toward the end of his long life, against the Vietnam War.

---

[15]   Although I should note that every single member of Trinity College serving in the war effort wrote to support Russell and protest his dismissal.

Figure 1.3 Pembroke Lodge, London. This is now a conference center and restaurant. The Bertrand Russell Suite is one of the fancier venues. Richmond Park is a royal park and the Russells lived here at the pleasure of the Crown. I made a pilgrimage here in 1998. This was before the house was restored, so I could not go inside. It is a sweet place, not too imposing, with sweeping views to the south and west. The park is vast (2360 acres – three times the size of Central Park) with herds of semi-tame deer roaming freely. What a charming place to grow up, and within London! Russell, as a boy, loved roaming and playing in the wilds of Richmond Park. The photo of Pembroke Lodge was made available by the kind permission of Sian Davies. I would also like to acknowledge and thank the photographer, Paul Fairbairn-Tennant.

Much of the writing and publishing that Russell did after his work in technical philosophy was directed more to politics, popular philosophy, and popular histories of philosophy. Russell published many dozens of books and was awarded the Nobel Prize for Literature in 1950. Some of the titles of his books indicate his ideas: *Why I am not a Christian* (1927); *Common Sense and Nuclear Warfare* (1959); *Has Man a Future* (1961); *War Crimes in Vietnam* (1967). Russell was an avid letter writer and wrote over 30,000 letters in his lifetime. I recall, when I was a graduate student at Cornell University, a friend and fellow graduate student wrote to Russell asking a technical question about his early philosophy. Not long after, he received a detailed reply from the great philosopher – a letter which my friend prized and framed and put on his wall over his desk. This was in the early 1960s. Russell is perhaps most famous in the

US as a result of his being denied by a New York court the opportunity to take a professorship at the City University of New York that he was offered in 1940. The court decided that Russell was morally unfit to teach our children.

Unlike Russell, Moore spent his life quietly at Cambridge University. He was the editor of *Mind* for many years and in many other ways continued to be a founder and leader of the analytic tradition in philosophy. He was a friend and supporter of Wittgenstein. Moore also lived a long life but never engaged in politics or disputes outside of philosophy.

Summary

Two initial sources of analytic philosophy are the application of the methods of symbolic logic to philosophical problems and the rejection of German metaphysics. If Russell gets the credit for introducing, popularizing, and applying the revolution in logic begun by Frege, Moore gets the credit for the rebellion against the metaphysical excesses of the German idealists and their English followers. Moore made simplicity, clarity, and careful non-technical analysis respectable in philosophy.

The logical positivists, the subject of the next chapter, were influenced by Russell but not much by Moore. The logical positivists took from Russell, or shared with him, a logicist analysis of mathematics, but rejected any form of platonism. The logical positivists prized Russell's *Principia Mathematica* and the revolution in logic that it represented. Perhaps the greatest cultural affinity that the positivists had with Moore and Russell was the rejection of the excesses of Continental metaphysics, especially in the traditions growing out of Kant and represented most egregiously by Hegel and his followers. Even today, philosophers brought up in the analytic tradition who study the German idealists and Hegel, and there are many who now do, do so with a sense of doing something slightly "naughty," "exotic," "off-beat," and perhaps more political than philosophical.

Final personal note: When I was a graduate student at Cornell in the 1960s, the philosophy department was thoroughly analytic. There were no courses on nineteenth-century philosophy in the philosophy department. We were forbidden to take a course on Nietzsche offered in the German department. There were no questions on Hegel, Kierkegaard, Marx, or Nietzsche on our PhD qualifying exam. The only philosophers that had any regard at all from that period were Frege and Mill, and they had a very high regard. I am confident that none of my teachers at Cornell would have described themselves as logical positivists. Norman Malcolm and Max Black, both leading analytic philosophers of the era, knew and studied with Moore, Russell, and Wittgenstein, but neither would have been comfortable with logicism or sense data theory. The main shared heritage was a distrust of mystification in philosophy and a scorn for anything that smacked of Hegelianism. Kant was highly regarded, but none of us accepted his synthetic *a priori*. I believe this was a lasting legacy of Moore and Russell.

Background 1.1 – Epistemology: empiricism versus rationalism

Epistemology is the area of philosophy that deals with questions about knowledge and belief. How do we know anything? When are beliefs justified? The central questions of epistemology are the nature of knowledge and skepticism. The philosophical skeptic denies that we have any knowledge of the external world (external to the subjective contents of our own minds). Modern skepticism began with Descartes, the father of modern philosophy. The philosophical project has been to demonstrate that we do have knowledge of the external world and how we have it. There is more extensive discussion of skepticism and contemporary analytic responses to it in the Epilogue.

The classical modern empiricists are John Locke (1632–1704), David Hume (1711–76), and George Berkeley (1685–1753). The classical modern rationalists are René Descartes (1596–1650), Baruch Spinoza (1632–77), and Gottfried Leibniz (1646–1716). Spinoza and Leibniz held that all ideas are innate in the mind, present at birth. Descartes held that most important ideas, like the idea of God and mathematical and geometrical notions, are innate. The rationalists argued that abstract ideas and ideas of God could not be derived from experience. Locke showed by laborious constructions how such ideas could be derived from experience by simple processes. Later rationalists shifted their ground somewhat and claimed that all knowledge is based, like math and geometry, on pure reason. The empiricists claimed that all knowledge is based on experience.

Background 1.2 – A priori, analytic, necessary

An *a priori* proposition is one that can be known independently of any particular experiences. An analytic proposition is one that is true in virtue of the definitions of the terms in the proposition. A necessary proposition is one that must be true, cannot be false. It is true in all possible worlds. All of this is admitted by philosophers to be murky. Empiricists tend to claim that *a priori* = analytic = necessary. Rationalists tend to deny that. Examples are "2 + 2 = 4." Most philosophers would agree that this is *a priori* and necessary. Many would also hold that it is analytic. "All grandmothers are mothers" is analytic (and *a priori* and necessary).Propositions that are not analytic are synthetic. Kant claimed that 5 + 7 = 12 is *a priori* and synthetic.

Background 1.3 – Mathematical logic of PM versus traditional Aristotelian logic and note on symbolism

Traditional Aristotelian logic, which was the only logic from about 400 BC until the publication of *PM*, held that every proposition was of the subject/predicate form, or compounds of such propositions. In "All zebras are animals," "zebras" is the subject term and "animals" is the predicate term. Traditional logic could not recognize relations nor handle singular terms. It treated "All zebras are animals" and "Socrates is an animal" as logically of the same form. The proposition "John is married to Betty" has "John" as its subject and attributes the predicate "married to Betty." "Betty is married to John" has "Betty" as subject term and attributes the predicate "married to John." This treatment misses the fact that "married to" is a relation.

Mathematical logic treats logic mathematically. Predicates represent functions from objects to truth-values. The two truth-values are true T and false F. So "x is an animal" is a function. "Socrates is an animal" is symbolized as "As" and it says that Socrates satisfies the function "animal," i.e. As gets the value T. "All zebras are animals" says that if any object satisfies the function "x is a zebra," then it satisfies the function "x is an animal." This would be symbolized as "$\forall x(Zx \supset Ax)$" which is read as "For all x, if x is a zebra, then x is an animal." The difference from traditional Aristotelian logic could not be more profound. Relations are just two, three, or more place functions. "John is married to Betty" says that the pair John/Betty satisfies the function "is married to." This is symbolized as "*Mjb*". The mathematical treatment of logic vastly increases the power, simplicity, and usefulness of logic. The original insights of the mathematical treatment of logic are due to Frege.

Note on symbolism: We have two quantifiers: the universal quantifier ∀ and the existential quantifier ∃. They are used with variables, x, y, z, etc. We also have symbols for truth-functional operators. **or** is symbolized by ∨, **and** by &, **not** by ∼, **implication** by ⊃, **equivalence** by ≡. We use upper-case letters as predicate symbols, lower-case letters as individual constants and variables. (See above.) We can make complex formulas by combining these symbols. Parentheses are used as punctuation marks. For example, $\exists x(Fx \& Gx) \supset \forall y(\sim Gy \supset \sim Fy)$. If something is F and G, then every nonG is nonF.

(See *Background 2.1* – Truth-tables, tautologies, etc. technical introduction to logical ideas in the *Tractatus*, p. 71, for the definition of the truth-functional operators in terms of truth-tables.)

Background 1.4 – Proofs that the sum of the interior angles of a triangle is 180° and that there are infinitely many prime numbers

Proof that the sum of the interior angles of a triangle is 180° (i.e. a straight line): This is an informal proof but is fully convincing. For this to work we need to assume the Euclidean parallel postulate. (At most one line can be drawn through any point not on a given line parallel to the given line in a plane., i.e. a line never gets closer to another line parallel to it.)

In Figure 1.4 Line 1 is parallel to Line 2. It is obvious (but can also be proved) that angle B = angle D, and C = E. D+A+E = B+A+C.

Proof that there are infinitely many prime numbers due to Euclid: Assume that there are finitely many prime numbers, i.e.

assume that there is a largest prime number. Say that l is the largest prime. Take all the finitely many primes and multiply them together, i.e. $2*3*5*\ldots *l$. The product is a huge composite number. Call it c. Now add 1 to c. This number, call it p, is equal to $c + 1$. p is larger than l, so it must be composite, since l is the largest prime. So p has some prime factors. But if we divide p by any of the prime numbers 2 to l, in each case we get a remainder of 1. So none of those primes is a factor of p. So either p is itself a prime greater than l, or p has a prime factor greater than l. This contradicts the assumption that l is the largest prime. Thus there is no largest prime.

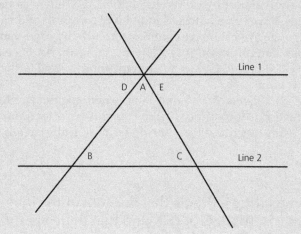

Figure 1.4

Background 1.5 – Technical explanation of Russell's paradox and other problems and a brief tour through Cantorian set theory

Russell's Paradox: Sets can contain themselves, e.g., intuitively, the set of big sets is a big set. Most sets do not contain themselves, e.g., the empty set does not contain itself. Now consider the set of all sets that do not contain themselves. Call it *S*. Is *S* a member of *S*? If it is, then *S* does not contain itself, since the members of *S* are the sets that do not contain themselves. On the other hand if *S* does not contain itself, then it does. In either case we get a contradiction. Thus there can be no such set as *S*.

Why is this a problem? The Comprehension Axiom was a vital part of the sort of set theory that Russell was using. The Comprehension Axiom says that any specification no matter how nutty specifies a set. This seems intuitively obvious, because if the specification is nutty enough (like, say, the set of round squares), we still get a set, i.e. the empty set. Russell's Paradox demonstrates that the Comprehension Axiom is not correct. At first Russell thought the problem would be easy to fix, but this turned out not to be the case.

Geog Cantor, the inventor of set theory, was able to demonstrate that there are ever larger sets without limit. By using an argument similar to Russell's demonstration of his paradox, but much earlier (by 1884), Cantor was able to establish that the set of subsets of any set has more elements than the set itself. Thus if we consider an infinite set, such as the natural numbers, we now know that the set of subsets of this set has more elements. Thus we get ever-higher levels of infinity. Also paradoxically there is no universal set – there can be no set of everything. It would have more subsets than itself. This is annoying because, e.g., each set should have a complement set – the set of things that are not in it. The complement of the empty set should be the universal set. But no such set exists. Problems mount, and are not easily solved by any intuitively satisfying methods.

Background 1.6 – German idealism and Bradley and McTaggart

German idealism was a loose school that grew out of the philosophy of Immanuel Kant in the nineteenth century. The main proponents were Fichte, Schelling, and Hegel, three thinkers often linked together. The term "idealism" in philosophy usually means a view that is opposed to both dualism and materialism. The idealists hold that everything, in some way or other, is mental or spiritual. The universe ultimately contains no matter or extra-mental energy. These are illusions. Very briefly, Kant held that the phenomena of our experience are the only things we can know about, but that they are generated by an unknown "thing-in-itself" which is non-mental, and not part of us. (Materialists hold that everything is matter, or physical; dualists hold that there are two kinds of substances: Mind and matter. Each ontological theory has problems.)

The German idealists get rid of Kant's unknowable thing-in-itself. The only things left are our mental phenomena and these are generated by the mind itself. For example, Fichte claimed that our representations, ideas, or mental images that make up our phenomenal world have their source in our ego, or knowing subject. No external thing-in-itself produces the ideas. Hegel and others expounded other bizarre ideas. For Hegel the world, universe, and history were manifestations of various stages of the development of Absolute Spirit. For the German idealists and their followers individuality was an illusion.

Hegel was much more influential than either Fichte or Schelling and by the end of the nineteenth century Hegelianism of one form or another was the dominant philosophy. Bradley and McTaggart were British Hegelians and idealists. Bradley denied the existence of individual things and, indeed, all of the deliverances of common sense. Instead there was just the one pure Hegelian Absolute. McTaggart famously denied the reality of time. For him, the universe is composed of timeless souls united by love.

Keep in mind that this is the barest snippet. No such snippet can do justice to the philosophers' ideas.

Further Reading

A good place to start for those interested in Frege is *The Frege Reader*, edited by Michael Beany (Wiley-Blackwell 1998). This also has an appendix with suggested further readings on Frege, which are voluminous. Also useful is *Frege: An Introduction to the Founder of Modern Analytic Philosophy* by Anthony Kenny (Wiley-Blackwell 1997).

Russell's autobiography is wonderful reading: *Russell Autobiography* (Routledge 1975).

The Cambridge Companion to Bertrand Russell (Cambridge University Press 2003) is a good place to find scholarly articles on Russell, with special emphasis on his early work and relations to Frege, Moore, and Wittgenstein.

Also *Russell, Idealism, and the Emergence of Analytic Philosophy* by Peter Hylton (Oxford University Press 1990) is a good source on the origins of British analytic philosophy but it is a tough slog.

The Philosophy of G. E. Moore, Vol. IV of *The Library of Living Philosophers*, edited by Paul A. Schilpp (Open Court 1999). This book contains articles by many leading philosophers, written for this volume, on aspects of Moore's philosophy. It includes Moore's replies to each article.

There is also a volume in the series devoted to Russell. *The Philosophy of Bertrand Russell (The Library of Living Philosophers Volume V)*, edited by Paul A. Schilpp (Open Court 1971).

Some Main Problems of Philosophy (Collier 1953) consists of 20 lectures that Moore gave in 1910–11 on many areas of philosophy.

A worthwhile book on Moore is *G. E. Moore* by Thomas Baldwin (Routledge 1990).

Origins of Analytical Philosophy by Michael Dummett (Harvard University Press 1996) supplements, and in some ways diverges from, the account of the subject that I give.

Contemporary Readings in Logical Theory (Macmillan 1967) edited by Irving M. Copi and James A. Gould is an extensive collection of classic articles on formal logic, its history, development, and many other aspects. This anthology contains several of the articles prominently featured in this and other chapters.

Symbolic Logic by Irving Copi (Prentice-Hall 1979) is a good introductory text.

2

Wittgenstein, the Vienna Circle, and Logical Positivism

It has long been one of my dreams to found a great school of mathematically-minded philosophers, but I don't know whether I shall ever get it accomplished. I had hopes of Norton, but he has not the physique, Broad is all right, but has no fundamental originality. Wittgenstein of course is exactly my dream. (Bertrand Russell to Lady Ottoline Morrell, December 29, 1912)

Introduction

Logical positivism, born in Vienna in the 1920s, was an energetic form of philosophy based on advances in mathematics and physics. Natural and social scientists, mathematicians, and philosophers came together to debate and develop the logical positivist program in what has come to be called the Vienna Circle. Even though the Vienna Circle was only a cohesive group from 1922 to the early 1930s, when the Nazis came to power, the views and ethos of the logical positivists spread throughout the English speaking world and beyond to Scandinavia, the Netherlands, and Poland. Logical positivism was a dominant focus in analytic philosophy until the early 1960s and much of analytic philosophy was dedicated to attacking, defending, elaborating, or questioning the central tenets of the Vienna Circle. Today these issues, although not as central as they once were, continue to be debated. The spirit of logical positivism is still alive, perhaps a bit subdued, but still there.

A Brief History of Analytic Philosophy: From Russell to Rawls, First Edition. Stephen P. Schwartz.
© 2012 John Wiley & Sons, Inc. Published 2012 by John Wiley & Sons, Inc.

Logical positivism developed from several sources. Among the most important were the philosophical methods and ideas of Frege and Russell, including their logicism especially as interpreted by Ludwig Wittgenstein in his *Tractatus Logico-Philosophicus* (Wittgenstein 1961b/1921). Since many of the early logical positivists were scientists and mathematicians, they were also inspired by recent innovations in physics, especially Einstein's theory of relativity. Although the logical positivists were not especially interested in the older traditions of philosophy, except to overthrow them, many of their views harked back to the classical British empiricists and more recent German-speaking empiricists such as the physicist Ernst Mach.[1]

Like Russell and Moore, the members of the Vienna Circle reacted against Hegelian German idealism. From the end of the eighteenth century to World War I, Germans (including German speaking Austrians, Swiss, Czechs, etc.) were dominant in philosophy, mathematics, and science.[2] Historical events help explain why a reaction against this German tradition in philosophy would arise in Germany and Austria. Germany and Austria had been disastrously beaten in a hideous war, World War I, which overturned all of society and the governments of Prussia and Austria. Many blamed the Prussian aristocratic traditions for starting the war and for not being able to pursue it successfully. Marxism, based on German philosophy, had taken over in Russia and was a real threat to German speaking nations. Philosophers were as fed up and disgusted with the traditions of Prussia, as was almost everybody else.[3]

In 1920 the air was right for a reaction against the traditions of Hegelian German idealism and Prussian rationalistic metaphysics, especially as represented by Kant and his followers.[4] The air in Germany and Austria was not quite right, however, for the intensity of the logical positivists' attack. Not surprisingly, the positivists and Wittgenstein were disliked or ignored in their own lands. They found a much

---

[1] The official name of the Vienna Circle was the "Ernst Mach Society."

[2] The list of great German-speaking scientists is, of course, immense, headed by Einstein. In philosophy the list starts with Leibniz, gets a tremendous boost from Immanuel Kant, and continues with Hegel, Schelling, Fichte, Feuerbach, Marx, Nietzsche, and many others.

[3] Sadly as it turns out not everybody in Austria and Germany was fed up. But those who still harbored hopes of Prussian glory were deeply subdued by the recent defeats – subdued that is until the Nazis gave them renewed vigor.

[4] Despite this reaction on the part of the logical positivists, they could not help being influenced by Kantian and neo-Kantian philosophy which was so much a dominant theme in late nineteenth- and early twentieth-century German philosophy. Recent scholarship has traced this influence. See Further Readings at the end of the chapter.

better reception in Britain and the United States. By 1938 most of the logical positivists had emigrated to England or America.

Ludwig Wittgenstein and the *Tractatus Logico-Philosophicus*

Although not a member of the Vienna Circle, Wittgenstein had a crucial influence on the development of the views of the logical positivists. He also later became one of the major critics of logical positivism and especially of his own philosophy as expounded in the *Tractatus*, as it is commonly called. Thus we have what philosophical scholars call the "early Wittgenstein" and the "later Wittgenstein." In this chapter the early Wittgenstein will be featured along with the Vienna Circle and other logical positivists and their allies. The later Wittgenstein will star in later chapters when we consider, more directly, problems with and criticisms of the logical positivist program and the ordinary language philosophy that grew up as one response to its downfall.

Wittgenstein is the most influential and the most widely read and studied of the analytic philosophers. (The Cornell University library lists 452 books on or about Wittgenstein, but only 139 for Russell.) If Frege is the pioneer and Bertrand Russell the father of analytic philosophy, then Wittgenstein's writings provide the backbone. And what an odd and creaky backbone it is! Just for the sake of comparison: Russell published dozens of philosophy books during his lifetime and hundreds of articles and pamphlets. Wittgenstein published only the *Tractatus* and one short article, and even the *Tractatus* was only published after Wittgenstein had essentially given up on it appearing in print. Shortly after Wittgenstein's death in 1951 a collection of his notes and writings appeared with the title *Philosophical Investigations*. Yet the *Tractatus* and *Philosophical Investigations* have attained almost biblical status among analytic philosophers and for many others as well. Like the books of the Bible, many nowadays love and revere them, others are dubious, and not a few are disdainful.

The members of the Vienna Circle accorded the *Tractatus* the honor of reading and discussing it line-by-line. It supplied an intellectual boost that helped to define the basic program of the logical positivists. The *Tractatus*, however, is a strange book to have played this role. It is short, and short on arguments. It is written in a unique oracular style that is aphoristic and terse. It has elements of mysticism and seems in places to verge on incomprehensibility. Nevertheless no real understanding of logical positivism and the further development of analytic philosophy is possible without grasping what the logical positivists took from the *Tractatus*.[5]

The story of Wittgenstein's early life and philosophical development is legendary among aficionados.

Wittgenstein came from a very wealthy and cultured Viennese family. His father was one of the most successful industrialists in Austria. After an undistinguished and sad childhood (two of Wittgenstein's older brothers killed themselves and he was often suicidal), Wittgenstein became interested in physics. On the advice of his father he moved to England and worked on engineering problems involving propellers at the University of Manchester. He became more interested in mathematics than physics and then turned to the philosophy of mathematics when he studied Russell's *Principles of Mathematics*. Wittgenstein consulted Frege during a visit to Germany and was encouraged by him to study with Russell at Cambridge. Russell soon recognized Wittgenstein's gift for philosophy and urged him to give up engineering and devote himself to logic and the foundations of mathematics. Wittgenstein started as a freshman in 1912 at Trinity College, Cambridge University. Soon Russell and Wittgenstein became close friends. Wittgenstein also had intellectual contacts with many of the famous people then at Cambridge, among them Moore, John Maynard Keynes, the leading economist of the day, and G. H. Hardy, the famous mathematician.

Wittgenstein was never happy at Cambridge although he spent the rest of his life, on and off, there. Because he was uncomfortable in the academic setting, he often fled to remote parts of Europe. He especially liked the coasts of Ireland and Norway. In 1914 Wittgenstein was living at a remote spot on a fjord in Norway working on philosophy and on his new ideas about how to simplify and improve the logic of Frege and Russell. He was especially concerned about the fundamentals of Whitehead and Russell's *Principia Mathematica*. Throughout his life Wittgenstein wrote voluminously in notebooks. These early notebooks from Norway are studied and combed by Wittgensteinians for clues to interpretation of difficult passages in the *Tractatus*.

When the Great War began Wittgenstein enlisted in the Austrian army. Because of his engineering background, he was appointed an artillery officer. He saw action and was decorated several times. He also began work on synthesizing and organizing his many notes in order to present them in book form. This was eventually to be published as the *Logisch-Philosophische Abhandlung – The Tractatus Logico-Philosophicus*. As Austria was collapsing militarily and socially,

---

[5]   I say "what the logical positivists took from the *Tractatus*," because claims about what the *Tractatus* actually contains philosophically are still the subject of intense disagreement.

Wittgenstein finished the manuscript of the *Tractatus* while on leave in Vienna. On November 3, 1918 he was taken prisoner by the Italians along with his entire unit. At this point in the war, the situation for Austria-Hungry was hopeless and entire divisions of the Austro-Hungarian army were surrendering to the Italians. Wittgenstein had two copies of the manuscript of the *Tractatus* in his backpack when he entered the prisoner-of-war camp. He managed to send one copy to Russell and the other to Frege. When Wittgenstein was released in 1919 he returned to Vienna and gave away the fortune he had inherited at the death of his father, and began training to be a grammar school teacher. He thought he had solved every outstanding problem in philosophy. There was nothing left to do in philosophy.

Understandably, given its obscure and difficult style and revolutionary ideas about logic expressed in a compressed format, Wittgenstein was unable to find a publisher for his masterpiece. Russell wrote an introduction to help get it published, but Wittgenstein disliked it and actually was offended by Russell's misinterpretations and mild criticisms. This was a disappointing time for Wittgenstein. He sent Frege a copy, but Frege was extremely critical and apparently only read a few pages before giving up. After a final failure to find a publisher Wittgenstein wrote to Russell in July 1920 "for the moment I shall take no further steps to have it published, so it is completely at your disposal and you can do with it whatever you want. (Only when you change something in the text, indicate that the alteration is yours)" (Cited in Monk 1990, p. 184).

How tragic and frustrating this must have been for Wittgenstein. He believed, not unjustifiably, that the *Tractatus* made major advances in clarifying the nature of the new logic and more hubristically contained the dissolution of all philosophical problems. Yet it was being ignored. In 1921 the *Tractatus* was finally published in an obscure periodical in German. After being refused by Cambridge University Press, it was published by Kegan Paul in an English translation with Russell's introduction. By 1924 Wittgenstein's ideas from the *Tractatus* were being discussed avidly in Vienna. The standard edition now is published with facing German and English pages by Routledge and Kegan Paul. I have my treasured copy next to my computer as I write this.

Wittgenstein's style in the *Tractatus* is declamatory and disdainful. You either "get" a claim he makes and accept it or not – not much argument and little discussion is there to help. Wittgenstein's personality was like that as well. Temperamentally he was far from the members of the Vienna Circle and philosophers in general, who argue with each other, interrupt each other, chide and provoke each other mercilessly. Philosophy thrives on this Socratic give and take. Wittgenstein was more like a prophet or seer whose pronouncements must be pondered in admiring silence. Of course, this irritates many philosophers and Wittgenstein has had as many detractors as admirers. Even Carnap did not get along with Wittgenstein, although he took many of his ideas from the *Tractatus*. Wittgenstein met with various members of the Vienna Circle but before long he refused to meet with Carnap present. Carnap in his autobiography gives a telling account of Wittgenstein:

> His [Wittgenstein's] point of view and attitude toward people and problems, even theoretical problems, were much more similar to those of a creative artist than to those of a scientist; one might almost say, similar to those of a religious prophet or a seer. When he started to formulate his view on some specific philosophical problem, we often felt the internal struggle that occurred in him that very moment, a struggle by which he tried to penetrate from darkness to light under an intense and painful strain, which was even visible on his most expressive face. When finally, often after a prolonged arduous effort, his answer came forth, his statement stood before us like a newly created piece of art or a divine revelation. Not that he asserted his views dogmatically. Although some of the formulations of the *Tractatus* sound as if there could not be any possibility of a doubt, he often expressed the feeling that his statements were inadequate. But the impression he made on us was as if insight came to him as through divine inspiration, so that we could not help feeling that any sober rational comment or analysis of it would be a profanation. (Carnap 1963, pp. 25–6)

Wittgenstein took up teaching grammar school, since he believed that neither he, nor anyone else, could make any further contributions to philosophy. He was not a successful schoolteacher, however, and soon quit. He did some architectural work for his sister in Vienna (Figure 2.1) and met occasionally with members of the Vienna Circle to discuss philosophy.

In 1929 Wittgenstein returned to Cambridge and received his PhD for the *Tractatus*, being examined by Russell and Moore. Due to the probing of several friends Wittgenstein began seriously to question his ideas. His notebooks and lectures from this period show him moving away from the *Tractatus*. The renowned Italian economist Piero Sraffa, who was in Cambridge at the time, had the most challenging questions. With the help of Russell, Wittgenstein got a fellowship at Trinity College, which he needed, since he had given away all his money. He was also meeting regularly with a coterie of followers. His lectures and notes, many of which were circulated informally and only published after his

Figure 2.1 The house in Vienna that Wittgenstein helped design for his sister. Today it is occupied by the Cultural Department of the Bulgarian Embassy

death, became pivotal for the movement away from the *Tractatus* and logical positivism.

Our concern in this chapter, however, is with the *Tractatus* and its influence. The *Tractatus* is impossible to summarize, but the heart of it is the application of Wittgenstein's ideas about logic to problems in the philosophy of language and foundations of mathematics. Although strikingly original and upsetting, his ideas are extensions and simplifications of the work of Frege and Russell. Wittgenstein, however, does not indulge in lengthy derivations; there are no axioms, no proofs, and hardly any symbolic logic, although his ideas provide the basics of the way symbolic logic is taught in universities today.

Wittgenstein is concerned to understand what language and thought have to be like in order to represent the world. The world consists of all the actual states of affairs, but language must also be able to represent non-actual states of affairs. All the possible ways that objects can be combined constitute the possible states of affairs. In order for us to be able to think about the world and talk about it, there must be a fundamental similarity of structure or isomorphism between thought and language, and between language and the world. This structure is represented by formal logic. Wittgenstein's guiding idea is that logic does not describe very abstract or fundamental facts or truths about the world or thought or even language, as all previous philosophers, including Frege and Russell, had assumed. Logic does not provide statements of facts at all. It is the framework or scaffolding that makes statements of facts possible.

Although Wittgenstein never used the term "logical atomism" his views are similar to Russell's. (See previous chapter, pp. 25–26.) Wittgenstein held that there are atomic or simple facts or states of affairs, each one of which is logically independent of all the others. Atomic propositions represent atomic states of affairs. All compound or complex propositions are built up of truth-functions of atomic propositions. These truth-functions are set out in truth-tables. Every undergraduate who takes a logic course learns about truth-tables, probably in the first week of the course. [*Background 2.1*– Truth-tables, tautologies, etc. technical introduction to logical ideas in the *Tractatus*] First introduced by Wittgenstein in the *Tractatus*, the idea is simple and elegant and has found numerous applications in philosophy, mathematics, engineering, and computer programming.

Tautologies and self-contradictions are limiting cases of truth-functions. A tautology is a compound sentence that comes out true no matter what propositions it is composed of. For example, sentences of the form *p or not p* and *if p, then p* and *if p, then if q, then p* are tautologies. These would be symbolized today as "$p \vee \sim p$" and "$p \supset p$" and "$p \supset (q \supset p)$".[6] Self-contradictions are just negations of tautologies. Thus for example "$\sim (p \vee \sim p)$" and "$\sim (p \supset p)$" are self-contractions as is "$p \& \sim p$" (*p and not p*). The point is that tautologies and self-contradictions are recognizable by a purely formal mechanical process – truth-tables. Also, according to Wittgenstein, tautologies and self-contradictions are without meaning in the sense that they contain no information, they do not represent or picture facts. I could enunciate endless tautologies about your favorite subject and each would be true, and at the end you would know no more about the subject than you did at the beginning. A tautology is compatible with every state of affairs, thus it contains no information.

Wittgenstein's use of truth-tables to demystify logic and mathematics provided the fuel for the logical positivist locomotive. Frege, Russell, and Whitehead, according to Wittgenstein, had accomplished a brilliant feat in showing that mathematics could be derived from logic, but they did not fully grasp what they had done. Frege and Russell still had ideas about self-evidence and pure reason floating around. Although Russell held that mathematics was analytic, he did not at first realize the implications of this. Russell was still yearning for some sort of intellectually satisfying certainty, whereas according to Wittgenstein the only certainty available is empty and formal.

---

[6] Wittgenstein used an awkward form of symbolization in the *Tractatus*. The symbols used in today's university courses are closer to Russell's in *PM*.

Throughout the modern era, and even before, philosophers have been somewhat confused about analytic "knowledge" and its relation to certainty.[7] No one really considered until Wittgenstein's *Tractatus* that analytic propositions contain no factual content and really do not represent knowledge at all. Whatever certainty they afford is worthless for support of knowledge. Analytic propositions, according to Wittgenstein, are tautologies and thus gain their self-evidence from their purely formal structure. They are not axioms in the traditional sense. Indeed for Wittgenstein there are no such axioms. All logical propositions are equal. Whether a proposition is tautological is not determined by deriving it from other more basic propositions, but by performing a mechanical truth-table test. Thus mathematics is purely tautological in character. Mathematical propositions do not represent any facts, do not have any content, and like all logical propositions are useful only in enabling us to transform one factual proposition into another one that follows from it. As we saw in the last chapter, Russell, after studying the ideas of the *Tractatus*, came grudgingly to accept Wittgenstein's deflationary view of mathematics. All the axioms, postulates, and theorems of logic and mathematics are tautological. They have the appearance of great depth and profundity but, when properly analyzed, one realizes that they are empty.

Although Wittgenstein never mentions empiricism in the *Tractatus* and does not seem to be interested in the empiricist program, his analysis of logic supported empiricism. Thus Rudolf Carnap, the most important and influential member of the Vienna Circle, in a section titled "The Tautological Character of Logic," says the following:

> On the basis of the new logic [the *Tractatus*], the essential character of logical sentences can be clearly recognized. This has become of the greatest importance for the theory of mathematical knowledge as well as for the clarification of controversial philosophical questions.
>
> The usual distinction in logic between fundamental and derived sentences is arbitrary. It is immaterial whether a logical sentence is derived from other sentences. Its validity can be recognized from its form.
>
> . . .
>
> Since all the sentences of logic are tautological and devoid of content, we cannot draw inferences from them about what was necessary or impossible in reality. Thus the attempt to base metaphysics on pure logic which is chiefly characteristic of such a system as Hegel's, is shown to be unwarranted. Mathematics as a branch of logic is also tautological. (Carnap 1959b/1930, pp. 141–2)

---

[7]   Leibniz, who developed precursors of modern logic, thought all true propositions were analytic and could be deduced by pure reason, if only we had enough time.

In a passage from an article by Hans Hahn, a leading mathematician and a member of the Vienna Circle, the problem that mathematics presents for empiricism is stated clearly.

> [E]mpiricism faces an apparently insuperable difficulty: how is it to account for the real validity of logical and mathematical statements? Observation discloses to me only the transient, it does not reach beyond the observed; there is no bond that would lead from one observed fact to another, that would compel future observations to have the same result as those already made. The laws of logic and mathematics, however, claim *absolutely universal* validity: . . .
>
> The conclusion seems inevitable: since the propositions of logic and mathematics have absolutely universal validity, are apodictically certain, since it must be as they say and cannot be otherwise, these propositions cannot be derived from experience. In view of the tremendous importance of logic and mathematics in the system of our knowledge, empiricism, therefore seems to be irrevocably refuted. (Hahn 1959/1933, pp. 149–50)

Hahn goes on to propound the response to this dilemma for empiricism:

> To sum up: we must distinguish two kinds of statements: those which say something about facts and those which merely express the way in which the rules which govern the application of words to facts depend upon each other. Let us call statements of the latter kind *tautologies*: they say nothing about objects and are for this very reason certain, universally valid, irrefutable by observation; whereas the statements of the former kind are not certain and are refutable by observation. The logical laws of contradiction and of the excluded middle are tautologies, likewise, e.g., the statement "nothing is both red and blue."
>
> . . .
>
> If I have succeeded in clarifying somewhat the role of logic, I may now be quite brief about the role of *mathematics*. The propositions of mathematics are of exactly the same kind as the propositions of logic: they are tautologous, they say nothing at all about the objects we want to talk about. (Hahn 1959/1933, pp. 157–8)

Although neither Hahn nor Carnap mention Wittgenstein in these passages they would readily acknowledge that these ideas were drawn from the *Tractatus*.

The original statements in the *Tractatus* are even more blunt:

6.1   The propositions of logic are tautologies.
6.11   Therefore the propositions of logic say nothing. (They are the analytic propositions.)

6.2   Mathematics is a logical method.

The propositions of mathematics are equations, and therefore pseudo-propositions.

6.22   The logic of the world, which is shown in tautologies by the propositions of logic, is shown in equations by mathematics.

(Wittgenstein 1961b/1921)

The *Tractatus* is written as a series of numbered statements. The whole numbers are assigned to the main propositions. The numerals after the point show the order of comment. Thus 6.22 is a comment on or elaboration of 6.2. (No number goes beyond four places after the point.) Seven propositions are assigned whole numbers. These are the main propositions to be elucidated. These seven are worth listing:[8]

1.   The world is all that is the case.

2.   What is the case – a fact – is the existence of states of affairs.

3.   A logical picture of facts is a thought.

4.   A thought is a proposition with a sense.

5.   A proposition is a truth-function of elementary propositions. (An elementary proposition is a truth-function of itself.)

6.   The general form of a truth-function is $[\bar{p}, \bar{\xi}, N(\bar{\xi})]$.
This is the general form of a proposition.

7.   What we cannot speak about we must pass over in silence.

Proposition 7 is the final sentence of the entire book.

Wittgenstein's *Tractatus* showed the logical positivists and other empiricists the way to respond to the threat of logic and mathematics, nevertheless there is much in the *Tractatus* that would make an empiricist uncomfortable. There is a sense of absoluteness, a lack of tentativeness, a deification of logic that seems inconsistent with the worldliness and messiness of experience as a source of knowledge. Wittgenstein mentions mysticism and ethics with reverence while denying that ethical or mystical utterances are cognitively meaningful. A selection of quotes gives the tone of Wittgenstein's attitude:

6.41   The sense of the world must lie outside the world. In the world everything is as it is, and everything happens as it does happen: *in* it no value exists – and if it did exist, it would have no value.

      . . . .

---

[8]   Thus 6.1 quoted above is a first level comment on 6 below, etc.

6.42   And so it is impossible for there to be propositions of ethics.
        Propositions can express nothing that is higher.
6.421   It is clear that ethics cannot be put into words.
        Ethics is transcendental.
        (Ethics and aesthetics are one and the same.)
6.522   There are indeed, things that cannot be put into words. They
        make themselves manifest. They are what is mystical.
        (Wittgenstein 1961b/1921)

The logical positivists would agree that there are no ethical or aesthetic propositions, assuming that by "proposition" we mean a statement that has a cognitive meaning. The logical positivists and their followers and allies[9] would not, on the other hand, like nor understand the claim that ethics is transcendental, and neither do I. Logical empiricists also rejected the view that the mystical makes itself manifest. This is exactly what they opposed. They held that mysticism reflects an interesting psychological condition but that is all. They would deny that mysticism reveals anything "higher." In any case, the mystical, the ethical, or anything "higher" would not be within the province of philosophy. Wittgenstein and the logical empiricists agree about that at least.

Although Wittgenstein never uses the word "metaphysics" in the *Tractatus* and uses "metaphysical" only three times and only once in the sense relevant to the logical positivists, the following passage foreshadows a key feature of the positivists' program – the rejection of metaphysics.

6.53   The correct method in philosophy would really be the following:
        to say nothing except what can be said, i.e. propositions of natural
        science – i.e. something that has nothing to do with philosophy – and
        then, whenever someone else wanted to say something metaphysical,
        to demonstrate to him that he had failed to give a meaning to certain
        signs in his propositions. Although it would not be satisfying to the
        other person – he would not have the feeling that we were teaching
        him philosophy – *this* method would be the only strictly correct one.
        (Wittgenstein 1961b/1921)

Wittgenstein states his grounds for the rejection of traditional metaphysics and indeed all of traditional philosophy.

---

[9] Usually lumped together as modern empiricists or logical empiricists, since they did not all follow the Vienna Circle in every detail and many found the term "positivism" to be divisive and irritating since it came with historical baggage.

4.11   The totality of true propositions is the whole of natural science
          (or the whole corpus of the natural sciences).
4.111   Philosophy is not one of the natural sciences.
          . . . .
4.112   Philosophy aims at the logical clarification of thoughts.
          Philosophy is not a body of doctrine but an activity.
          A philosophical work consists entirely of elucidations.
          Philosophy does not result in 'philosophical propositions', but
      rather in the clarification of propositions. (Wittgenstein 1961b/1921)

This is the view of philosophy that was adopted by the logical empiricists. The job of philosophers is to analyze and elucidate propositions,
to clarify the language of science, to root out all vestiges of metaphysical
thought-wandering and expose them to criticism. The title of an early
article by Carnap sums it up: "The Elimination of Metaphysics through
Logical Analysis of Language."

The Vienna Circle is infamous for its uncompromising attack on metaphysics. Of course this "elimination" of metaphysics also extended to
ethics and theology and, just as Wittgenstein says, anything other than
natural science. Naturally, many non-scientists found this attack irritating, invidious, and disturbing. Did this bother the logical positivists?
Not at all. Philosophers are supposed to be gadflies. If we're not annoying folks we're not doing our job. Most philosophers, even if we did not
enjoy membership in the Vienna Circle or agree with the logical positivists, feel that they presented a fair challenge to the metaphysicians,
theologians, and ethicists.

Historical Note: The Vienna Circle and their Allies

Only one, Herbert Feigl, of the original members of the Vienna Circle
was trained as a philosopher. In fact Feigl gave the name "logical positivism" to the group's doctrines in 1931. Moritz Schlick, the
leader of the group, was a physicist who trained under Max Planck.
Kurt Gödel, a mathematician, met with the group. Other members
included Hans Hahn, a mathematician with many theorems and results
named after him; Otto Neurath was an economist, Phillip Frank a
physicist, Friedrich Waismann also was a physicist. Rudolf Carnap
came late to the group and had been trained as a physicist and
philosopher. He became one of the most important and influential
philosophers of the twentieth century and was the leading exponent of the logical empiricism that grew out of the discussions of
the group.

The Vienna Circle had a branch in Berlin headed by Hans Reichenbach, a philosopher who had studied with Ernst Cassirer, David Hilbert, Max Planck, and Max Born. Carl Hempel was a member of the Berlin Circle who became a leading twentieth-century philosopher. He is perhaps second only to Carnap as an exponent (and critic) of logical empiricism (the term he introduced and preferred). Karl Popper, a well-known philosopher of science and political philosopher, was on the fringe of the Vienna Circle. The logical positivists of the Vienna Circle had many followers in Scandinavia, Australia, New Zealand, and the United States, who spread their doctrines as missionaries to the benighted hordes. The holy task was to inspire a sense of metaphysical sin in the natives.

The Elimination of Metaphysics and the Logical Positivist Program

A. J. Ayer, a British philosopher, is the best known and most famous exponent of logical positivism. Although he was not a member of the Vienna Circle and barely understood German,[10] Ayer's book *Language, Truth and Logic* published in 1936 did more to popularize the ideas of the Vienna Circle in English-speaking lands than any other text. *Language, Truth and Logic* (Ayer 1946/1936) is a summary and somewhat simplified version of the ideas of the *Tractatus* and the Vienna Circle, put in a clear, direct, and often blunt style. (Note of caution: Many now would hold that the view of logical positivism derived from Ayer is a caricature of a varied, motley, and creative family of views. Nevertheless this "caricature" had been the standard view of logical positivism until the last 20 or so years when it was questioned by recent historians of the Vienna Circle. (See further readings.) Given its historical importance, the exposition I give here is essentially that standard view. The standard view is derived from Ayer, Quine, and others including logical positivists themselves. Ayer, Quine, and other proponents of the standard view knew the members of the Vienna Circle intimately or were members themselves. So I trust their story isn't too much of a caricature. No doubt their story will be picked apart and modified, but it is *the* story that is the subject of the pickings apart and modifications.)

---

[10] A. J. Ayer, from Oxford, and W. V. O. Quine, from Harvard visited the Vienna Circle. A. J. Ayer spent the year 1933 meeting with the Circle. Quine visited Vienna in 1932 but followed Carnap to Prague. Quine and Carnap remained close friends although they were at odds with each other philosophically. Ayer and Quine also differed philosophically. Ayer was an avid supporter of logical positivism, while Quine was the leading critic.

Despite its simple style and dubious argumentation, *Language, Truth and Logic* is a classic of twentieth-century philosophy. It has sold more copies than any other academic work of philosophy. It is still in print, and read and cited, and used for target practice, by budding philosophers. I read *Language, Truth and Logic* as a freshman in college and it changed my life or at least my way of thinking about philosophy. And I was not the only one so affected among my companions.

The first sentence of Ayer's *Language, Truth and Logic* is "The traditional disputes of philosophers are, for the most part, as unwarranted as they are unfruitful" (Ayer 1946/1936, p.33). This is from Chapter 1 "The Elimination of Metaphysics." The key feature emphasized by the logical positivists was that their attack on metaphysics was not pragmatic; it was semantic or logical. According to Ayer: "one cannot overthrow a system of transcendent metaphysics merely by criticizing the way in which it comes into being. What is required is rather a criticism of the nature of the actual statements which comprise it" (Ayer 1946/1936, p. 34). The utterances of the metaphysicians are found to be meaningless – without cognitive content. According to Carnap, they are devoid of literal sense: "In the domain of *metaphysics*, including all philosophy of value and normative theory, logical analysis yields the negative result *that the alleged statements in this domain are entirely meaningless*" (Carnap 1959a/1932, pp. 60–1). The logical positivists thought that their logical or semantic elimination of metaphysics was more solid and decisive than any attack on metaphysics that was based on such pragmatic considerations as the inability of metaphysicians to solve real world problems, their inability to agree on any results, or on psychological claims about the supposed weakness of the human intellect.

The positivists' elimination caught on. It especially appealed to those hard-minded scientists and mathematicians who disliked philosophy anyway. They felt this was a salutary clearing away of the vestiges of medieval pseudo-science posing as deep thinking. (As a young professor in the mid-1970s I proposed to teach a course titled "Introduction to Metaphysics." Offering this new course required approval by a faculty curriculum committee composed of non-philosophers. Approval was denied on the grounds that "there is no such subject. It has been eliminated." The committee changed its decision when I explained somewhat disingenuously that I meant to teach the *history* of metaphysics – you know, Plato, Aristotle, Descartes, those guys.)

The logic-based attack on metaphysics (and ethics, aesthetics, and theology) was distilled into what is one of the most famous slogans of philosophy – the verifiability criterion of meaningfulness. "We say that a sentence is factually significant to any given person if, and only if, he knows how to verify the proposition which it purports to express ..." (Ayer 1946/1936, p. 35). Of course, this needs to be qualified in many ways. Verification need not be conclusive or no general propositions would be meaningful. Also there may be practical problems involved with verification, so a proposition need only be verifiable in principle. The statements of mathematics, including geometry and logic, are meaningful according to Ayer and Carnap (pace Wittgenstein) but are tautologies. So a more complete and guarded version of the verifiability criterion of meaningfulness would go as follows: "A putative proposition is meaningful if and only if it is weakly verifiable in principle or it is a tautology or self-contradiction." "Weakly verifiable" means that it need not be conclusively verifiable, and "in principle" is intended to avoid practical limits to verification.

Most utterances of metaphysicians, ethicists, aestheticians, and theologians do not meet this criterion, therefore they are meaningless. Or so the logical positivists claimed.[11]

This is the first major part of the logical positivist program:

The elimination of metaphysics, ethics, aesthetics, and theology by the verifiability criterion of meaningfulness.

The elimination of metaphysics leaves an obvious puzzle. If the utterances of the metaphysicians (ethicists, theologians, etc.) are literally meaningless how can the grand history of these "disciplines" be explained? How can one explain the devotion of generations of brilliant minds to them, to the pursuit of nonsense?

The answer given by the logical positivists, and again this is based on the *Tractatus*, is that metaphysicians have been bewitched by language. (Ethics and religion would be explained biologically, psychologically, or in a Marxist/Leninist fashion as instruments of class oppression.)

We have already seen one example of bewitchment by language in the previous chapter. Philosophers were misled by superficial grammar to assume that each apparent referring term must have a referent. If no "real" referent was available, such as for "Santa Claus" or "the president of Canada," then there must be an "unreal" one that has being but not physical reality. Russell's analysis of definite descriptions was a paradigm of what philosophy should be according to the logical

---

[11]   I am suppressing criticisms of the logical positivists until later. All these doctrines came under heavy fire from Wittgenstein, Quine, and ordinary language philosophers. Those criticisms played such an important role in the development of analytic philosophy that they require chapters of their own and will be surveyed in the following two.

positivists. It dissolved metaphysical puzzlement by logical analysis of language.

Because of statements such as "There is a prime number between 5 and 9," philosophers were led to believe in the real existence of less dubious entities such as numbers. A number is not a physical object. So it must be an abstract object that exists eternally and perfectly as a metaphysical object outside of time and space. Now we are off and running, intoxicated by our metaphysical discoveries. That is until the demystification project of the Vienna Circle saves us from our linguistic illusions. Frege, Russell, and Whitehead had shown that we have no need to postulate such entities as numbers, or rather that talk of numbers could be translated into talk about logic and sets or properties. Sets and properties, alas, are still a bit suspicious. Wittgenstein accomplishes the final demystification with his analysis of such talk as consisting of nothing but formal tautologies which carry no ontological or referential weight at all.

The logical positivists believed that all metaphysical mystification rested on confusions engendered by language. The basic problem is the unstated but pervasive assumption that every term must have a referent. Thus, for example, in English every adjective can be made into a noun. We have "redness," "quickness," "beauty," and "justice." I heard this sentence last Sunday afternoon while watching TV: "The quickness of the wide receiver enabled him to score." The subject of the sentence is quickness. We are all taught in grade school that a noun stands for a person, place, or thing. "Quickness" is not a person or place, so it must be a thing; but what kind of thing? Ah! Enter the metaphysicians with their abstract objects that cannot be seen but can be known. Wait a minute! The quickness of the wide receiver can be seen, I saw it, but justice cannot be. But can quickness *itself* be seen as opposed to quick people or objects? Quickness itself is a universal that we apprehend with the help of seeing quick things. It is easy to understand how this kind of thread can spin off endless paragraphs of apparently profound thought – or nonsense. When represented in symbolic logic such terms as "quickness" would not be the subject of sentences. They appear only as predicates. Although Russell sometimes treated properties and universals as real entities in themselves, in Wittgensteinian first order symbolic logic they only appear as represented by predicate letters.

The treatment of existence is another example of how symbolic logic relieves metaphysical puzzlement. An awful lot of metaphysical thought has been devoted to being and existence, as though these were deep metaphysical attributes. What is the nature of Being? And even more fascinatingly what is the nature of Not Being? Endless midnight ponderings have been aroused by these sorts of questions. All of which are (or should be according to the logical positivists) eliminated by attention to logical symbolism – in particular to the quantifiers. Consider the claim "Zebras exist." This looks like a straightforward claim that zebras have the property of existing, just as "Zebras run" attributes the property of running to zebras. Despite the superficial similarity these two sentences are logically very different. "Existence" is not a property at all; it is expressed by a quantifier. "Zebras run" is translated into the symbolism as "$\forall x(Zx \supset Rx)$. For any x, if x is a zebra, then x runs. (Don't worry about whether this is true, we are only concerned with its form.) On the other hand, "Zebras exist" is translated as "$\exists xZx$." There is an x, such that x is a zebra. The contrast could not be more evident. In the same vein consider "Unicorns do not exist." Do not get metaphysical over this and wonder how something could have the property of not existing. Is "not existing" having the property of non-existence or just lacking the property of existence? These metaphysical questions are going nowhere. (Oops. Where is nowhere?) Eliminate this nonsense. Just recall your sophomore logic class and symbolize it: $\sim \exists xUx$. Metaphysics? – Poof! If you insist that existence is a property, it is not a property of individuals but is a property of properties. It is the property a property has when at least one thing has the property. Thus it makes no sense to say, e.g., that God exists (or does not exist). The logical positivists "eliminated" the jewel of metaphysics, the ontological argument for the existence God, in this way. [*Background 2.2* – The ontological argument, substance and property, etc.] Ayer insisted that he was not an atheist, because an atheist denies the existence of God, which of course Ayer claimed was just as meaningless as asserting the existence of God. In Ayer's view either to assert or deny the existence of God is meaningless.

We've now arrived, slightly out of breath, at the second major tenet of the logical positivists:

The cause of metaphysical puzzlement is the superficial grammar of language; its cure is logical analysis.

Despite their protestations, there was more than intellectual fastidiousness motivating the logical positivists' attack on metaphysics. We have already noted that German post-Kantian idealism was redolent of Prussian arrogance. Thus Marxist-leaning members of the Vienna Circle such as Neurath considered metaphysics to be reactionary, a tool of class oppression allied with traditional religion. Ironically the logical positivists in turn were accused of being bourgeois ideologues because of their resistance to dialectical materialism, which they would classify as a metaphysical view. The Marxists and Communists followed Lenin in his scathing attack on empiricism delivered in his inflammatory style in the book *Materialism and Empirio-Criticism: Critical Comments on a Reactionary Philosophy* (1909). *Materialism and Empirio-Criticism* was considered to be a classic of Marxist-Leninist philosophy and was required reading in the Soviet Union well into the 1970s. Lenin's extremely hostile attack on empiricism was applied ferociously to the logical empiricism that grew out of the Vienna Circle. The fact that all of the members of the Vienna Circle were anti-fascists and political liberals and several were Marxists or socialists earned them no sympathy at all from the Bolsheviks.

The third and fourth tenets are familiar from earlier passages:

> *Logic and mathematics consist of nothing but tautologies. These are formal truths that have no referential content.*

This can be made more general:

> *All propositions that are necessary or a priori are tautologies. All propositions that are contingent or a posteriori are synthetic. Analytically true = tautologous = a priori = necessary. Synthetic = a posteriori = contingent. There are no synthetic a priori propositions.*

The fifth major tenet of the Vienna Circle and their followers is also prefigured in the *Tractatus*. This is the doctrine of the unity of science.

> *All of science consists of a single unified system with a single set of natural laws and facts. There are no separate methods or systems in the psychological or social sciences.*

The idea of unified science influenced many thinkers who were not otherwise associated with logical empiricism. Carnap, Charles Morris, and Neurath edited the *International Encyclopedia of Unified Science* which published articles elaborating and promulgating the logical empiricist point of view. Volumes of this series have been published until recently, although later editions take a dubious view of logical positivism. For example, the second volume contains Thomas Kuhn's classic and influential work *The Structure of Scientific Revolutions* (originally published in 1962) which takes a very different view of science than that of the logical positivists. (See the next chapter.)

The sixth major tenet – *Reductionism* – of logical positivism is a cluster of views which were controversial and led to consternation even within the Vienna Circle.

Reductionism is a program whereby talk about one kind of entity is "reduced" or translated into talk about another, presumably simpler, kind of entity. For example, we have seen that logicists claimed to reduce mathematics to logic. The reduced "entities" are constructed out of the more basic stuff. Reductionism was partly inspired by one of Russell's famous slogans.

> The supreme maxim in scientific philosophizing is this:
> *Wherever possible, logical constructions are to be substituted for inferred entities.* (Russell 1914, p. 155)

One version of positivists' reductionism that was embraced at times by Ayer, Carnap, and a few others is that talk about physical objects such as tables and chairs is to be reduced to talk about elements that are given in perception. The most obvious candidates for the given elements are sense data. Likewise, for Russell our ordinary physical objects would be inferred entities known only by description thus to be replaced by constructions out of sense data.

Of course, no such translation of even one sentence was ever accomplished. Russell states that such a reduction remains an ideal.

The view that all meaningful statements about physical objects must be translatable, in principle, into equivalent statements about sense data is called phenomenalism. The most ambitious attempt at a phenomenalist reduction was undertaken by Carnap. His book *The Logical Structure of the World* (published in German in 1928 and usually known as "the *Aufbau*") is an ambitious and sustained attempt to construct the language of science on the basis of what Carnap calls "the autopsychological foundation." He describes his project in his preface to the 1967 translation. "The main problem concerns the possibility of the rational reconstruction of the concepts of all fields of knowledge on the basis of concepts that refer to the immediately given" (Carnap 1967/1961, p. v). This would be a key feature of the positivists' empiricism. The program's negative side was the elimination of metaphysics. The reconstruction of all knowledge – i.e. natural science – on the basis of immediate experience would be the positive side. The dominant view among philosophers was that the project was a failure. Even Carnap came to accept this verdict.

Despite its evident problems, A. J. Ayer explicitly embraces phenomenalism in *Language, Truth and Logic*. He uses the term "sense contents" rather than "sense data" because he wants to include immediate introspection. "[W]e shall use ['sense contents'] to refer to the immediate data not merely of 'outer' but also of 'introspective' sensation. ..." (Ayer 1946/1936, p. 53).

> On the contrary, we know that it must be possible to define material
> things in terms of sense-contents, because it is only by the occurrence of
> certain sense-contents that the existence of any material thing can ever be
> in the least degree verified. And thus we see that we have not to enquire
> whether a phenomenalist "theory of perception" or some other sort of
> theory is correct, but only what form of phenomenalist theory is correct.
> (Ayer 1946/1936, p. 53)

Phenomenalism was an ideal that was a theoretical necessity – or
seemed to be – for empiricists.[12]

According to Ayer and the logical positivists, phenomenalism is not
a form of idealism although it was inspired by Berkeley's subjective
idealism. [*Background 2.3*– The way of ideas of Locke, Berkeley, and
Hume, and the subjective idealism of Berkeley] Idealism of any sort
would be considered to be a metaphysical "theory" and thus unverifiable, and thus cognitively meaningless. Phenomenalism is a claim
solely about language:

> [T]he symbol "table" is definable in terms of certain symbols which stand
> for sense-contents, ... And this, as we have seen, is tantamount to saying
> that sentences which contain the symbol "table," ... can all be translated
> into sentences of the same language which do not contain that symbol,
> nor any of its synonyms, but do contain certain symbols which stand for
> sense-contents; a fact which may be loosely expressed by saying that to say
> anything about a table is always to say something about sense-contents.
> ... For example, the sentence, "I am now sitting in front of a table" can,
> in principle, be translated into a sentence which does not mention tables,
> but only sense-contents. (Ayer 1946/1936, p. 64)

And finally, from Ayer:

> But, in fact, we have seen that sense-contents are not in any way parts of
> the material things which they constitute; the sense in which a material
> thing is reducible to sense-contents is simply that it is a logical construction
> and they are its elements; and this, as we have previously made clear,
> is a linguistic proposition which states that to say anything about it is
> always equivalent to saying something about them. (Ayer 1946/1936,
> pp. 140–1)

---

[12] Phenomenalism has had a long run and is perhaps still not completely moribund. The
final sustained attempt at a phenomenalist reduction was made by the eminent Harvard
philosopher Nelson Goodman. Although the work was begun in the 1930s, in 1951 he
published his famous book *The Structure of Appearance*. This was an attempt to fix the
problems with Carnap's *Aufbau* and to proceed with a more sophisticated phenomenalist
reduction. No one, not even Goodman, thinks that he succeeded.

Presumably the phenomenalist language of sense-contents was intended by its adherents to be the unified language of unified science.

Phenomenalism was always unacceptable to some members of the Vienna Circle especially those with Marxist leanings. Neurath felt that a much more solid ground for reduction would be provided by the ordinary language of physical objects with some additions from science. This is a version of physicalism, the chief rival of phenomenalism.

> The unified language of unified science, which is derivable by and large from modifications of the language of everyday life, is the language of physics.
> . . .
> Science endeavors to transform the statements of everyday life. They are presented to us as "agglomerations," consisting of physicalistic and pre-physicalistic components. We replace them by the "unification" of physicalistic language. (Neurath 1959/1931, pp. 287–8)

Carnap also claimed in the *Aufbau* that physicalism was a legitimate alternative to phenomenalism. Physicalism would serve different purposes than phenomenalism.

Physicalism turns phenomenalism on its head, or rather puts it back on its feet. "Sense-contents" would be physically defined in terms of neurophysiological processes and behavior. All of psychology and sociology would be translated into physics via descriptions of behavior and neurophysiological processes in living human bodies. As we will see in the next chapter, Carnap formulated an approach to philosophy that would accommodate both phenomenalism and physicalism. Struggles over reductionism and what might provide a suitable reductive base continue among philosophers today.

Finally we come to the seventh major tenet of the logical positivists. This will have to wait until Chapter 8 for a full discussion, since it concerns ethics.

> *Ethical utterances have no cognitive content but are expressive of attitudes and emotions.*

"But in every case in which one would commonly be said to be making an ethical judgment, the function of the relevant ethical word is purely 'emotive.' It is used to express feeling about certain objects, but not to make any assertion about them" (Ayer 1946/1936, p. 108). For example, when someone says "Stealing is wrong," this means something like "I find stealing to be repulsive and I would urge you to have the same attitude to stealing." This view has come to be called "emotivism" and unlike the other major tenets of logical positivism is still today a live option taken seriously by philosophers.

Like the reductionist tenet of logical positivism emotivism was not accepted by all members of the Vienna Circle. They all did accept that ethics could not be normative. It could not result in verifiable value judgments. The most that philosophical ethicists could aspire to would be the analysis of ethical language, the explication of ethical concepts and their role in our social systems.

> For if ethics furnishes a justification it does so only in the sense just explained, namely, in a relative-hypothetical way, not absolutely. It "justifies" a certain judgment only to the extent that it shows that the judgment corresponds to a certain norm; that this norm itself is "right," or justified, it can neither show nor, by itself, determine. (Schlick 1962/1930, p. 17)

Schlick suggested that at the heart of our moral systems and sentiments lies a desire for happiness, but he firmly rejected utilitarianism as unverifiable. Instead he proposed as the fundamental moral principle "Be ready for happiness!" The moral ideal is to maximize our individual and collective capacity for happiness. Schlick says we cannot argue for this principle rationally, only propose it as a definition. "I would hold it practical to accept this definition, because the end it establishes is that which *de facto* is most highly valued by mankind" (Schlick 1962/1930, p. 197). My emotive response to this is: "I like this! I want to be ready for happiness, and I would urge you to adopt the same attitude."

The Demise of the Vienna Circle

By 1936 the Vienna Circle was already splitting up. The logical positivists were leaving Austria and Germany. The reasons for this were partly philosophical but primarily political. Since all the members of the Vienna Circle and allied Berlin Circle were liberals, socialists, or Marxists, the rise of Nazism made them uncomfortable in their native land.[13] A tragic event in 1936 that unambiguously raised the level of

---

[13]   In 1936 Carnap went to the University of Chicago and eventually spent many years teaching at UCLA. Hans Reichenbach also made it to UCLA after emigrating to Turkey. Moritz Schlick was murdered. Herbert Feigl also emigrated to the United States and joined the faculties at Iowa and then Minnesota. Waismann and Neurath moved to England where Wittgenstein, Russell, and others welcomed them. Ayer had already returned to London. Hempel left Berlin in 1937 and had an eminent career at Princeton until he retired as emeritus professor in 1964. He taught at the University of Pittsburgh's leading philosophy of science department until 1984. Phillip Frank left Austria in 1938 and took up a chair in physics at Harvard.

discomfort to clear danger was the murder of Moritz Schlick by a former student of his. At the trial the student claimed he was offended by Schlick's arrogant Jewish attitude to religion and morality. (Schlick was not even Jewish!) The local Nazis vigorously supported the criminal and made him a hero. Sentenced to ten years in prison, he was paroled after only two and joined the Austrian Nazi party.

Modern empiricists enjoy the privilege of being their own most penetrating critics. None of the original members of the Vienna Circle continued to defend their main tenets after the mid-1930s. Instead they devoted their philosophical energies to moving away from what they considered to be the crude and overly simplified views of their earlier period. Only A. J. Ayer continued tenaciously to defend the fundamentals of logical positivism, in spirit at least if not in detail. He suffered a lot of abuse and scorn, and still to this day has an ambiguous reputation among analytic philosophers. As we will see, J. L. Austin, wittier and cleverer than Ayer, wrote scornful and ridiculing refutations of Ayer's phenomenalism. Ayer was made something of a laughingstock or whipping boy of philosophy. Despite his struggles as a philosopher to maintain his dignity, Ayer became a celebrity, and was popular at fashionable parties. And he was always feisty. The story is that Ayer once confronted (successfully!) Mike Tyson at an upscale New York party – verbally, that is. Mike Tyson was harassing a young model who later became famous (Naomi Campbell). When Ayer demanded that Tyson stop, the boxer said: "Do you know who I am? I'm the heavyweight champion of the world," to which Ayer replied: "And I am the former Wykeham Professor of Logic. We are both pre-eminent in our field. I suggest that we talk about this like rational men." Ayer and Tyson then began to talk, while Naomi Campbell slipped out.

No doubt Ayer's courage was fueled by his assurance that Tyson was a construct out of his own sense-contents.[14]

The Influence of the Logical Positivists

Ridiculing the doctrines of the logical positivists, especially as propounded by Ayer, is easy and fun, nevertheless the Vienna Circle had a wide influence among philosophers, and natural and social scientists.

The influence of the logical positivists is evident in the doctrines of operationalism and instrumentalism in the natural and social sciences

---

[14] Given her bellicose history, I have the feeling, that Naomi could have handled Tyson herself and didn't need Ayer's intervention.

and behaviorism in psychology. Of course, the influence went both ways. The scientists also influenced the philosophers. Ideas flowed back and forth. (See Chapter 3 for a discussion of behaviorism.)

From the 1920s until well into the 1950s some form of operationalism was embraced by large numbers of scientists. Operationalism is a form of verificationism applied to scientific terms. It rests on the principle that all terms used by a scientist need to be defined by means of operations that can be carried out with observable results. Operationalism in physics was advocated most famously by the Nobel Prize winning physicist Percy Bridgman. Bridgman, in his influential book *Logic of Modern Physics* (1927), argued that all physical entities, processes, and properties must be definable by means of operations and procedures whose results can be observationally apprehended. Verificationism and operationalism developed in parallel and supported each other. By the mid-twentieth century it was fashionable to attempt to "operationalize" all sorts of concepts in physics and in the rest of the natural sciences, and in the social sciences including economics, operations research, business management, and so on. "To operationalize" is now a standard verb of English and refers to a process that is basic to all research and management.[15]

Verificationism was fundamental to quantum physics and was still being espoused in the 1950s. According to Max Born:

> [Heisenberg (in 1925)] cut the Gordian knot by a philosophic principle [which] asserts that concepts and pictures that do not correspond to physically observable facts should not be used in theoretical description. (Born 1955a, p. 258)

Born attributes the great success of modern physics to verificationism.

> Modern physics has achieved its greatest successes by applying the methodological principle that concepts which refer to distinctions beyond possible experience have no physical meaning and ought to be eliminated. (Born 1955b, p. 4)

The standard interpretation of the epistemology underlying quantum physics is verificationism.

Behaviorism in psychology was given a tremendous boost by verificationism. Since the nineteenth century, psychologists had been

---

[15]   Just for an example: "Operationalization is the process of defining a fuzzy concept so as to make the concept measurable in form of variables consisting of specific observations" (en.wikipedia.org/wiki/Operationalize).

examining human and animal behavior. In the twentieth century it took a more methodological turn due in part to the influence of verificationism. Methodological behaviorism is the view that psychology should only concern itself with behavior. Inner mental states are not publicly observable and therefore not subject to meaningful scientific description or investigation. A directly verificationist form of behaviorism is the view that all mental terms referring to inner states and events such as anger, thoughts, and intentions must be definable in terms of publicly observable behavior. The idea is that inner introspectable mental events and processes are not publicly verifiable, whereas the outer behavior is observable, measurable, and verifiable publicly. Since the "inner" manifestations of, say, anger are not verifiable, any attempted reference to them would be meaningless. The word "anger" is meaningful, so it must refer to "outer" publicly verifiable behavior including verbal behavior. This view raises all sorts of issues because, of course, my inner events of anger are observable and verifiable by me. Thus we must distinguish between first and third person psychological reports and their various meanings and verifications. Despite its evident difficulties and apparent denial of the "inner," behaviorism was popular among social scientists until the cognitive science revolution, which is still going on.

My sense is that most philosophers and scientists feel that operationalism and behaviorism were salutary as reactions against wild speculation and abstruse German metaphysics, and that the attitude of the logical positivists is still useful in certain contexts. Nevertheless no one any longer subscribes to all of the doctrines of the logical positivists, nor are operationalism or behaviorism still considered mainstream in natural science or psychology despite their widespread applications. In fact, much of the development of philosophy and methodology in the sciences since the 1950s has been driven by the criticisms of the doctrines of the logical positivists. This is the subject of the next three chapters.

Background 2.1 – Truth-tables, tautologies, etc. technical introduction to logical ideas in the *Tractatus*

The basic truth-functions are "not," "or," "and," "if . . . , then . . . ," and " . . . if and only if . . . "

Where P is any proposition, not P is true when P is false, and false when P is true. P or Q is true when P is true, Q is true, or both are true, and false when both P and Q are false. And so on. These truth-functions can be set out in tables called "truth-tables."

P	Not P	P	Q	P or Q	P	Q	P and Q	P	Q	If P, then Q	P	Q	P if and only Q
t	f	t	t	t	t	t	t	t	t	t	t	t	t
f	t	t	f	t	t	f	f	t	f	f	t	f	f
		f	t	t	f	t	f	f	t	f	f	t	f
		f	f	f	f	f	f	f	f	t	f	f	t

Usually these functions are symbolized. For example, not P, ∼P. P or Q, P ∨ Q. P and Q, P & Q. If P, then Q, P ⊃ Q. P if and only if Q, P ↔ Q. Then larger and more complex formulas can be constructed. Tautologies are so constructed that they automatically come out true no matter what.

P or not P	P	not P	P ∨ ∼ P
	t	f	t
	f	t	t

If P, then if Q, then P	P	Q	Q ⊃ P	P ⊃ (Q ⊃ P)
	t	t	t	t
	t	f	t	t
	f	t	t	t
	f	t	f	t

Of course, infinitely many different tautologies can be constructed. Tautologies contain no information. They do not "picture" anything, since they "picture" everything. One of Wittgenstein's central claims is that all necessary propositions, such as those of mathematics, turn out to be tautologies.

Background 2.2 – The ontological argument, substance and property, etc.

According to traditional metaphysics a substance is just an individual thing. Aristotle says: "The individual man or horse." A property (attribute, quality) is a mode of a substance, such as white, round, wooden, tall, heavy, etc. "The horse is white" says that the substance – the horse – has the property of being white. This is true if and only if the indicated horse is, indeed, white. Problems mount, as we've seen, when the substance supposedly indicated does not exist as in "The present king of France is bald." These problems intensify when we treat existence as a property of substances. It seems we cannot deny existence to anything. "The present king of France does not exist" seems to assert of the indicated substance that it does not exist. But how can we indicate a substance that does not exist and say something about it? These problems are eliminated by symbolic logic and Russell's treatment of definite descriptions as explained in the text. (Other problems remain at this time unsolved. For example, we talk intelligently about fictional characters.)

The ontological argument for the existence of God, first introduced by Anselm of Canterbury about AD 1100, is an *a priori* argument that relies on treating existence as a property. The books and articles on the ontological argument would fill a small library, which is astonishing since no one would be brought to faith by it. Even the Catholic Church rejects it. Very briefly, Anselm claims that God is the unsurpassable being. God must have all great-making properties (such as power, wisdom, benevolence) to the maximal degree. This is true by definition – it is God's job description. No lesser beings need apply. Now Anselm asks "Is there actually a being that fills that job description or is it just an idea, a myth?" He answers that it cannot be just an idea or myth because existence is itself a great-making property, so since God has all great-making properties God must exist. The logical positivist response, derived from Frege and based on symbolic logic, is that existence is not a (first-order) property at all so it cannot be a great-making property. [See also *Background 6.7* – The ontological argument, for a more technical discussion.]

Background 2.3 – The way of ideas of Locke, Berkeley, and Hume, and the subjective idealism of Berkeley

The rationalists argued that many, most, or all ideas were innate, because they could not be derived from experience. For example, we have no sensory experience of the basic geometrical objects such as points, lines, circles, and so on. All physical realizations of these perfect objects are imperfect. Also any idea involving infinite magnitudes – such as the idea of God – could not be derived from experience since we and all creation are finite.

John Locke responded that ideas of things that we could never experience are still derived from experience by compounding, subtracting, and comparing ideas that do come from experience. Most ideas are compound or complex ideas built up out of simple ideas. Locke's view is sort of a chemical theory of the mind. (A close friend of Locke's was Robert Boyle, one of the founders of modern chemistry.) Just as chemical compounds are built up from elements, so our compound ideas are built from elemental ideas, all of which are derived from sensory impressions. For example, the idea of a unicorn is based on the idea of a horse and a horn, both of which we have seen, and compounding them, or putting them together in our imagination. The idea of God is derived from the idea we have of ourselves and compounding "without limit" this idea.

Both David Hume and George Berkeley agreed with Locke that no ideas are innate; they are all derived from sensory impressions, the complex ones being built up out of the simpler ones. Berkeley went on to argue that there are only ideas; there is nothing else except our souls and God. In particular Berkeley held that the idea of matter is self-contradictory. The universe contains no matter, only immaterial souls and God. God coordinates all the perceptions so that the finite souls can interact. Berkeley's theory is a version of idealism. It is often called subjective idealism in contrast to the absolute idealism of Hegel.

Further Reading

Logical Positivism edited by A. J. Ayer (Free Press 1959) contains key articles by logical positivists. The introduction by Ayer provides a good overview of the movement.

A classic book on the *Tractatus* is G. E. M Anscombe's *An Introduction to Wittgenstein's Tractatus* (Harper & Row 1959).

For those interested in a very detailed scholarly treatment there is Max Black's *A Companion to Wittgenstein's Tractus* (Cornell University Press 1964).

The Library of Living Philosophers has volumes on Ayer and Carnap. These are invaluable resources for those seeking to know more about the lives and ideas of these thinkers. *The Philosophy of Rudolf Carnap (Library of Living Philosophers, Volume XI)*, edited by Paul A. Schilpp (Open Court 1963) and

The Philosophy of A. J. Ayer (Library of Living Philosophers, Volume XXI) edited by Lewis E. Hahn (Open Court 1992).

Several seminal works have been published more recently that question the standard or received view of the Vienna Circle and logical positivism. It is agreed that the positivists rejected the synthetic *a priori* and speculative metaphysics, but their attitudes toward empiricism, reductionism, and epistemological foundationalism, not to mention the unity of science are more nuanced, various, and philosophically sophisticated than is recognized in the standard view. For the revisionist view of logical positivism see for example *Reconsidering Logical Positivism* by Michael Friedman (Cambridge University Press 1999). Friedman's Preface and Introduction are excellent overviews of the current revised view of the Vienna Circle and logical positivism.

Useful anthologies of recent articles are *The Cambridge Companion to Logical Empiricism* edited by by Alan Richardson and Thomas Uebel (Cambridge University Press 2007) and *The Vienna Circle and Logical Empiricism: Re-Evaluation and Future Perspecitives* edited by Friedrich Stadler (Kluwer 2003).

3

Responses to Logical Positivism: Quine, Kuhn, and American Pragmatism

> *For my part I do, qua lay physicist, believe in physical objects and not in Homer's gods; and I consider it a scientific error to believe otherwise. But in point of epistemological footing the physical objects and the gods differ only in degree and not in kind. Both sorts of entities enter our conception only as cultural posits. The myth of physical objects is epistemologically superior to most in that it has proved more efficacious than other myths as a device for working a manageable structure into the flux of experience.* (Quine 1961b/1951, p. 44)

Introduction

The main theme of analytic philosophy since World War II and well into the 1960s and 1970s has been the dismantling of logical positivism and the philosophical ideas of Wittgenstein's *Tractatus*. The logical positivist program was attacked and overturned point by point by the positivists themselves and others who were sympathetic to positivism. Even Wittgenstein, when he returned to philosophy in the mid-1930s, devoted his philosophical attention to attacking, rejecting, and refining his earlier views. Today, those working within the analytic tradition are still considering the central issues that moved the positivists, but a more relaxed and expansive mood is welcomed among young philosophers. Some are even considering reviving parts of the logical positivists'

A Brief History of Analytic Philosophy: From Russell to Rawls, First Edition. Stephen P. Schwartz.
© 2012 John Wiley & Sons, Inc. Published 2012 by John Wiley & Sons, Inc.

program. This is understandable since the spirit of the logical positivists' motivation was never really abandoned or defeated. When pushed, the positivist program gave ground rapidly, but the methods, standards, and attitudes are still with us.

In England, mainly at Oxford, the attack on logical positivism was carried on by philosophers still respectful of Russell and Moore, but the foremost influence was Ludwig Wittgenstein. John Austin, Gilbert Ryle, and others at Oxford were opposed to the use of formal logic to "solve" philosophical problems and moved in the direction of the ordinary language and common sense philosophy derived from Moore and from the later Wittgenstein, who had turned against the use of symbolic logic to dissolve philosophical problems. [*Background 3.1* – The distinction between the early and late Wittgenstein and why this is a necessary distinction to make]

In the United States, the most relentless critic of positivism was Willard Van Orman Quine of Harvard University. Quine studied in Vienna, met with the Vienna Circle, and was close friends with Carnap who, along with Ayer, staunchly attempted to defend and refine positivism even as it was crumbling around them. The legendary Carnap-Quine correspondence, dialogue, and debate went on for years. In his influence and stature in analytic philosophy, Quine ranks just barely behind the founders of analytic philosophy: Frege, Russell, Moore, and Wittgenstein. Although Quine called himself an empiricist, his philosophy was also rooted in the tradition of the American pragmatists John Dewey and William James, thus adding an American flavor to the mainline of analytic philosophy. While not opposed to the motivations of the Vienna Circle, Quine and his pragmatist followers were dissatisfied with the basic tenets of the *Tractatus* and the positivists.

In this chapter we will discuss problems with the positivist program and Quine's criticisms of it, and the contemporary pragmatism that grew out of his work. In the next chapter we will survey Oxford ordinary language philosophy. Both can be understood only against the background of the logical positivism of the Vienna Circle.

The problem with logical positivism was that it did not go far enough, that it was not true to its own empiricist ideals. It had too many remnants of the old ways of philosophy.[1] Logical positivism was still infected with rationalism and metaphysics – the stuff it was trying to get rid of.

---

[1]   Even the term "positivism" suggests older nineteenth-century outmoded materialistic philosophy. For this reason many of the followers of the Vienna Circle preferred the label "logical empiricism." The terminology can be a bit confusing. Quine and Hempel refer to them as "modern empiricists."

The reliance on sense data theory, reductionism of one flavor or another, meanings, formal logic, and a rigidly applied principle of meaningfulness needed to be expunged or at least critically examined before the empiricism of the logical positivists could be self-respecting. Quine calls this project "tidying up empiricism." It needed it.

The Demise of the Verifiability Criterion of Meaningfulness

The most protracted and painful story in the dismantling of logical positivism is the history of the permutations of and revisions to and ultimate demise of the verifiability criterion of meaningfulness – the claim that an utterance is meaningful if and only if it is either a tautology (or a self-contradiction) or empirically verifiable (or falsifiable). (For the sake of brevity, we will suppress the parenthetical elements in future formulations.) This principle was close to the heart of logical positivism and is its most famous doctrine. Without the verifiability criterion of meaningfulness logical positivism loses much of its sting and its aura of clearing the air of unscientific mists. According to Carl Hempel, a leading philosopher of science and one of the staunchest allies of the Vienna Circle, "The fundamental principle of modern empiricism is the view that all non-analytic knowledge is based on experience" (Hempel 1950, p. 41). As Hempel points out, this fundamental principle does not entail the verifiability criterion of meaningfulness, but the verifiability criterion is the way the fundamental principle of empiricism is applied. The positivists' elimination of metaphysics, theology, ethics, and aesthetics is not based on psychology or the limits of human cognition, but on the semantics of language. This is part of the meaning of the "logical" in "logical positivism" and "logical empiricism." It is the elimination of metaphysics by the application of logic.

> In the domain of *metaphysics*, including all philosophy of value and normative theory, logical analysis yields the negative result *that the alleged statements in this domain are entirely meaningless*. Therewith a radical elimination of metaphysics is attained, which was not possible from the earlier antimetaphysical standpoints. (Carnap 1959a/1932, p. 61)

Despite Carnap's heady claims, the basic problem with the verifiability criterion of meaningfulness is that it cannot be formulated in a satisfactory way. It cannot be formulated in such a way that it eliminates metaphysics but retains the positivists' beloved natural science.

Hempel states the problem in his classic essay "Empiricist Criterion of Cognitive Significance: Problems and Changes" (Hempel 1965). (This is a revision of Hempel, 1950. "The empiricist criterion of cognitive significance" is another name for the verifiability criterion of meaningfulness.)

> I think that the general intent of the empiricist criterion of meaning is basically sound, and that notwithstanding much oversimplification in its use, its critical application has been, on the whole, enlightening and salutary. I feel less confident, however, about the possibility of restating the general idea in the form of precise and general criteria which establish sharp dividing lines (a) between statements of purely logical and statements of empirical significance, and (b) between those sentences which do have cognitive significance and those which do not. (Hempel 1950, p. 102)

Hempel was right to be dubious; satisfying (a) and (b) has never been accomplished despite prodigious labor.

The seeds of the destruction of the verifiability criterion of meaningfulness are already present in Wittgenstein's *Tractatus* but were ignored by the members of the Vienna Circle. Directly after his claim that the only correct method in philosophy would be to demonstrate the meaninglessness of metaphysical sentences (see Chapter 2, p. 57) Wittgenstein says the following:

> 6.54   My propositions serve as elucidations in the following way: anyone who understands me eventually recognizes them as nonsensical, when he has used them – as steps – to climb up beyond them. (He must, so to speak, throw away the ladder after he has climbed up it.) (Wittgenstein 1961b/1921, p. 151)

The next sentence is one of the most famous of twentieth-century philosophy. It is the final sentence of the *Tractatus*:

> 7.   What we cannot speak about we must pass over in silence.[2]

Unfortunately, as with the other uncomfortable aspects of Wittgenstein's *Tractatus*, the members of the Vienna Circle ignored this admonition, as it turns out, unwisely.

The verifiability criterion of meaningfulness came to be viewed as either nonsense or a dubious slogan. According to the verifiability

---

[2]   This is worth giving in the original German since it is poetic compared to the awkward English translation: *Wovon man nicht sprechen kann, darüber muss man schweigen.*

criterion of meaningfulness, cognitively meaningful sentences are either tautologies, i.e. analytic, or empirically verifiable. Any other sentence is cognitively meaningless. But this criterion can now be turned on the verifiability criterion of meaningfulness itself. If it is a tautology, then it is analytic and has no force. It just represents how someone has chosen to define some terms. As a statement of the standard meaning of "meaningful," it is surely incorrect. On the other hand, it is not an empirical proposition, at least not one that has any hope of being true. Thus the verifiability criterion of meaningfulness turns out to be an example of the very metaphysical nonsense that it was intended to eliminate.

In response, Ayer, Carnap, and Hempel had to agree that the verifiability criterion of meaningfulness was itself cognitively meaningless, and consequently suggested that it was a proposal, a recommendation. But why anyone who was inclined to metaphysical pondering or moral theorizing would accept this recommendation remained unanswered. Of course, they wouldn't and didn't. The self-referential problem was not enough to end the campaign of the verifiability criterion of meaningfulness, but there were other technical problems as well. One of the more engaging and entertaining philosophical sports well into the 1950s was finding technical flaws in any particular formulation of the verifiability criterion of meaningfulness. One defender of it would revise it to meet some technical objection, then another critic would find yet another technical flaw in the new formulation. We have, fortunately, no need to summarize the episode. There is voluminous literature on it – much of it is explored in the Hempel article. By the 1960s no one any longer embraced the verifiability criterion of meaningfulness, except a few hotheaded sophomore philosophy majors who hadn't yet gotten the news. I blush to admit that I was among them. I still haven't quite overcome the disappointment.

One of the more promising reactions to the demise of the verifiability criterion of meaningfulness was Karl Popper's attempt to replace it with a principle of falsification. Popper was a Viennese philosopher and social theorizer of the same vintage as the members of the Vienna Circle, but Popper was not associated with them. He considered himself to be the "official opposition." In philosophical temperament, however, Popper was close to the Vienna Circle and he was always in the stream, if not the mainstream, of analytic philosophy.

Besides his opposition to the verifiability criterion of meaningfulness another key issue that separated Popper from the logical positivists and so many other analytic philosophers was that he did not idolize Wittgenstein sufficiently. Popper idolized himself.

Like most of the members of the Vienna Circle, Popper was a refugee from Nazism. Although he had been brought up as a Christian and both his parents considered themselves Christians, his ancestry was Jewish. That was Jewish enough for the Nazis. Popper's story is similar in outline to many other leading German and Austrian philosophers and scientists. First he emigrated to New Zealand, then in 1946 moved to England where he became professor of philosophy at the London School of Economics. Life in England was good to Popper. He became Sir Karl Popper in 1965.

The idea behind Popper's principle of falsification is that instead of focusing on verifiability one should consider only those observations that would falsify a claim or theory.

> Thus there clearly was a need for a different criterion of demarcation; and I proposed (though years elapsed before I published this proposal) that the refutability or falsifiability of a theoretical system should be taken as the criterion of its demarcation. According to this view, which I still uphold, a system is to be considered as scientific only if it makes assertions which may clash with observations; and a system is, in fact, tested by attempts to produce such clashes, that is to say by attempts to refute it. Thus testability is the same as refutability, and can therefore likewise be taken as a criterion of demarcation. (Popper 1963, p. 256)

To be scientific a theory must be falsifiable in principle. We must know what tests would refute it. As an application of his principle Popper notoriously argued that Marxism is unfalsifiable. The Marxists, on the other hand, always vehemently insisted that their theories were scientific. The exchange was not friendly. Empiricists were calling Marxism unscientific, while the Marxists accused empiricism of being a reactionary bourgeois doctrine, especially if linked with phenomenalism. (See Chapter 2, p. 65.) The official philosophy of Marxism was dialectical materialism. Popper's attack on Marxism as metaphysical or, worse, religious was not popular among leftists. It turns out the Marxists were right and Popper was wrong. Marxism is falsifiable. Most of the central tenets of Marxism have been falsified by history. Later Popper continued his attacks on Communism, claiming that it was inconsistent with democracy and freedom. Instead he favored the "open society" based on liberal democracy. (See the discussion of Popper's political philosophy, Chapter 8, pp. 287–9.)

Alas, the falsifiability criterion runs into the same sorts of problems as the verifiability criterion. The main objection is that scientific theories and claims are not testable or falsifiable in the direct way that Popper seems to envision. Even Popper recognized that Darwin's theory of natural selection fails his test. It is not susceptible to crucial experiments. According to Popper it is useful metaphysics. This in itself is enough to damn his criterion. The problems are more systematic, however. Quine argued that scientific theories and claims are enmeshed in an entire web of beliefs and theories in such a way that tests and trials only bear on the entire web, not on individual theories or claims. (This is discussed in detail below.) Popper's falsifiability criterion is still too narrow, formal, and rigid. If we applied his falsifiability criterion, too much would turn out to be unscientific, just like Darwin's theory and dialectical materialism.

Popper's falsifiability criterion is not, however, as rigid as the verifiability criterion. Popper never intended his criterion as a criterion of meaningfulness. According to Popper testability serves to demarcate or distinguish science from metaphysics, but metaphysics is not meaningless, it is merely unscientific. Popper is critical of verifiability and the positivist program.

> Put in a nut-shell, my thesis amounts to this. The repeated attempts made by Rudolf Carnap to show that the demarcation between science and metaphysics coincides with that between sense and nonsense have failed. The reason is that the positivistic concept of 'meaning' or 'sense' (or of verifiability, or of inductive confirmability, etc.) is inappropriate for achieving this demarcation – simply because metaphysics need not be meaningless even though it is not science. In all its variants demarcation by meaninglessness has tended to be at the same time too narrow and too wide: as against all intentions and all claims, it has tended to exclude scientific theories as meaningless, while failing to exclude even that part of metaphysics which is known as 'rational theology'. (Popper 1963, p. 253)

This is a fair statement of the failure of the verifiability criterion.

Quine's Rejection of the Analytic/Synthetic Distinction

The analytic/synthetic distinction is also central to the logical positivist program. It plays a role in the statement of the verifiability criterion of meaningfulness – "a putative proposition is meaningful if and only if it is a tautology or empirically verifiable."[3] The distinction also plays a role in the first, third, and fourth, parts of the logical positivists'

---

[3] For the purposes of this discussion "tautology" and "analytically true proposition" mean the same thing, and in most contexts they can be used interchangeably, although there is distinction that Quine notes. Also we use "analytic" to mean "analytically true" unless otherwise indicated.

program as set out in the previous chapter, and Quine claimed it was closely involved in the positivists' reductionism as well. These parts are the following:

The elimination of metaphysics, ethics, aesthetics, and theology by the verifiability criterion of meaningfulness.

Logic and mathematics consist of nothing but tautologies. These are formal truths that have no referential content.

All propositions that are necessary or a priori are tautologies. All propositions that are contingent or a posteriori are synthetic. Analytically true = tautologous = a priori = necessary. Synthetic = a posteriori = contingent. There are no synthetic a priori propositions.

All these are definitive of logical positivism and logical empiricism in general.

Unlike the verifiability criterion of meaningfulness, the analytic/synthetic distinction is intuitive and useful and not nearly as invidious. In more-or-less its contemporary form the analytic/synthetic distinction was popularized by Kant and has been widely used by philosophers and logicians since his time. And unlike the verifiability criterion of meaningfulness, the analytic/synthetic distinction has been used enthusiastically by non-empiricists and empiricists alike. It has become, and remains, part of the fundamental equipment of philosophers regardless of affiliation.

Quine readily acknowledges the appeal of the distinction, but claims that empiricists in assuming it are thereby indulging in metaphysics.

But, for all its a priori reasonableness, a boundary between analytic and synthetic statements simply has not been drawn. That there is such a distinction to be drawn at all is an unempirical dogma of empiricists, a metaphysical article of faith. (Quine 1961b/1951, p. 37)

As with the verifiability criterion, the logical positivists were being accused of being metaphysical by their own sympathizers. If Quine is right about this, modern empiricists must reformulate their entire program. Quine's challenge cannot be ignored.

Quine's criticisms of logical positivism are best known from his classical article "Two Dogmas of Empiricism"(Quine 1961b/1951). This is the most widely read, cited, and reprinted article in the history of analytic philosophy.[4] "Two Dogmas of Empiricism" is only one of a

---

[4] Its only possible equal would be Russell's "On Denoting." According to Google Scholar, Quine's article has 3660 citations online whereas Russell's has only 2430.

series of articles and writings by Quine that elaborated his criticisms of the "dogmas" of empiricism, but the publication of "Two Dogmas of Empiricism" was the turning point of the attack on the logical positivist program by those sympathetic to empiricism.

Quine, in the first paragraph, states his target clearly:

> Modern empiricism has been conditioned in large part by two dogmas. One is a belief in some fundamental cleavage between truths which are *analytic*, or grounded in meanings independently of matters of fact and truths which are *synthetic*, or grounded in fact. The other dogma is *reductionism*: the belief that each meaningful statement is equivalent to some logical construct upon terms which refer to immediate experience. Both dogmas, I shall argue, are ill founded. (Quine 1961b/1951, p. 20)

The second of the two so-called "dogmas" – reductionism – is the sixth part of the logical positivists' program. Far from being a dogma, it was disputed by members of the Vienna Circle at least in its phenomenalist form. True, some central figures of logical empiricism such as Ayer embraced phenomenalist reductionism as did Carnap early on, but they were not dogmatic about it. The first "dogma," however, as we have seen, is fundamental to the entire philosophy of logical positivism. It was never questioned by them.

From such a famous and admired source as Quine's article we would expect a demolition of the analytic/synthetic distinction based on an argument that is greeted by gasps of "Ah ha! Amazing! Insightful!" Ironically no such arguments are to be found in Quine's "Two Dogmas" (as it is usually called). Philosophers are still debating what his arguments are – not just the premises and reasoning, but even the conclusions. Did Quine claim that there are no analytic propositions or did he claim that the notion of analytic proposition makes no sense?

The general idea of Quine's arguments is understandable even if the details are disputed. Through various technical considerations, Quine argues that the notion of analyticity cannot be made clear or else the clarification is circular. In order to explain the notion of analyticity, philosophers need to appeal to other notions such as synonymy which are either hopelessly unclear or depend on the notion of analyticity.

A favorite example of an analytic proposition, which is now becoming somewhat dated, is "All bachelors are unmarried." How is the analyticity to be explained? It rests on the definition of the word "bachelor" plus standard logic. By definition the term "bachelor" is synonymous with "unmarried man." But what does it mean that they are synonymous? That they mean the same thing. In other words, just that "All bachelors are unmarried men" is analytic. Here we have a vicious circle.

> Analyticity at first seemed most naturally definable by appeal to a realm of meanings. On refinement, the appeal to meanings gave way to an appeal to synonymy or definition. But definition turned out to be a will-o'-the-wisp, and synonymy turned out to be best understood only by dint of a prior appeal to analyticity itself. So we are back at the problem of analyticity. (Quine 1961b/1951, p. 32)

According to Quine, there is no way to break out of this circle.

Quine's attack on the analytic/synthetic distinction is really an attack on the notion of meaning used by the positivists and inherited uncritically from traditional philosophy and common sense. Quine in "Two Dogmas" and in other famous writings attacks the view that associated with a term, purely semantically (linguistically or conventionally), there is a concept or idea that is the meaning of the term. According to this common sense view linguistic meaning is to be sharply distinguished from non-linguistic empirical facts. Despite Quine's qualms the distinction seems intuitive enough. Consider the definition of "cigarette":

> *cigarette*: a slender roll of cut tobacco enclosed in paper and meant to be smoked; *also*: a similar roll of another substance (as marijuana). (Merriam-Webster Dictionary)

Presumably this gives the meaning of the word "cigarette." This would, also presumably, generate analytic propositions. For example, "Cigarettes are meant to be smoked." On the other hand, an empirical fact about cigarettes is, for example, that smoking cigarettes causes lung cancer. This fact does not follow from the definition of "cigarette." It required empirical research to establish it. No one would empirically research whether cigarettes were for smoking. That is true by definition. This is precisely the distinction that Quine is contesting – and not just contesting but reviling.

> My present suggestion is that it is nonsense, and the root of much nonsense, to speak of a linguistic component and a factual component in the truth of any individual statement. (Quine 1961b/1951, p. 42)

Convincing us of this is going to be an difficult job for Quine. The distinction is commonsensical, supported by lots of examples, and the claim that it is the source of much nonsense seems exaggerated at best.

Nevertheless, Quine's claim is not entirely unconvincing upon deeper reflection. We can get something of an idea of the problems with analyticity if we consider that parts of the "definition" seem to be empirical – e.g., a similar roll of another substance (as marijuana). Is the extension of "cigarette" to include marijuana a misuse, an extension, or part of the original meaning of the term "cigarette"? And isn't even the claim that cigarettes are enclosed in paper just a general empirical claim? Is it really analytic? Can't there be cigarettes made with other substances than paper? In fact, aren't there such? Cigarettes wrapped in thin leaves? Or are there? Isn't this an empirical question? And what exactly is the definition of "paper" anyway? We begin to see the difficulty of distinguishing pure elements of the linguistic meaning of "cigarette" from empirical facts or generalizations about cigarettes. The notion that the term "cigarette" has a pure linguistic meaning begins to dissolve.

While philosophers often still do use the terms "analytic" and "synthetic" and many accept a distinction between truths by definition and empirical ones, we do not do so with a clear conscience. In any case, no one now believes that the analytic/synthetic distinction or the notion of linguistic meaning can do all the work that the positivists tried to get them to do.

Quinean Empiricism without the Dogmas

Holism

Quine is no anti-empiricist. Quine would prefer to be seen as a less dogmatic and more practical empiricist than the logical positivists. In a late passage Quine sounds like Russell. Quine uses the term "relative empiricism."

> [M]axim of *relative empiricism:* Don't venture farther from sensory evidence than you need to. We abandoned radical empiricism when we abandoned the old hope of translating corporeal talk into sensory talk; but the relative variety still recommends itself. (Quine 1974, p. 138)

What does this Quinean empiricism look like in detail? In order to get an idea we must consider Quine's criticism of the second "dogma" – the "dogma" of reductionism. Getting rid of this dogma distinguishes relative empiricism from unsupportable radical empiricism.

According to Quine the two dogmas are interchangeable and based on the same error.

> The dogma of reductionism ... is intimately connected with the other dogma – that there is a cleavage between the analytic and the synthetic. ... [T]he one dogma clearly supports the other in this way: as long as it is taken to be significant in general to speak of the confirmation and infirmation of a statement, it seems significant to speak also of a limiting kind of statement which is vacuously confirmed, *ipso facto*, come what may; and such a statement is analytic.
>
> The two dogmas are at root identical. (Quine 1961b/1951, p.41)

The mischief according to Quine is caused by the view that the unit of significance is the statement.

Philosophy has seen a steady broadening of the base of meaning. Classical empiricists, such as Locke and Hume, viewed the individual term as the unit of significance. Each term was associated with a sensory concept or idea which was its meaning. For example, "gold" named the complex concept "yellow malleable incorruptible metal." Frege and, following him, Russell and Wittgenstein argued that a term only has meaning in the context of a statement – the statement is the unit of meaning. According to Quine we must go still further.

> Russell's concept of definition in use [e.g., his analysis of definite descriptions] was, as remarked, an advance over the impossible term-by-term empiricism of Locke and Hume. The statement, rather than the term, came with Russell to be recognized as the unit accountable to an empiricist critique. But what I am now urging is that even in taking the statement as unit we have drawn our grid too finely. The unit of empirical significance is the whole of science. (Quine 1961b/1951, p. 42)

The modern empiricists of the Vienna Circle and their allies got into dogmatic trouble because they drew the "grid too finely." Quine's objection is that a statement cannot be verified or falsified individually or even have a meaning taken individually. His view that "The unit of empirical significance is the whole of science" is called "holism." Holism is the basis of Quine's philosophy. It is the source of his criticism of logical positivism and his more constructive views, which we will describe shortly.

Quine is a self-proclaimed empiricist, so experience according to him plays a crucial role in the adjustment of belief and the attainment of knowledge. This role is not the statement by statement verification (or even Popperian falsification) that the positivists envisioned. Experience does not directly determine the truth or falsity of individual statements, according to Quine. According to Quine the positivists and other modern empiricists failed to recognize the holistic character of knowledge.

> The totality of our so-called knowledge or beliefs, from the most casual matters of geography and history to the profoundest laws of atomic physics or even of pure mathematics and logic, is a man-made fabric which impinges on experience only along the edges. Or, to change the figure, total science is like a field of force whose boundary conditions are experience. A conflict with experience at the periphery occasions readjustments in the interior of the field. Truth values have to be redistributed over some of our statements. Re-evaluation of some statements entails re-evaluation of others, because of their logical interconnections – the logical laws being in turn simply certain further statements of the system, certain further elements of the field. (Quine 1961b/1951, p. 42)

The web of belief, the single web of all of knowledge or science, is the root metaphor of Quinean holism.

The Quine–Duhem Thesis

The web of belief, of course, is a somewhat disordered conglomeration, not a geometrically constructed spider's orb. Furthermore, different people, or segments of the culture, may have somewhat different webs. There are many and diffuse complicating factors. The ways in which the web, or webs, get adjusted, fitted together, and reconciled with experience, and the ways in which internal conflicts when they arise are resolved are not mechanical or formal processes. Which statements and which parts of the fabric of knowledge are adjusted to meet exigencies is not determined by experience or anything else. There is a lot of play in the system.

According to holism, experience meets the web only at its edges. Adjustments to the system to accommodate recalcitrant experiences are not determined in any direct way. We have many options about how to adjust the system when observations do not turn out the way we expected.

> But the total field is so undetermined by its boundary conditions, experience, that there is much latitude of choice as to what statements to re-evaluate in the light of any single contrary experience. No particular experiences are linked with any particular statements in the interior of the field, except indirectly through considerations of equilibrium affecting the field as a whole. (Quine 1961b/1951, pp. 42–3)

Even the laws of logic and mathematics are not immune to revision. Nor are statements about immediate experiences directly falsifiable by apparently contradictory observations. Everything is always up for grabs, or rather more formally, subject to revision. Nothing is sacrosanct: not analytic, not a priori, not purely observational.

> [I]t is misleading to speak of the empirical content of an individual statement – especially if it be a statement at all remote from the experiential periphery of the field. Furthermore it becomes folly to seek a boundary between synthetic statements, which hold contingently on experience, and analytic statements which hold come what may. Any statement can be held true come what may, if we make drastic enough adjustments elsewhere in the system. Even a statement very close to the periphery can be held true in the face of recalcitrant experience by pleading hallucination or by amending certain statements of the kind called logical laws. Conversely, by the same token, no statement is immune to revision. Revision even of the logical law of the excluded middle has been proposed as a means of simplifying quantum mechanics. (Quine 1961b/1951, p. 43)

This view of theory or knowledge revision is based on the "Quine–Duhem Thesis."[5] The Quine–Duhem thesis is the claim that any theory can accommodate any observations. Despite what Popper claimed, a scientific theory cannot be directly refuted by supposed falsifying evidence. Such falsifying evidence can always be accommodated by making changes elsewhere than in the theory. For example, accommodations can be made in the supporting assumptions, logic, or intellectual environment. Furthermore, any observations can be accommodated or explained by an infinite number of different and inconsistent theories. Thus scientific theories are radically under-determined by observational evidence. Verification and falsification of theories always rests on numerous subsidiary assumptions and hypotheses about how things work. Rather than changing the theory, these assumptions or hypotheses can be readjusted to accommodate the observations. Since the observations themselves are also theory laden – they rely on equipment or the functioning of sense organs, or cooperation among groups of people – they can be discounted or reinterpreted. Thus the Quine–Duhem Thesis and holism support and explain each other.

The Indeterminacy of Radical Translation

Quine used the Quine–Duhem Thesis for a further assault on meanings. In his most famous book, *Word and Object* (Quine 1960), Quine treats

---

[5]   Pierre Duhem was a French physicist and philosopher of science who was active in the late nineteenth and very early twentieth centuries, and is known today among analytic philosophers primarily because of his eponymous thesis.

translation as a form of theory construction. He has us think about what he calls "radical translation." An anthropologist or linguist is attempting translation from an entirely unknown and unrelated language. The translator must rely entirely on observing the behavior of informants and listening to the verbal sounds they make. As he works on his translation the linguist is creating a theory of native word meaning. The linguist notes that an informant says "Gavagai" as a rabbit scampers by, and writes down "'gavagai' means 'rabbit.'" But wait a minute! Not so fast:

> For consider 'gavagai'. Who knows but what the objects to which this term applies are not rabbits after all, but mere stages, or brief temporal segments of rabbits? In either event the stimulus situations that prompt assent to 'Gavagai' would be the same as for 'Rabbit'. Or perhaps objects to which 'gavagai' applies are all and sundry undetached parts of rabbits; . . . When from the sameness of stimulus meanings of 'Gavagai' and 'Rabbit' the linguist leaps to the conclusion that a gavagai is a whole enduring rabbit, he is just taking for granted that the native is enough like us to have a brief general term for rabbits and no brief general term for rabbit stages or parts. (Quine 1960, pp. 51–2)

Quine wants to suggest that there is no fact of the matter about what "gavagai" means.

This point applies to translation in general:

> [M]anuals for translating one language into another can be set up in divergent ways, all compatible with the totality of speech dispositions, yet incompatible with one another. In countless places they will diverge in giving, as their respective translations of a sentence of one language, sentences of the other language which stand to each other in no plausible sort of equivalence, however loose. (Quine 1960, p. 27)

This under-determination of translation is a manifestation of the more general under-determination of theory by data.

> To the same degree that the radical translations of sentences is under-determined by the totality of dispositions to verbal behavior, our own theories and beliefs in general are under-determined by the totality of possible sensory evidence time without end. (Quine 1960, p. 78)

The Structure of Scientific Revolutions

Quine's claims seem to be purely theoretical in the sense that we would all know how to verify or falsify the claim that there are brick houses on our street and no one would disagree, and most likely no one would disagree about the translation of a native word.[6] True enough, and Quine would not deny this. But in the natural sciences things have not proceeded so straightforwardly. The renowned historian and philosopher of science Thomas Kuhn documented that in scientific theory revision and replacement, events proceed in much the way suggested by the Quine–Duhem Thesis and Quinean holism.

Kuhn's vocabulary from his justly famous and influential book *The Structure of Scientific Revolutions* (Kuhn 1970/1962) has been incorporated into the fabric of contemporary philosophy of science and culture in general. Today the terms "paradigm" and "paradigm shift" are widely used (and misused) in every area, including the popular media, in more-or-less the sense introduced by Kuhn.

Kuhn denies that the process of theory replacement in science (and the growth of knowledge generally) is a process where old faulty theories are verified or falsified by crucial experiments and replaced by truer ones. His view is that old paradigms, which involve entire worldviews based on scientific theories, are replaced by new paradigms. These paradigm shifts have often been intellectually violent revolutions. The overthrow of a paradigm is not determined just by the experimental data. It is a multifaceted cultural phenomenon involving religion, ways of life, technological advances, fashions of thinking, and every other facet of scientific life. The process does certainly involve experimental results, observations, and the data they generate. These cannot be ignored. However, contrary to the views of the positivists and Popper, they play a subsidiary role and depend on the surrounding cultural milieu in a holistic way.

The view of science that emerges from Kuhn's historical work is close to Quine's and supports his criticisms of the logical positivists.

> To the historian, at least, it makes little sense to suggest that verification is establishing the agreement of fact with theory. All historically significant theories have agreed with the facts, but only more or less. There is no more precise answer to the question whether or how well an individual theory fits the facts. (Kuhn 1970/1962, p. 146)

Typically the adherents of the old scientific paradigm are not defeated by the results of experiments or observations. They are defeated by the grim reaper. Older scientists are replaced in positions of scientific power by younger colleagues with fewer intellectual commitments. The younger scientists find it easier to embrace the new paradigm. "How then are scientists brought to make this transition [from one

---

[6] Except for vagueness and ambiguity, which are nothing special and no news.

paradigm to another]? Part of the answer is that they are very often not" (Kuhn 1970/1962, p.150). Kuhn cites with approval Max Planck:

> A new scientific truth does not triumph by convincing its opponents and making them see the light, but rather because its opponents eventually die, and a new generation grows up that is familiar with it. (Kuhn 1970/1962, p. 151)

Competing scientific paradigms are incommensurable. This means that members of the disparate paradigms can only partially communicate with each other. Neither can defeat the other with decisive verifications or falsifications.

> The proponents of competing paradigms are always at least slightly at cross-purposes. Neither side will grant all the non-empirical assumptions that the other needs in order to make its case. ... Though each may hope to convert the other to his way of seeing his science and its problems, neither may hope to prove his case. The competition between paradigms is not the sort of battle that can be resolved by proofs. (Kuhn 1970/1962, p. 148)

The term "matter" may mean one thing to an Aristotelian physicist and something different to a Newtonian, and something else again to an Einsteinian. This is like the Quinean problem of radical translation. There is no fixed eternal meaning of the term "matter." A scientific term gets its meaning by being embedded in a theory and ultimately in the whole of science of the time. Members of different scientific schools are talking past each other when they discuss and disagree about, e.g., matter. "[T]he proponents of different paradigms practice their trades in different worlds" (Kuhn 1970/1962, p. 150). This partly explains why one physicist's crucial falsifying experiment is another's merely annoying anomaly.

> What had previously been meant by space was necessarily flat, homogeneous, isotropic, and unaffected by the presence of matter. If it had not been, Newtonian physics would not have worked. To make the transition to Einstein's universe, the whole conceptual web whose strands are space, time, matter, force, and so on, had to be shifted and laid down again on nature whole. ... Copernicus' innovation was not simply to move the earth. Rather, it was a whole new way of regarding the problems of physics and astronomy ... (Kuhn 1970/1962, p. 149)

Because of Kuhn's work, philosophers have come to accept that the *Tractarian* and verificationist views of the Vienna Circle and their followers are an unrealistic idealization. The logical positivists' notion of science was a fantasy that ignored the messy, holistic, and "unscientific" nature of scientific "progress." Even the term "scientific" does not have a strict meaning. How are we to settle the question of whether Marxism is scientific? The discussion is full of value judgments, presuppositions, and cultural prejudices. It is not a question with a clear, verifiable, and objective answer.

Kuhn's book *The Structure of Scientific Revolutions* was published as Volume II, No. 2 of the *International Encyclopedia of Unified Science*.[7] This was a series of publications started by positivists. Many positivists and former members were on the editorial board. This irony reveals the extent to which they themselves were engaged in and sympathetic to overturning their own philosophical paradigm. Is this a counterinstance to Kuhn's views about theory change? Not really. Kuhn's historical analysis was meant to apply to natural science. Despite the hopes of Russell and the logical positivists, philosophy is not a science.

Pragmatism

If scientific theories are radically under-determined by data, how are they validated? How do scientists decide which theory to adopt? As we have seen, part of the answer is cultural predilections, but this cannot be the whole answer. It leaves unexplained the success of science.

Both Quine and Kuhn argue that pragmatic considerations guide the direction of science and explain its success. According to Quine natural science is a tool for making predictions. It is not a *Tractarian* picture of reality, which must be judged by how accurately it depicts the natural world. "As an empiricist I continue to think of the conceptual scheme of science as a tool, ultimately, for predicting future experience in the light of past experience" (Quine 1961b/1951, p. 44). Since science is a tool, it is judged in the way we judge any tool. How useful is it? How well does it work? Does it do the job for which it was designed? Changes in the web of science are evaluated by whether they improve the tool. Do they make it easier to use? Do they increase the system's predictive capacity? This is pragmatism. We shape the tool for the job it is intended for and for those who will be using it, and judge it by how well it works.

Data are the raw materials, but what we do with them is a matter of choosing the most convenient and useful organization. According

---

[7] Recall part five of the logical positivist program: All of science consists of a single unified system with a single set of natural laws and facts. There are no separate methods or systems in the psychological or social sciences – or at least there ought not to be.

to Quine, particular sensory experiences impinge on the whole of science, including common sense,[8] geography, history, etc. only at the periphery. Experiences that are anomalous can be accommodated in an endless and under-determined number of different ways. How do we choose what to change? We should and must consider what have come to be called "extra-empirical" or "pragmatic" virtues. The most important virtues are simplicity, conservatism, modesty, elegance, and fruitfulness. Two or more different hypotheses may accommodate a particular set of data, but we should choose the one that is the simplest, that disturbs the rest of the web the least, that makes the fewest ancillary assumptions, and so on. None of this is rigidly or mechanically determined by the logic of verification. The decision that we make in a particular case "turns upon our vaguely pragmatic inclination to adjust one strand of the fabric of science rather than another in accommodating some particular recalcitrant experience. Conservatism figures in such choices, and so does the quest for simplicity" (Quine 1961b/1951, p. 46).

Kuhn emphasizes the divergence from the mechanical or strictly logical procedures imagined by the logical positivists.

> Debates over theory-choice cannot be cast in a form that fully resembles logical or mathematical proof. ... Nothing about that relatively familiar thesis implies either that there are no good reasons for being persuaded or that those reasons are ultimately decisive for the group. Nor does it even imply that the reasons for choice are different from those usually listed by philosophers of science: accuracy, simplicity, fruitfulness, and the like. What it would suggest, however, is that such reasons function as values and that they can thus be differently applied, individually and collectively ... (Kuhn 1970/1962, p. 199)

Pragmatic considerations, despite the somewhat businesslike sound of the term, are not opposed to ideals of rationality. For Quine pragmatic considerations are what rationality is:

> Each man is given a scientific heritage plus a continuing barrage of sensory stimulation; and the considerations which guide him in warping his scientific heritage to fit his continuing sensory promptings are, where rational, pragmatic. (Quine 1961b/1951, p. 46)

Quinean (and Kuhnian) pragmatism is in the great tradition of American pragmatism. [*Background 3.2* – Peirce, James, and Dewey]. The term "pragmatism" was coined by C. S. Peirce but the most prominent and famous pragmatist was the leading American philosopher

---

[8] "Science is a continuation of common sense." (Quine 1961b/1951, p. 45).

William James. William James was born in New York in 1842 and died in 1910. Besides doing influential work in philosophy, James was a prominent psychologist and wrote important works on religion. William James is not to be confused with his brother, the novelist Henry James.

James, like Quine, considered himself an empiricist first and foremost. James asserts that pragmatism is a form of empiricism, but empiricism shorn of its more difficult burdens and dogmas.

> Pragmatism represents a perfectly familiar attitude in philosophy, the empiricist attitude, but it represents it, as it seems to me, both in a more radical and less objectionable form than it has ever yet assumed. A pragmatist turns his back resolutely and once and for all upon a lot of inveterate habits dear to professional philosophers. He turns away from abstraction and insufficiency, from verbal solutions, from bad *a priori* reasons, from fixed principles, closed systems, and pretended absolutes and origins. (James 1955/1907, p. 45)

James is writing (1907) well before the Vienna Circle came together, but the issues do not seem to have changed much by the time of Quine's confrontation with logical positivism. They just became more technical and articulated. In tune with the style of his times, James' writing is more flowery and less specific than Quine's, but Quine's empiricism is in the tradition of James and American pragmatism. Quine was after a more radical and less objectionable form of empiricism than logical positivism.

Empiricism, of course, has its origins in Europe, but the pragmatist version is a singularly and uniquely American movement in philosophy. Quine is the first and foremost American philosopher of the twentieth century. He was born in Ohio in 1908. He graduated from Oberlin College and then, like William James, spent almost his entire professional life at Harvard University. Alfred North Whitehead was Quine's PhD thesis advisor at Harvard, which partly explains Quine's lifelong interest in and brilliance at mathematics and mathematical logic. Quine, from his position as professor of philosophy at Harvard from 1956 to 1978, had the chance to associate with and influence many leading American philosophers. Many (but not all) of them adopted and extended his holism and pragmatism. Interestingly, Thomas Kuhn also was born in Ohio and was at Harvard at the same time as Quine was getting his PhD and starting his career. Clearly they influenced each other. Kuhn later took positions at the University of California, Princeton University, and MIT but the two always remained closely connected.

Unlike his most famous predecessors, Russell and Wittgenstein, Quine continued to publish and remain in the forefront of philosophy throughout his long life. Quine published seven books and numerous articles *after* he retired in 1978. For sheer energy and volume Quine can hardly be equaled among the top philosophers of the twentieth century. I have not even mentioned, nor will I be able to discuss here, Quine's vast contributions to formal logic, set theory, and the foundations of mathematics.

Despite his contributions to many areas of philosophy of science, logic, and philosophy of mathematics, Quine's revivification of American pragmatism is his most enduring contribution to philosophy. American pragmatism had fallen into neglect and disfavor primarily because of the tremendous force of European logical positivism. This battle between positivism and pragmatism was renewed and continued in the United States in the exchange between Quine and Carnap, who was teaching at The University of Chicago and then UCLA. [*Background 3.3* – "Warfare" in philosophy] Today logical positivism is dead and Quinean pragmatism is alive and kicking. Does that mean that Quine is closer to the truth than Carnap and the logical positivists? Pragmatists would hesitate to objectify truth in the way suggested by the phrasing of this question. There is no first or fundamental philosophy that discovers truth or rather TRUTH underlying or separate from science.

One result of Quine's attacks on the dogmas of empiricism is a reconceptualization of philosophy. Quine sees philosophy as continuous with natural science. "One effect of abandoning them [the two dogmas of empiricism] is ... a blurring of the supposed boundary between speculative metaphysics and natural science. Another is a shift toward pragmatism" (Quine 1961b/1951, p. 20). The quest for knowledge is embodied in science, and the quest is pursued pragmatically. Philosophy and philosophizing are part of the enterprise and we philosophers make what contributions we can. Aligning philosophy with science seems to give philosophers a definite down-to-earth job to do, but at the same time it diminishes the pretensions of philosophy. Quine and the American pragmatists, like the logical positivists, viewed traditional philosophy as a forlorn project of trying to solve obsolete problems. Quine was not much interested in the history of philosophy. He was given to saying "There are those who study the history of philosophy, and then there are those who do philosophy." He also famously said "philosophy of science is philosophy enough" (Quine 1966a/1953, p. 149).

Metaphysics and Science

Quine was more lenient toward metaphysics than the positivists were, but nothing in Quine would give solace to any traditional metaphysician. Quine and his followers did not have that fervid "We must eliminate any whiff of metaphysics without mercy" attitude of the Vienna Circle. Quine soothes: "[T]he question what ontology actually to adopt still stands open, and the obvious counsel is tolerance and an experimental spirit" (Quine 1961a/1948, p. 19). Much that the positivists would have rejected as meaningless turns out to be part of the web of science and thus is not to be rejected on the basis of dubious theories of meaning. Quine, we saw, refers approvingly to the blurring of the distinction between speculative metaphysics and natural science. Still, Quine has enough of the positivist spirit that he cannot bring himself to allow metaphysics under that name; he countenances "ontology." Nowhere in his writings does he explicitly recommend metaphysics as such, nor would he allow any metaphysics that is independent of the work of scientists.

Quine inherited his focus on ontology from Carnap. Carnap in a famous article titled "Empiricism, Semantics, and Ontology" (Carnap 1956b/1950), distinguishes between two kinds of questions – internal questions and external questions. According to Carnap ontological issues are external questions, which means that they concern only semantics – which kind of terms to use. The answers to external questions are not true or false. The "answers" to external questions are decisions not discoveries. External questions are misleadingly formulated as factual questions.

> Are there properties, classes, numbers, propositions? In order to understand more clearly the nature of these and related problems, it is above all necessary to recognize a fundamental distinction between two kinds of questions concerning the existence or reality of entities. If someone wishes to speak in his language about a new kind of entities, he has to introduce a system of new ways of speaking, subject to new rules; we shall call this procedure the construction of a linguistic *framework* for the new entities in question. And now we must distinguish two kinds of questions of existence: first, questions of the existence of certain entities of the new kind *within the framework;* we call them *internal questions;* and second, questions concerning the existence or reality *of the system of entities as a whole,* called *external questions.* Internal questions and possible answers to them are formulated with the help of the new forms of expressions. The answers may be found either by purely logical methods or by empirical

methods, depending upon whether the framework is a logical or a factual one. An external question is of a problematic character which is in need of closer examination. (Carnap 1956b/1950, p. 206)

According to Carnap, a question such as "Are there numbers?" could be meant as an internal question in which case the answer is obvious once we have adopted a language form that allows talk of numbers. Asked as an external question about the entire system of mathematics it makes no sense. It is a pseudo-question. This is Carnap's approach to traditional ontological questions such as whether there are physical objects, whether there are propositions, properties, (the gods of Homer?) and so on.

> Internal questions are here, in general, empirical questions to be answered by empirical investigations. On the other hand, the external questions of the reality of physical space and physical time are pseudo-questions. A question like 'Are there (really) space-time points?' is ambiguous. It may be meant as an internal question; then the affirmative answer is, of course, analytic and trivial. Or it may be meant in the external sense: 'Shall we introduce such and such forms into our language?'; in this case it is not a theoretical but a practical question, a matter of decision rather than assertion, and hence the proposed formulation would be misleading. (Carnap 1956b/1950, p. 213)

Carnap held that the dispute between the phenomenalists and physicalists (see Chapter 2, p. 67) was a dispute about external questions. He suggested that this is a pragmatic issue, and that one could adopt phenomenalism for some purposes and physicalism for others.

One might assume that Quine would approve of Carnap's approach, since the decision about which linguistic framework to adopt is pragmatic according to Carnap. Although Quine had the highest regard for Carnap, "[N]o one has influenced my philosophical thought more than Carnap" (Quine 1966b/1951, p. 126), he does not agree with Carnap. Quine rejected Carnap's distinction between factual statements and pseudo-statements based on linguistic conventions. Nor would Quine allow a distinction between internal and external questions. He would certainly not agree that answers to some internal questions are analytic, as Carnap holds. Despite elements of pragmatism, Carnap is still working on improving, explaining, and clarifying the basic positions of the logical positivists.

> A brief historical remark may here be inserted. The non-cognitive character of the questions which we have called here external questions was recognized and emphasized already by the Vienna Circle ... (Carnap 1956b/1950, p. 215)

Carnap does not confront doubts about the analytic/synthetic distinction, the rigid notion of meaning, or the Quinean claim that ontological questions are just as much empirical as any other questions in science.

Quine cannot use Carnap's terminology, because he rejects the distinction. The following is from "On Carnap's Views on Ontology" (one of several in which Quine attacked Carnap's ideas).

> I have set down my misgivings regarding the distinction between analytic and synthetic in a recent paper "Two dogmas of empiricism," and will not retrace those steps here. Let me merely stress the consequence: if there is no proper distinction between analytic and synthetic, then no basis at all remains for the contrast which Carnap urges between ontological statements [external questions] and empirical statements of existence [internal questions]. Ontological questions then end up on a par with questions of natural science. (Quine 1966b/1951, p. 134)

Recall that for Carnap internal questions such as "Are there (really) space-time points?" can get answers that are analytic, whereas external questions are psuedo-questions. If we reject the analytic/synthetic distinction, Carnap's distinction vanishes. Both what Carnap would have fancied as external questions and what he fancied as internal questions end up "on a par." They are empirical questions of natural science, according to Quine.

Epistemology Naturalized

Quine's approach to epistemology is similar to his handling of metaphysics. Epistemology, or what is left of it, like metaphysics, and what is left of it, is part of natural science. Quine proposes that epistemology be included in empirical psychology. The title of an article, only slightly less famous and influential than "Two Dogmas," puts it succinctly: "Epistemology Naturalized" (Quine 1969).

Quine's view that epistemology is part of natural science has been even more influential than his views on metaphysics. The claim that questions about how human beings form beliefs and get knowledge are questions of psychology is plausible and independent of more contentious issues involving the analytic/synthetic distinction. Quine is rescuing epistemology from the atrophied clutches of traditional philosophy and from those who would eliminate it along with metaphysics.

> Carnap and the other logical positivists of the Vienna Circle had already pressed the term "metaphysics" into pejorative use, as connoting meaninglessness; and the term 'epistemology' was next. Wittgenstein and his

followers, mainly at Oxford, found a residual philosophical vocation in therapy: in curing philosophers of the delusion that there were epistemological problems. [See Chapter 4]

But I think that at this point it may be more useful to say rather that epistemology still goes on, though in a new setting and a clarified status. Epistemology, or something like it, simply falls into place as a chapter of psychology and hence of natural science. It studies a natural phenomenon, viz., a physical human subject. (Quine 1969, p. 82)

Here again Quine is in the tradition of American pragmatism. Dewey anticipated Quine's naturalized epistemology. Dewey also suggests Quine's view of science as prospective rather than mirroring. (Dewey does not use Quine's words, instead he talks of "reflection," and connects it to human evolution.)

Reflection is an indirect response to the environment, and the element of indirection can itself become great and very complicated. But it has its origin in biological adaptive behavior and the ultimate function of its cognitive aspect is a prospective control of the conditions of the environment. The function of intelligence is therefore not that of copying the objects of the environment, but rather of taking account of the way in which more effective and more profitable relations with these objects may be established in the future. (Dewey 1973/1922, p. 54)

Many would question whether psychology is all there is to epistemology, but Quine is expansive and tolerant. His main concern is to challenge the traditional view that epistemology (and metaphysics) is a foundational enterprise prior to and independent of empirical science. There would still be room for the kinds of things that the old epistemologists did.

Such a study could still include, even, something like the old [epistemological] rational reconstruction, to whatever degree such reconstruction is practicable; for imaginative constructions can afford hints of actual psychological processes, in much the way that mechanical simulations can. But a conspicuous difference between old epistemology and the epistemological enterprise in this new psychological setting is that we can now make free use of empirical psychology. (Quine 1969, p. 83)

And natural science can also make free use of philosophical epistemology. In an engaging image Quine imagines epistemology and natural science mutually containing each other.

The old epistemology aspired to contain, in a sense, natural science; it would construct it somehow from sense data. Epistemology in its new setting, conversely, is contained in natural science, as a chapter of psychology. But the old containment remains valid too, in its way.... There is thus reciprocal containment, though containment in different senses: epistemology in natural science and natural science in epistemology. (Quine 1969, p. 83)

The idea is that epistemology represents science studying the scientific process itself. This is a circle but not a vicious one. According to a metaphor often repeated by Quine, science is like a ship that the sailors have to rebuild and repair while sailing in it.[9]

American Pragmatists after Quine: Nelson Goodman, Richard Rorty, and Hilary Putnam

Many leading American philosophers have been closely associated with Quine, and been influenced in one way or another by his holism and pragmatism. The most prominent among them are Nelson Goodman, Richard Rorty, and Hilary Putnam. Only Rorty and Putnam (and only later in his career) would be happy styling themselves pragmatists, but each is beholden to the American pragmatist tradition. They share a rejection of traditional philosophical questions and are suspicious of the notion of absolute truth embodied by science mirroring reality. They revel in dismantling the pretensions of the logical positivists.

Each of the prominent neo-pragmatists, as they are often called, was born in the United States and educated there. Nelson Goodman, born in Needham, Massachusetts, got his BA and PhD from Harvard and was on and off a professor of philosophy there, intersecting with Quine. He was older than Quine but took years off to run an art gallery and enjoy an artistic career. Rorty, born in New York City, is the least closely associated with Quine, and never spent time at Harvard, but he often cites Quine as a major influence on his ideas.[10] Hilary Putnam, born in Chicago, was a close associate of Quine's and has been professor of philosophy at Harvard for many years. He is now, in 2011, the only one of this group still living. Happily, he is professor emeritus at Harvard and the grand old man of American philosophy and justly revered.

Quine and Goodman both served in military intelligence in the US Armed Forces during World War II. As we will see, many of their

---

[9]   The metaphor is due to Otto Neurath of the Vienna Circle.

[10]   But then Rorty cites almost every philosopher since 1910 as a major influence. Rorty is nothing if not eclectic and wide-ranging. He once quipped that he was the transitory professor of trendy studies.

generational colleagues in Britain served in various branches of the British forces, but most in intelligence. Some of them had fascinating military careers. Putnam and Rorty were too young to serve in the war.

World War II did not have the same sort of discernible effect on epistemology and metaphysics as did World War I. One effect, however, of the Nazis and World War II was the emigration of many German and Austrian philosophers to English speaking countries. We must not underestimate the influence of the logical positivists. Each of the American neo-pragmatists was philosophically formed in the atmosphere of the early Wittgenstein and the Vienna Circle. Quine, Putnam, and Rorty studied with Carnap. Quine traveled to Vienna and followed Carnap to Prague. Putnam studied with Carnap and Reichenbach at UCLA. Goodman was influenced by Carnap, especially in his early work. The arrival in this country of Carnap, Hempel, and others was a tremendous boon for American philosophy.

Unlike the members of the Vienna Circle, the American pragmatists were not part of a movement that met together or published manifestoes or had anything like a party line. Each of them is fiercely independent and individualistic in thought, writing, and style. Part of the idea of pragmatism is an irreverent attitude to traditional philosophy and its traditional preoccupations, and resistance to anything resembling a manifesto or program. The American neo-pragmatists knew each other, were influenced by Quine, especially his holism and pragmatism, and were reacting against traditional philosophy and Carnap, despite revering him. Beyond that they had little in common.

The most prominent theme shared by the neo-pragmatists is a rejection of the correspondence theory of truth. [*Background 3.4 –* Correspondence, coherence, and pragmatic theories of truth] "For the pragmatist, true sentences are not true because they correspond to reality, and so there is no need to worry about what sort of reality, if any, a given sentence corresponds to – no need to worry about what 'makes' it true" (Rorty 1982, p. xvi). Contrary to the *Tractatus*, we do not need to look for the one sort of thing that makes a sentence true – a fact or objective state of affairs for it to correspond to. The "truth-makers" are as diverse and multifarious as our purposes and projects.

Rorty

Rorty, the quintessential and self-described pragmatist, has been prominent beyond philosophy departments. He has had a large following among other humanists, especially those in literature departments. Consistent with his pragmatism, Rorty is dubious about philosophy as an academic field. Given a chance, he would have shut down philosophy departments and have philosophers do more useful things. At any rate he said things to this effect. This helps to explain the tendency among his analytic colleagues to dismiss his work as cultural pandering.

Rorty's "cultural pandering" consists in his trying to engage and include Continental philosophers in dialogue. Rorty more than anyone else has worked to bridge the gap between analytic philosophy – especially the pragmatist wing of it – and Continental philosophy.

There is something to this rapprochement. Just as the pragmatists have been trying to overcome the "paradigm" of traditional philosophy and reset the questions and dialogue in a new key, so too the major Continental philosophers have been bent on expunging remnants of the tradition of Western metaphysics that begins with Plato. And as I mentioned earlier, both the analytic and Continental traditions include philosophers who exhibit a modernist tendency.

Rorty did not deny that major differences between the analytic and Continental camps persist, especially their differing attitudes to science. According to Rorty, the analytic philosophers tend to revere science and mathematics and are inspired by them. As we have seen, analytic philosophers have gained many of their issues from work in philosophy of science and the foundations of mathematics. The Continental philosophers, on the other hand, distrust and dislike science as much as they do traditional Platonist metaphysics. Heidegger and Sartre detested modern science and technology. Following Nietzsche, they see science as a continuation of Platonist metaphysics. They argue that modern technology is destructive of individuality and freedom.

Unfortunately for Rorty's attempt at rapprochement, this difference in attitude to science goes deeper than he realizes. It is not just a matter of style and inclination. American pragmatism is nothing and not true to its roots if it does not embrace natural science as the most reliable and fruitful way to truth and knowledge. William James and John Dewey were both engaged in science and technology and accorded them the highest respect. Natural science is what pragmatism is about and where it comes from. The differing attitudes to science represents a wide gulf between the Continental philosophers and analytic pragmatists, and analytic philosophers in general.

Ironically, Continental philosophers seem to share a view of science that is reminiscent of the logical positivists. Or rather I should say they both indulge in an extreme view of science – in the one case adulation, in the other fear and scorn. Kuhn and Quine tried to overcome the idea that science is a rigidly organized description of independent reality that gets closer and closer to absolute truth. Thus they would disparage as naïve and uninformed the Continental view of science as recast Platonist metaphysics. The Continentals are attacking an institution that never existed. James, Dewey, and Quine viewed science as a cultural phenomenon that is to be judged by a diffuse set of values and interests, not by how well it mirrors "reality."

Rorty also worked to depose the metaphor of the mind and knowledge as mirrors. In his major work *Philosophy and the Mirror of Nature* (Rorty 1979) he criticizes the dominant and traditional Western view of the mind and thus scientific knowledge as containing pictorial representations of external, independent physical reality. The attempt to mirror reality by thought and language is forlorn because it is an incoherent endeavor. It is a relic of the enlightenment inherited from Plato and Aristotle. We see this mirroring also in Wittgenstein's picture theory. To some extent the logical positivists with their focus on verifiability inherited the notion from Wittgenstein, but when pressed would have likely rejected the metaphor as metaphysical. Putnam, Goodman, and Rorty labored to dismantle the traditional view of science as an attempt, by rigid and formal methods, to get an ever more accurate picture or mirror of a fixed lawlike world. They rejected a view of science according to which it proceeded to get ever nearer to ultimate truth, to achieve an ever more accurate picture. Dewey in his 1922 article on pragmatism says: "A phrase of James' very well summarizes its [pragmatism's] import: 'the popular notion that 'Science' is forced on the mind *ab extra*, and that our interests have nothing to do with its constructions, is utterly absurd'" (Dewey 1973/1922, pp. 53–4). A well-defined line can be traced from Dewey and James, through Quine and Kuhn, to Putnam, Goodman, and Rorty.

One aspect that would, however, distinguish the later American pragmatists and make them more congenial with the Continentals is that, contrary to Quine, the early Wittgenstein, and the Vienna Circle, they did not see science as containing all of knowledge. The pragmatists, given their view of science as value-laden, are more tolerant of non-scientific endeavors than were early Wittgenstein and the logical positivists. Rorty, Goodman, and Putnam insisted that disciplines outside of science are also ways of knowing. Art, music, literature, morality, and perhaps even religion, contribute to the web of knowledge.

> A view of knowledge that acknowledges that the sphere of knowledge is wider than the sphere of 'science' seems to me to be a cultural necessity if we are to arrive at a sane and human view of ourselves *or* of science. (Putnam 1978, p. 5)

Once one frees oneself from the toils of the correspondence theory of truth and the metaphysical notion of reality that accompanies it, one abandons the idea that knowledge is a mirror of external reality. This opens us to viewing literature and art as offering, among other things of course, cognitive content with pragmatic value.

Still, science is the Queen. The pragmatic attitude toward science is based on respect and admiration for science. As Putnam puts it, the anti-traditional view of science is the only sane and human one. The neo-pragmatists aimed to dismantle the rigid theories of the logical positivists, and thus to save science from its friends – friends who wanted to impose an unrealistic formal structure on it.

Goodman

Nelson Goodman's contribution to unraveling the traditional view of science was his modestly named "new riddle of induction." Goodman announced this in the early 1950s and it quickly made him famous. Much more than a mere riddle, it caused major upheavals in the philosophy of science. The scientific method which proceeds by empirical induction is one of the key elements of the traditional view of science, but the logic of induction has always been beset by problems. As opposed to deductive logic, the logic of confirmation – inductive logic – had never been successfully formalized. Several annoying puzzles or paradoxes ("riddles") of induction have surfaced, each requiring ever more elaborate and technical solutions. Both Carnap and Hempel had tried to develop purely mechanical or syntactic methods of inductive confirmation to deal with these riddles. [*Background 3.5* – Induction versus deduction and the traditional problems of induction] In tune with the positivists' faith in formal logic, they thought that the problems of inductive logic could be solved by fiddling with the symbolic logic.

Goodman swept away all such attempts. He was able to devise understandable but unnatural predicates that defeated any purely mechanical system of inductive logic.

> So long as what seems to be needed is merely a way of excluding a few odd and unwanted cases that are inadvertently admitted by our definition of [inductive] confirmation, the problem may not seem very hard or very pressing. We fully expect that minor defects will be found in our definition and that the necessary refinements will have to be worked out patiently one after another. But some further examples will show that our present difficulty is of a much graver kind. (Goodman 1965/1955, p. 73)

105

Goodman's best known cooked up predicate is "grue." An item is grue if and only if it is green and examined before *t* (any specific time in the future, say 2 p.m. EDT, March 30, 2030) or is unexamined before *t* and is blue. The time now being well before our arbitrarily chosen *t*, we rattle around places where emeralds are found and examine a bunch of them. Naturally each of them is green. This supports the induction that all emeralds are green. (It confirms the claim that all emeralds are green, but of course does not absolutely prove it. That is why it is inductive, not deductive.)

But wait, our observations of emeralds also support the induction that all emeralds are grue. They confirm the claim that all emeralds are grue. Each observed emerald is green and examined before *t*, so it is grue. Clearly this is a problem, because if our supported induction confirms that all emeralds are grue, then when *t* rolls around we should expect every newly examined emerald to be blue. This merits a bit of an explanation: If we examine an emerald just after *t* and we expect it to be grue (on the basis of our grue-induction), then since we know it was not examined before *t*, we must expect it to be blue. It is either examined before *t* and green or it is blue.

The rub is that of course it is not blue and we do not expect it to be. Nobody would. The induction with "grue" is crazy. Unfortunately, nothing in the most complex syntactic formalizations explains why induction does not work for "grue" but does for "green." Goodman concludes on the basis of such cooked up predicates that "we are left once again with the intolerable result that anything confirms anything. This difficulty cannot be set aside as an annoying detail to be taken care of in due course" (Goodman 1965/1955, p. 75).

The response to the "grue" riddle which surely occurs to the reader is that induction does not work with such cooked up artificial predicates as "grue" and was never meant to. Induction was only meant to work with natural predicates like "green." This is quite correct. It is a main point of Goodman's argument. No normal person would ever use a grue-like predicate, but that is a natural fact about us, not a result of logic or metaphysics. "Grue" and "green" are logically equal. From the point of view of formal systems "grue" is just as good a predicate as "green." Formal systems recognize no difference between "natural" and "cooked up" predicates. Goodman shows how, surprisingly, all of our inductions with "green" can be done with "grue," although they would be much more complex. "Green" has no logical superiority to "grue."

Goodman's example may seem highly contrived and technical, and by itself perhaps it would not have had much of an effect. The point is that combined with Quine's attack on the analytic/synthetic distinction, and the attacks on the verifiability criterion of meaningfulness, it helped to show the bankruptcy of the mechanical, rigid, formal approach of the logical positivists and their allies. A more pragmatic and eclectic approach to philosophical problems came to seem inevitable, and even beneficial and salutary.

Goodman calls predicates and hypotheses that are inductive-friendly "projectible," and ones like "grue" that are not good for induction "nonprojectible." The problem is to define or describe a way to distinguish the projectible from the nonprojectible predicates. This cannot be done in any syntactic, mechanical way. Again, pragmatic conditions must come into play.

> Categories that are inductively right tend to coincide with categories that are right for science in general; but variations in purpose may result in variations in relevant kinds. (Goodman 1978, p. 128)

Note especially the final phrase. The kinds that we recognize in nature are partly, perhaps even largely, a result of our purposes.

Putnam

Hilary Putnam, in a prodigious series of publications from 1954 to the present day, has expressed opinions and given arguments on almost every topic in philosophy. He has also changed his positions on those topics many times. Putnam has been one of his own most relentless critics. In later chapters we will describe his important role in the revival of metaphysics and his seminal contributions to the philosophy of mind. In the 1980s he became dissatisfied with his ideas in that sphere. He then advanced a version of pragmatism that he called "internal realism." (He said that he wished he had called it "pragmatic realism.")

Putnam distinguishes between two philosophical perspectives – the externalist and the internalist. (This distinction is only distantly related to Carnap's distinction between external and internal questions.)[11] Putnam's internalist perspective is influenced by Quine and the pragmatists.

---

[11] Putnam's terminology has not caught on and is doubly confusing, because not only is it derived obliquely from Carnap, but "externalism" came to be widely used to name a completely different theory that is also partly based on Putnam's arguments. (See Chapter 7, pp. 259–60.) A better-known and less confusing terminology for the distinction he is offering is that between metaphysical realists and anti- or non-realists. Alas, "realism" also has many and varied uses in philosophy and in ordinary language.

First his description of the externalist perspective:

> One of these perspectives is the perspective of metaphysical realism. On this perspective, the world consists of some fixed totality of mind-independent objects. There is exactly one true and complete description of 'the way the world is'. Truth involves some sort of correspondence relation between words or thought-signs and external things and sets of things. I shall call this perspective the *externalist* perspective, because its favorite point of view is a God's Eye point of view. (Putnam 1981, p. 49)

There is no reason to believe that we will ever arrive at the one true and complete description (unless we are God), but it is there nevertheless, according to externalism. It is what science aims at.

The internalist (or anti-realist) perspective rejects this belief in a mind-independent truth.

> The perspective I shall defend has no unambiguous name. ... I shall refer to it as the *internalist* perspective, because it is characteristic of this view to hold that *what objects does the world consist of?* is a question that it only makes sense to ask *within* a theory or description. Many 'internalist' philosophers, though not all, hold further that there is more than one 'true' theory or description of the world. 'Truth', in an internalist view, is some sort of (idealized) rational acceptability – some sort of ideal coherence of our beliefs with each other and with our experiences *as those experiences are themselves represented in our belief system* – and not correspondence with mind-independent or discourse-independent 'states of affairs'. There is no God's Eye point of view that we can know or usefully imagine; there are only the various points of view of actual persons reflecting various interests and purposes that their descriptions and theories subserve. (Putnam 1981, pp. 49–50)

The final clauses of this quote could serve as a definition of pragmatism – "there are only the various points of view of actual persons reflecting various interests and purposes that their descriptions and theories subserve." Putnam calls his view "internal *realism*" because he wants to emphasize his rejection of any form of relativism or subjectivism. Even though most philosophers would balk at calling his internalist perspective "realist," Putnam insists that there are enough empirical constraints on our theories to make the term "realism" appropriate. Frankly, this is a bit of philosophical cake-eating and at the same time wanting to have it on the part of Putnam.

Putnam's view is influenced by Quine's holism and epistemological naturalism.

Internalism is not a facile relativism that says, 'Anything goes'. Denying that it makes sense to ask whether our concepts 'match' something totally uncontaminated by conceptualization is one thing; but to hold that every conceptual system is therefore just as good as every other would be something else. If anyone really believed that, and if they were foolish enough to pick a conceptual system that told them they could fly and to act upon it by jumping out of a window, they would, if they were lucky enough to survive, see the weakness of the latter view at once. Internalism does not deny that there are experiential *inputs* to knowledge; knowledge is not a story with no constraints except *internal* coherence; but it does deny that there are any inputs *which are not themselves to some extent shaped by our concepts,* by the vocabulary we use to report and describe them, or any inputs *which admit of only one description, independent of all conceptual choices.* Even our description of our own sensations, so dear as a starting point for knowledge to generations of epistemologists, is heavily affected (as are the sensations themselves, for that matter) by a host of conceptual choices. The very inputs upon which our knowledge is based are conceptually contaminated; but contaminated inputs are better than none. If contaminated inputs are all we have, still all we have has proved to be quite a bit.

What makes a statement, or a whole system of statements – a theory or conceptual scheme – rationally acceptable is, in large part, its coherence and fit; coherence of 'theoretical' or less experiential beliefs with one another and with more experiential beliefs, and also coherence of experiential beliefs with theoretical beliefs. Our conceptions of coherence and acceptability are, on the view I shall develop, deeply interwoven with our psychology. They depend upon our biology and our culture; they are by no means 'value free'. But they *are* our conceptions, and they are conceptions of something real. They define a kind of objectivity, *objectivity for us,* even if it is not the metaphysical objectivity of the God's Eye view. Objectivity and rationality humanly speaking are what we have; they are better than nothing. (Putnam 1981, pp. 54–5)

Quine's influence on Putnam's philosophy of science is evident also from the following passage. It is a good description of Quine's holistic views of science.

What I have been saying is that the procedures by which we decide on the acceptability of a scientific theory have to do with whether or not the scientific theory as a whole exhibits certain 'virtues'. I am assuming that the procedure of building up scientific theory cannot be correctly analyzed as a procedure of verifying scientific theories *sentence by sentence.* I am assuming that verification in science is a holistic matter, that it is whole theoretical systems that meet the test of experience 'as a corporate body', and that the judgment of how well a whole system of sentences meets the test of experience is ultimately somewhat of an intuitive matter which could not be formalized short of formalizing total human psychology.(Putnam 1981, p. 133)

We see from the above passages, quoted at length, that Putnam's internal realism is something of a synthesis of Carnap and Quine. From Quine he's taken holism, from Carnap the notion that ontology is relative or internal to a theory or system. (*"What objects does the world consist of?* is a question that it only makes sense to ask *within* a theory or description."* (Quoted above).)

Putnam is given to fanciful but engaging metaphors and slogans. One of his favorites of his internal realist phase is that "the mind and the world jointly make up the mind and the world" (Putnam 1981, p. xi). Putnam's defense of internalism consists, however, of much more than slogans and programmatic pronouncements. Like Quine and Goodman, he offers technical and sophisticated arguments, often based on advances in symbolic logic, to support his views. And like Quine's and Goodman's, Putnam's technical arguments are mostly negative. He dismantles what he takes to be the rigid and mechanical views of earlier empiricists, especially the logical positivists and their followers – a rigid notion of meaning, of sentence by sentence verification, and reductionism, and a rigid distinction between science and other forms of intellectual life.

Putnam diverges from Quine in his treatment of values. Quine shared with the positivists a dismissive attitude to values. He had a rather crude behaviorist theory of morality. Putnam, on the other hand, takes values seriously. He argued that the fact/value distinction, which was almost as dear to the positivists as the analytic/synthetic distinction, is unsupportable. Our descriptions, theories, and judgments are saturated with values. Such ordinary words as "cruel" and "kind" are descriptive and applicable empirically, but they are also evaluative. To speak of someone as cruel or an act as cruel is to make a moral judgment. Vast numbers of our words are value-laden. Even such factual sounding terms as "rational," "logical, " "irrational," are evaluative.

When we think of facts and values as independent we typically think of 'facts' as stated in some physicalistic or bureaucratic jargon, and the 'values' as being stated in the most abstract value terms, e.g. 'good', 'bad'. The independence of value from fact is harder to maintain when the facts themselves are of the order of 'inconsiderate', 'thinks only about himself', 'would do anything for money'. (Putnam 1981, p. 139)

I believe that Putnam would consider his rescuing values from positivist exclusion to be his most important contribution to philosophy. This marks a fundamental break with previous empiricist philosophy.

The Third Dogma of Empiricism

Rorty includes Donald Davidson among the neo-pragmatists, he says, because Davidson is a major contributor to the "holistic 'pragmatizing' strain in analytic philosophy ... "[12] (Rorty 1982, p. xix). Davidson is another American philosopher who was trained at Harvard and is closely associated with Quine, but he is more likely to be seen as an opponent of pragmatism than a supporter. (There is much more on Davidson, especially his contributions to philosophy of language and philosophy of mind, in Chapter 5 including biographical information.) Davidson, unlike Putnam and Rorty, explicitly rejects the label "pragmatist" (and likewise the labels "anti-realist," "empiricist," "transcendental idealist" and so on).

Davidson claims to have exposed a third dogma of empiricism. He accuses Quine himself, as well as Kuhn, of subscribing unwittingly to this one. In a 1974 presidential address to the American Philosophical Association titled "The Third Dogma of Empiricism,"[13] Davidson aims his critique at Quine. The third dogma of empiricism according to Davidson is the idea that we have conceptual schemes for organizing the data of experience.

> I want to urge that this second dualism [the first is analytic/synthetic] of scheme and content, of organizing system and something waiting to be organized, cannot be made intelligible and defensible. It is itself a dogma of empiricism.(Davidson 1985e/1974, p. 189)

Quine and others certainly speak in terms of conceptual schemes. A key Quine statement cited by Davidson for criticism is from "Two Dogmas": "As an empiricist I continue to think of the conceptual scheme of science as a tool, ultimately, for predicting future experience in the

---

[12] I think Davidson would agree with the "holistic" label but he is too focused on the classical notion of truth to be comfortable with the "pragmatizing" label. Much of Davidson's work has been a systematic approach to language, thought, and action based on the contributions of Alfred Tarski to formal logic, in particular his explication of the notion of truth in formal systems. Indeed, Davidson has built his approach to philosophy on Tarski's work on truth.

[13] Later reprinted (Davidson 1985e/1974) with the title "On the Very Idea of a Conceptual Scheme."

light of past experience" (Quine 1961/1951, p. 44). The long quote from Putnam starting "Internalism..." contains several references to our conceptual system or scheme, our conceptual choices and so on. Particularly problematic according to Davidson is the notion that science is a conceptual scheme for organizing and predicting experiences.

Davidson is bothered by the conceptual relativism that he believes emerges from the "dogma" of scheme and content. Conceptual relativism is based on the idea that there are data or sense impressions, or some sort of basic facts. These are the contents that are organized differently by different schemes. One of the problems with conceptual relativism is that it seems to imply that different conceptual schemes cannot be translated into each other's terms. The adherents of differing conceptual schemes cannot really understand each other. Davidson cites Kuhn as a particularly egregious example of a conceptual relativist, because he claimed that differing scientific paradigms are incommensurable.

Davidson likens the problem of conceptual relativism to one in which another language is flatly untranslatable into our own. But, Davidson asserts, a "language" that is untranslatable into our language is not something that we could perceive as a language at all. We could hear the sounds, or see the marks, but we could not recognize them as linguistic. Likewise, a conceptual scheme too different from ours could not be recognized by us as a conceptual scheme. In order for a scheme to be recognized by us as a scheme it must have enough of an overlap with ours to be understandable to us, in which case it is not really a different conceptual scheme. Perhaps we disagree with others who supposedly have a different conceptual scheme, but in order to disagree with someone about something, Davidson argues, we must agree with them about almost everything else.

Doesn't this just show that we humans have our one and only conceptual scheme, not that the notion of conceptual scheme is incoherent? Davidson anticipates this thought and rejects it. "It would be equally wrong to announce the glorious news that all mankind – all speakers of language, at least – share a common scheme and ontology. For if we cannot intelligibly say that schemes are different, neither can we intelligibly say that they are one" (Davidson 1985e/1974, p. 198).

The exposure of this third dogma spells doom for empiricism, according to Davidson (and I suppose he would gleefully add it dooms pragmatism as well). The dogma of scheme and content "is itself a dogma of empiricism, the third dogma. The third, and perhaps the last, for if we give it up it is not clear that there is anything distinctive left to call empiricism" (Davidson 1985e/1974, p. 189).

Davidson coyly hedges his claims with "perhaps" and "it is not clear" and so on, but Quine in his response to Davidson takes his point seriously. In an article titled "On the Very Idea of a Third Dogma" Quine gives a pragmatist response to Davidson. The pragmatist is dubious about the notion of truth especially if a lot of weight is put on it as Davidson does. Quine grants much that Davidson says but deflects it from harming his pragmatic or relative empiricism. Quine's counter-Davidson claim is that "the proper role of experience or surface irritation is as a basis not for truth but for warranted belief" (Quine 1981a, p. 39).

> If empiricism is construed as a theory of truth, then what Davidson imputes to it as a third dogma is rightly imputed and rightly renounced. Empiricism as a theory of truth thereupon goes by the board, and good riddance. As a theory of evidence, however, empiricism remains with us, minus indeed the two old dogmas. (Quine 1981a, p. 39)

Quine's point is that experience is still recognized as the only reliable source of knowledge, or as Quine puts it "warranted belief." Quine's idea is, I think, that we should drop talking about a pragmatist or empiricist theory of truth and instead focus on what we are justified in believing, and rationally acting upon. The best and maybe only evidence for our beliefs that we ultimately have is the common experience of humanity especially as interpreted by natural science. This much is still distinctive of empiricism. It is not as exciting, radical, or revolutionary as the views of the classical British empiricists or the logical positivists. But empiricism rid of its outmoded epistemological and metaphysical presuppositions is sounder. As Quine says, empiricism "has indeed wanted some tidying up, and has had it" (Quine 1981a, p. 39). This process of "tidying up" was a main theme of analytic philosophy after the Vienna Circle. The main elements have been pragmatism, holism, and naturalized epistemology. It was a labor of love.

Background 3.1 – The distinction between the early and late Wittgenstein and why this is a necessary distinction to make

This is a summary of material that is in the text at various places. The early Wittgenstein (from about 1911 to about 1922) is represented by the *Tractatus*. This is a highly formal system based on the conception of isomorphism among our ideas, our language, and the world. Language can represent or picture facts in the world because there is a common structure shared between language and the world. Likewise language can express our ideas because there is a commonality of structure between language and our thoughts; and our thoughts can represent the world because there is also a commonality of structure. The structure is logic, and in particular modern symbolic of the Frege–Russell variety, somewhat streamlined and simplified. This is a version of logical atomism.

After publishing the *Tractatus* Wittgenstein left philosophy because he thought that he had solved/eliminated all philosophical problems. He could not stay away, however, and was soon convinced by friends in Cambridge that his *Tractatus* theory was too crude. Wittgenstein devoted the remainder of his life (from about 1930 to his death in 1951) to criticizing his *Tractatus* theory. His approach and style entirely changed. He wrote now mostly in short paragraphs in aphoristic form. He used no symbolic logic and was suspicious of formalism. His theory of language was entirely different. Instead of a picture of reality or a fact, the meaning of a statement was its use in practical life. Like tools, the point of the elements of language was to do jobs, only one of which might be on some occasions to picture, but usually not. Rather, language is used to elicit a response in listeners, to coordinate our activities, and so on. The later Wittgenstein published nothing, but wrote voluminously in notebooks, lectured, and met with small groups of students, many of whom went on to be leading philosophers. Some of Wittgenstein's notebooks were informally copied and circulated privately. Soon after his death the classic work of the later Wittgenstein – *The Philosophical Investigations* – was published.

Thus there is an important contrast between Wittgenstein's early life, style, and ideas and his later approach to philosophy.

Background 3.2 – Peirce, James, and Dewey

Charles Sanders Peirce (1839–1914), William James (1842–1910), and John Dewey (1859–1952) are the most famous American philosophers until Quine.

Peirce was foremost a mathematician, logician, and scientist. He made many disparate contributions to philosophy that were characterized more by brilliance and insight than by system. He contributed two main ideas that have lasted in philosophy: Fallibilism and pragmatism. Fallibilism is the view that any of our beliefs might be false. It is a call for epistemological modesty without thereby falling into despair and skepticism. Although Peirce coined the term "pragmatism" he was not a pragmatist.

William James, the brother of Henry James, was famous for writing classic works on psychology, religion, and philosophy. He is the outstanding American pragmatist. Both Peirce and James were closely associated with Harvard University. James was a member of the Harvard faculty from 1873 until his death.

Dewey wrote and published major works in many areas of philosophy. He also was active as a journalist and educational reformer. He was a leading public intellectual. In the latter half of the twentieth century Dewey's reputation was in eclipse. Both James and Peirce were considered more interesting and important as philosophers. Dewey called his philosophy "instrumentalism" rather than "pragmatism" but he is considered to be, along with James, one of the leading American pragmatists.

Background 3.3 – "Warfare" in philosophy

The battle or warfare analogy is inapt perhaps, because philosophical interchange is supposed to be friendly. Philosophers are committed to seeking the truth together, not to winning an argument. The "loser" of a philosophical argument is no loser if he gets a closer or clearer vision of the truth. The dialectical nature of philosophy requires that intellectual opponents are both seeking enlightenment. Disagreement always rages in philosophy – it is the nature of the Socratic enterprise always to dispute and question – so, on the other hand, it is not inapt to speak in a limited sense of winners and losers. The battle or warfare analogy is apt because the philosophical opponents must struggle against each other and attempt to defeat their opponent intellectually. The idea is that thereby they will gain truth or enlightenment. Philosophers seeking the truth cannot adopt an accommodating and accepting attitude to the other or we will never get anywhere. Just as jurists believe that the way to justice is by the struggle between defense attorney and prosecutor, philosophers believe that the way to truth is via dialectical struggle and combat. Although this is the traditional and dominant view of philosophy, not all philosophers accept it. Some feminist philosophers reject the battle metaphor of philosophy in the sense that they view philosophical progress as possible on the basis of non-combative cooperation. Also Russell and the logical positivists tried to reformulate philosophy as a cooperative scientific enterprise with objective results. To the extent that philosophy is restricted to logic and formal analysis of language, this is appropriate.

Background 3.4 – Correspondence, coherence, and pragmatic theories of truth

The correspondence theory of truth is like a *Tractarian* view of representation. A proposition is judged true if it accurately represents or "pictures" independent reality, it is false otherwise.

The coherence theory of truth is the view that truth is a matter of fittingness to a system. A proposition is true if it coheres or fits in with the rest of the propositions in the system to which it belongs. If it conflicts with other accepted propositions it is false.

The pragmatic theory of truth is the view that a proposition is true if it is useful, if it works in practice. A failed proposition is useless. We call this falsity.

All sorts of modifications and combinations of these three theories have been proposed by philosophers. Nothing satisfactory has been established. Each of the theories has serious problems. The nature of truth is still an area of intense philosophical disagreement.

Background 3.5 – Induction versus deduction and the traditional problems of induction

Deductive Logic: This is the standard sort of formal logic that is taught in symbolic logic courses. Deductive inferences are defined as inferences in which the truth of the premises necessitates the truth of the conclusion. For example: All men are mortals. Socrates is a man. Therefore Socrates is a mortal. Another example: If P, then Q. Not Q. Therefore not P.

Inductive Logic: This is the study of inferences where the premises do not necessitate the conclusion but make it likely. Inductive logic has not been successfully formalized. It merges into probability theory and statistics. There are several well-known paradoxes of induction. We support a generalization such as "All A are B" by examining As. If every examined A is a B, then this supports the generalization. It does not prove it, because the next A may not be a B.

Here's an older "riddle of induction" due to Hempel, called the paradox of confirmation or the raven paradox: According to deductive logic "All A are B" is logically equivalent to "All non-B are non-A, " so support for one should equivalently be support for the other. Consider the claim that all crows (or ravens) are black things. As we examine more crows and find that they are black, this increases our confidence in this claim. Note, however, that it is equivalent to "All non-black things are non-crows." So each non-black thing that is not a crow supports the claim that all crows are black. So we can just as well support the claim that all crows are black by examining snowy egrets (they are non-black things) and determining that they are non-crows. We don't even need to look at any crows to support the claim that all crows are black. This of course is ridiculous, but no clear solution to the paradox is available at present.

Further Reading

The Philosophy of W. V. Quine (Library of Living Philosophers, Volume XVIII) edited by Paul Schilpp and Lewis E. Hahn (Open Court 1982) has many excellent articles by leading philosophers and replies by Quine.

The Web of Belief (Random House 1978) by Quine and J. S. Ullian was written as an intro textbook, but has a lot of Quine's philosophy in it.

Among the many useful books on Quine are *Quine: Language, Experience and Reality* by Christopher Hookway (Stanford University Press 1988) and *The Philosophy of W. V. Quine: An Expository Essay* by Roger Gibson (University Press of Florida 1982). Gibson has written or edited several other worthwhile books on Quine.

Criticism and the Growth of Knowledge (Cambridge University Press 1970) edited by Imre Lakatos and Alan Musgrave is an early and influential collection of essays by leading philosophers of science on Kuhn's work. It contains a preface and reply by Kuhn.

Putnam's *The Many Faces of Realism* (Open Court 1987) is a discussion of many topics that revolve around Putnam's pragmatic realism.

Realism with a Human Face (Harvard 1992) is another book of interesting essays by Putnam.

Rorty now has a volume in the Library of Living Philosophers: *The Philosophy of Richard Rorty (The Library of Living Philosophers, Volume XXXII)* edited by Randall E. Auxier and Lewis Edwin Hahn (Open Court 2009).

A Companion to Pragmatism edited by John R. Shook and Joseph Margolis (Wiley-Blackwell 2009) has interesting essays by Putnam and Rorty, and many other leading philosophers. It also has some essays by the original American pragmatists.

4

Oxford Ordinary Language Philosophy and Later Wittgenstein

Our language can be regarded as an ancient city: a maze of little streets and squares, of old and new houses, and of houses with extensions from various periods; and this surrounded by a multitude of new suburbs with straight and regular streets and uniform houses. (Wittgenstein 2009/1953, p.11e, #18)

Introduction

During and just after World War II the center of gravity of British analytic philosophy shifted from Cambridge University to Oxford. The three stars of the analytic world, Bertrand Russell, G. E. Moore, and Ludwig Wittgenstein, were no longer active at Cambridge. Russell was out of mainstream philosophy. Moore retired from his professorship in 1939 at the age of 66. He wrote very little after that. Wittgenstein was still active but no longer at Cambridge, and his influence was strongest at Oxford, as was Moore's. Wittgenstein had succeeded Moore in his professorship, but resigned in 1947 and left Cambridge to live in Ireland. During the war, obviously a difficult time for Germans and Austrians living in Britain, Wittgenstein worked in a hospital in London. At Oxford a new group of analytic philosophers emerged in the late 1940s and 1950s. The leading ones among them were John Austin, Gilbert Ryle, and Peter Strawson.

A Brief History of Analytic Philosophy: From Russell to Rawls, First Edition. Stephen P. Schwartz.
© 2012 John Wiley & Sons, Inc. Published 2012 by John Wiley & Sons, Inc.

The change from Cambridge to Oxford was more than a change of location. The philosophical orientation of the Oxford philosophers was different from and opposed to that of the Cambridge philosophers. The Oxford philosophers had been trained in Latin and Greek, the traditional education of British elites, whereas Russell and Wittgenstein brought their background in mathematics and formal logic to their philosophical work. Several features characterized the thought of the post-war Oxford philosophers, but the unifying theme was rejection of formalism in philosophy. This trend was aimed at the work of Russell and Wittgenstein's *Tractatus* as well as their followers in the Vienna Circle such as Carnap. The Oxford philosophers, although proficient in and knowledgeable about symbolic logic, rejected the notion that formal logic and the study of formal languages could offer solutions to philosophical problems. Indeed, they tended to view symbolic logic as an attractive snare for the philosophical intellect. Their attack on the formalism of Russell, the *Tractatus*, and the logical positivists was partly influenced by G. E. Moore's common sense philosophy, but the main inspiration was Wittgenstein's attack on his own *Tractatus*. The Oxford philosophers were not so much relying on common sense as on natural language as it is spoken and used in non-scientific and non-academic discourse. They focused on ordinary language. Thus they came to be called "ordinary language philosophers." Their influential approach to philosophical issues was called "ordinary language philosophy" or "Oxford ordinary language philosophy" or simply just "Oxford philosophy."

The Oxford philosophers examined ordinary language with great subtlety and cleverness, and some of their observations enlighten and charm. In the foreground, however, is the question "How can the study of ordinary language lead to philosophical insights and the solution, or dissolution, of philosophical problems?" This is an important challenge. The basic response is this: We illuminate concepts by investigating the use of words. For example, "We investigate the concept of knowledge by studying the usage of sentences in which 'know' and cognate words occur" (Malcolm 1951, p. 336). Such an investigation will not increase our knowledge of facts, but will help us to understand the difference between, e.g., knowledge, certainty, and belief. "One way of determining what knowledge is is, first of all, determining what the standard uses or jobs of the verb 'to know' are" (Weitz 1953, p. 189).

Suppose, just to take a different example, you want to investigate philosophical issues involving the nature of intentions (the same would apply to knowledge, certainty, belief, thoughts, actions, sensations, emotions, etc.). If you want to know what intentions are, then investigate the use of the term "intention" and its cognates such as "intend," "intending," and "intentional." When we discover, or rather uncover, the correct use of "intention" and its cognates, we will have elucidated the concept of intention, and thus the essential nature of intentions. "*Essence* is expressed by grammar" (Wittgenstein 2009/1953, p. 123e). Words express concepts. In philosophy, the solutions to our problems will come from the elucidation of concepts.

One of the most famous and influential applications of ordinary language philosophy was Elizabeth Anscombe's book *Intention* (Anscombe 1969/1957). Anscombe was a close friend and devoted student of Wittgenstein. She translated his *Philosophical Investigations* and was one of his literary executors on his death.

Anscombe's book is a close and perceptive examination of how we use ordinary terms and talk about our intentions. She arrives at insights that have influenced philosophers and created an entire area of philosophy of action.

For example, Anscombe distinguishes between knowledge by observation and practical knowledge that is embodied in our intentions. She asks us to consider the difference between someone following me around the grocery store listing what I buy and my use of a grocery list that I have created to determine my shopping. If what I buy does not accord with my list – I come home with nonfat yogurt instead of the whole milk yogurt I intended to buy – then we do not say that the list is wrong, but that the action is wrong.

> Let us consider a man going round a town with a shopping list in his hand. Now it is clear that the relation of this list to the things he actually buys is the same whether his wife gave him the list or it is his own list; and that there is a different relation where a list is made by a detective following him about. If he made the list itself, it was an expression of intention; if his wife gave it to him, it has the role of an order. What then is the identical relation to what happens, in the order and the intention, which is not shared by the record? It is precisely this: if the list and the things that the man actually buys do not agree, and if this and this alone constitutes a mistake, then the mistake is not in the list but in the man's performance (if his wife were to say: "Look, it says butter and you have bought margarine", he would hardly reply: "What a mistake! we must put that right" and alter the word on the list to "margarine"); whereas if the detective's record and what the man actually buys do not agree, then the mistake is in the record. (Anscombe 1969/1957, p. 56)

Practical knowledge exercised in action is different from theoretical knowledge (represented by the list based on observation). Anscombe says that practical knowledge unlike theoretical knowledge is not derived from the objects known. When acting intentionally we know what we are doing because we intend it, not because we observe it.

One of the influential points that Anscombe makes is that much of our ordinary language is not descriptive, is not meant to correspond to, reflect, or be derived from external states of affairs. Rather it is practical in the sense that it is meant to change, control, or affect the external states of affairs. (Also see in this connection Austin on speech acts later in this chapter.) This is a direct challenge to the picture theory of meaning of the *Tractatus*.

Toward the end of her book Anscombe distinguishes between actions that are voluntary and those that are intentional. The distinction is elaborate – for example, mere doodling would be described as voluntary action, but not intentional – and has many facets. At the end she says (and I just offer this as an example of ordinary language philosophy at work) "Every intentional action is also voluntary, though ... intentional actions can also be described as involuntary from another point of view, as when one regrets 'having' to do them. But 'reluctant' would be the more commonly used word" (Anscombe 1969/1957, p. 90).

Anscombe also relies on ordinary language to distinguish between wanting, wishing, and hoping. You can wish for anything even what you know to be impossible. For example, I can wish that 2 plus 2 didn't equal 4. I cannot hope for that. This is not a psychological difficulty, but a linguistic or grammatical one. The difference between wanting and hoping is that wanting entails trying to get.

The analysis of our ordinary concepts is not a scientific exercise in empirical linguistics or psychology. The ordinary use must already be in place before the empirical psychological or linguistic investigations can get started. The scientific use of the term "intention," if there is one, is parasitic upon the ordinary uses that we learned at our mothers' knees. Nor is this an empirical linguistic investigation involving surveys and polls. Each of us is a competent speaker and user of our language. To the extent that we share that language and concepts, we can fruitfully engage in philosophy together using our own linguistic intuitions. The relevant intuitions that we use are not our intuitions about what intentions are. These intuitions are most likely to be confused and derived from suspect sources. The intuitions that we start with are our intuitions about what we would say in ordinary non-philosophical contexts, contexts in which our language is at work. These intuitions are powerful, active, and shared.

When we start investigating philosophical issues by looking at the ordinary use of terms, we realize that many of the terms used by philosophers have no ordinary use, or if they do, their ordinary uses are divergent from the ways they have been used by philosophers. This leads to the suspicion that the philosophical uses of such terms are muddled or empty. The attempt to rectify the problem by the use of formal logic only exacerbates it by creating the illusion of mathematical clarity. The solution to the failures of historical philosophers is to return to the ordinary uses of ordinary terms in ordinary contexts. This has a refreshing air of clearing out a lot of musty philosophical refuse.

Consistent with their interest in ordinary language in ordinary contexts, Oxford philosophers were much less interested in philosophy of mathematics and philosophy of science than were the Cambridge philosophers and the logical positivists. Like their Continental existentialist counterparts, the Oxford philosophers took inspiration from literature, the arts, and politics. Several Oxford ordinary language philosophers went on to become important figures in other fields. Isaiah Berlin became a leading public intellectual and political thinker. Iris Murdoch, although she did valuable work in ordinary language philosophy as a young woman, achieved fame as a novelist.

The Oxford philosophers were opposed to formalism in philosophy, but they were not averse to using it elsewhere. Austin, Ryle, Strawson, and other Oxford philosophers worked in British intelligence during World War II. Ryle was fluent in German from his philosophical studies and this proved useful in intelligence work. Austin was especially meticulous and demanding and soon became the expert in charge of major sections. "[H]is superiors in rank very quickly learned that he was an outstanding authority on all branches of intelligence work ... " (Warnock 1969, p. 8). Other philosophers used their linguistic sensitivity in code breaking during the war.

As with Quine and the American neo-pragmatists, Oxford ordinary language philosophy can be seen as a struggle with and against Frege, Russell, early Wittgenstein, Carnap, and logical positivism. The ordinary language philosophers were sympathetic to the positivists' attack on speculative metaphysics, but were opposed to their doctrinaire use of verification and formal logic. The ordinary language philosophers saw philosophy as primarily the elucidation of concepts by the examination of the ordinary use of words, the application of the results of these investigations to philosophical problems, and the uncovering of the errors that traditional philosophers fell into by ignoring the ordinary uses of expressions.

In the rest of this chapter we will consider in more detail the Oxford philosophers' and Wittgenstein's attack on formalism, the philosophy of language on which this is based, and the application of ordinary language methods to issues about perception and the philosophy of mind.

The Attack on Formalism – Strawson and Ryle

The Oxford philosophers rejected the idea that using the logic of *Principia Mathematica* should replace other methods in philosophy. The ordinary language philosophers felt that the reliance on formal logic in philosophy gave the illusion of clarity, precision, and scientific results. Russell justifies the use of symbolic logic in just those terms in a counterattack.

> They [the Oxford ordinary language philosophers] are persuaded that common speech is good enough not only for daily life, but also for philosophy. I, on the contrary, am persuaded that common speech is full of vagueness and inaccuracy, and that any attempt to be precise and accurate requires modification of common speech both as regards vocabulary and as regards syntax. Everybody admits that physics and chemistry and medicine each require a language which is not that of everyday life. I fail to see why philosophy alone, should be forbidden to make a similar approach towards precision and accuracy. (Russell 1957, p. 387)

According to Ryle the error in Russell's approach is the confusion of form with content. Philosophy is messy and the messy problems it confronts cannot be resolved by mathematical formulas.[1] Just as mathematics cannot solve problems of urban planning or economic forecasting, but can still be useful, symbolic logic cannot solve philosophical problems, but can on occasion be a useful tool. Of course, philosophers need to proceed with precision and accuracy, but this does not require symbols and formulas. Philosophers need precision and accuracy of thought and argument, not the precision of the physicist, chemist, or medical doctor.

> But patently fighting cannot be reduced to drill, cartography cannot be reduced to geometry, trading cannot be reduced to balancing accounts. Nor can the handling of philosophical problems be reduced to either derivation or the application of theorems about logical constants. The philosopher is perforce doing what might be called 'Informal Logic', and the suggestion that his problems, his results or his procedures should or could be formalized is as wildly astray as would be the corresponding suggestions about the soldier, the cartographer and the trader. (Ryle 1962, pp. 123–4)

---

[1] Here we are referring to the areas of philosophy outside of logic. Since the early twentieth century logic is Russellian symbolic logic.

As we've seen in Chapter 1, an exemplary result of the methods of symbolic logic is Russell's analysis of definite descriptions. This seemed to solve philosophical problems, remove mystification, and clarify fuzzy language and thinking. Followers of Russell argued that only the interpretation of the problem using the symbolic logic methods of *Principia Mathematica* could offer these results. Consequently the Oxford philosophers' attack on formal methods in philosophy focused on Russell's analysis.

Strawson emerged as a leader of the ordinary language philosophy movement when he challenged Russell's theory of definite descriptions, and along with it Russell's entire approach to solving philosophical problems. In "On Referring" (Strawson 1971/1950) Strawson offers an alternative account of definite descriptions based on ordinary language and usage rather than symbolic logic. Strawson's "On Referring" was for Oxford ordinary language philosophy what Russell's "On Denoting" was for the Cambridge formalist school.

Strawson argues that Russell's theory is the direct result of being misled by formal logic. Strawson uses no symbols in his article. In fact he does not even quote any symbolic formulas, not even Russell's, as though their very presence would taint his text. Oxford philosophers recognized that ordinary language can also be misleading,[2] but the cure is philosophical analysis not substitution of logical formulas.

According to Russell's theory, the "The present king of France is wise" is false if currently there is no king of France. According to Strawson it is not false; rather, it lacks a truth-value: it is neither true nor false. This in itself is an affront to classical symbolic logic where a fundamental assumption is that every statement is either true or false (and not both). Strawson's move is not a minor technical adjustment. It is an attempt to derail Russell's formal logic.

> The mere occurrence of truth-value gaps, as we may call them – cases where, in Strawson's phrase, the question of truth value does not arise – would add irksome complications to deductive theory if allowed for. (Quine 1960, p. 177)

Strawson says of "The present king of France is wise" that

> . . . it will be used to make a true or false assertion *only* if the person using it *is* talking about something. If, when he utters it, he is not talking about anything, then his use is not a genuine one, but a spurious or pseudo-use:

---

[2]   Ryle catalogues many instances in his early article "Systematically Misleading Expressions" (Ryle 1968/1931).

he is not making either a true or a false assertion, though he may think he is. And this points the way to the correct answer to the puzzle to which the [Russell's] Theory of Descriptions gives a fatally incorrect answer. (Strawson 1971/1950, p. 182)

Strawson supports these claims by appealing to our ordinary usage.

What are the false things which Russell would say about the sentence ["The present king of France is wise"]? They are:

(1)   That anyone now uttering it would be making a true assertion or a false assertion;
(2)   That part of what he would be asserting would be that there at present existed one and only one king of France.

   I have already given some reasons for thinking that these two statements are incorrect. Now suppose someone were in fact to say to you with a perfectly serious air: 'The king of France is wise'. Would you say, 'That's untrue'? I think it is quite certain that you would not. But suppose he went on to *ask* you whether you thought that what he had just said was true, or was false; whether you agreed or disagreed with what he had just said. I think you would be inclined, with some hesitation, to say that you did not do either; that the question of whether his statement was true or false simply *did not arise*, because there was no such person as the king of France. (Strawson 1971/1950, p. 183)

Strawson seems to be correct about how we would respond, assuming we knew no king presently reigns in France. (But on this see p. 177.) And just as surely Russell need not disagree with Strawson about how we would in fact react. Why, then, isn't Russell troubled by it? According to Strawson, formal logicians are misled by infatuation with their formal systems. They assume, almost unconsciously, that if it holds in their formal systems, then it must also in some way or other hold in natural language, regardless of our naïve reactions. As noted above, in formal systems such as *PM* statements must be either true or false, and none can be both. So, for Russell, a statement such as "The present king of France is wise" must be either true or false. According to Strawson this is an error foisted on philosophy by an uncritical acceptance of formal methods.

[Ordinary linguistic] conventions for referring have been neglected or misinterpreted by logicians. The reasons for this neglect are not hard to see ... (1) the preoccupation of most logicians with definitions; (2) the preoccupation of some logicians with formal systems. .... The influence of the preoccupation with mathematics and formal logic is most clearly seen (to take no more recent examples) in the cases of Leibniz and Russell. (Strawson 1971/1950, p. 189)

The more recent examples that Strawson had in mind, but did not mention, would certainly include Rudolf Carnap. After Russell left the mainstream of philosophy, Carnap became the champion of formal methods and the use of symbolic logic in philosophy. (We will see in more detail his influential contributions in the next two chapters.) In 1947 Carnap published a book titled *Meaning and Necessity: A Study in Semantics and Modal Logic* (Carnap 1956a/1947) that was to provide the methods and set the issues for a generation of philosophers intent on applying formal methods in philosophy. Naturally these philosophers were scornful of Oxford ordinary language philosophers. The feeling was mutual.

Shortly after its publication Ryle wrote a review of Carnap's *Meaning and Necessity*. The ridicule that Ryle heaps on Carnap is typical of the attitude of his Oxford colleagues.

> He [Carnap] still likes to construct artificial "languages" (which are not languages but codes), and he still interlards his formulae with unhandy because, for English speakers, unsayable Gothic letters. But the expository importance of these encoded formulae seems to be dwindling. Indeed I cannot satisfy myself that they have more than a ritual-value. They do not function as a sieve against vagueness, ambiguity or sheer confusion, and they are not used for the abbreviation or formalization of proofs. Calculi without calculations seem to be gratuitous algebra. Nor, where explicitness is the desideratum, is shorthand a good substitute. (Ryle 1949a, p. 69)

Ryle offers detailed criticisms of substantive parts of Carnap's views, in particular his theory of meaning. (In the next section we will see how notions about meaning significantly divided the ordinary language philosophers from the formalists.) But Ryle was not averse to merely mocking Carnap's pretensions to rigor.

> Instead of speaking of expressions as "names," he gives them the intimidating title "designators." (He likes to coin words ending in " . . . tor." He speaks of "descriptors" instead of "descriptions," "predicators" instead of "predicates," "functors" instead of "functions," and toys with the project of piling on the agony with "conceptor," "abstractor," "individuator," and so on. But as his two cardinal words "designator" and "predicator" are employed with, if possible, even greater ambiguity and vagueness than has traditionally attached to the words "term" and "predicate," I hope that future exercises in logical nomenclature will be concentrated less on the terminations than on the offices of our titles.) (Ryle 1949a, p. 71)

The concluding two paragraphs of Ryle's review summarize his scorn for Carnap and his formal methods.

> My chief impression of this book is that it is an astonishing blend of technical sophistication with philosophical naiveté. . . .
>
> Carnap's influence on philosophers and logicians is very strong. The importance of semantic problems in philosophy and logic cannot be over-estimated. It is because I fear that the solutions of these problems may be impeded by the dissemination of his mistakes that I have reviewed so scoldingly the treatise of a thinker whose views are beginning to be regarded as authoritative. (Ryle 1949a, p. 76)

Alas for poor Ryle, the methods and ideas that Carnap pioneered in *Meaning and Necessity* grew in authoritativeness and continue to be central in analytic philosophy today. Despite his tremendous influence and popularity in the 1940s to 1960s, Ryle has diminished as an active influence. Carnap, on the other hand, despite his apparent defeat in his struggle with Quine about analyticity and other issues, remains an important and influential figure.

Philosophy of Language – Austin and Wittgenstein

The disagreement between the advocates of the use of formal methods to solve philosophical problems and the Oxford philosophers who reject it is not just a disagreement about methodology. The disagreement has deep roots in views about the nature of language, thought, and reality.

In his notebooks written before the *Tractatus*, Wittgenstein says "The great problem round which everything that I write turns is: Is there an order in the world *a priori*, and if so what does it consist in?" (Wittgenstein 1961a/1915, p. 53e). According to the philosophy of logical atomism expounded by Russell and embodied in Wittgenstein's *Tractatus* the answer is "Yes! There is such an order and it consists of logical structure." One basic presupposition of logical atomism is that there is an isomorphism of structure between language and the world, language and thought, and thus between thought and the world. Because of this isomorphism we can think about the world and express our thoughts in language. Language, thought, and the world have the same structure, the same skeleton. This structure is represented by symbolic logic. Wittgenstein calls it "the all-embracing world-mirroring logic" (Wittgenstein 1961a/1915, p. 39e). The formalists believed that the logic of *Principia Mathematica* captured the common structure of language, thought, and reality. "The shortest account of logical atomism that can be given is that the world has the structure of Russell's mathematical logic" (Urmson 1956, p. 6).

Unfortunately the ability of language and thought to represent the world is only potential. Ordinary thought and talk is sloppy and loose, unfit to accurately represent the crystalline purity of the world. Ordinary terms like "red" and "tall" are vague and much of our language is imprecise. We say things like "P is truer to the facts than Q." Thought and language need to be regimented by means of symbolic logic. They need to be perfected, not necessarily for mundane practical affairs, but for the high and edifying purposes of philosophy and science. Only such regimentation by symbolic logic will allow the solution and dissolution of philosophical problems, according to the formalists. Only an ideal language constructed with symbolic logic can accurately reflect the structure of the world.

Since symbolic logic represents the isomorphism of language, thought, and the world, investigations with the tools introduced by Frege, Russell in *Principia Mathematica*, and Wittgenstein in the *Tractatus* are the way to get at the ultimate nature of things. "Propositions show the logical form of reality. They display it" (Wittgenstein 1961b/1921, p. 51, #4.121). The deployment of symbolic logic is philosophy's best chance to be scientific and to accomplish anything worthwhile.

The ordinary language philosophers and later Wittgenstein reject this view. Wittgenstein, in his *Philosophical Investigations*, calls the idea of an *a priori* order an illusion. Talking about features of his Tractarian view Wittgenstein writes:

96. Other illusions come from various quarters to join the particular one spoken of here. Thought, language, now appear to us as the unique correlate, picture, of the world. These concepts: proposition, language, thought, world, stand in line one behind the other, each equivalent to each. . . .

97. Thinking is surrounded by a nimbus. – Its essence, logic, presents an order: namely, the a priori order of the world; that is, the order of *possibilities*, which the world and thinking must have in common. But this order, it seems, must be *utterly simple*. It is *prior* to all experience, must run through all experience; no empirical cloudiness or uncertainty may attach to it. (Wittgenstein 2009/1953, p. 49e)

In order to undermine logical atomism and the idea of an isomorphism between language and the world and between language and thought the Oxford philosophers and Wittgenstein attacked the formalists' theories of language and thought. We will focus on the alternative view of language in this section. In the next, we will examine the alternative view of thoughts and other mental phenomena.

Early Wittgenstein embraced the picture theory of meaning, which fits neatly with the isomorphism view. (See Chapter 2, pp. 113–14.) According to the picture theory, statements get their meaning by directly representing possible facts and have the same complexity as those facts. Statements are true when they correspond to the facts, and false otherwise. Ryle attributes a congruent theory of meaning for terms to Frege, Russell, Carnap and other formalists. Ryle calls it the "Fido"-Fido Theory.

> Frege, like Russell, had inherited (directly, perhaps, from Mill) the traditional belief that to ask What does the expression "E" mean? is to ask, To what does "E" stand in the relation in which "Fido" stands to Fido. The significance of any expression is the thing, process, person or entity of which the expression is the proper name. (Ryle 1949a, p. 69)

Ryle calls this a "grotesque theory." Ryle is being somewhat unrestrained, but Strawson, Austin, and later Wittgenstein would agree that the picture theory and the "Fido"-Fido theory are grossly mistaken.

The fundamental problem with the formalists' theories of meaning is that the formalists assume that all of the elements of language work either to picture or to name. Wittgenstein famously begins his *Philosophical Investigations* with a quote from Augustine expressing a version of the "Fido"-Fido Theory. Augustine states that he learned language from his elders by learning what objects the words stand for. Wittgenstein constructs various language games in which words actually do function in this way. The point is that this is a simplified and naïve view of language and how it functions. Only in contrived and simplified situations would words only stand for things. Wittgenstein and the ordinary language philosophers held that the picture theory was an oversimplification that focused on one sort of function and assumed that all of language functioned that way. (Recall our earlier discussion of Anscombe's analysis of practical versus theoretical knowledge.)

According to Wittgenstein and Austin, words, statements, and utterances generally are tools for doing various jobs. Naming and picturing are only two of the vast number of tasks that language users perform with their utterances. Wittgenstein and Austin would agree with Quine that the traditional notion of meaning is outmoded and misleading. They urge that we get rid of the formalists' meanings and think instead of uses. The most trenchant slogan of the Oxford philosophers is:

> 43. For a *large* class of cases of the employment of the word "meaning" – though not for *all* – this word can be explained in this way: the meaning of a word is its use in the language. (Wittgenstein 2009/1953, p. 25e)

"Meaning is use" was the cry of the anti-formalists. To know how to use a word correctly is to know its meaning. To know how to use a word or phrase correctly is to know rules and conventions for correct use. Rules and conventions are not pictures or things. Rules and conventions only exist in a social context of institutions and customs.

> To follow a rule, to make a report, to give an order, to play a game of chess, are *customs* (usages, institutions).
>
> To understand a sentence means to understand a language. To understand a language means to have mastered a technique. (Wittgenstein 2009/1953, p. 87e, #199)

The tool analogy is crucial to Wittgenstein's philosophy of language. Just as there are many different kinds of tools that operate in different ways, there are many different tasks that language is used for, and many different ways that words and phrases work to accomplish those tasks.

> 11. Think of the tools in a toolbox: there is a hammer, pliers, a saw, a screwdriver, a rule, a glue-pot, glue, nails and screws. – The functions of words are as diverse as the functions of these objects. (And in both cases there are similarities.)
> Of course, what confuses us is the uniform appearance of words when we hear them in speech, or see them written or in print. For their *use* is not that obvious. Especially when we are doing philosophy!

> 12. It is like looking into the cabin of a locomotive. There are handles there, all looking more or less alike. (This stands to reason, since they are all supposed to be handled.) But one is the handle of a crank, which can be moved continuously (it regulates the opening of a valve); another is the handle of a switch, which has only two operative positions: it is either off or on; a third is the handle of a brakelever, the harder one pulls on it, the harder the braking; a fourth, the handle of a pump: it has an effect only so long as it is moved to and fro. (Wittgenstein 2009/1953, p. 10e)

The formalist may reply "Surely every word must stand for something; it has to signify something in order to be useful. The thing that it signifies is its meaning. Signifying is something that meaningful words have in common, just as tools have in common that they serve to modify something."

13. If we say: "Every word in language signifies something", we have so far said nothing *whatever*; unless we explain exactly *what* distinction we wish to make. (It might be, of course, that we wanted to distinguish the words of language ... from words 'without meaning' such as occur in Lewis Carroll's poems, or words like "Tra-la-la" in a song.)

14. Suppose someone said, "*All* tools serve to modify something. So, the hammer modifies the position of a nail, the saw the shape of the board, and so on." – And what is modified by the rule, the glue-pot and nails? – "Our knowledge of a thing's length, the temperature of the glue, and the solidity of the box." – Would anything be gained by this assimilation of expressions? (Wittgenstein 2009/1953, p. 10e)

Presumably not.

Wittgenstein uses the term "language game" to emphasize that the uses of the elements of language are like moves in a game governed by rules and are part of the entire web of our lives – our "form of life" as he puts it. This is a direct attack on the picture theory of meaning of the *Tractatus*. There the meaning is a formal property of the words and statements that they have independently of any use. It attaches to them by means of the picturing relationship. An accurate photo of me is a picture of me in itself and apart from the use to which it is put or the context in which it occurs. Sometimes language is like that, but mostly it is not. Only in the context of active life do symbols have meaning. "432. Every sign *by itself* seems dead. *What* gives it life? – In use it *lives*" (Wittgenstein 2009/1953, p. 128e). The uses are endlessly multifarious – as multifarious as our active lives.

23. But how many kinds of sentence are there? Say assertion, question, and command? – There are *countless* kinds: countless different kinds of use of all the things we call "symbols", "words", "sentences". And this diversity is not something fixed, given once for all; but new types of language, new language-games, as we may say, come into existence, and others become obsolete and get forgotten. (We can get a *rough picture* of this from the changes in mathematics.)

    The word "language-game" is used here to emphasize the fact that the *speaking* of language is part of an activity, or of a form of life ... [Wittgenstein here lists fifteen different examples of language use] – It is interesting to compare the diversity of the tools of language and of the ways they are used, the diversity of kinds of word and sentence, with what logicians have said about the structure of language. (This includes the author of the *Tractatus Logico-Philosophicus*.) (Wittgenstein 2009/1953, pp. 14e–15e)

According to Wittgenstein, the formalists' assumption that a word stands for one thing is an error. To assume, for example, that the word "game" stands for the property of being a game is a grotesque over-simplification. Most general nouns are "family resemblance" words. Consider the different kind of activities that we call games and the different sorts of uses for the word "game." There is nothing common to all things we call games, no essence of game, no necessary and sufficient condition for being a game. Various threads and similarities underlie our use of the word "game" but there is no one thread that is common to all.

> 67.   I can think of no better expression to characterize these similarities than "family resemblances"; for the various resemblances between members of a family – build, features, colour of eyes, gait, tem-perament, and so on and so forth – overlap and criss-cross in the same way. – And I shall say: 'games' form a family. (Wittgenstein 2009/1953, p. 36e)

A word like "game" is also vague, and open-textured in the sense that it can be applied creatively to new cases as they come up. No definition determines once and for all whether something is a game. Frege and Russell considered vagueness and open texture to be defects of ordinary language. No vagueness would be allowed to infect their ideal language. Each term would have exactly one perfectly precise meaning. But vagueness and open texture are essential to any language that human beings could use. These are not defects of language.

> 71.   One can say that the concept of a game is a concept with blurred edges. – "But is a blurred concept a *concept* at all?" – Is a photograph that is not sharp a picture of a person at all? Is it even always an advan-tage to replace a picture that is not sharp by one that is? Isn't one that isn't sharp often just what we need? (Wittgenstein 2009/1953, p. 38e)

The formalists' project is a forlorn one. Perfecting language, creating an ideal language, is a struggle against our lives as active, engaged people. There are no atomic propositions and there cannot be. Simplicity is always relative to a context, a purpose. Using another metaphor, Wittgenstein says that for some purposes the broom in the corner is a single simple object, for others it is a complex of a stick with a brush attached. Wittgenstein says of Russell's attempts at an ideal language

"We feel as if we had to repair a torn spider's web with our fingers" (Wittgenstein 2009/1953, p. 51e, #106).

Language and meaning necessarily involve following rules and conventions for the use of expressions in our active day-to-day lives. To know a language is to be able to apply the rules that govern it, although we need not be able to articulate those rules. But Wittgenstein insists these rules must be public. No private language is possible, because no private rules are possible. The most famous part of Wittgenstein's *Philosophical Investigations* is his private language argument, where he argues that a private language is impossible. This is no trivial point. It is a direct attack on Russell's logical atomism. Russell claimed that the language of logical atomism "would be largely private to one speaker" (Russell 1971/1918, p. 198). Russell held that ultimately all meanings must be analyzable into names of items that are immediately known such as sense data and universals such as whiteness.

Wittgenstein argues, on the contrary, that language is essentially public. It cannot be private. His argument involves several steps. With the use of an item of language, say a word, there must be a distinction between correct uses and incorrect uses, just as in a game of chess there are correct (allowed) moves and incorrect (disallowed) moves. A rule determines which moves are correct and which incorrect, what is allowed or disallowed. Thus the correct use of a word necessarily involves following rules. But whether or not the user is following the rule correctly must be publicly checkable. A private rule where only the single user determines whether the use is correct or incorrect is no rule at all. Whatever the user decides is automatically correct; whatever the user does accords with the private rule. This is only a sham rule because there is no distinction between correct and incorrect moves.

> 202. That's why 'following a rule' is a practice. And to *think* one is following a rule is not to follow a rule. And that's why it's not possible to follow a rule 'privately'; otherwise thinking one was following a rule would be the same thing as following it. (Wittgenstein 2009/1953, pp. 87e–88e)

> But in the present case [a private language where a sign stands for a private sensation], I have no criterion of correctness. One would like to say: whatever is going to seem correct to me is correct. And that only means that here we can't talk about 'correct'. (Wittgenstein 2009/1953, p. 99e, #258)

Wittgenstein's private language argument has been subject to continuing intense scrutiny and controversy. If the argument is sound, it is a refutation of logical atomism (at least when it involves the privacy that Russell insists on), phenomenalism, and any other attempt to ground language or knowledge in the contents of the individual mind.

Both Strawson and Austin embraced the meaning-as-use point of view. Strawson says: "I explain and illustrate the conventions governing the use of the expression. This *is* giving the meaning of the expression" (Strawson 1971/1950, p. 182). Austin went on to develop a technical and elaborate approach to expounding the meaning-as-use slogan, while Strawson devoted his energies to "descriptive metaphysics" as we will see later in this chapter.

Austin did not publish any book-length treatments – his only publications were brilliant articles – but two of his lecture series were published after his untimely death in 1960. The book *How to do Things with Words* was compiled from his William James Lectures delivered at Harvard in 1955. The editor was J. O. Urmson, a close friend and associate of Austin, and also an ordinary language philosopher of note. Urmson and G. J. Warnock edited and published a collection of Austin's papers and wrote tributes to him after his tragic death from cancer when he was only 49. Urmson and Warnock were part of a group of philosophers who gathered around Austin at Oxford and admired his ordinary language philosophy.

Austin was persuasive, charming, and clever, and devoted immense energies to minute investigations of ordinary language. He and his colleagues were fascinated by very fine distinctions. As an amusing and charming example and defense of his group's careful attention to linguistic detail Austin pointed out that we can distinguish "by accident" and "by mistake." This distinction is often fudged.

> [P]eople will say 'almost anything', because they are so flurried, or so anxious to get off. 'It was a mistake', 'It was an accident' – how readily these can *appear* indifferent, and even be used together. Yet, a story or two, and everybody will not merely agree that they are completely different, but even discover for himself what the difference is and what each means. [At this point Austin inserts the following as a footnote.] You have a donkey, so have I, and they graze in the same field. The day comes when I conceive a dislike for mine. I go to shoot it, draw a bead on it, fire: the brute falls in its tracks. I inspect the victim, and find to my horror that it is *your* donkey. I appear on your doorstep with the remains and say – what? 'I say, old sport, I'm awfully sorry, &c., I've shot your donkey *by accident*'? Or '*by mistake*'? Then again, I go to shoot my donkey as before, draw a bead on it fire – but as I do so, the beasts move, and to my horror yours falls. Again the scene on the doorstep – what do I say? 'By mistake'? Or 'By accident'? (Austin 1961/1956–7, pp. 132–3)

Austin wrote cleverly like this on many topics: truth, knowledge of other minds, sense data (as we shall see in the next section), and free will and determinism. His approach is always characterized by cleverness, close attention to ordinary language, and a deflationary attitude to traditional philosophy. But Austin's most lasting contribution is his introduction of the notion of a speech act.

Before his William James Lectures, Austin had indicated his line of thought in an article titled "Performative Utterances." Like Wittgenstein, Ryle, and Strawson, Austin is critical of traditional philosophers' exclusive attention to the stating or describing function of language. "We have not got to go very far back in the history of philosophy to find philosophers assuming more or less as a matter of course that the sole business, the sole interesting business, of any utterance – that is, of anything we say – is to be true or at least not false" (Austin 1961b, p. 221). Austin points out that many significant utterances have the role, not of reporting an occurrence, but of actually performing one. For example, saying "I promise that...," "I do..." (in a marriage ceremony), "I name this ship..." (in a ship naming ceremony), "I warn you...," "I sentence you..." Uttering any of these is to perform an act – promising, marrying, naming, warning, sentencing. And of course there are many other such examples. Austin calls these sorts of utterances "performative utterances." The point of a performative utterance is not to make a true or false report of some sort of inner event or spiritual occurrence – the inner act of intention, say – but to perform the action in question. Performative utterances are not judged as true or false, but by other criteria. To be effective they have to be performed in the appropriate setting, by the appropriate person, in the proper way. I may say "I sentence you to pay a fine of $10" but unless I'm a judge in the appropriate setting no act is performed. "Statements ... were to be true or false; performative utterances on the other hand were to be felicitous or infelicitous" (Austin 1961b, p. 234).

But, now, this won't quite do after all. No one is more finicky about getting the details just right than Austin is. He points out that stating, describing, and asserting are speech acts too. We can say "I state that...," "I hereby describe...," or "I assert..." and these are parallel to, e.g., "I promise that..." but are performing the actions of stating, describing, and asserting.

> What we need to do for the case of stating, and by the same token describing and reporting, is to take them a bit off their pedestal, to realize that they are speech-acts no less than all these other speech-acts that we have been mentioning and talking about as performative. (Austin 1961b, pp. 236–7)

Austin is also at pains to demote "true" and "false" from their pedestals. The ways in which we assess performatives as apt or inapt, justified or unjustified, accurate or inaccurate, etc. shade off to "true" or "false."

> 'True' and 'false' are just general labels for a whole dimension of different appraisals which have something or other to do with the relation between what we say and the facts. If, then, we loosen up our ideas of truth and falsity we shall see that statements, when assessed in relation to the facts, are not so very different after all from pieces of advice, warnings, verdicts, and so on. (Austin 1961b, pp. 237–8)

Thus speech act is unveiled as the essence of language. And we see why saying "P is truer to the facts than Q" can make perfectly good and useful sense.

Austin points out that in saying anything we are doing a great many different things. In *How to do Things with Words* Austin examines in detail the types of forces that utterances can have. The locutionary act or force of an utterance is its sense, its meaning, in the traditional usage. The illocutionary act or force of an utterance is the use that we put that meaning to, what we do with the utterance.

> When we perform a locutionary act, we use speech: but in what way precisely are we using it on this occasion? ... I explained the performance of an act in this new and second sense as the performance of an 'illocutionary' act, i.e. performance of an act *in* saying something as opposed to performance of an act *of* saying something; and I shall refer to the doctrine of the different types of function of language here in question as the doctrine of 'illocutionary forces'. (Austin 1962, p. 99)

Then there is the perlocutionary act or force. In saying something one produces some consequences or results. This is the perlocutionary act. Example: I say "Take the bus, don't drive." Locutionary act: I said something that meant take the bus, don't drive. Illocutionary act: I advised or suggested or recommended taking the bus. Perlocutionary act: I persuaded someone to take the bus (assuming she acted on my advice, suggestion, recommendation). This all gets rather complex and technical and in the course of the book ever more and detailed distinctions and categories are introduced. It is all more technical and formal than Wittgenstein ever would have approved of. On the other hand, Austin didn't admire Wittgenstein and expressed his disdain for him on several occasions. Austin said "Moore is my man."

Austin's terms and distinctions have become part of the philosophical heritage of analytic philosophy. The notion of speech act is widely used outside of philosophy in linguistics, social sciences, and literary criticism. It is now part of the jargon of academia.

Philosophy of Mind – Ryle, Strawson, and Wittgenstein

The best-known and most popular work of Oxford ordinary language philosophy has been Ryle's *The Concept of Mind* (Ryle 1949b). I say "has been" because although it was a sensation for a decade or two after it was published, Ryle's book and the position he argued for has disappeared from center stage in the philosophy of mind. Nevertheless his position, which he reluctantly acknowledged was a version of behaviorism, was an important and widely held view, in one form or another, in both philosophy and psychology. The philosophical leanings of the ordinary language philosophers and later Wittgenstein on the nature of mind and thought all tend toward behaviorism.

The attraction of behaviorism was that the only alternatives were Cartesian dualism and identity theory. Behaviorism is appealing, although problematical, because it is better than the alternatives. Dualism smacked both of traditional metaphysics and traditional religion, while identity theory, besides being very implausible and suffering from crippling technical problems (see pp. 184–5), sinned by abjectly worshiping at the feet of the scientists. Nor did the scientists invite such worship, being far more cautious than philosophical proponents of the identity theory. [*Background 4.1* – Dualism, behaviorism, and identity theory] Oxford ordinary language philosophers and later Wittgenstein rejected traditional metaphysics, were dubious about traditional religion, and unimpressed by natural science. Neither dualism nor the identity theory was acceptable. (Also see Chapter 5 for specific philosophical objections to dualism and identity theory.) This left behaviorism.

Behaviorism is also tainted, however. As a program in psychology, it partly derived its motivation from the logical positivists' verifiability criterion. Other people's behavior is publicly observable, but their inner mental states are not. Another problem with behaviorism is that it is far from any common sense views of the mind. Ryle and Wittgenstein are uneasy behaviorists at best; Strawson rejects behaviorism. Ryle's and Wittgenstein's rejection of dualism and the identity theory caused them to back uneasily into positions that they admitted resemble behaviorism. "The general trend of this book [*The Concept of Mind*] will undoubtedly, and harmlessly, be stigmatised as 'behaviourist'" (Ryle 1949b, p. 327). Wittgenstein also acknowledged that his ideas sound behaviorist: "307. 'Are you nevertheless a behaviourist in disguise?

Aren't you nevertheless basically saying that everything except human behaviour is a fiction?'" He answers his imagined interlocutor: "If I speak of a fiction, then it is of a *grammatical* fiction" (Wittgenstein 2009/1953, p. 109e). (We will see what he means by "grammatical fiction" shortly.)

Ryle launches an attack on dualism at the beginning of *The Concept of Mind*. The first and most influential chapter of this famous book is titled "Descartes' Myth." The myth that Ryle attributes to dualists he calls "with deliberate abusiveness" the myth of "the ghost in the machine" (Ryle 1949b, pp.15–16). The machine is the human body. The ghost is the human mind. "Ghost," of course, is meant to suggest something spooky, and something that isn't really there. Etymologically Ryle's coinage is clever, as the English word "ghost" is related to German "Geist," which means mind or spirit. Ryle's point is that the mind is not a thing; not a substance in the philosophical sense. Our bodies are things, material things, but our minds are not things, not immaterial things, not any *thing*. We are misled into assuming that minds are things by our language. Since we have the noun "mind" we assume that it stands for a thing. There's that pervasive error again of assuming that a word must stand for a thing. The error is deepened when we suppose that since it cannot be a material thing that obeys physical laws, the mind must be an immaterial thing that is free of physical causation.

Ryle claims that this mistake – taking the mind for a thing – is an example of a fundamental type of confusion that he calls a category mistake.

> It [the myth of the ghost in the machine] is one big mistake and a mistake of a special kind. It is, namely, a category mistake. It represents the facts of mental life as if they belonged to one logical type or category (or range of types or categories), when they actually belong to another. (Ryle 1949b, p. 16)

Suppose someone is visiting our university and wants to be shown about. We tour the classrooms, visit lectures taking place, the laboratories, the theatre, the dorms, and the dining halls. Our visitor says "Fine, I've seen the classrooms, faculty offices, dorms, labs, etc. but I want to see the university, where is it?" The visitor has made a category mistake. The mistake is to assume that the university is another thing alongside the classrooms, dorms, etc. "The University is just the way in which all that he has already seen is organized" (Ryle 1949b, p. 16). Naturally in ordinary life we do not make silly category mistakes like this, but when pondering abstract philosophical questions we are prone to such confusions.

Ryle does not want to deny that people think, have feelings, sensations, get ideas in their heads, and so on.

> I am not, for example, denying that there occur mental processes. Doing long division is a mental process and so is making a joke. But I am saying that the phrase 'there occur mental processes' does not mean the same sort of thing as 'there occur physical processes' . . . . (Ryle 1949b, p. 22)

When we use mental terms such as "intelligent," "thoughtful," "clever," "insightful," and so on to describe actions or speeches, "we are not referring to occult episodes of which the overt acts and utterances are effects . . ." (Ryle 1949b, p. 25). Rather we are describing the ways in which the overt acts and utterances are done. "We are referring to those overt acts and utterances themselves" (Ryle 1949b, p. 25). Just as the university is the organization of the classrooms, lectures, faculty, dorms, administration, and so on, and not a separate thing, our minds are not separate things, but are the organization of our behavior. Mental terms refer to ways of behaving.

> . . . [W]hen we speak of a person's mind, we are not speaking of a second theatre of special-status incidents, but of certain ways in which some of the incidents of his one life are ordered. (Ryle 1949b, p. 167)

The ways of behaving need not all be manifested directly. If I think that French vanilla yogurt is delicious, this need not mean that I will always behave in overt ways. But, according to Ryle, I must at least have a disposition to behave in ways that I may not immediately manifest. Dispositions are tendencies to exhibit traits or behaviors that manifest themselves under certain conditions. To say that a glass is brittle is to say that it will break given certain conditions and events. To say that I think that French vanilla yogurt is delicious is to say that I will behave in certain ways given certain conditions and events. The connection is not strict, however. Just as the glass may break in various, countless different ways, I may manifest my thoughts about yogurt in countless different but typical ways. Of course, behavior includes verbal behavior.

Mental terms are conceptually grounded in behavior and behavioral dispositions. This is logical behaviorism. To understand a mental term such as "desire," "fear," or "belief" is to understand how it is manifested in behavior and dispositions to behave. The behavior and dispositions are not evidence for the mental states, as tracks in the snow would be evidence for the presence of deer. We do not infer the mental states from the behavior. The mental terms are descriptions of behavior and dispositions to behave.

> It is being maintained throughout this book that when we characterise people by mental predicates, we are not making untestable inferences to any ghostly processes occurring in streams of consciousness which we are debarred from visiting; we are describing the ways in which those people conduct parts of their predominantly public behavior. (Ryle 1949b, pp. 50–1)

As Strawson points out in his celebrated book, *Individuals* (Strawson 1963/1959), behaviorism of the sort Ryle is arguing for has the advantage that it avoids the skepticism inherent in dualism. The appeal of behavioral meanings for mental terms is that behavior is observable. If mental terms refer to private inner mental occurrences, we are mired in the problem of other minds. "It would follow [from dualism] that no one has ever yet had the slightest understanding of what anyone else has ever said or done" (Ryle 1949b, p. 53). With dualism we cannot avoid skepticism about other people and their minds. [*Background 4.2* – The problem of other minds] "580. An 'inner process' stands in need of outward criteria" (Wittgenstein 2009/1953, p. 161e).

However, Strawson rejects behaviorism because behaviorists cannot account for first person uses of mental terms. We do not ascribe sensations and states of mind to ourselves on the basis of our behavior. Even though others' behavior is criteria for their being in mental states, behavior does not play that role in our first person statements about our own mental states. I do not judge that, e.g., "I am dizzy" or "I am sleepy" on the basis of my behavior (although self-observations of behavior can be relevant in some cases). To suppose that mental terms have two different meanings – one when used in second and third person contexts, and another in first person – introduces a needless complication. Strawson insists that such terms are univocal.

> ... [I]t is essential that they [mental predicates] should be both self-ascribable and other-ascribable to the same individual, where self-ascriptions are not made on the observational basis on which other-ascriptions are made, but on another basis. It is not that these [mental] predicates have two kinds of meaning. Rather, it is essential to the meaning that they do have, that both ways of ascribing them should be perfectly in order. (Strawson 1963/1959, p. 107)

Strawson attempts to forge a synthesis of dualism and behaviorism that would include the advantages of each. He argues that persons are "primitive" items of our conceptual scheme. The special feature of persons is that both material predicates (called "M-predicates by Strawson), such as weight and location, and psychological predicates (called "P-predicates"), such as "is dizzy" or "sees a red patch" can be attributed to them.

> [T]he concept of a person is to be understood as the concept of a type of entity such that *both* predicates ascribing states of consciousness *and* predicates ascribing corporeal characteristics, a physical situation &c. are equally applicable to an individual entity of that type. I have said ... that this concept is primitive.... (Strawson 1963/1959, p. 101)

A person is not the same as his body nor his mind, nor a combination of the two. The point of saying that the concept of person is primitive is that it is not analyzable into anything else. This, likewise, is contrary to Russell's logical atomism. For Russell the concept of person, including myself, is complex. A person is a logical construct out of sense data.

Self-ascription of P-predicates requires that one is able to ascribe them to others. Strawson argues that I would not be able to say of myself, e.g., "I am dizzy" unless I were able to say similar things correctly of others on appropriate occasions.

> There would be no question of ascribing one's own states of consciousness, or experiences, to anything, unless one also ascribed, or were ready and able to ascribe, states of consciousness, or experiences, to other individual entities of the same logical type as that to which one ascribes one's own states of consciousness. (Strawson 1963/1959, p. 100)

Individuals of the "same logical type" are, as we have seen, persons. One must be able not only to ascribe P-predicates to others but to do so correctly and truly.

> Clearly there is no sense in talking of identifiable individuals of a special type, a type, namely, such that they possess both M-predicates and P-predicates, unless there is in principle some way of telling, with regard to any individual of that type, and any P-predicate, whether that individual possesses that P-predicate. And, in the case of at least some P-predicates, the ways of telling must constitute in some sense logically adequate kinds of criteria for the ascription of P-predicates. (Strawson 1963/1959, p. 103)

The logically adequate criteria in the case of other people involve their behavior, including their linguistic behavior.

The advantages of Strawson's position are striking. It is a refutation of dualism and solves the problem of other minds. A person is not a ghost in a machine nor a compound of two separate substances. A person is a single substance that has both material properties and psychological properties. We cannot doubt the existence of other minds, because we have logically adequate observable criteria for the ascription of mental properties to others.

Strawson's position has been influential but not entirely satisfactory. He gains his advantages too easily. The invocation of the primitive concept of a person, which is essential to Strawson's position, seems to be a facile device. Russell once quipped: "The method of 'postulating' what we want has many advantages; they are the same as the advantages of theft over honest toil" (Russell 1919, p. 71). Of course, Strawson would deny that he is postulating the concept of person. Rather he would claim that he is discovering it, by philosophical analysis, at the center of our conceptual scheme.

Discovering the concept of person in our conceptual scheme, Strawson is tip-toeing back into metaphysical waters. In his book *Individuals: An Essay in Descriptive Metaphysics*, Strawson contrasts descriptive and revisionary metaphysics. "Descriptive metaphysics is content to describe the actual structure of our thought about the world, revisionary metaphysics is concerned to produce a better structure" (Strawson 1963/1959, p. xiii). Descriptive metaphysics is an extended form of conceptual analysis.

> How should it [descriptive metaphysics] differ from what is called philosophical, or logical, or conceptual analysis? It does not differ in kind of intention, but in scope and generality. Aiming to lay bare the most general features of our conceptual structure, it can take far less for granted than a more limited and partial conceptual inquiry. (Strawson 1963/1959, p. xiii)

His analysis of the concept of person is the best known and most influential part of Strawson's book, but he tackles many difficult topics, among them the possibility of disembodied consciousness and whether we can conceive of an entirely auditory world.

But is it metaphysics? Ryle, in a BBC discussion of metaphysics, asserts that Strawson's descriptive metaphysics emphatically is not metaphysics, and even what Strawson calls revisionary metaphysics falls short of being metaphysical. "But a philosopher would not usually rank as a metaphysician just for his contributions to the task of conceptual revision" (Ryle 1957, p. 144). I suspect that Ryle has in mind Russell and early Wittgenstein. They might well be viewed as conceptual revisionists, but would recoil at being labeled metaphysicians. Certainly Wittgenstein would. So what, according to Ryle, is the metaphysician properly so-called expected to do?

> What is commonly expected of a metaphysician is that he should assert
> the existence or occurrence of things unseen and give for these assertions
> purely philosophical or conceptual reasons. If he is not an ontologist he is
> not a metaphysician.
>
> More specifically, the metaphysician is widely expected to argue for
> existence-conclusions which either belong to theology or are at least
> theologically interesting. (Ryle 1957, p. 144)

In Chapter 6, "The Rebirth of Metaphysics," we will see that Ryle is right
at least to the extent that the possible worlds metaphysics at the center
of the rebirth of metaphysics in analytic philosophy has theologically
interesting applications. Unlike Strawson's descriptive metaphysics, it
is genuine metaphysics according to Ryle's criteria.

As (quasi-)behaviorists both Ryle and Wittgenstein must confront
the question of first-person ascriptions of mental states, as Strawson
insists. Wittgenstein urges us not to assimilate first-person ascriptions
to descriptions or referential statements. Rather our first-person mental
statements are learned expressions of those mental states. To say "My
foot hurts" can be a report, if, say, we are being diagnosed by a doctor.
In most ordinary uses, however, we have learned to replace crying
and other primitive forms of pain behavior by using words. "The
verbal expression of pain replaces crying ... " (Wittgenstein 2009/1953,
p. 95e, #244).

> Here is one possibility: words are connected with the primitive, the natural,
> expressions of the sensation and used in their place. A child has hurt
> himself and he cries; then adults talk to him and teach him exclamations
> and, later, sentences. They teach the child new pain-behaviour.
>
> "So you are saying that the word 'pain' really means crying?" – On
> the contrary: the verbal expression of pain replaces crying and does not
> describe it. (Wittgenstein 2009/1953, p. 89e)

Ryle calls first-person self-ascription of mental states "avowals."

> Now many unstudied utterances embody ... what I have elsewhere been
> calling 'avowals', like 'I want', 'I hope', 'I intend', 'I dislike', 'I am
> depressed', 'I wonder', 'I guess' and 'I feel hungry'; and their grammar
> makes it tempting to misconstrue all the sentences in which they occur
> as self-descriptions. But in its primary employment 'I want... ' is not
> used to convey information, but to make a request or demand. ... Nor,
> in their primary employment, are 'I hate... ' and 'I intend... ' used for
> the purpose of telling the hearer facts about the speaker ... They are
> the utterances of persons in revolted and resolute frames of mind. They
> are things said in detestation and resolution and not things said in order

to advance biographical knowledge about detestations and resolutions. (Ryle 1949b, pp.183–4)

Often avowals are performatives in Austin's sense. Utterances of "I wish to," "I love that," "I hate that," "I regret that," "I'm afraid that," are often performances of actions rather than reports of mental states. The point is the illocutionary force. Saying "I love that painting" is a speech act of praising or, perhaps, requesting. It is not a report of an interior loving mental state.

But surely I know my own mental states directly and immediately and can report that knowledge. Wittgenstein denies that the grammar of "knowledge" supports this philosophical claim. We can only speak of knowledge where there is a possibility of error, where there is a difference between merely believing and knowing. With our own sensations we can find no such contrast. "One says 'I know' where one can also say 'I believe' or 'I suspect'; where one can satisfy oneself" (Wittgenstein 2009/1953, p. 232e).

> 246. In what sense are my sensations *private?* – Well, only I can know whether I am really in pain; another person can only surmise it. – In one way this is false, and in another nonsense. If we are using the word "to know" as it is normally used (and how else are we to use it?), then other people very often know if I am in pain. – Yes, but all the same, not with the certainty with which I know it myself! – It can't be said of me at all (except perhaps as a joke) that I *know* I am in pain. What is it supposed to mean – except perhaps that I *am* in pain?
> ...I cannot be said to learn of them [my sensations]. I *have* them.
> This much is true: it makes sense to say about other people that they doubt whether I am in pain; but not to say it about myself. (Wittgenstein 2009/1953, pp. 95e–96e)
>
> Whether I *knew* something depends on whether the evidence backs me up or contradicts me. For to say one knows one has a pain means nothing. (Wittgenstein 1969/1951, p. 66e, #504)

Wittgenstein does not deny that we have pains and they hurt, that we have sensations and feelings. He does not deny that I have inner mental states. He *does* deny that the "inner" plays any role in the language game. It is a wheel that turns nothing. In one of his most famous metaphors Wittgenstein has us imagine that each of us has a box that no one else can look into. This is one of the key passages in Wittgenstein's philosophy of mind and language.

Well, everyone tells me that he knows what pain is only from his own case! – Suppose that everyone had a box with something in it which we call a "beetle". No one can ever look into anyone else's box, and everyone says he knows what a beetle is only by looking at *his* beetle. – Here it would be quite possible for everyone to have something different in his box. One might even imagine such a thing constantly changing. – But what if these people's word "beetle" had a use nonetheless? – If so, it would not be used as the name of a thing. The thing in the box doesn't belong to the language-game at all; not even as a *Something:* for the box might even be empty. – No, one can 'divide through' by the thing in the box; it cancels out, whatever it is.

That is to say, if we construe the grammar of the expression of sensation on the model of 'object and name' the object drops out of consideration as irrelevant. (Wittgenstein 2009/1953, pp.106e–107e, #293)

The beetle in the box is the grammatical fiction that Wittgenstein mentions in the passage quoted earlier.

Wittgenstein says in one of his more provocative statements that the sensation of pain is not a something nor is it a nothing. What is it then? A grammatical fiction.

304. "But you will surely admit that there is a difference between pain-behaviour with pain and pain-behaviour without pain?" – Admit it? What greater difference could there be? – "And yet you again and again reach the conclusion that the sensation itself is a Nothing." – Not at all. It is not a Something, but not a Nothing either! The conclusion was only that a Nothing would render the same service as a Something about which nothing could be said. We have only rejected the grammar which tends to force itself on us here. (Wittgenstein 2009/1953, pp. 108e–109e)

Wittgenstein's use of grammar and the notion of grammatical fiction indicates how closely his philosophy of mind is tied to his philosophy of language. A main point of his private language argument is that a dualist cannot explain language. For the dualist, language, even a private language, is impossible. If word meanings are "inner" private ideas in the mind, no one can know what anyone else means and I cannot even know what I mean, since my memory might be constantly deceiving me. In the final paragraph of Section I of his *Philosophical Investigations* Wittgenstein states: "And nothing is more wrong-headed than calling meaning something a mental activity! Unless, that is, one is setting out to produce confusion" (Wittgenstein 2009/1953, p.181e, #693). Only in the context of our social life is language possible.

Wittgenstein's private language argument and many features of his philosophy of mind continue to be influential, but not widely accepted.

Dualism is getting a bit of attention these days even though Ryle and his fans thought that he buried it. Ryle came to regret his behaviorism, and to reject it and dualism as well.

> [L]ike plenty of other people, I deplored the perfunctoriness with which *The Concept of Mind* had dealt with the Mind *qua* pensive. But I have latterly been concentrating heavily on this particular theme for the simple reason that it has turned out to be at once a still intractable and progressively ramifying maze. Only a short confrontation with the theme suffices to make it clear that and why no account of Thinking of a Behaviorist coloration will do, and also why no account of a Cartesian coloration will do either. (Ryle 1971, p. xii)

In the next chapter we will see how philosophers of mind attempted to deal with the demise of both dualism and behaviorism without falling into the identity theory.

So was Wittgenstein a behaviorist?

> 281. "But doesn't what you say amount to this: that there is no pain, for example, without *pain-behaviour*?" – It amounts to this: that only of a living human being and what resembles (behaves like) a living human being can one say: it has sensations; it sees; is blind; hears; is deaf; is conscious or unconscious. (Wittgenstein 2009/1953, p. 103e)

For me, this is not quite close enough to answer unequivocally "Yes."

The Rejection of Sense Data Theory

We can already see that sense data theory is incompatible with the anti-formalists' philosophy of language and mind. The most direct ordinary language attack on sense data theory is Austin's *Sense and Sensibilia* (Austin 1964). Like *How to do Things with Words, Sense and Sensibilia* was neither written nor published by Austin himself. It was reconstructed by Warnock from notes and drafts left by Austin.

The target of Austin's attack is Ayer. This led to some bitterness. "[H]e [Austin] sets about my book [*Foundations of Empirical Knowledge*] especially in a rather scornful way. It may even be questioned whether he is always scrupulously fair" (Ayer 1969, p. 284). Ayer admits that the philosophical public has sided with Austin and that sense data theory has succumbed to his attacks. He is a bit of a sore loser. "It is a tribute to his [Austin's] wit and to the strength of his personality that he was able to persuade so many philosophers that he had succeeded [in refuting sense data theory]" (Ayer 1969, p. 308).

Although *Sense and Sensibilia* did more than any other work to discredit the notion of sense data, the demise of sense data theory was not just a result of Austin's celebrated wit and philosophical acuity. Sense data theory – which had been featured in the philosophies of Russell, Moore, Carnap, and other logical positivists – was under attack from many leading philosophers. Ryle devoted a section of his *The Concept of Mind* to sense data theory. He rejects it flat out on the basis of ordinary language.

> A linguistic consequence of all this argument is that we have no employment for such expressions as 'object of sense', 'sensible object', 'sensum', 'sense datum', 'sense-content', 'sense field' and 'sensibilia'; the epistemologist's transitive verb 'to sense' and his intimidating 'direct awareness' and 'acquaintance' can be returned to store. (Ryle 1949b, p. 221)

The American philosopher Wilfrid Sellars pursued another attack on sense data. His classic essay "Empiricism and the Philosophy of Mind" (Sellars 1973/1956) was a lengthy, difficult criticism of sense data theory and the myth of the given.[3] Sellars claims on the basis of detailed arguments many of which derive from ordinary language that

> ... the idea that epistemic facts can be analyzed without remainder – even "in principle" – into non-epistemic facts, whether phenomenal [i.e. sense data] or behavioral, public or private ... is, I believe, a radical mistake – a mistake of a piece with the so-called "naturalistic fallacy" in ethics. [See Chapter 8 for a discussion of the naturalistic fallacy.] (Sellars 1973/1956, p. 475)

This is an attack on Carnap and the logical positivists' phenomenalism. Carnap describes his project in an early work: "The main problem concerns the possibility of the rational reconstruction of the concepts of all fields of knowledge on the basis of concepts that refer to the immediately given" (Carnap 1967/1925, p. v). His book, titled *The Logical Structure of the World*, is an attempt at just such a construction of the world out of sense data. Carnap explicitly states that he is motivated by Russell's supreme maxim of scientific philosophy: Substitute logical constructions for inferred entities (see p. 65). Sellars critique came a little late, however. Carnap had already given up this sort of project, at least in its phenomenalist form, partly on the basis of criticisms offered by Neurath.

---

[3] This is a nod to Ryle. Sellars includes an extensive discussion of Ryle and the myth of the ghost in the machine in his article. He questions Ryle's behaviorism. Sellars studied at Oxford as a Rhodes Scholar in the 1930s. He was influenced by Ryle and Wittgenstein.

Even a brief summary of Sellars' article would be impossible here. One of Sellars' basic points, reminiscent of Ryle but much more elaborately argued, is that the sense data theorists do not have any language or conceptual structure adequate to their purposes. For example, expressions such as "The tie seems red to me" or "The tie looks red to me" are not used to report basic sensations, but to indicate that some question about the appearance of the color of the tie is appropriate in the context of observation – it's too dark to see clearly or there's a funny light coming in the window. The sense data theorists need generous portions of ordinary language in order to formulate their theories, but they end up distorting the ordinary meanings to the point of incoherence. Sellars' basic point, which has been influential, is that we have no access to epistemically untainted sources of pure data. Whatever data we have, sense or otherwise, whatever is "given" to us comes already theory-laden. This is a point that Putnam emphasizes in expounding his internal realism, as we saw in the last chapter.

Sellars' assimilation of the myth of the given to the naturalistic fallacy in ethics is unfortunate, however. By the 1950s philosophers no longer considered the naturalistic fallacy to be a genuine fallacy.

Another way of undermining sense data theory was proposed by Roderick Chisholm. Chisholm was an American philosopher who is usually considered analytic in orientation, but who always went his own way independent of philosophical fashion. He even devoted several works to Continental philosophers unpopular with his analytic colleagues. He did minutely ingenious and extensive work in every major area of philosophy. As an expositor and teacher of philosophy Chisholm was unexcelled. He spent his entire career at Brown University.

Chisholm proposed the adverbial theory of sensing. The point is to be able to describe subjective experiences of perception but without reference to sense data. This would enable us to talk about sensation without talking about suspect items such as sense data, appearances, or seemings. According to Chisholm, treating appearances as objects, as sense data theorists do, leads to several puzzles. For example, if we say that a chicken appears spotted to me, does the appearance have a definite number of spots? If it is an object, then can it be shared? Does it have properties that I do not observe? And do I observe my appearances? Puzzles like these helped to bury sense data theory.

Of course, things do appear certain ways to us. We have subjective sensations. The problem arises when we slide from "x appears blue to me" to "There is a blue appearance that I am having."

We should be on our guard, therefore, when locution (1) [x appears ... to S] above is transformed as

(2) x presents a ... appearance to S.

For statements of the form of (2) are deceptively like such statements as "John presents an expensive gift to Mary," where the adjective attributes a property to the thing designated by the noun following it. The locutions "x takes on a ... appearance for S," "S senses a ... appearance of x," and "S is acquainted with a ... sense-datum belonging to x," which may be thought of as variants of (2), are equally misleading. Whatever else appearances may be, then, they are not "objects to a subject." (Chisholm 1957, pp. 116–17)

The way to avoid the temptation to speak of appearances, and thus sense data, in the philosophical analysis of perception is to be cautious in the way we paraphrase "x appears blue to S." Chisholm proposes, as a philosophical paraphrase, the admittedly awkward expression "S is being appeared to bluely by x." This proposed adverbial paraphrase has the advantage, according to Chisholm, of avoiding reference to an appearance as an "object to a subject." Thus it avoids multiplying entities needlessly. "But when we speak in terms of appearing we have only the original external objects. Thus we avoid multiplying entities and we avoid puzzles concerning the status and whereabouts of sense-data" (Chisholm 1950, p. 102). In addition, a perceptual state such as being appeared to bluely is, Chisholm holds, self-presenting, in that the subject cannot be mistaken about how she is being appeared to. Chisholm built an epistemology with such self-presenting states as base. Unfortunately the adverbial paraphrase seems artificial and only barely comprehensible. If we attempt adverbial paraphrases of other senses such as smell or hearing the results are incomprehensible. Chisholm attempted to give more natural sounding paraphrases in terms of sensing, but his adverbial theory was not generally adopted by philosophers.

Austin's attack on the sense data theory was more accessible and biting than either Chisholm's or Sellars' and was, consequently, more popular and, ultimately, more effective.

Austin gives a concise statement of the theory he will attack.

The general doctrine, generally stated, goes like this: we never see or otherwise perceive (or 'sense'), or anyhow we never *directly* perceive or sense, material objects (or material things), but only sense data (or our own ideas, impressions, sensa, sense-perceptions, percepts, &c.). (Austin 1964/1959, p. 2)

One of the key arguments that sense data theorists have used to support the need for sense data is the argument from illusion. Recall the Checker Shadow Illusion from Chapter 1, p. 31. The areas A and B are physically the same but we are seeing *some things* that are different. (Here, perhaps, we can see the appeal of Chisholm's adverbial theory. We might better say "We are being appeared to differently by A and B.") What else could these be but sense data? Ayer uses as an example a straight stick that looks bent when it is partially immersed in water. Since the image is of a bent stick, it cannot be the real straight stick that we are directly seeing. The sense data theorist wants to generalize from these kinds of cases. The object that we are directly aware of in perception is never a physical object. It is an intermediary between us and the object. It is "in" us, not at the object. It is a sense datum. Our perceptual world is a veil of perception composed of sense data. We can never directly sense physical objects including other people.

Austin's response is worth quoting at length. This is Austin at his best.

> Well now: does the stick 'look bent' to begin with? I think we can agree that it does, we have no better way of describing it. But of course it does *not* look *exactly* like a bent stick, a bent stick out of water – at most, it may be said to look rather like a bent stick partly immersed *in* water. After all, we can't help seeing the water the stick is partly immersed in. So exactly what in this case is supposed to be *delusive*? What is wrong, what is even faintly surprising, in the idea of a stick's being straight but looking bent sometimes? Does anyone suppose that if something is straight, then it jolly well has to *look* straight at all times and in all circumstances? Obviously no one seriously supposes this. So what mess are we supposed to get into here, what is the difficulty? For of course it has to be suggested that there *is* a difficulty – a difficulty, furthermore, which calls for a pretty radical solution, the introduction of sense-data. But what is the problem we are invited to solve in this way?
>
> Well, we are told, in this case you are seeing *something*; and what is this something 'if it is not part of any material thing'? But this question is, really, completely mad. The straight part of the stick, the bit not under water, is presumably part of a material thing; don't we see that? And what about the bit *under* water? – we can see that too. We can see, come to that, the water itself. In fact what we see is *a stick partly immersed in water*; and it is particularly extraordinary that this should appear to be called in question – that a question should be raised about *what* we are seeing – since this, after all, is simply the description of the situation with which we started. It was, that is to say, agreed at the start that we were looking at a stick, a 'material thing', part of which was under water. (Austin 1964/1959, pp. 29–30)

Austin is pulling the rug out from under the sense data theorist – Ayer in this case. The poor chap can't even get started with his argument from illusion. Good old down to earth English common sense will clear away a lot of this rubbish.

I think that Austin's argument can be summed up, anachronistically, by a passage from G. E. Moore's "The Refutation of Idealism" (1959/1903).

> I am directly aware of the existence of material things in space as of my own sensations; and *what* I am aware of with regard to each is exactly the same – namely that in one case the material thing, and in the other case my sensation does really exist. The question to be asked about material things is thus not: What reason have we for supposing that anything exists *corresponding* to our sensations? but: What reason have for supposing that material things do *not* exist, since *their* existence has precisely the same evidence as that of our sensations.[4] (Moore 1959/1903, p. 30)

Austin says: "It was ... agreed at the start that we were looking at a stick, a 'material thing'...." The sense data theorist cannot get any traction to get his problem or issue moving without using distorted or misleading language. Austin treats other arguments for sense data with similar bluff appeals to ordinary language and common sense.

The veil of perception story is common to a lot of traditional philosophy, as Austin points out. He cites in this regard Locke, Berkeley, Hume, and Kant. Ayer has simply given this old story a new technical-sounding linguistic boost.

> Now of course Ayer's exposition of this very old story is (or at any rate was when it was written) very up to date, very linguistic. ... However, as we have seen, this relative sophistication does not prevent Ayer from swallowing whole almost all the old myths and mistakes incorporated in traditional arguments. (Austin 1964/1959, p. 105)

As this passage indicates, Austin's ultimate target is not just sense data theory, but the project of traditional epistemology itself. The entire tradition has been one of trying to solve problems that do not exist. Note the use of "myths" again. Traditional philosophy is a collection of myths with which philosophers spook themselves and others who abandon their common sense and their working, everyday use of language. "For philosophical problems arise when language *goes on a holiday*" (Wittgenstein 2009/1953, p. 23e, #38).

---

[4]   Moore later rejected this direct realism and embraced sense data theory.

Like Sellars and Wittgenstein (but not Chisholm), Austin rejects the idea that knowledge has or needs foundations.

> For even if we were to make the very risky and gratuitous assumption that what some particular person knows at some particular place and time could systematically be sorted out into an arrangement of foundations and super-structure, it would be a mistake in principle to suppose that the same thing could be done for knowledge *in general*. And this is because there *could* be no *general* answer to the questions what is evidence for what, what is certain, what is doubtful, what needs or does not need evidence, can or can't be verified. If the Theory of Knowledge consists in finding grounds for such an answer, there is no such thing. (Austin 1964/1959, p. 124)

Austin's point in all this is not that sense data do not (or do) exist. Austin's point and Sellars' is that they cannot do the job they were intended for – supplying foundations for empirical knowledge. And, in any case, there is no need or place for that job anyway.

Although the ordinary language philosophers rejected sense data – which were so beloved by Ayer and Carnap – the Oxford philosophers were extending the project of the logical positivists. Austin, Ryle, Strawson, and the later Wittgenstein and their students were getting rid of the last remnants of speculative metaphysics and eliminating or dismissing the problems of traditional epistemology which still bewitched the positivists. Like the positivists, the ordinary language philosophers saw the problems of philosophy as rooted in language and its misuse. Unlike the positivists they did not think the solution was to regiment language by formal logic.

The Legacy of Ordinary Language Philosophy

Ordinary language philosophy reflected changes in society. The Oxford philosophers and later Wittgenstein approached philosophy in a way that was more expansive, more humane, and less regimented than the logical atomists and logical positivists. Their methods represented a looser, even more modernist version of philosophy: Sweeping away traditional methods and issues, calling them myths, and avoiding the technical, linear argumentation, full of jargon, of traditional philosophy. This appealed to people after two world wars, a depression, and then a frightening nuclear standoff between the US and the Soviet Union. Young intellectuals into the 1960s found the patter of later Wittgenstein and Austin to be entrancing. It was a groovier philosophy than symbolic logic and the technicalities of logical atomism or logical syntax of language. I wonder if I am going too far in suggesting that the layered view of language that the atomists and reductionists had mirrored a hierarchical view of society that was out of fashion in the 1960s. In any case, it could be viewed in that way and thus found to be distasteful.

Despite Oxford philosophers' intensifying the logical positivist program of sweeping away traditional philosophical problems, ordinary language philosophy was expansive in that it encouraged examining the discourse, and thus the concepts and "form of life," of many areas of activity – religion, politics, ethics, art, and literature.

> The recognition of this richer variety of uses of language is one of the marks of the new period. The tendency now will be, though not always perfectly realized, to ask questions like 'What are people doing when they use ethical, scientific, metaphysical language, claim knowledge, or express belief, make promises, or express sympathy?' without trying to fit them all into a few *a priori* categories. (Urmson 1956, p. 172)

In the US, many philosophers were influenced by Oxford philosophers and Wittgenstein. John Searle devoted a great deal of energy to expanding and expounding Austin's philosophy of language. His book *Speech Acts* (Searle 1969) is a detailed elaboration of speech act theory and the application of it to dissolving outstanding philosophical issues. Stanley Cavell's article "Must We Mean What We Say?" (Cavell 1964/1958) was a much-admired defense of the methods of ordinary language philosophy. Cavell captures both the expansiveness and detail of ordinary language philosophy in this passage from his article.

> What they [the philosophically perplexed] had not realized was what they were saying, or, what they were *really* saying, and so not known *what they meant*. To this extent, they had not known themselves, and not known the world. I mean, of course, the ordinary world. That may not be all there is, but it is important enough: morality is in that world, and so are force and love; so is art and a part of knowledge (the part which is about the world); and so is religion (wherever God is). Some mathematics and science, no doubt, are not. This is why you will not find out what "number" or "neurosis" or "mass" or "mass society" mean if you only listen to our ordinary uses of these terms. But you will never find out what voluntary action is if you fail to see when we should say of an action that it is voluntary. (Cavell 1964/1958, p. 109)

One of the results of this expansiveness and the overthrow of positivistic constriction was the reintroduction of ethics as an area of philosophic interest. Full discussion of this will have to wait until Chapter 8, but several Oxford philosophers engaged in the analysis of ethical language. The leaders in this effort were R. M. Hare, H. L. A. Hart, and Charles L. Stevenson. At first this was marketed as "metaethics" – investigations into the logic of moral discourse. But soon more substantive moral philosophy emerged. Elizabeth Anscombe in a groundbreaking article "Modern Moral Philosophy" (Anscombe 1968/1958) helped to change the direction of moral thinking toward Aristotelian virtue ethics.

Despite the efforts of Cavell, Searle, and others, ordinary language philosophy went into decline in the late 1960s. The early deaths of Austin and Wittgenstein abetted the decline. Other causes were dissatisfaction with the more-than-a-whiff of behaviorism and the meaning-as-use doctrine. As we will see in the next chapter this dissatisfaction led to a strong reaction and the development of new ideas and methods in philosophy. As with the logical positivists, the reaction was as fertile as the original movement.

Quine and the American neo-pragmatists and the ordinary language philosophers ended the reign of the logical positivists. The ordinary language philosophers removed sense data from the foundations of knowledge and helped us to see that knowledge could not have such a foundation, and did not need it. However, neither Quine nor the ordinary language philosophers eliminated epistemology as a central concern of philosophers. Nor did they eliminate formal philosophy and the use of formal logic in analytic philosophy. As we will see in the next two chapters formal methods in philosophy grew in importance. Since the decline of ordinary language philosophy, analytic philosophy has become more eclectic. Ordinary-language-type arguments are used alongside formal logic and have led to major insights and advances. [*Background 4.3* – The Gettier problem and contextualism and other examples] No major all-encompassing movements have dominated analytic philosophy since the heyday of Oxford philosophy. Metaphysics, even speculative metaphysics that would meet Ryle's expectations, is no longer a taboo area. It has experienced a startling rebirth that will be the topic of Chapter 6. Analytic philosophy after the Oxford movement, largely because of it and Quine, became more expansive, more inclusive, more eclectic.

Background 4.1 – Dualism, behaviorism, and identity theory

Mind/body dualism, introduced by Descartes, is the view that there are two kinds of substances: bodies and minds. These substances are different in nature and obey different laws. A person is identical with a mind. The mind is housed in a body but need not be. It could exist as a purely spiritual entity – a disembodied consciousness. A serious problem for dualists is explaining how mind and body could interact. Another problem is the problem of other minds. (See *Background 4.2* – The problem of other minds.)

Behaviorism comes in several different forms. Methodological behaviorism is the idea that psychologists should only study behavior. Logical behaviorism or philosophical behaviorism, which is relevant to our discussion here, is the view that all mental words and concepts are definable in purely behavioral terms. We mean by "thinking," "intending," "loving," "seeing," etc. something about behavior including verbal behavior. A serious problem for behaviorists is explaining the use of first person mental statements. They do not seem to be based on behavior.

The identity theory rests on the claim that all mental events, states, and processes are neuro-physiological events, states, or processes. Each mental event is identical with some physical event in the nervous system. My "mental" event of thinking that the identity theory is crazy is actually an electro-chemical event in my brain. A serious problem for identity theorists is explaining the subjective experience of consciousness. There is much more about the identity theory and its problems in Chapter 5.

Background 4.2 – The problem of other minds

According to Descartes, the classical mind/body dualist, I am a mind or soul. I have no physical properties although I am intimately related to a body. I have no weight and no spatial location. This is true of each of us or whoever is a conscious person. All I can see or hear are another body and the sounds it makes. I can never have direct contact with another person. How then do I know that there are other people? All those bodies might be zombies for all I can tell. And if there are other people I can never tell what they are thinking, feeling, sensing. Their minds, thoughts, emotions, and mental states are opaque to me.

One proposed solution to the problem of other minds is the argument from analogy. I know how I feel when I act in a certain way, so I can reason that a similar thing is going on in the mind of another when he behaves in the same way. I can see his behavior so I can by analogy with myself reason to his mental states. Most philosophers agree that the argument from analogy does not succeed. For analogical reasoning to work you have to have access to more than one case. But with the problem of other minds I have access to only one case – myself – so it will not work.

Ryle and Austin dismiss the problem. Austin is particularly incisive.

> One speaker at Manchester said roundly that the real crux of the matter remains still that 'I ought not to say that I know Tom is angry, because I don't introspect his feelings': and this no doubt is just what many people do boggle at. The gist of what I have been trying to bring out is simply:
>
> (1) *Of course* I *don't* introspect Tom's feelings (we should be in a pretty predicament if I did).
> (2) *Of course* I *do* sometimes know Tom is angry.
>   Hence
> (3) to suppose that the question 'How do I know that Tom is angry?' is meant to mean 'How do I introspect Tom's feelings?' (because, as we know, that's the sort of thing that knowing is or ought to be), is simply barking our way up the wrong gum tree. (Austin 1961c/1946, pp. 83–4)

This is the sort of sequence that motivates logical behaviorism.

Background 4.3 – The Gettier problem and contextualism and other examples

In the shortest article ever to create an entire area of philosophy Edmund Gettier (Gettier 1963) demonstrated in his three-page paper that knowledge could not be defined as justified true belief. Gettier offered examples where a belief is true and justified but would not be knowledge because it was true by coincidence. Smith has applied for a job and he has a justified belief that "Jones will get the job." (It does not matter how.) He also has a justified belief that "Jones has ten coins in his pocket." Smith therefore (justifiably) concludes that "the man who will get the job has ten coins in his pocket." In fact, Jones does not get the job. Instead Smith does. However Smith (by sheer chance) also had ten coins in his pocket, but he does not realize this. So his belief that "the man who will get the job has ten coins in his pocket" was justified and true. But it does not appear to be knowledge. Although epistemologists dealing with Gettier problems do not often write about what we would say, they are analyzing the ordinary concept of knowledge embodied in ordinary language. They are working with our ordinary intuitions about when we would say that someone knows something. The attempt by philosophers to get clear about knowledge led to a theory of language that seems obvious and would be favored by the Oxford philosophers even if they would have been suspicious of the formal methods used in formulating it. Contextualism holds that terms can only be understood in context; that important philosophical terms can only be understood relative to a context. The contexts they are most concerned with are nonphilosophical.

Kripke and Putnam used our ordinary linguistic intuitions to defend bold theories about proper names and natural kind terms while at the same time using sophisticated formal logic. These are topics of Chapter 7.

Further Reading

There are libraries of books on Wittgenstein's later philosophy. One of my favorites is David Pears' volume in the Modern Masters series. Pears was a leading figure in the Oxford school. His book also covers early Wittgenstein: *Ludwig Wittgenstein* (Viking Press 1970).

Norman Malcolm's memoir is a classic in its own right and supplies the view that most people have of Wittgenstein: *Ludwig Wittgenstein, A Memoir* (Oxford University Press 1966).

Readings in the Philosophy of Language (Prentice-Hall 1971) edited by Jay Rosenberg and Charles Travis is focused entirely on analytic philosophy of language and includes many classic articles.

Ryle: A Collection of Critical Essays (Doubleday 1970) edited by Oscar P. Wood and George Pitcher contains many essays on Ryle's philosophy. Contributors include Austin, Ayer, Strawson, Urmson, and Warnock.

Symposium on J. L. Austin (Routledge and Kegan Paul 1969) edited by K. T. Fann is an anthology of 26 original articles on Austin and his philosophy. Contributors include Ayer, Urmson, Warnock, Strawson, Pears, Searle, and other leading philosophers.

The Philosophy of P. F. Strawson (The Library of Living Philosophers, Volume XXVI) edited by Lewis E. Hahn (Open Court 1998) is another invaluable edition.

Philosophy of Mind: A Contemporary Introduction by John Heil (Routledge 1998) is a very good introduction to dualism, behaviorism, identity theory, and later theories of mind, and all their difficulties.

5

Responses to Ordinary Language Philosophy: Logic, Language, and Mind

It is no more sensible to complain that philosophy is no longer capable of solving practical problems than it is to complain that the study of the stars no longer enables one to predict the course of world events. (Grice 1989b, pp. 179–80)

Since the decline of ordinary language philosophy in the 1960s, no single movement or school has dominated analytic philosophy. Analytic philosophers began working in every area of philosophy including metaphysics and used a variety of methods. Ordinary language arguments were (and are) combined with formal logic. Philosophers of a formal bent appeal to our linguistic intuitions; writers working on aesthetics or the emotions use methods of mathematical logic. This trend continues to the present day. Recently some analytic philosophers have become interested in nineteenth-century German idealism, others are attempting to resurrect Cartesian dualism and rationalism. Nothing is taboo except carelessness and pretentious obscurity.

Analytic philosophy, since the 1960s, has been characterized less by shared doctrines and methods than by lines of influence and style. A disputed question is whether any unified tradition of analytic philosophy persisted after the decline of the Oxford philosophers. The philosophers we discuss in this chapter fall under the heading "analytic," because they are focused on the same issues that gripped Austin, Wittgenstein, Ryle, and Strawson and they are working with questions and methods derived from Frege, Russell, Wittgenstein, and Quine.

A Brief History of Analytic Philosophy: From Russell to Rawls, First Edition. Stephen P. Schwartz.
© 2012 John Wiley & Sons, Inc. Published 2012 by John Wiley & Sons, Inc.

They saw themselves and those they argued with as in the analytic tradition. The disagreements, often ferocious, were intramural.

The two areas in which philosophers unhappy with ordinary language philosophy lavished most of their attention were philosophy of language and philosophy of mind. The ordinary language philosophers' attack, especially Austin's, on sense data was successful and went unchallenged.

The area in which analytic philosophers made the most striking and impressive advances was the philosophy of language. These advances were due to the applications of the sort of formal methods eschewed by the Oxford philosophers. Formal methods withstood the attacks of Ryle, Wittgenstein, Strawson, and their followers because of the advances in the foundations of mathematics and logic due to the work of Kurt Gödel and Alfred Tarski, and formal philosophical work of Carnap. Philosophy of language achieved a level of sophistication that made the sort of scorn that Ryle heaped on Carnap seem like resentful kicking-one's-feet-in-the-spokes. Formal philosophy of language was abetted by revolutionary developments in linguistics due to Noam Chomsky. The combination of formal sophistication and scientific linguistics gave to philosophy of language the sort of mathematical and scientific imprimatur that philosophers had only dreamed of. Areas of special progress were in the formal treatment of contextual features and pragmatics; the sorts of aspects of language use that Strawson and others claimed could not be explicated by formal methods. [*Background 5.1* – Are Frege, Gödel, Tarski, and Chomsky analytic philosophers?]

PART 1: FORMAL LOGIC AND PHILOSOPHY OF LANGUAGE

Gödel and Tarski

Kurt Gödel and Alfred Tarski were both émigrés from the Nazi onslaught. Gödel was a mathematician who had been a member of the Vienna Circle (but did not share their views). He went to the United States in 1940 and became a US citizen in 1947. Gödel spent his entire time in the United States at the Institute for Advanced Study in Princeton, New Jersey, where he was a close associate of Einstein. Although he continued to make important contributions to physics, mathematics, and logic, Gödel became increasingly unstable mentally. He died of self-starvation in 1978.

Tarski was a Polish Jew who was a leader of an active group of Polish logicians before World War II. He went to the United States in 1939, leaving just before the Nazi invasion of Poland. In 1940 he was at Harvard with Carnap, Quine, Russell, and other leading philosophers. He spent some time at the Institute for Advanced Study with Gödel and then went to the University of California, Berkeley where he spent the rest of his teaching career.

Carnap, Gödel, Tarski, Russell and so many others went to the United States as a result of the upheavals in Europe in the late 1930s – a disaster for Europe but a boon for American philosophy! Because of the presence of such as Carnap, Gödel, Russell, and Tarski, formal approaches to philosophy flowered in the United States. Oxford and later Wittgenstein had less and less influence.

Gödel is best known to philosophical logicians for his completeness theorem *and* for his incompleteness theorem. This sounds odd. One cannot prove a thing and its opposite. Of course not: Gödel's completeness theorem establishes that any fairly simple logical system of the sort that we learn in symbolic logic courses is adequate to derive every logical consequence of a set of axioms. This is worth knowing. It means that if a statement or set of statements, such as the premises of an argument, logically imply another statement, such as a proposed conclusion (when properly translated into the symbolism), then we can logically prove this using the rules of proof of our symbolic logic. [*Background 5.2* – Consistency and completeness of symbolic logic]

What about Gödel's *incompleteness* theorem? Axioms systems can have properties that interest logicians. Are the axioms consistent? If not, then one can prove a statement and its negation from them. That would be very bad. Are the axioms independent of each other? If not, then we don't need all of them. Are they complete? This can mean various things but usually means "Do they entail every truth about the objects they are meant to describe?" The easiest way of thinking about this is to ask if every statement that can be formulated in the axiom system is either provable or disprovable. Gödel's completeness theorem states that every logical consequence of a set of axioms is provable. Gödel's incompleteness theorem, which he proved in 1931, states that for systems complex enough to be axioms for arithmetic or number theory there are statements that are neither provable nor disprovable (assuming that the axioms are consistent). These are usually called undecidable propositions of arithmetic. Essentially this means there are statements of arithmetic that are true of the natural numbers but unprovable. They are true but are not logical consequences of the axioms for arithmetic.

Gödel's result seems to have astonishing implications. It gave the tottering logicist program of Frege and Russell the final deathblow. Arithmetic cannot be reduced to logic and set theory. Since proof is our only method of verification in mathematics, it shows that some mathematical facts are beyond the reach of human knowledge.[1] Gödel's completeness proof surprised no one. His incompleteness proof rearranged people's mental furniture.

An awful lot of the major developments in twentieth-century mathematical logic have depended upon, in various ways, versions of the liar paradox. "This statement is false." It is true if it is false and false if it is true. Why would anybody want to make such statements? Nobody does, but they can arise whenever self-reference is possible. Liar-paradox-type problems of self-reference are the basis of Russell's paradox, which led to Frege's despair and to the failed complexities of Whitehead and Russell's *Principia Mathematica*; they were used by Gödel to make his incompleteness proof; and played a central role, as we will see, in Tarski's work.

The idea of Gödel's incompleteness proof is simple, although the technical devices he employed are ingenious. Gödel showed that arithmetic contains statements that say of themselves that they are not provable. The statement "I am not provable" is true if it is not provable, and false if it is provable. So if arithmetic is consistent (no false statements are provable), then there are true statements that are not provable. The trick for Gödel was to show that such a statement could be formulated in the language of number theory. He devised a technique called Gödel numbering that has become widely used in mathematics and logic. Every arithmetic statement in the language of number theory is given a unique natural number. This is done with all sorts of fussy and technical mathematical tricks, but it works. Groups of statements in number theory, such as proofs, can also be given unique numbers. So every statement in the language of number theory has a unique Gödel number and every proof has one too. Gödel formulated statements in the language of number theory like the following: "There is a Gödel number of the proof of the statement with Gödel number n," and more interestingly "There is no Gödel number of the proof of the statement with Gödel number m." This second one says that there is no proof of the statement represented by Gödel number m. This second statement also has a Gödel number. Let's say it is j. Then we can put j where m is and get "There is no Gödel number of the proof of the statement with

---

[1] Although Gödel did not accept this. He had rationalist leanings and held that mathematicians could use intellectual intuition in some areas where proofs were unavailable.

Gödel number *j*." This, then, says "There is no proof of me." Furthermore, we can easily see that the incompleteness cannot be repaired by adding more axioms or even adding "There is no proof of me" to the axioms. Another unprovable but true statement which says "There is no proof of *me*" will still be lurking.

"There is no proof of me" may not be a very interesting statement, but there are several interesting mathematical propositions that have been shown to be undecidable given current methods. Another well-known claim – that every even number greater than two is the sum of two primes (Goldbach's Conjecture) – is almost certainly true but no one yet has been able to find a proof of it. Other simple statements about prime numbers have also resisted proof. Gödel also established that the consistency of the axioms of number theory cannot be proven within number theory. Gödel's undecidability results can be applied not only to number theory, but also to set theory in which some of the undecidable statements include statements about how large the infinite number of real numbers is. [*Background 5.3* – Infinite sets and the continuum hypothesis]

Gödel's actual result, as startling as it was, is less important than the techniques he developed to prove it. He showed that the set of truths of arithmetic is more complex than the set of theorems, of provable statements. This required formal techniques for describing complexity. These have had crucial applications in logic, mathematics, computer science, and philosophy of language. For example, the notion of recursion developed by Gödel played a key role in linguistics and philosophy, as we will see. A set of objects or group of statements is recursive (even if it is infinite), if each item can in theory be reached from a finite base of items in a finite number of steps by the application of a finite number of rules. For example, if a system has finitely many axioms and proofs have to have finitely many steps (as in axiom systems for geometry and arithmetic), then the set of theorems is recursive. Gödel showed that the set of truths of arithmetic is not recursive. The connection between recursion and computability is obvious.

Tarski also used the notion of recursion. Tarski showed how to give a recursive definition of "truth" for formal systems. Of course, as we have seen, no such definition is possible for formal systems that are complex enough to allow self-reference. They will always succumb to paradox and contradiction. Such is the case also with all natural languages.

Tarski starts with a simple truism: "*P*" is true if and only if *P*. When *P* is replaced by a declarative sentence of English we get, for example:

"Snow is white" is true if and only if snow is white.

Now this may seem so simple as to be simpleminded. But it is not. First, it shows that a statement is logically equivalent to the statement that it is true. This in itself tends to demystify and clarify the notion of truth. Second, any acceptable theory of truth would have to have as a consequence every schema of the form: "*P*" is true if and only if *P*. Third, this schema shows how contradiction arises from the liar paradox.

The only sentence on this page printed in bold is not true. Call this sentence *S*.

According to the truth schema: *S* is true if and only if the only sentence on this page printed in bold is not true. But *S* is the only sentence on this page printed in bold. So:

S is true if and only if *S* is not true.

Thus any system or language with sufficient resources to talk about its own sentences as true or false will be inconsistent. In such a system or language no predicate *T* of the system or language holds of just the true sentences. Truth cannot be defined.

Tarski's solution is to forbid formal systems to contain their own truth-predicate, as he puts it. If we want to talk about the truth or falsity of the sentences of a language, we have to use another system or language. The language we talk about is called the object-language. The language we use to talk about the object-language is called the meta-language. The distinction between object-language and meta-language, introduced by Tarski, has become fundamental to logic, philosophy, and linguistics.

> [W]e have to use two different languages in discussing the problem of the definition of truth and, more generally, any problems in the field of semantics. The first of these languages is the language which is "talked about" and which is the subject-matter of the whole discussion; the definition of truth which we are seeking applies to the sentences of this language. The second is the language in which we "talk about" the first language, and in terms of which we wish, in particular, to construct the definition of truth for the first language. We shall refer to the first language as "*the object-language*," and to the second as "*the meta-language*." (Tarski 1949/1944, p. 60)

This is from Tarski's groundbreaking article "The Semantic Conception of Truth" (Tarski 1949/1944). [*Background 5.4* – Syntax, semantics, and pragmatics] Tarski's goal was to put semantics on a scientific and mathematical basis. The notion of proof had been investigated mathematically and been formalized by Gödel and others. The notion of truth and other semantic notions were, according to Tarski, still in a primitive and unformalized state. Tarski showed how to give a mathematically rigorous recursive definition of truth for formal systems. The method is not hard to understand, although the details, as always, are fussy. Students who take symbolic logic are familiar with a recursive definition of well-formed formula. This is syntax. P, Q, R, etc. are well-formed formulas. If P is a well-formed formula, then so is $\sim P$. If P and Q are well-formed formulas, then so is $P \vee Q$. If P and Q are well-formed formulas, so is $P \,\&\, Q$. If P and Q are well-formed formulas, then so is $P \supset Q$. Anything not built up from these rules is not well-formed. When we get to the quantifiers, with variables free and bound, things get a bit more complex. We can also give a recursive definition of proof, still within the realm of syntax.

Tarski's recursive semantic truth definition basically follows the definition of well-formed formula. The problem is he cannot use the notion of truth, since that is being defined. Instead he uses a more basic notion – satisfaction. Nevertheless, when the dust settles, the idea is that $\sim P$ is true if and only if is P not true; $P \vee Q$ is true if and only if either P is true or Q is true; and so on. Again with the quantifiers, things get a bit more complex. In fact, they get quite complex. This is another reason that Tarski had to use the notion of satisfaction. So that he could define truth for quantified statements. The idea, at least in current form, is that a universal quantification – e.g., $\forall x R x$ – is true if and only if R is satisfied by everything in the model, domain, or possible world that is the range of the quantifiers. All this has become a basic indispensable tool of those working in logic, philosophy of language, metaphysics, and every other formal area. And, by the way, clarifies a key claim of Wittgenstein's *Tractatus*. Wittgenstein claimed that logical relations and facts cannot be stated, only shown. He was right, in a way. They cannot be stated in the object-language, but they can in a meta-language. Facts about the meta-language can be stated in a meta-meta-language, and so on.

Davidson

Donald Davidson, who emerged as one of the leading analytic philosophers in the 1960s and 1970s, famously claimed that Tarski truth-definitions provide the key to the solution and dissolution to fundamental problems in the philosophy of language. Davidson starts from two undisputed facts: 1) Languages must be learnable; and 2) we who speak a language can make and understand a potentially infinite number of different sentences. We are able to grasp the meanings of arbitrary sentences that we have never seen before. Indeed most of the sentences we interpret every day are ones we haven't seen or heard before, e.g., the ones in this text. No limit can be set to such sentences. This fact about language is emphasized also by Chomsky and makes trouble for a behaviorist approach to language learning, as we will see. So one task of philosophers and linguists is to explain how this ability of ours is possible.

> I have assumed that the speakers of a language can effectively determine the meaning or meanings of an arbitrary expression (if it has a meaning), and that it is the central task of a theory of meaning to show how this is possible. (Davidson 1985a/1967, p. 35)

According to Davidson, one's language must consist of a finite number of basic items that are combined to make complex items (e.g., complex sentences) according to a finite set of rules. A fundamental principle, first emphasized by Frege, is that the meaning of a complex item such as a sentence is a function of the meanings of its component items. This is called compositionality. The potential combinations are infinite, but we can decode the combinations, because the meanings of the complex items are functions of the meanings of the simpler items. In other words, the structure of a natural language is recursive. The form of the semantic recursion, according to Davidson, is similar to a Tarski-style truth-definition for a formal system. A theory of meaning for a natural language is similar to a Tarski truth theory. Davidson's idea is that a theory of meaning will give the truth conditions of complex items, such as compound sentences, in terms of simpler items, such as simpler sentences, and the simpler sentences in terms of words. This is as far as the philosophy of language can go in explicating meaning, according to Davidson. That is, the most we can do is exhibit the recursive structure of learnable languages.

> I suggest that a theory of truth for a language does, in a minimal but important respect, do what we want, that is, give the meanings of all independently meaningful expressions on the basis of an analysis of their structure. And on the other hand, a semantic theory of a natural language cannot be considered adequate unless it provides an account of the concept of truth for that language along the general lines proposed by Tarski for formalized languages. (Davidson 1985b/1968, p. 55)

In summary: "My present interest ... is to urge the general relevance and productiveness of requiring of any theory of meaning (semantics) for a natural language that it give a recursive account of truth" (David-son 1985b/1968, p. 57).

Despite his invocation of Tarski, Davidson's method is not Tarski's. Tarski held that such a theory cannot be given for a natural language. Since natural languages contain their own truth predicate, they are sub-ject to self-referential paradoxes. Davidson recognizes this, of course, and many other problems that would not arise in giving a truth defi-nition for a formal language: Besides self-reference, natural languages contain such features as quotations; sentences about beliefs, hopes, and desires; tenses, and demonstratives. Davidson's Program, as it is called, involved tackling all of these problems. Many philosophers enthusiastically joined in. The idea was to use the resources of first-order symbolic logic to explicate the structure of language, or at least of various aspects of it. Great ingenuity was lavished on this project. This was great work for logicians who distained the slogan "meaning is use." For Davidsonians "meaning is truth-conditions."

Davidson was encouraged by Frege's groundbreaking demon-stration that the meanings of the quantifiers "all," "some," and "none" could be fully explicated by symbolic logic. We've seen also how the meanings of "or," "and," "not," and "if . . . , then," at least in some uses, can be explicated by formal means (although the ordinary language philosophers questioned this. More on this soon). Davidson's approach to semantics appealed to philosophers who were suspicious of meanings. Truth-conditions are objective, "out there," extensional [*Background 5.5* – Intension and extension and the problem of non-extensional contexts], whereas meanings are ontologically suspect. This, however, was not Davidson's objection to meanings.

> My objection to meanings in the theory of meaning is not they are abstract or that their identity conditions are obscure, but that they have no demonstrated use. (Davidson 1985a/1967, p. 21)

The fundamental idea is to use nothing but the resources of first order predicate symbolic logic to explicate the structure of natural language. Davidson's program is a spare, formal, minimalist approach to philosophy that appeals to those who question the pretensions of traditional philosophers. It also offered philosophers scientific-seeming work with palpable results.

Davidson's appeal to truth conditions as meanings is reminiscent of the logical positivists who held that a meaningful statement must have verifiable truth conditions. One difference between Davidson and the positivists was that the positivists insisted that the truth conditions be empirical and ultimately explainable in terms of direct observations.

Davidson makes no such commitment. Indeed, Davidson embraces a version of Quine's anti-positivist holism, as well as Quine's dim view of meanings.

> We decided a while back not to assume that parts of sentences have meanings except in the ontologically neutral sense of making a systematic contribution to the meaning of the sentences in which they occur. Since postulating meanings has netted nothing, let us return to that insight. One direction in which it points is a certain holistic view of meaning. If sentences depend for their meaning on their structure, and we understand the meaning of each item in the structure only as an abstraction from the totality of sentences in which it features, then we can give the meaning of any sentence (or word) only by giving the meaning of every sentence (and word) in the language. Frege said that only in the context of a sentence does a word have meaning; in the same vein he might have added that only in the context of the language does a sentence (and therefore a word) have meaning. (Davidson 1985a/1967, p. 22)

Davidson owes as much to Quine as he does to Tarski. He was a student of Quine's at Harvard in 1940 when Carnap, Russell, and Tarski were there. Harvard (Figure 5.1) then was the world center of formal philosophy and Davidson picked up on it.

> Reading Carnap as a graduate student [at Harvard] had helped to persuade me that traditional philosophical problems could be treated with clarity and insight using the formal resources of logic. In 1940 Carnap taught at Harvard. I attended his lectures, and even met him briefly. Bertrand Russell, Tarski, and, of course, Quine were all there that year. (Davidson 1999, p. 34)

Philosophy was flowering, but war was too. Davidson joined the Navy in 1942 and served in the Mediterranean. He was present at the invasions of Sicily, Anzio, and Salerno. After the war he taught at Queens College in New York. From 1951 to 1967 he was at Stanford University where he was able to consult Carnap and Tarski (both also in California). Davidson subsequently held positions at Princeton, Rockefeller, and the University of California, Berkeley. He received many awards and travelled widely giving lectures and seminars all over the world. Davidson was prolific and contributed to many areas of philosophy besides philosophy of language. (His contributions to the philosophy of mind figure later in this chapter.) Initially, an article undermining the Oxford philosophers' philosophy of action explanation made him famous. Followers of Wittgenstein, such as Anscombe, had argued that action explanations in terms of beliefs and desires

Figure 5.1 Emerson Hall, Harvard University. The philosophy department occupies the entire building on Harvard Yard. From the time of William James this has been a center of philosophy in America. Photo provided by Ellen Usher.

must be sharply distinguished from causal explanations. Davidson ingeniously argued that reasons are causes and explanations of actions in terms of beliefs and desires are causal explanations. His analysis of discourse about events using symbolic logic is a model of such techniques and is equally influential.

Another topic derived from Quine, which Davidson explored extensively, was radical translation (see pp. 89–90). He called it radical interpretation because it involves not just making a translation manual of the native's language, but in addition an interpretation of the other's beliefs, actions, and emotions.

> Since we cannot hope to interpret linguistic activity without knowing what a speaker believes, and cannot found a theory of what he means on a prior discovery of his beliefs and intentions, I conclude that in interpreting utterances from scratch – in *radical* interpretation – we must somehow deliver simultaneously a theory of belief and a theory of meaning. (Davidson 1985d/1974, p. 144)

Davidson claims that by observing the informant's behavior, the interpreter should be able to formulate a theory of truth for the informant's language. We should be able to tell when an informant holds an utterance to be true.

Of course, the interpreting will be radically indeterminate. There will be no one correct theory.

> What is important is that if meaning and belief are interlocked as I have suggested, then the idea that each belief has a definite object, and the idea that each word and sentence has a definite meaning, cannot be invoked in describing the goal of a successful theory. (Davidson 1985d/1974, p. 154)

Interpreting is guided by Davidson's version of the principle of charity.[2] We must interpret the alien language and speaker in such a way that almost all of the speaker's beliefs agree with ours. In other words, any speaker of a language must be massively right, according to our lights.

> This method is intended to solve the problem of the interdependence of belief and meaning by holding belief constant as far as possible while solving for meaning. This is accomplished by assigning truth conditions to alien sentences that make native speakers right when plausibly possible, according, of course, to our own view of what is right. What justifies the procedure is the fact that disagreement and agreement alike are intelligible only against a background of massive agreement.... If we cannot find a way to interpret the utterances and other behavior of a creature as revealing a set of beliefs largely consistent and true by our standards, we have no reason to count that creature as rational, as having beliefs, or as saying anything. (Davidson 1985c/1973, p. 137)

Davidson uses the principle of charity to argue against epistemological relativism, and against the widely held idea – held by Quine, Kuhn, and Putnam among many others, according to Davidson – that there are different conceptual schemes. If speakers must massively agree, we all must share a single conceptual scheme. This means that the notion of conceptual scheme drops out of the picture of language, thought, and knowledge (see pp. 111–13 for more on this). Davidson even uses the principle of charity to field an argument against philosophical skepticism.

As is the nature of philosophy, every claim and argument of Davidson's has been challenged. Michael Dummett, who became the leading British philosopher in the 1970s and 1980s, had a famous head to head confrontation with Davidson at All Souls College at Oxford when Davidson spent the academic year 1973–74 there. Davidson visited Oxford several times, gave the prestigious John Locke Lectures in 1970,

---

[2] In introduction to logic we teach that an argument must always be interpreted in the way that makes the most sense given the context and other information that we have. This is called the principle of charity.

and gave various other lectures and seminars over the years – right in the heart of enemy territory! If you know anything about the culture of philosophy, you know that he was received with the deepest respect, honor, and adulation, while being subjected to a blizzard of counter-arguments and criticisms. (But I'm not quite sure that Carnap would have been received with the same courtesy in the time of Ryle.)

Davidson and Dummett together gave a joint seminar on truth. Dummett, while not exactly in sympathy with ordinary language philosophy, represented an evolved version of Oxford methods, incorporating the ideas of Frege of whom Dummett was a leading expositor. Davidson describes his encounter with Dummett.

> The seminar was apparently viewed by the Oxford community as a sort of gladiatorial contest, and a large crowd turned out. At the first session I sketched the gist of my "Truth and Meaning". The burden of Dummett's two articles on what a theory of meaning should be were his response, and this took up most of the rest of the seminar. (Davidson 1999, p. 53)

Dummett's objections to Davidson's program are complex and changed even within the articles mentioned. Dummett holds that use, as in the slogan "meaning is use," cannot be ignored, and constrains a formal theory of meaning. He raises a rather obvious point: How can a theory of truth be informative? Sentences like " 'Snow is white' is true if and only if snow is white" can be known and uttered without the utterer knowing what "Snow is white" means. Even if we rewrite it as "'Snow is white' means snow is white" what have we gained? Surely the statement that " 'Snow is white' means snow is white" is true, but it seems to be uninformative unless we already understand the meta-language in which it is formulated. In order to understand a sentence we have to be able to use it correctly in communicative contexts, not just be able to spout formal truth conditions which amount to nothing more than removing the quotation marks.

At this point Davidson would invoke holism. On a sentence by sentence recounting, the sentences of a truth theory are trivial. But if we once had an entire truth theory for a language that exhibited the language's compositional structure, with basic terms interpreted by the behavior of speakers, we would have something that would be nontrivial and that would exhibit as much about meaning as we can.

Did Davidson and his followers, or anyone else for that matter, think that such a theory could in practice ever be formulated? Of course not. What then is the point of all this wrangling over what form a theory of meaning should take if we have no hope of ever having such a theory? According to Dummett:

> It is not that the construction of a theory of meaning, [of the sort Davidson proposes], for any one language is viewed as a practical project; but it is thought that, when once we can enunciate the general principles in accordance with which such a construction could be carried out, we shall have arrived at a solution of the problems concerning meaning by which philosophers are perplexed. (Dummett 1975, p. 97)

Meaning in the philosophers' sense is not a concept like knowledge, belief, or thought. It is not a concept that is entwined with our everyday activities and that grew up with human life. It is an artifact of those who study language, who make dictionaries, or translate poetry. Yet the notion of meaning has been central to philosophy, especially analytic philosophy, and, according to those influenced by Quine, like Davidson, has done a lot of mischief. Getting a view of how meanings ought to be philosophically represented and described should go a long way to clarifying what meanings are, or are not.

In what sense is Davidson's work a response to ordinary language philosophy? Davidson had little to say directly about Austin or Wittgenstein. The response of Davidson and Carnap and the other proponents of formal methods was shown rather than stated. "Look at what we are doing, and then judge if formal methods are worthwhile."

Dummett describes the scorn, absorbed from Ryle, that Oxonians had for Carnap and his methods. In an article titled "Can Analytical Philosophy be Systematic, and Ought it to Be?" Dummett says:

> In those English philosophical circles dominated by the later Wittgenstein or by Austin, on the other hand [than those in the US influenced by Carnap], the answer given to this question was a resounding 'No'; for them, the attempt to be systematic in philosophy was a primal error, founded upon a total misconception of the character of the subject. (Dummett 1978, p. 438)

In a response to an essay of Strawson's where he attacks formalism, Carnap is conciliatory. He makes a plea for eclecticism. "I share Goodman's feelings when he says that the verbal analyst [ordinary language philosophers] appears to him 'as a valued and respected, if inexplicably hostile ally'" (Carnap 1963, p. 940). Carnap goes on to say:

> We all agree that it is important that good analytic work on philosophical problems be performed. Everyone may do this according to the method which seems to be the most promising to him. The future will show which

of the two methods [ordinary language philosophy versus formalism], or which of the many varieties of each, or which combination of both, furnishes the best results. (Carnap 1963, p. 940)

The formalists' response to Oxford ordinary language philosophy is right here. "Judge us by our results."

And what have analytic philosophers judged? Formal methods, the use of formal logic, mathematical models, and the results of scientific linguistics have been and continue to be widely, and effectively, used in analytic philosophy of language and other areas of philosophy.

Nevertheless, ordinary language philosophy has been by-passed (and to some extent absorbed) rather than defeated by Carnap's challenge. Carnap's plea: "Judge us by our results" is only applicable if everyone addressed agrees on what counts as results and how to evaluate them. Later Wittgenstein, Ryle, Austin, and Strawson did not share a notion of philosophical results with Carnap. As Dummett says, according to the Wittgensteinians and Austinians, Carnap's work was "founded upon a total misconception of the character of the subject." And, I fear, Carnap did not appreciate the divergence between his goals and Wittgenstein's. Wittgenstein states his purpose in philosophy: "What is your aim in philosophy? – To shew the fly the way out of the fly-bottle" (Wittgenstein 2009/1953, p. 110e, #309). Showing flies the way out of fly-bottles is not the sort of task that Carnap would recognize as a legitimate philosophical enterprise; nor would Wittgenstein consider a better theory of modal logic or a formalization of meaning based on a recursive notion of truth to be a way out of a fly-bottle. Carnap and Wittgenstein have fundamentally different ideas about the goals, methods, and nature of philosophy. Ordinary language philosophers, especially Wittgenstein and his followers, thought that philosophy should be primarily transformative, rather than informative.

Grice

Paul Grice was an Oxford philosopher who was closely associated with Oxford ordinary language philosophers. Grice was educated at Oxford and taught there until 1967, when he also moved to California and took a position at Berkeley. He co-authored a famous article with Strawson questioning Quine's dismissal of the analytic-synthetic distinction, considered himself a member of the Oxford school, and devoted some effort to explaining and defending some aspects of ordinary language philosophy. Nevertheless, Grice did more to discredit ordinary language philosophy than any other critic. His critique of ordinary language philosophy was an inside job.

Grice's arguments that were most damaging to ordinary language philosophy were expounded, appropriately, at Harvard. In 1967 Grice gave Harvard's William James Lectures. Even though these were highly influential, they were not published until 1989. Previously they were passed around in unauthorized editions, in a similar way to Wittgenstein's notebooks.

The title of Grice's lecture series is "Logic and Conversation." Grice strove to distinguish between the literal meaning of an utterance, including its logical implications, and the other senses that it merely suggests in conversation, often forcefully. People often say things which have a different force than the literal meaning. Everybody knows how the expression "Everybody knows..." is abused and not to be taken literally. At the swimming pool there is a threatening sign that reads "You are required to shower before entering the pool." Unless someone is truly hydrophobic they have already showered many times. (And if they *are* hydrophobic why would they be entering the pool?) So the sign is pointless. But it isn't. It is understood that the sign intends "immediately before" or "after reading this sign and before entering the pool" but it does not *literally* mean that. Grice offered a careful and detailed analysis of many such non-literal suggestions or meanings. He called them conventional or conversational implicatures (as opposed to logical implications). Ordinary language philosophers failed to distinguish between the meaning of an utterance and its other contextual, conventional, and conversational implicatures. Many of the use-meanings noted by ordinary language philosophers are not, after all, part of the literal meanings of the utterances, but are more loosely related by implicatures.

According to Grice, conversation is governed by several conversational norms. Among them are ones like "Be relevant," "Be as informative as is required by the context," "Do not say what you believe to be false," and so on. We assume that speakers are abiding by these norms. We will naturally fit a speaker's utterance to the norms. Grice offered several examples to illustrate conversational implicature.

A: I am out of petrol.
B: There's a garage round the corner.

(Gloss: B would be infringing the maxim "Be relevant" unless he thinks, or thinks it possible, that the garage is open, and has petrol to sell; so he implicates that the garage is, or at least may be open, etc.) (Grice 1989a/ 1967, p. 32)

Try this sometime. At a party, before everyone is too far gone, say to some fellow revelers "I came in by the door." Your hearers will thrash around trying to figure out how else one would enter the room. The assumption is that you believe your statement to be true and relevant. Why would you say it if the room is perfectly normal and everyone always enters it by the door? Note that your statement is literally true, but is bizarre, because it violates conversational norms.

Grice offers ways to determine if an implicature is in play. The most important is that an implicature is cancelable, unlike a logical implication. The speaker, in the petrol example, can say "but the garage isn't open" without contradicting himself.

Strawson and others in their attack on formalism argued that symbolic logic failed to capture the meanings of the logical connectives. For example, in formal logic *P* & *Q* is equivalent to *Q* & *P*. In English usage these seem often not to be equivalent, however. For example:

1) Bob got sick and he went to the hospital.
2) He went to the hospital and Bob got sick.

Most notoriously the symbolic logic version of "if . . . , then . . . " seems to vary widely from the standard meaning. $P \supset Q$ is true whenever P is false or Q is true. So for example:

3) If John is walking, then he'll be late for the meeting.

is true if John is driving or doing anything other than walking. This does not seem to square with our sense of the meaning of 3.

Conversational implicature can explain many or all of these divergences. In example 2 the suggestion that Bob got sick in the hospital is an implicature. It is not part of its literal meaning. It is cancelable: "He went to the hospital and Bob got sick, but not in that order." The topic of the meaning or meanings of "if . . . , then . . . " is complicated and a huge literature is devoted to it, so no simple way to resolve this issue is at hand, but Grice argued with subtlety that even with "if . . . , then . . . " the divergence in meaning between symbolic logic and ordinary language can be explained by conversational implicature. His analysis supports the view that the literal meanings of "and," "or," "if . . . , then . . . " (in many standard uses) are those assigned them by symbolic logic. Strawson failed to distinguish literal meaning from implicature.

Grice also examined that centerpiece of ordinary language philosophy – Strawson's alternative to Russell's theory of definite descriptions. Recall that Strawson held, on the basis of ordinary usage, that a statement of the form "The *X* is *Y*" lacks a truth-value when *X* fails to refer. Russell held that it is false if *X* fails to refer or fails to refer uniquely (see p. 24 and pp. 125–6). Part of Strawson's argument is that no one would say "The X is Y" if he knew that X did not exist. Grice points out that a use of, for example, "The present king of France is not bald" could be appropriate even though the speaker knew that France is currently kingless. Suppose two people are ardently debating whether the present king of France is bald. I knowingly interrupt their dispute and insist "the present king of France is not bald – because there is no king of France!" So Strawson cannot be quite right. (Take a look again at the quote from Strawson on p. 126.) We do sometimes use a definite description that we know fits nothing. The issues involving definite descriptions and implicatures are quite complex and Grice did not claim to refute or even dispute Strawson's views on definite descriptions.[3] Later philosophers have attempted to use Grice's notion of implicature to defend Russell's analysis against Strawson.

Ordinary language philosophers also scoffed at Russell's uniqueness condition. In ordinary language if I say "The book is on the table" my statement is not falsified because many books are on many tables all over the world. Surely, they claimed, I do not mean "There is one and only one book and there is one and only one table and the book is on that table." So, they claimed, Russell cannot be right. But my statement is like the one at the pool. Hearers and speakers understand, given the context, that it would be absurd for me to claim that there is one and only one book and it is on the table. So I must have in mind a particular book and believe that, in the context, my hearer knows which book I am referring to. I am using a statement that is literally false, just as Russell claims (and would be pointless if taken literally), to communicate information. The information gets communicated because of contextual features, rather than just literal meaning.

Grice's analysis served to disarm many other arguments and considerations deployed by ordinary language philosophers. For example, Ryle and others claimed that the ordinary concept of voluntary action only applies when something is wrong about the action. Philosophers have improperly extended the concept beyond its normal range.

> It should be noticed that while ordinary folk, magistrates, parents, and teachers, generally apply the words 'voluntary' and 'involuntary' to actions in one way, philosophers often apply them in quite another way.

---

[3] In his essay in which he outlines a Russellian response to Strawson based on implicature, Grice begins with the footnote: "This essay is intended as a tribute to the work, in this and other philosophical domains, of my friend, former pupil, and former Oxford colleague and collaborator Sir Peter Strawson" (Grice 1989c, p. 269). In a personal conversation with Grice many years ago I asked him "So who's right Strawson or Russell?" He answered without a moment's hesitation "Russell of course."

> In their most ordinary employment 'voluntary' and 'involuntary' are used, with a few minor elasticities, as adjectives applying to actions which ought not to be done. We discuss whether someone's action was voluntary or not only when the action seems to have been his fault. (Ryle 1949b, p. 69)

If I am sitting of an evening in my easy chair comfortably reading, asking whether I am doing so voluntarily is very odd. To say that I am sitting there reading voluntarily seems to be meaningless or nonsensical unless something is amiss or questionable about my doing so. But this is like saying that I entered the room by the door. The oddness or apparent meaninglessness is a result of contextual features and conversational norms. The suggestion that something is amiss is an implicature. The claim that I am sitting in my chair reading voluntarily is meaningful and (usually) literally true just like the statement that I came in by the door.

This last point casts doubt on Cavell's claim that I quoted in the previous chapter. "But you will never find out what voluntary action is if you fail to see when we should say of an action that it is voluntary" (Cavell 1964/1958, p. 109). The problem that the ordinary language philosophers failed to recognize, as was made clear by Grice, is that of distinguishing conversational constraints on "what we should say" from aspects of literal meaning. This failure undermines many of the ordinary language philosophers' arguments. If I shouldn't say of an action that it is voluntary because that would be boring and irrelevant, this does not shed any light on what voluntary action is.

Carnap – Meaning and Necessity

Did Rudolf Carnap's *Meaning and Necessity* deserve the scorn that Ryle lavished on it? Dummett came to think not.

> Of course, the Carnap that Ryle taught us to reject was a caricature of the real Carnap; but so strong was this prejudice, that it took me, for one, many years to realize that there is much worthy of study in Carnap's writings. (Dummett 1978, p. 437)

Dummett's slightly patronizing tone leaves one wondering, however, if he had quite recovered from his anti-Carnapian prejudice. In any case, Dummett is right that Ryle's Carnap was a caricature.

In his summary of *Meaning and Necessity*, Carnap says that "The chief purpose of this book is to develop a method for the analysis of meaning in language, hence a semantical method" (Carnap 1956a/1947,

p. 202). His ambitions are in fact rather more modest. The point and contribution of the work is to revitalize the notions of intension and extension and apply them via various formal systems to some technical puzzles in semantics. [*Background 5.5* – Intension and extension and the problem of non-extensional contexts] Frege, Russell, and Quine had also offered technical solutions to problems of non-extensional contexts. Carnap argues that his solution using the notions of intension and extension, in certain very restricted ways, is superior – not closer to the truth but better in that it is simpler and easier to use.

The most influential part of Carnap's book is not in fact his intension/ extension method, but his system of modal logic, which is primitive by today's standards. (Modal logic extends standard symbolic logic by adding symbols for necessity and possibility. See the first section of Chapter 6 for an extensive discussion of modal logic.) As we will see in the next chapter, advances in modal logic had a tremendous effect, and Carnap's *Meaning and Necessity* helped to stimulate those advances.

The formal systems that Carnap propounded in *Meaning and Necessity* were not meant to describe natural languages. Carnap hesitates to claim that they even explicate natural language notions. In an appendix to *Meaning and Necessity* he says: "Our explication ... will refer to semantical language systems, not to natural languages. It shares this character with most of the explications of philosophically important concepts given in modern logic, e.g. Tarski's explication of truth" (Carnap 1956a, p. 222). He viewed his explications as restricted in philosophical application.

> The use of symbolic logic and of a constructed language system with explicit syntactical and semantical rules is the most elaborate and most efficient method [of explication]. For philosophical explications the use of this method is advisable only in special cases, but not generally. (Carnap 1963, p. 936)

Recall from the last chapter that Ryle wrote in criticism of the Carnapian approach that

> ... patently fighting cannot be reduced to drill, cartography cannot be reduced to geometry, trading cannot be reduced to balancing accounts. Nor can the handling of philosophical problems be reduced to either derivation or the application of theorems about logical constants. (Ryle 1962, pp. 123–4)

I cannot imagine that Carnap would have disagreed. He would say that just as drill is a form of discipline and preparation for military operations, and geometry is indispensable for map-making, the construction of formal systems is useful, even indispensable, for those struggling with the difficult and puzzling questions of philosophy.

Ryle's criticism is more apt when formalist-leaning philosophers, including Carnap himself at times, lose sight of the philosophical context of their formal systems, and become absorbed in technical minutiae. According to the leading contemporary logician, Saul Kripke, "Surely a little common sense is needed to check the philosophical tendency to build formal castles in the air" (Kripke 1976, p. 414).[4]

Kripke eloquently summarizes the dangers of unrestrained formalism:

> In recent but past times some circles of English-speaking philosophy, especially in Great Britain, were said to have greatly underestimated the applicability of formal and logical techniques to philosophical questions.... I hardly need defend the genuine philosophical contribution made by modern logic here. To some extent the pendulum seems to have swung again in the other direction, and cautions of a different kind are required. Logical investigations can obviously be a useful tool for philosophy. They must, however, be informed by a sensitivity to the philosophical significance of the formalism and by a generous admixture of common sense, as well as a thorough understanding both of the basic concepts and of the technical details of the formal material used. It should not be supposed that the formalism can grind out philosophical results in a manner beyond the capacity of ordinary philosophical reasoning. There is no mathematical substitute for philosophy. (Kripke 1976, p. 416)

Chomsky

Noam Chomsky revolutionized the field of linguistics and helped to found contemporary cognitive science. Chomsky is not in the tradition of analytic philosophy, however. He championed rationalism and rejected empiricism, which in one form or another remained near the heart of analytic philosophy. Behaviorism, as a form of empiricism, came in for especially heated attacks from Chomsky. In the previous chapter I emphasized that Wittgenstein was keen to show that the dualist cannot explain language as a form of communication. Chomsky argued, tellingly, that the behaviorist cannot explain our ability to learn a language. Chomsky claimed that language learning was innate and that all normal humans are born with a universal grammar already

---

[4] We will see a great deal more of Kripke and his contributions to logic and philosophy in the next chapter.

hard-wired in their brains. He called his theory Cartesian linguistics, indicating its rationalist foundations.

Chomsky's innateness hypothesis has been controversial, but his assault on behaviorist theories of language helped to bury behaviorism. The most serious attempt to carry out the behaviorist program was B. F. Skinner's book *Verbal Behavior*. Skinner was an eminent Harvard psychologist and a friend of Quine's. Quine's behaviorist leanings owed much to Skinner. Chomsky's famous review of Skinner's book figures prominently in obituaries of behaviorism.

Behaviorism was on its way out anyway. Even the supposed "logical behaviorists" Ryle and Wittgenstein were hesitant and coy, never happy with behaviorism. Ryle regretted his behaviorist leanings, as we saw in the last chapter. Wittgenstein said that he subscribed to no philosophical doctrines, and defended himself somewhat obliquely against the charge that he was committed to behaviorism. Logical behaviorism never had any plausibility. No definitions in terms of behavior and dispositions to behave were ever formulated nor could they be. The sorts of behaviors and dispositions that would be criterial for a desire for French vanilla yogurt are too multifarious as is the desire itself. The way in which even a simple perception or sensation is manifested in behavior depends on other mental states. If I desire a cup of French vanilla yogurt, I'll open the fridge only if I believe there's some of that delicious yogurt in there, I have nothing more pressing to do, etc. The behaviorist needs to invoke other mental states to explain behavior. Furthermore, thoughts and day dreams are interior and private and need never be manifested in anything exterior. Behaviorism was an artifact of verificationism and its days were numbered when verificationism went out the window. Behaviorism was still echoing dully in Quine's philosophy of language, but Chomsky quashed that.

Children learn language with astonishing rapidity and from very limited behavioral sources. Given a defective and limited source of inputs, the normal child by the age of five or six is able to speak grammatically, and formulate new sentences and understand them. This cannot be learned merely on the basis of repetition and stimulus/response.

> We constantly read and hear new sequences of words, recognize them as sentences, and understand them. It is easy to show that the new events that we accept and understand as sentences are not related to those with which we are familiar by any simple notion of formal (or semantical or statistical) similarity or identity of grammatical frame. (Chomsky 1980/1959, p. 59)

For example, the sentences "John is easy to leave" and "John is eager to leave" are superficially similar (just differ in three letter places) but entirely different in structure and meaning. Such examples could be multiplied endlessly.

> To attribute the creative aspect of language use to "analogy" or "grammatical patterns" is to use these terms in a completely metaphorical way, with no clear sense and no relation to the technical usage of linguistic theory. It is no less empty than Ryle's description of intelligent behavior as an exercise of "powers" and "dispositions" of some mysterious sort, or the attempt to account for the normal, creative use of language in terms of "generalization" or "habit" or "conditioning." A description in these terms is incorrect if the terms have anything like their technical meanings, and highly misleading otherwise ... (Chomsky 1966, pp. 22–3)

Chomsky in his 1959 review of Skinner suggested a proto-version of the view that later was so closely associated with Davidson – that natural languages are like a formal logical system.

> It is not easy to accept the view that a child is capable of constructing an extremely complex mechanism for generating a set of sentences ... which has many of the properties of an abstract deductive theory. Yet this appears to be a fair description of the performance of the speaker, listener, and learner. (Chomsky 1980/1959, p. 59)

The ordinary language philosophers viewed the nature of language as determined by its role as a tool for coordination of our activities and for communication. Wittgenstein, in particular, opposed the view that the purpose of language was to express our thoughts. Chomsky, on the other hand, embraces exactly this view. He insists that language has many purposes and uses, but he opposes what he calls the instrumentalist theory of language. Chomsky has said in many different ways and places that "language serves essentially for the expression of thought" (Chomsky 1977, p. 88). Davidson comes very close to this view as well: "The dependence of speaking on thinking is evident, for to speak is to express thoughts" (Davidson 1985f/1975, p. 155). This is the point at which the divergence from ordinary language philosophy is sharpest and most philosophical, not merely methodological. For the next step is not far: And the structure of language is isomorphic to the structure of thought, and the world. Here we have the view, familiar from the logical atomists, that the Oxford philosophers and later Wittgenstein opposed. These are the first two sentences of a Davidson article titled "The Method of Truth in Metaphysics":

> In sharing a language ... we share a picture of the world that must, in its large features, be true. It follows that in making manifest the large features

of our language, we make manifest the large features of reality. (Davidson 1985g/1977, p. 199)

I find this statement of Davidson's startling and inspiring in its boldness. It is in the spirit of Russell of "The Philosophy of Logical Atomism" and Wittgenstein of the *Tractatus*. It also denies skepticism and every sort of post-structuralist relativism, and explains in one way the intense attention that philosophers have paid to language – a way that is different from Austin's and Wittgenstein's. The ordinary language philosophers investigated the ordinary uses of language to get at our concepts, but they made no claim that these concepts were absolute, the truth about metaphysical reality, or universal. They are our concepts because they are useful, but others with other ways of life might have other or different concepts. Our ordinary concepts need to be illuminated primarily because they have been abused by previous philosophers, not because they express the deep metaphysical nature of reality. Like the logical positivists, the ordinary language philosophers shunned what they saw as metaphysical intoxication of the sort that Davidson expresses in the above quote.

As we will see in the next chapter, although analytic philosophers learned to be wary of abusing ordinary concepts, inspired by Davidson and the developments in formal logic they enjoyed a new sense of metaphysical euphoria.

PART 2: PHILOSOPHY OF MIND

Functionalism

If behaviorism is implausible, why did ordinary language philosophers flirt with it? One reason is that they were still flirting with verificationism. Another is that the alternatives to behaviorism were even less appealing. Identity theorists hold that mental events, states, and processes are nothing but physical and chemical processes in our nervous systems. This view violates common sense and ordinary language strictures. For example, often I know the mental state of another, but I have no idea what is going on with her neurophysiology. My first person avowals of my own sensations are incorrigible, but I certainly do not appeal to awareness of my brain states when making them, nor are the brain states in any way linguistically relevant. Furthermore, identity theory seems to be abjectly kneeling at the feet of neurophysiologists; an idolatry that the scientists in turn did not particularly welcome. The ordinary language philosophers were suspicious of such science worship. Dualism has severe problems too, as we have seen. Other minds would be unknowable and the dualist has no explanation of how a non-physical mind could interact with a physical body. Furthermore, as Wittgenstein argued, the dualist has no explanation for language. The dualist's language would be a private language with private meanings that are incommunicable, which is no language at all. Finally dualism was in the service of traditional religion, which was not a whole lot more popular with ordinary language philosophers than was natural science. Unlike dualism, which is unscientific, behaviorism was a key methodology in scientific psychology during the first half of the twentieth century. It was just scientific enough, but not too much, unlike the identity theory.

As Sherlock Holmes said: "If every theory but one has been eliminated, then the only one left must be true, no matter how implausible." ~~Dualism~~; ~~identity theory~~; leaves behaviorism as the only alternative left.[5]

Holmes' dictum is fine as long as we are sure that we have considered every theory. In the 1960s philosophers of mind, led by Hilary Putnam and David Lewis, developed a new alternative that fits well with materialism, is compatible with dualism (although this was not important), and is a descendant of behaviorism. Functionalism was born as an attempt to repair the problems with behaviorism and the identity theory, and came to dominate the philosophy of mind.

The problem with behaviorism is that it is not possible to define mental terms using only observable behavior and dispositions to behave. The behaviorist cannot forgo appeal to mental states. The problems with identity theory turned out to be even more serious than those that bothered the ordinary language philosophers. Scientific identities of the sort the identity theorists entertained must be lawlike – the same mental state must be identical with the same physical state all the time. This is called type-type identity. [*Background 5.6* – Type/token distinction and scientific identities] Human beings experience pain and have desires, so do dogs and whales, but our brains are different, so the underlying physical states must be different. Also human brains vary considerably in size and structure. Thus pain, hunger, fear, etc. could not each be identical with its own specific type of neurophysiological state. This is called multiple realizability. Pain cannot be identified with one type of underlying physical state or process. Pain is multiply realized. The

---

[5] This is an explanation of why some philosophers were attracted to behaviorism. Plenty of analytic philosophers embraced identity theory, especially as ordinary language philosophy declined. Very few, if any, were outright dualists. Still, today, I think that most analytic philosophers consider Cartesian dualism to be a bankrupt theory.

neurophysiological processes that underlie pain in human beings are different from the processes that underlie pain in, say, whales. Certainly, more complex mental states are multiply realizable.

> Finally, the hypothesis [identity theory] becomes still more ambitious when we realize that the brain-state theorist is not just saying that *pain* is a brain state; he is, of course, concerned to maintain that *every* psychological state is a brain state. Thus if we can find even one psychological predicate which can clearly be applied to both a mammal and an octopus (say 'hungry'), but whose physical-chemical 'correlate' is different in the two cases, the brain-state theory has collapsed. (Putnam 1975a/1967, pp. 436–7)

A complex mental state, such as a desire for French vanilla yogurt, is likely to be realized by different physical states in different people, and different physical states in the same person at different times. Thus the lawlike connections between physical state and mental state required for identity are not to be found.

Functionalism is the view that mental states (events, properties, processes) are not identical with brain-states, nor are they dispositions to behave; rather, mental states are functional states of an organism. A functional state is defined by what it does and its relations to other mental states. It is a state that brings about or causes the behavior of an organism under specific conditions. It is a state that plays a particular causal role in the organization of an animal's behavior.

David Lewis, a leading analytic philosopher and early proponent of functionalism, gives a concise description of the theory. (We will see more of David Lewis in the next chapter.)

> Our view is that the concept of pain, or indeed of any other experience or mental state, is the concept of a state that occupies a certain causal role, a state with certain typical causes and effects. It is the concept of a state apt for being caused by certain stimuli and apt for causing certain behavior. Or, better, of a state apt for being caused in certain ways by stimuli plus other mental states and apt for combining with certain other mental states to jointly cause certain behavior . . . .
> If the concept of pain is the concept of a state that occupies a certain causal role, then whatever state does occupy that role is pain. (Lewis 1980, p. 218)

The key statement in this passage is worth repeating: Pain is "a state apt for being caused in certain ways by stimuli plus other mental states and apt for combining with certain other mental states to jointly cause certain behavior." (Other mental states are like pain in this way.) The functionalist, thus, views a mental state as a function that takes an input stimulus, *plus other mental states*, and generates an output that depends on both the input and the other mental states. In fact, it takes an input plus the entire mental state of the organism and generates an output – and the outputs can also be changes to the mental state of the organism. This is an improvement over behaviorism. Behaviorism also, in a way, sees a mental state as a function, but a very simple function. It takes an input stimulus to output behavior (or is a disposition to take a stimulus to an output). This is too simple – the behavioral output given an input always depends on other mental states of the organism. My story about my desire for French vanilla yogurt showed that it must combine with other mental states if it is to result in behavior, and those other mental states will help determine the behavior. So the behavioral output given a stimulus will vary depending on the other desires, beliefs, fears, and so on of the organism. Behaviorists could not account for this without postulating real internal mental states, which is to give up behaviorism. For the functionalist, mental states are genuine internal states of the organism, not just redescriptions of behavior and dispositions to behave, as they are for behaviorists.

Functionalism was inspired by the computer revolution. Function-alists like Putnam use a computer analogy to develop their theory. According to Putnam we are Turing machines.[6] [*Background 5.7* – Alan Turing and Turing machines] A computer does not just take an input and spit out an output. The output depends on the input plus the pro-gram the machine is running – its machine state. So the computer takes an input and given its total machine state generates an output. This is a much better picture of how our minds work than the behaviorist's. What we do with a given input depends on our entire mental system when we receive the input.

> [Functionalism] . . . allows us to distinguish between psychological states not only in terms of their behavioral consequences but also in terms of the character of their interconnections. This is because the criterion of identity for machine table states acknowledges *their relations to one another* as well as their relations to inputs and outputs. (Block and Fodor 1980/1972, pp. 241–42)

Thus with input I, mental state s_1 will produce output B, when other states $s_2, s_3,$ and s_4 are present. Given the injury to my toe when I stub it, I will go to the refrigerator to get ice, if I feel pain, and if I believe

---

[6] Lewis' version of functionalism is somewhat different from Putnam's in that Lewis did not emphasize the analogy to a computer program.

there is ice in the fridge and that ice will help relieve the pain, and I have no more pressing needs than the need to relieve the injury.

> ... [T]his does *not* mean that the Machine will always *avoid* being in the condition in question ('pain'); it only means that the condition will be avoided unless not avoiding it is necessary to the attainment of some more highly valued goal. Since the behavior of the Machine (in this case, an organism) will depend not merely on the sensory inputs, but also on the Total State (i.e. on other values, beliefs, etc.), it seems hopeless to make any general statement about how an organism in such a condition *must* behave.... (Putnam 1975a/1967, p. 438)

Computers offer a perfect example of multiple realizability. Several different computers can each be calculating, for example, the first ten prime numbers. Each computer is running a program on different hardware. The hardware, of course, can be highly variable. A computer could be made of cogs and wheels and have no electric parts. A Mac is different from a Dell, and so on, but they can each compute the first ten primes. In fact, given the complexity of a modern computer, it would probably compute the first ten prime numbers differently, in terms of the electronic processes, each time it does it. The computer state or process "computing the first ten primes" is multiply realizable.

Computer states and processes can be described on different levels. On one level – the functional level – we can say the computer is "computing the first ten prime numbers." An electrical engineer can explain how the computer is doing this process this time at the underlying lower level of silicon chips. No strict correlations between the functional level and the lower level are to be found. At another time or with another computer the lower level processes will be different when computing the first ten prime numbers.

The neurophysiological processes in our nervous systems that realize our mental states are like the level of silicon chips. Given an input "10," a computer will display the first ten prime numbers when it is in a particular functional organization – for example, it has been programmed when given a number n as input to compute n many prime numbers in order starting with 2 and to display them as output. The computer's actions and states at this level are the result of the input, the program, and the computer's functional organization. (It has to be able to run the program.) My desire to gobble some French vanilla yogurt is like the part of a computer program that gets it to compute the first n prime numbers. Given an input – I see a tub of French vanilla yogurt in the fridge – the desire produces the output of my behaving in a certain way given the other functional states I am in. I grab for the tub, open it, etc. In this way a mental state takes an input (which could be other mental states) and produces an output. The output depends on the input plus the other mental states of the organism. So same input and same mental state could and probably would result in differing outputs at different times, because the rest of the functional organization of the organism will be different. For example, if I recall that I am saving the yogurt for dessert, I will not gobble it now, but put it aside.

The basic idea, then, behind functionalism is that mental states are like functional computer states. They are multiply realizable in terms of "hardware." A mental state is a state that produces an outcome or output depending on the input and the other states of the organism. The nature of the mental state is determined by the characteristic way in which it does this.

Functionalism improves on the identity theory in that it does not require that a given mental state is always realized by a particular underlying neurophysiological state. Functionalism is still congenial to materialists in that they can claim that the processing all ultimately depends on the hardware, just like with a computer. Mental states are not identical with physical states of the organism, but they do supervene on the physical states. [*Background 5.8* – Supervenience] Functionalism improves on behaviorism in that a mental state is not defined in terms of specific behaviors or dispositions to behave. Functionalism is welcome to disappointed behaviorists in that ultimately the inputs are sensory and the outputs behaviors, even though a lot is going on in between.

Objections to Functionalism – Bats and the Chinese Room

Like the identity theory, functionalism has been attacked because it leaves out of the account the subjective nature of our mental lives. Consciousness does not play a role in functional explanations. This is made explicit by the computer analogy. Consciousness, the subjective aspects of mental states such as pain – philosophers call these qualia – play no role in computer operations, since computers have no qualia, as far as we know. The particular character that makes a sensation a sensation of pain is the way it feels, its peculiar and unpleasant subjective aspect. If an organism were in a functional machine state that filled the role of pain, but lacked qualia, it would not experience pain, it would not have pain sensations, but functionalism says it would be in pain regardless of the missing qualia. This is a conundrum for functionalists.

Since Putnam referred to octopuses to refute the identity theory, anti-functionalists, in all fairness, could also appeal to lower animals to attack functionalism. Thomas Nagel, in his influential article "What Is It Like to Be a Bat?" (Nagel 1980/1974), claims that neither the identity theory nor functionalism can account for mentality.

> It [the subjective character of experience] is not captured by any of the familiar, recently devised reductive analyses of the mental, for all of them are logically compatible with its absence. It is not analyzable in terms of any explanatory system of functional states, or intentional states, since these could be ascribed to robots or automata that behaved like people though they experienced nothing. (Nagel 1980/1974, p. 160)

Nagel claims that we all believe that bats have experiences. As we also know, bats hunt and navigate by echolocation. Since we have no idea what perceiving by echolocation is like, we cannot conceive of what it is like to be a bat, no more than we can conceive of what it is like to be, say, blind and deaf from birth. We can, theoretically, give an objective scientific description of bat neurophysiology and, presumably, a functional analysis of bat mentality – at least the difficulties here are merely practical – but none of this helps us to understand what it is like to be a bat. Nagel concludes that descriptions of neurophysiology and functional analyses leave out essential features of mentality – namely, what it is like. They leave out consciousness – qualia. A philosophy of mind that does not account for consciousness is left with a mystery, according to Nagel.

> If we acknowledge that a physical theory of mind must account for the subjective character of experience, we must admit that no presently available conception gives us a clue how this could be done.... If mental processes are indeed physical processes, then there is something it is like, intrinsically, to undergo certain physical processes. What it is for such a thing to be the case remains a mystery. (Nagel 1980/1974, p. 165)

Nagel proposes, in the final paragraphs of his essay, that philosophers develop a new kind of phenomenology to describe the subjective character of experience and thus to prepare the way for relating it to neurophysiological realizations. As far as I know, no one has pursued this path.

Another attack on identity theories, functionalism, and the closely related project of AI (artificial intelligence) is based on a much-discussed thought experiment – called the Chinese room – proposed by John

Searle.[7] Searle's conclusion is similar to Nagel's in that he claims that functionalism leaves out something essential to mentality. Searle's thought experiment is meant to show that a system could pass the Turing test and not understand anything. The Turing test was introduced by Alan Turing, one of the pioneers of computer science, as an operational test for the success of AI. Turing originally described it in his "Computing Machinery and Intelligence," which was published in *Mind* in 1950. Here is a slightly simplified version of the test: Hidden in one room is a normal person, in another is the computer being tested. It has been programmed to respond to written questions and comments. We pose questions and engage in conversations with the occupants of the two rooms. They answer and converse in written form. If we are consistently unable to tell which is the computer and which the person, then the computer passes the test. Of course, so far no actual computer can pass the Turing test. Turing's view is that a machine that passes the test could be, without serious distortion, described as thinking. The machine would be functionally thinking in the functionalists' sense, if it is indistinguishable (in all relevant respects) from a normal person; in other words, if its input and output were functionally indistinguishable from a normal thinking person.

Searle has us imagine that he is in a sealed-off room with batches of Chinese symbols. Searle knows no Chinese, but he has instructions in English about how to output Chinese symbols when new ones come in through a slot.

> Suppose also that after a while I get so good at following the instructions for manipulating the Chinese symbols and the programmers get so good at writing the programs that from the external point of view – that is, from the point of view of somebody outside the room in which I am locked – my answers to the questions are absolutely indistinguishable from those of native Chinese speakers. Nobody just looking at my answers can tell that I don't speak a word of Chinese. (Searle 1981, p. 355)

In other words, Searle in the Chinese room would pass the Turing test even though he does not understand a word of Chinese.

According to Searle, the Chinese room thought experiment proves two things: One is that the Turing test is not a test of thinking, intelligence, understanding, or anything similar. A computer could pass the Turing test and not understand anything. The other is that no purely

---

[7] Recall from last chapter that Searle is also the North American expositor of speech act theory.

functional account can capture the nature of thinking, understanding, or intelligence.

> But I do see very strong arguments for saying that we could not give such a thing [understanding English or Chinese] to a machine where the operation of the machine is defined solely in terms of computational processes over formally defined elements; that is, where the operation of the machine is defined as an instantiation of a computer program. It is not because I am the instantiation of a computer program that I am able to understand English and have other forms of intentionality ... but as far as we know it is because I am a certain sort of organism with a certain biological ... structure.... (Searle 1981, p. 367)

Nagel's and Searle's articles generated storms of controversy. Searle's 1980 article "Minds, Brains, and Programs" is probably the second most cited article in the history of analytic philosophy and Nagel's is not far behind. (The first would be Quine's "Two Dogmas of Empiricism.") Searle's article is a classic of cognitive science as well as philosophy.

Although most of the responses were negative, these articles have undercut the appeal of functionalism. Putnam himself has given up on it.

> Starting around 1960, I developed a view in the philosophy of mind based on the analogy between a mind and a digital computer. I gave my view the name "functionalism," and under this name it has become the dominant view – some say the orthodoxy – in contemporary philosophy of mind.... [T]he computer analogy, call it the "computational view of the mind," or "functionalism," or what you will, does not after all answer the question "What is the nature of mental states?" (Putnam 1994, p. 441)

The defenders of functionalism have not settled on an adequate response to the challenges of Nagel and Searle. Nor have they given up on functionalism, despite Putnam's defection. Some have adopted desperate measures. They have denied qualia. Accordingly we cannot conceive of what it is like to be a bat, because there is no such thing to conceive. And no such thing as what it is like to be me! If that is the cure, functionalism is not worth saving.

The functionalists do, however, have a more reasonable response to Nagel and Searle. Consciousness and qualia are undeniable, and so far unexplainable by functionalists, but they are also unexplainable by everyone else. They are a mystery for everybody who embraces a scientific, materialist view. We know of no way to fit consciousness with a materialist ontology. Do we see Descartes smiling and beckoning to us from ages ago? Functionalists say "Don't panic at the first whiff of trouble. Dualism still has worse problems and also has no explanation of consciousness. We are only at the very beginning of the science of mind. No one knows, at this point, how, when, or if consciousness and qualia can be explained functionally or in some other way consistent with scientific principles."

Unfortunately, functionalism has another "whiff" of trouble that comes from the direction of science, as we will see in the final section of this chapter.

Anomalous Monism

Anomalous monism is a version of the identity theory proposed and defended by Davidson. The virtue of anomalous monism is that it is a token identity theory that avoids the problems of type identity theory. Anomalous monism is not defeated by the multiple realizability of mental states. Davidson offers another alternative besides functionalism to frustrated materialists.

Davidson begins his article "Mental Events" (Davidson 1980/1970) (he prefers to discuss mental events rather than states, processes, or properties) with a puzzle. The following three principles are true, he claims, and yet seem inconsistent.

> *Some mental events interact causally with physical events.* E.g. having desires, intentions, and beliefs cause me to make bodily movements, like going to the freezer to get some ice when I stubbed my toe. The stubbing causes me to feel pain (and stupid).

> *"The second principle is that where there is causality, there must be a [natural] law: events related as cause and effect fall under strict deterministic laws."* (Davidson 1980/1970, p. 108. Italics added)

> *"The third principle is that there are no strict deterministic laws on the basis of which mental events can be predicted and explained."* (Davidson 1980/1970, p. 108. Italics added) This principle is the anomalism of the mental.

Davidson proposes a solution to the puzzle which, at first, is more puzzling than the puzzle.

> The three principles will be shown consistent with one another by describing a view of the mental and the physical that contains no inner contradictions and that entails the three principles. According to this view [anomalous monism], mental events are identical with physical events. (Davidson 1980/1970, p. 109)

For Davidson, events are single datable individuals. Thus according to anomalous monism each mental event is identical with a particular physical event, presumably a neurophysiological event in some organism's brain. This is token identity.

How does this solve the puzzle, since the second and third principles still conflict with the first?

An event can be described in many different ways. Every particular event or action falls under many different descriptions. For example, my raising my arm is also my voting for the motion, my helping to defeat the benighted fools, my raising my left arm, my exercising my rights, my contracting certain muscles, my raising my left arm enthusiastically at 4:30 p.m. August 3, 2007 and so on. The event of the defeat of the motion is also the start of a battle with the dean, the end of a long rancorous process, an event that took place at 4:30 p.m. August 3, 2007 in room 213 of Faculty Hall, etc.

According to Davidson, all events are physical events, but some physical events (such as certain neurophysiological events in our nervous systems) also have mental descriptions. An event of which some mental term is true – has a mental description – is a mental event. Causal laws link events causally only under special descriptions but not under all descriptions that are true of them. For example, I may correctly report that an event described in my email of 3 January caused an event described in my email of 4 January. No natural laws link events described as mentioned in emails. An event described in my 3 January email was my having excessively lolled out in the sunshine in Florida. An event described in my 4 January email was my having got sunburned. Laws do connect those types of events. Notice, however, an event described in my email of 3 January *did* cause an event described in my email of 4 January. Davidson concludes that causality is a relation that holds between events no matter how they are described, but laws only apply to events when they are described in ways amenable to natural science. Mental events are not subject to lawlike regularities under their mental descriptions. But mental events cause physical events and vice versa in as much as the mental events *are* physical events. Since they cause physical events, mental events are physical events.

> The demonstration of identity follows easily. Suppose *m*, a mental event, caused *p*, a physical event; then under some description *m* and *p* instantiate a strict law. This law can only be physical ... But if *m* falls under a physical law, it has a physical description; which is to say it is a physical event. An analogous argument works when a physical event causes a mental event. (Davidson 1980/1970, p. 117)

Finally, we would only need the premise that every mental event is a cause or effect of some physical event. This is a proof of anomalous monism, given the premises.

Davidson's solution is ingenious, but ingenuity is not the same as philosophical wisdom. I do not think that Davidson would deny that his solution is arcane and not needed if you reject any of the three principles. The first is unquestionable, the other two are problematic. Davidson's point is that you can accept the three principles – many philosophers do – and still consistently embrace a version of the identity theory. He is right about that, and for some philosophers this is a valuable result.

The Problem of Mental Causation

Anomalous monism is consistent, but it is afflicted with another serious problem – a problem that challenges any form of nonreductive materialism, including functionalism. (As mentioned earlier, materialism is optional for functionalists, but almost all are materialists.) Once philosophers gave up reductive materialism, i.e., type identity theory, functionalism offered a way to be a nonreductive materialist, as did anomalous monism.

Jaegwon Kim has been the most persistent philosopher articulating the problems of mental causation. In his 1989 presidential address to the American Philosophical Association "The Myth of Nonreductive Materialism" Kim argues that materialists are stuck with either reductionism – type identity theory – or eliminativism – the desperate measure of denying qualia, consciousness, and other mental events. The sorts of nonreductive materialism proposed by the functionalists and Davidson cannot, after all, accommodate the fact that mental events, states, properties, and processes cause and are caused by physical events, states, properties, and processes.

The problem of mental causation is generated by Davidson's first principle. Mental events cause and are caused by physical events. Kim argues that nonreductive materialists are in a hopeless tangle regarding mental causation. Kim rests his case on two claims that he insists materialists cannot deny.

The Causal Closure of the Physical: "*[A]ny physical event that has a cause at time t has a physical cause at t.*" (Kim 1989, p. 43)

Certainly Davidson and the other nonreductive materialists would accept this principle.

> Is the abandonment of the causal closure of the physical domain an option for the materialist? I think not: to reject the closure principle is to embrace irreducible nonphysical causes of physical phenomena. It would be a retrogression to Cartesian interactionist dualism ... (Kim 1989, p. 47)

> *The Exclusion Principle*: If an event has a physical cause, it does not also have a mental cause.

> Could it be that the mental cause and the physical cause are each an *independent sufficient* cause of the physical effect? The suggestion then is that the physical effect is *overdetermined*. So if the physical cause hadn't occurred, the mental cause by itself would have caused the effect. This picture is again absurd ... (Kim 1989, p. 44)

Materialists would have to agree. The idea that nature indulges in widespread and systematic causal overdetermination violates our basic notion of the natural economy. Denying the exclusion principle, without some sort of deep explanation, simply to save a philosophical position is not an option. And to deny either of Kim's principles would be unscientific. The last thing a modern materialist wants is to be branded unscientific.

The causal closure of the physical and the exclusion principle entail that mental events have no causal work to do in the physical realm; they have no causal power to effect physical movements. This violates Davidson's first principle. This result is unacceptable. This is the problem of mental causation.

Is Davidson really prey to this argument? Recall that according to Davidson's anomalous monism each mental event is a physical event. So anomalous monism is tailor-made to avoid Kim's problem of mental causation. The mental enters into causal relations with the physical because the mental is physical. No overdetermination is in play here, because the mental event is not a different event from the causing physical event, it is only the event under a different form of description.

Unfortunately, Davidson cannot wriggle out of Kim's clutches so easily. The problem of mental causation can be reformulated as involving properties. An event causes another event in virtue of the causal powers of its properties. The rock's dropping in the water caused a splash, because the rock has the properties of being dense, heavy, and so on. So the dropping event had the property of being a dropping of a heavy object, etc. If the physical properties of an event are sufficient to explain the causation, then there is no role for the mental properties of an event.

Functionalists distinguish between mental properties and physical properties, because the mental properties are multiply realized at the physical level. The mental properties supervene on the physical properties of an organism. But Davidson toys with the same line.

> Although the position I describe denies there are psychophysical laws, it is consistent with the view that mental characteristics are in some sense dependent, or supervenient, on physical characteristics. (Davidson 1980/1970, p. 111)

As soon as one allows the distinction between physical properties and mental properties – this view is called property dualism – one cannot avoid the problem of mental causation. Davidson is going to have to deny that mental events have mental characteristics that are distinct from physical characteristics. Otherwise he is in the same boat as the functionalists. If physical properties are doing all the causal work, providing all the causal powers, there is nothing for mental properties to provide. They would play no explanatory role in the physical realm. They would be epiphenomenal.

The problem of mental causation is particularly annoying to materialists. Philosophers initially moved toward materialism, because Cartesian dualism has no explanation of how the mental and physical realms can interact. Materialists had to move to more sophisticated versions of their ontology, such as property dualism, when type identity theory and behaviorism proved untenable. Now they find themselves grappling with the same problem of mind/body interaction as the Cartesian substance dualists. According to Kim, property dualists are no better off than substance dualists. If Davidson's anomalous monism does avoid the problem of mental causation, then that makes it extremely attractive to materialists.

The problem of mental causation and the problem of consciousness are today the central problems in the philosophy of mind.

Background 5.1 – Are Frege, Gödel, Tarski, Turing, and Chomsky analytic philosophers?

During this period and to the present day the reputation and influence of Frege continues to grow. He is now included among the world-historical philosophers. Gödel, Tarski, and Chomsky have also had a large influence on analytic philosophy. Nevertheless, I hesitate to call any of these four "analytic philosophers." Frege,

Gödel, and Tarski were trained as mathematicians and published in mathematics journals. Chomsky is a linguist and is listed as a professor of linguistics in the Department of Linguistics and Philosophy at MIT. Frege revolutionized logic, which is a traditional area of philosophy. He also founded contemporary philosophy of language. Gödel and Tarski made fundamental contributions to mathematical logic. Despite my hesitations I include them in my list of major analytic philosophers (with asterisks indicating I do not consider them to be analytic philosophers) and devote space to their work because of the influences they had on analytic philosophy. Turing was a mathematician and is considered to be one of the founders of computer science. Again I hesitate to call him a philosopher except in the sense in which everyone is a philosopher.

Background 5.2 – Consistency and completeness of symbolic logic

One of the purposes of propositional symbolic logic is to test the validity of arguments. We can do this using truth-tables. An argument (when properly symbolized) is valid if and only if there is no way to assign Ts (true) and Fs (false) such that the premises come out true and the conclusion false. Symbolic logic textbooks also have systems of proof or deduction. There are many different systems of deduction. A deduction system allows one to deduce the conclusion of an argument from its premises. Some use axioms, others dispense with axioms and just have rules for writing new lines of a proof, and so on. The truth-table method is the same in every symbolic logic text, but the methods or systems of deduction vary. Every deduction system of symbolic logic must be consistent and complete. This means that it gives the same answers about validity for propositional logic as the truth-table method. That a system of deduction is consistent means that no invalid arguments are provable. That it is complete means that for every valid argument there is a deduction or proof of the conclusion from the premises using that system. Consistency is easy to prove for a particular system. That a system is complete is not easy to prove. Gödel's completeness proof provided a method for showing that the standard deduction systems for symbolic logic are complete.

Alternatively truth-tables can be used to establish that a statement is a tautology, that is, it comes out true for every assignment of Ts and Fs to its component parts. Systems of deduction can be formulated so that tautologies are deducible according to the rules. A system of deduction of tautologies is consistent if no nontautologies are deducible. It is complete if every tautology is deducible. To every truth-functionally valid argument there corresponds a unique tautology.

This is a bare-bones explanation. Readers interested in pursuing these notions further should consult the works indicated in the suggested further readings at the end of the chapter.

Background 5.3 – Infinite sets and the continuum hypothesis

Not all infinite sets have the same cardinality – basically, size. The cardinality of the real numbers is strictly greater than the cardinality of the integers. (The real numbers are comprised by the rational and irrational numbers.) The integers are countable whereas the real numbers are uncountable. The real numbers represent the points on a line segment, and so are called the continuum. Between every two points there are infinitely many points. Between every two real numbers there are infinitely many real numbers. In general the power set P^s of any set S has a strictly greater cardinality than the set S. (The power set of set is the set of all the set's subsets.)

The continuum hypothesis is "There is no set whose cardinality is strictly between that of the integers and that of the real numbers." In 1940 Gödel showed that the continuum hypothesis could not be disproved using standard set theory (assuming set theory is consistent). In 1963 Paul Cohen, a mathematician at the University of Chicago, showed that the continuum hypothesis cannot be proven from the same basis. This established the independence of the continuum hypothesis.

Background 5.4 – Syntax, semantics, and pragmatics

These are terms used to describe features of formal and natural languages and have become standard members of the philosophical lexicon. The syntax of a language is its grammar and other purely structural features. In symbolic logic the syntax includes the rules for making well-formed formulas. The syntax of a formal system also includes the rules of deduction or proof. The idea is that the syntax can be described formally without any mention of meaning, truth, or interpretation. The semantics of a system or language includes the interpretation of the symbols of the system and their relation to things outside it such as models or the world. Syntax is grammar and proof, semantics is meaning, reference, and truth. In formal systems such as mathematical theories the notions of well-formed formula and proof are syntactical notions, the notion of truth, usually truth in a model, is a semantical notion. Truth-tables are a semantic method. Proof theory studies proofs mathematically, whereas model theory studies truth. These are both highly developed areas of logic and meta-mathematics.

Pragmatics has only recently come in for formal study. Pragmatics includes all the social and contextual features of language. Speech act theory and Grice's conversational implicature come under the heading of the pragmatics of language.

I say: "Larry made it to class on time today." Syntax: This is a grammatical English sentence. Semantics: The meaning and truth conditions of this sentence, the reference of "Larry" and so on. Pragmatics: We could easily imagine a context in which my saying this would suggest that Larry is often late to class.

Critics of ordinary language philosophy claimed that the ordinary language philosophers failed to distinguish semantics from pragmatics.

Background 5.5 – Intension and extension and the problem of non-extensional contexts

The intension of a term such as "grandmother" is usually considered to be the property or properties that define the term – in this case being the mother of a parent. The extension of the term grandmother includes all and only those things to which the term correctly applies. This may include only actual grandmothers or include all possible grandmothers. The extension is often relativized to possible worlds. (See the next chapter for discussion of possible individuals and possible worlds.) The notions of intension and extension are clearest when considering general terms, but Frege and Carnap applied them to many other sorts of terms and to sentences. Frege called the intension "sense" and extension "denotation." For Frege and Carnap the intension (sense) of a sentence is the proposition it expresses, its extension (denotation) is its truth-value.

Philosophers distinguish between extensional contexts and non-extensional and intensional contexts. In an extensional context a term can be substituted for any equivalent term (i.e. has the same extension) without changing the reference or truth-value. For example, Bill Clinton = the 42nd president of the US. "The 42nd president of the US was impeached." "Bill Clinton was impeached." No change of truth-value. Frege famously pointed out that this is not so in non-extensional contexts. For example, "Ralph believes that Bill Clinton was impeached" could be true and "Ralph believes that the 42nd president of the US was impeached" false. There are many non-extensional contexts. For example, "necessarily" creates one. "Necessarily Bill Clinton is Bill Clinton" is true but "Necessarily Bill Clinton is the 42nd president of the US" is false. Someone else is the 42nd president in other possible worlds. Non-extensional contexts create puzzles for philosophers, since it is not clear how to interpret the intensions and extensions of phrases in non-extensional contexts. Frege, Russell, Quine, and others had different theories about this. Carnap in *Meaning and Necessity* offered his own solution that he claimed was simpler than the others. His theory is the same as Frege's in extensional contexts but differs in the interpretation of phrases in non-extensional contexts.

Background 5.6 – Type/token distinction and scientific identities

{dog dog cat cat} Between the brackets are four word tokens but only two word types. A particular lightning bolt at a particular time and place is a token. It is a particular electrical discharge. This is a token-token identity. Lightning is a discharge of electricity in the atmosphere. Heat is molecular motion. Gold is the element with atomic number 79. These are type-type identities. They tell us what a certain type of thing is. The sorts of identities that scientists hope to discover are mostly type-type. For example, the cause of AIDS is HIV. But some interesting scientific discoveries are token-token identities. For example, the cause of the dinosaur extinction was the Chicxulub meteor impact.

Background 5.7 – Alan Turing and Turing machines

Alan Turing was a mathematician and computer scientist. He did crucial work for the British war effort in World War II, cracking German secret codes. Turing is credited with the invention of the modern computer and programming techniques for it.

A Turing machine is an abstract or theoretical computer. It is usually visualized as involving a strip of paper with squares marked off and a head or device that moves back and forth along the strip one square at a time. The device has orders about what to do depending on what it sees in the square it is viewing. The number of symbols can be very limited. Just a 1 will do. A Turing machine can be described very precisely mathematically and has been studied in great detail.

Anybody can work one with a pencil and piece of paper. Here is an informal description of how to add two numbers. The input is a row of 1s, single blank square, then another row of 1s. The two rows of 1s represent the two numbers to be added together. The output will be a single number – their sum – which will be a single row of 1s. Here is the program: Start at the beginning of the tape. Move along the tape to right. If you see a 1 move one square to the right. Continue until you see a blank. Print a 1. Continue moving to the right as long as the squares contain 1s. When you get to another blank, move one square to the left and erase the 1 in that square. Stop. Done. Your tape will now show a single string of 1s equal to the sum of the two original strings.

Astonishingly, a Turing machine can compute anything that is computable. Theoretically. If you wanted to compute, say, the first ten prime numbers by Turing machine using pencil and paper, you would need a pad of paper and a lot of patience. But the procedure would be pretty simple.

According to Putnam our mentality can be described as a Turing machine. "I have argued for the hypothesis that (1) a whole human being is a Turing machine, and (2) that psychological states of a human being are Turing machine states ..." (Putnam 1975b, p. 298). This is the basis of Putnam's functionalism. He gave up this view.

Background 5.8 – Supervenience

Supervenience is a relation of dependence. A characteristic, property, or quality that supervenes on other characteristics, properties, or qualities strictly depends on them in the following sense: If *A* properties supervene on *B* properties, then there can be no difference in *A* properties without a difference in *B* properties. Initial examples of supervenience came from value theory. If two paintings differ in aesthetic properties – for example, how good they are – then they must differ in some other material properties – for example, what they look like. They cannot be materially identical, indistinguishable, except in their aesthetic properties.

Non-reductive materialists (non-reductive because they have given up on type-type identities) usually hold that the mental supervenes on the physical. If two people differ in mental properties, then there must be some neurophysiological difference between them. They cannot be in exactly the same type of neurophysiological state. Of course, because of multiple realizability, two people can be in exactly the same type of mental state but not in the same exact type of neurophysiological state.

Supervenience is a technical concept in philosophy that is now widely used in many different contexts, and takes several different forms.

Further Reading

Gödel's Proof by James Newman and Ernest Nagel (NYU Press, new edition 2008) is a readable introduction to the famous incompleteness proof.

The Philosophy of Donald Davidson (Library of Living Philosophers, Volume XXVII) edited by Lewis E. Hahn (Open Court 1999).

For a readable introduction to Chomsky and his contributions to linguistics and philosophy there is *Noam Chomsky* by John Lyons in the Modern Masters series (Viking Press 1970).

Two classic articles by Grice are "In Defense of a Dogma" co-authored with Strawson (*The Philosophical Review* 1956) and "Meaning" (*The Philosophical Review* 1957). "Meaning" has been especially influential. Both are reprinted in *Readings in the Philosophy of Language* (Prentice-Hall 1971) edited by Jay Rosenberg and Charles Travis along with many other classic articles in analytic philosophy of language.

Michael Dummett also has a volume in the Library of Living Philosophers: *The Philosophy of Michael Dummett (Library of Living Philosophers, Volume XXXI)* edited by Randall E. Auxier and Lewis E. Hahn (Open Court 2007).

There are two excellent surveys of analytic philosophy of mind: *Philosophy of Mind* by John Heil (Routledge 1998) and *Philosophy of Mind* by Jaegwon Kim (Westview Press 1998).

6

The Rebirth of Metaphysics

We must associate with each world a domain of individuals, the individuals that exist in that world. Formally, we define a quantificational model structure *(q.m.s.) as a model structure (**G, K, R**), together with a function ψ which assigns to each **H** ∈ **K** a set ψ(**H**), called the* domain of **H**. *Intuitively ψ(**H**) is the set of all individuals existing in **H**. Notice, of course, that ψ(**H**) need not be the same set for different arguments H, just as, intuitively, in worlds other than the real one, some actually existing individuals may be absent, while new individuals, like Pegasus, may appear. (Kripke 1971/1963, p. 65)*

Modal Logic

The most remarkable development in the recent history of analytic philosophy is the resurgence of metaphysics – traditional metaphysics – as an area for analytic philosophers. No philosophy-watcher at mid-twentieth century could have imagined the avalanche of work by analytic philosophers in the sort of metaphysics that the logical positivists imagined they had eliminated. A dam burst that released philosophical energy that had been pent up since the heyday of the Vienna Circle. The primary cause of the rebirth of metaphysics was developments in formal modal logic in the 1960s. Again, a major surge of analytic philosophy was provoked by developments in formal logic.

Modal logic is the logic of necessity and possibility. Modal logics are developed by adding to standard propositional or quantificational

A Brief History of Analytic Philosophy: From Russell to Rawls, First Edition. Stephen P. Schwartz.
© 2012 John Wiley & Sons, Inc. Published 2012 by John Wiley & Sons, Inc.

logic new symbols for necessity and possibility. The usual symbols are □ for necessity and ◇ for possibility. Thus, □*P* (read "box P") means that *P* is necessarily true. ◇*P* (read "diamond P") means that *P* is possibly true. Unlike standard first order predicate logic, many different non-equivalent systems of modal logic compete for attention, and logicians were not agreed on which, if any, were correct.

C. I. Lewis, another Harvard philosopher, is the founder of modern modal logic. Lewis distinguished several different modal logic systems in his early symbolic logic text in 1918. Lewis distinguished modal systems S1-S5 and others soon added additional systems. The systems differed in the modal propositions that they included as axioms or theorems. The most important systems have been Lewis' S4 and S5, and B (named for a mathematician L. E. J. Brouwer). S4, S5, and B share a base but S4 adds the axiom □ *P* ⊃ □□ *P*, B adds *P* ⊃ □ ◇ *P*, and S5 adds ◇ *P* ⊃ □ ◇ *P*. S4 and B are distinct, but S5 includes both S4 and B. S5 is the most inclusive modal system and is the one that philosophers and logicians use most of the time. The details of the various modal systems will not trouble us here. When relevant, we will just assume that we are using S5. [*Background 6.1* – The modal system S5] (Those interested in more details will find sources in the suggested further readings at the end of the chapter.)

The point that we need to focus on is that various distinct systems of modal logic were developed and that logicians did not agree on which was the correct one or even on what their differences reflected. Furthermore, modal logic is not truth functional. □*P* could be false even though *P* is true. This will be the case whenever *P* is contingently true but not necessarily true. Knowing the truth-value of *P* does not by itself allow one to know the truth-value of □*P*. Carnap, in *Meaning and Necessity*, developed a primitive but influential semantics for modal logics. Carnap's system of modal logic reproduces the positivists' dubious view that all necessity is analyticity. He treated □*P* as meaning that *P* is analytic and ◇*P* as meaning that *P* is not self-contradictory. (In all modal systems ◇*P* is equivalent to ∼ □ ∼ *P* and □*P* is equivalent to ∼ ◇ ∼ *P*. Possibly *P* means not necessarily not *P*. So "possible" in Carnap's system means "not analytically false.") The sentence "The earth has one natural satellite" is true but not analytic. Thus, ◇ The earth has one natural satellite, but ∼ □ The earth has one natural satellite. To repeat: □ is not truth-functional.

Despite the fact that no one knew which if any of the modal systems was correct, modal logic seemed useful and interesting, even vital. Look at any newspaper: it is full of sentences using modal terms such as "may," "might," "could," "must," "need not," "had to," etc. Our language and thought is full of notions about what could have been, could not have been, must have been, and so on. Analysis and regimentation of such notions promised to be a fertile area of logical work – the logical next step after working out the logic of the truth-functional operators "not," "and," "or," "if. . ., then,. . .," and the quantifiers "all," "some." Furthermore, other systems are analogous to the logic of necessity and possibility. Logicians developed modal-logic-type systems for ethics with an ought symbol, for epistemology with symbols for belief and knowledge, tense logic (before and after), and found several other applications. Modal logic is also useful in explaining distinctions that would otherwise be difficult to express. For example, I urge you not to separate "cannot." It should be one word. It means something different from "can not." I cannot go to the store $= \sim \Diamond S$. I can not go to the store $= \Diamond \sim S$. These are not the same.

The disarray of modal logic was a source of sorrow. Logicians and mathematicians do not like uncertainty. Philosophers are used to it and thrive on it, of course, but not in their formal systems. The existence of different formal systems for a subject would in itself not be so much of a problem if practitioners knew what the differences represented and how they represented them. The trouble with the competing modal systems is that logicians' intuitions and reflections could not help them decide among the systems nor even gain insight into what the differences represented. Logicians and philosophers shared a vague idea that a necessary truth is true no matter what, true in all possible situations or worlds. Is that the same as analytic, as in Carnap's system? A contingent truth is one that is true but not necessarily true – it could have been false if things had been different. Is that the same as not analytic and not self-contradictory? If so, this seems to be defining the unclear by means of the murky.

Carnap utilized what he called state descriptions – complete consistent descriptions of everything. Every complete consistent set of sentences is a state description. A state description is a linguistic representation of a possible world. $\Box P$ means that P holds in every state description, and $\Diamond P$ means that P holds in at least one state description. Carnap was trying to replace something murky and metaphysical – possible worlds or total states of affairs – with something clear and definite – state descriptions. This replacement that Carnap makes of possible worlds by state descriptions is an example of what he considers to be a translation from what he calls a material mode of speech into a formal mode of speech. [*Background 6.2* – Material mode versus formal mode and semantic ascent] According to Carnap to be scientific philosophers must replace statements about things, properties, or whatever philosophically concerns them including possible worlds, with statements about language. In his 1937 book *The Logical Syntax of Language*, Carnap gives page after page of such translations from the material mode to the formal mode. For example, "The moon is a *thing*; five is not a thing, but a *number*" (material mode); "'Moon' is a thing-word (thing-name); 'five' is not a thing-word, but a number-word" (formal mode) (Carnap 1937, p. 297). Carnap claims that *"Translatability into the formal mode of speech constitutes the touchstone for all philosophical sentences"* (Carnap 1937, p. 313). He would have us translate statements about possible worlds (material mode) into statements about state descriptions (formal mode). Carnap claimed material mode statements in philosophy led to inexhaustible confusion, whereas formal mode statements allowed for the confusions to be dispelled scientifically. Often the issues turned out to be nothing more than a decision about which sorts of language to adopt. Despite Carnap's attempts at clarity, the situation with modal logic continued to be murky, unlike classical first-order predicate logic, which is the paragon of clarity.

Adding to the dismay of would-be modal logicians, W. V. Quine, the leading analytic philosopher of the time, was opposed to modal logic. According to Quine modal logic is worse than useless – "modern modal logic was conceived in sin" (Quine 1966d, p. 175). First of all, as we saw in Chapter 3, Quine rejected Carnap's notion of analyticity, so a logical system based on representing that notion is doomed from the start. Quine also objected to combining the modal operators $\Box$ and $\Diamond$ with quantifiers. The problems are most pointed with such modal sentences as $\exists x \Box (x>7)$, where we quantify into a modal context. Quine's objections to quantified modal logic had modal logicians stymied for awhile and led to a huge number of responses, which in turn led to developments of and increasing sophistication of modal logic, and to the actualization of Quine's worst fears – a resurgence of proscribed metaphysics.

Quine had various technical objections to quantified modal logic, which modal logicians handled with technical responses and fixes, but his fundamental objection is that quantifying into modal contexts leads unavoidably to essentialism. Essentialism of the sort involved in quantified modal logic – Aristotelian essentialism – is good old-fashioned metaphysics.

> There is yet a further consequence [of quantified modal logic], and a
> particularly striking one: Aristotelian essentialism. This is the doctrine

that some of the attributes [i.e. properties and relations] of a thing (quite independently of the language in which the thing is referred to, if at all) may be essential to the thing, and others accidental. E.g. a man, or talking animal, or featherless biped (for they are in fact all the same *things*), is essentially rational and accidentally two-legged and talkative, not merely qua man but qua itself. (Quine 1966c/1953, pp. 173–4)

Evidently this reversion to Aristotelian essentialism is required if quantification into modal contexts is to be insisted on. An object of itself and by whatever name or none, must be seen as having some of its traits necessarily and others contingently. (Quine 1961c, p. 155)

[*Background 6.3* – Essence versus accident] For Quine this is enough to disqualify quantified modal logic and modal logic in general. "[Quantified modal logic] ... leads us back into the metaphysical jungle of Aristotelian essentialism" (Quine 1966c/1953, p. 174). "And in conclusion I say, as Carnap and Lewis have not: so much the worse for quantified modal logic. By implication, so much the worse for unquantified modal logic as well ... " (Quine 1961c, p.1 56).

Quine's argument that quantifying into modal contexts leads to essentialism depends on the fact that objects fall under different descriptions. A well-known example of Quine's involves the number of planets:

The number of planets $= 9$.

The datedness of this identity is instructive, but the problem this identity poses for modal logic has nothing to do with the shifting truths of astronomy. Consider the modal sentence:

$$\exists x \Box (x > 7)$$

If we substitute "9" for "x" in "$\Box(x > 7)$" we get a true statement:

$$\Box (9 > 7)$$

We should be able to substitute any name for the same object without changing the truth-value. However, when we do this we get the falsehood:

$$\Box(\text{the number of planets} > 7)$$

(Surely, another supposed planet might get demoted just as Pluto did.) This demonstrates that $\Box$ creates a non-extensional context.

As Quine puts it, the modal context is referentially opaque. [*Background 6.4* – Identity of indiscernibles, substitutivity, referential opacity, and more on extensional versus intensional] The only way to make sense of this situation is to hold that the number nine, that object itself, is necessarily greater than seven, but it only contingently numbers the planets. This is essentialism, which Quine so adamantly rejects.

Quine insists that "Being necessarily or possibly thus and so is in general not a trait of the object concerned, but depends on the manner of referring to the object" (Quine 1961c, p. 148). According to Quine, the descriptions entail the necessity or contingency, not the object itself. One way of putting this, although not adopted by Quine, is that modality is only *de dicto*, not *de re*. *De dicto* means of the word or speech, and *de re* means of the thing itself. Quine rejects *de re* modality. In a famous passage, he tries to get us to sense his puzzlement about *de re* modality.

> Perhaps I can evoke the appropriate sense of bewilderment as follows. Mathematicians may conceivably be said to be necessarily rational and not necessarily two-legged; and cyclists necessarily two-legged and not necessarily rational. But what of an individual who counts among his eccentricities both mathematics and cycling? Is this concrete individual necessarily rational and contingently two-legged or vice versa? Just insofar as we are talking referentially of the object, with no special bias toward a background grouping of mathematicians as against cyclists or vice versa, there is no semblance of sense in rating some of his attributes as necessary and others as contingent. Some of his attributes count as important and others as unimportant, yes; some as enduring and others as fleeting; but none as necessary or contingent.
>
> Curiously, a philosophical tradition does exist for just such a distinction between necessary and contingent attributes. It lives on in the terms 'essence' and 'accident', 'internal relation' and 'external relation'. It is a distinction that one attributes to Aristotle (subject to contradiction by scholars, such being the penalty for attributions to Aristotle). But, however venerable the distinction, it is surely indefensible. (Quine 1960, pp. 199–200)

Quine, of course, did not stop at rejecting modal logic and its attendant essentialism. He rejected any intensional objects, such as attributes (properties, relations), propositions, and meanings, as we have seen. Quine was an extensionalist in the sense that he held that first-order predicate logic plus set theory was adequate for philosophy and science.

> Such a [extensional] language can be adequate to classical mathematics and indeed scientific discourse generally, except in so far as the latter involves debatable devices such as contrary-to-fact conditionals or modal adverbs like 'necessarily'. (Quine 1961b/1951, p. 30)

Anything intensional such as properties (instead of sets), meanings, propositions, and *de re* modality, leads to metaphysics.

> Most of the logicians, semanticists, and analytical philosophers who discourse freely of attributes, propositions, or logical modalities betray a failure to appreciate that they thereby imply a metaphysical position which they themselves would scarcely condone. (Quine 1961c, p. 157)

But condone it they did! – rather than give up quantified modal logic, attributes, etc. they became outright metaphysicians. They wantonly used *de re* modalities, embraced various forms of essentialism, and in general basked in the joys of unrestrained intensional logic. And we still do. The most amazing thing is that no outbreaks of self-hatred plagued analytic philosophy, little shame or embarrassment, and only slight hesitations about all that metaphysics. Analytic philosophers have enjoyed and continue to enjoy a flowering of metaphysics.

Most of us (I say "us" because I am of this school) not only did not suffer from a bad conscience but were rather smug. My view is that Aristotelian essentialism is intuitive and commonsensical and, contrary to Quine, defensible – not spooky and weird. When we gave up the restrictions against metaphysics that had encumbered analytic philosophy, we felt a sense of relief and exhilaration. In embracing metaphysics, however, we did not give up commitment to clarity, care, and careful sequential reasoning, nor to honoring science and mathematics.

Quine's objection to intensional objects is that they lacked clear criteria of identity. An often-repeated slogan of Quine's is "No entity without identity."

> We have an acceptable notion of class, or physical object, or attribute, or any other sort of object, only insofar as we have an acceptable principle of individuation for that sort of object. There is no entity without identity. (Quine 1981b/1975, p. 102)

According to Quine, we have principles of individuation for physical objects (spatial location and spatio-temporal continuity), for classes (classes or sets that have the same elements are identical), but not for attributes. Attributes, i.e. properties or relations, can have exactly the same members but be different, e.g. triangular and trilateral; having a heart, having a kidney. We have no criteria, according to Quine, of when attributes are the same or different. The same goes for meanings, as he argued in "Two Dogmas," and propositions. For the same reason, Quine rejects unactualized possibles.

> Take, for instance, the possible fat man in that doorway; and, again, the possible bald man in that doorway. Are they the same possible man, or two possible men? How do we decide? How many possible men are there in that doorway? Are there more possible thin ones than fat ones? How many of them are alike? ... These elements are well-nigh incorrigible. (Quine 1961a/1948, p. 4)

Analytic metaphysicians responded in various ways to Quine's argument. They pointed out that criteria for identity of persons and physical objects are not as clear as Quine supposes. Philosophers have puzzled over personal identity and the temporal reidentification of physical objects. Often we do not have clear answers about whether an object is the same as or different from a past object. [*Background 6.5* – The ship of Theseus] Yet we get along fine with physical objects. If we followed Quine's strictures, we would have to get rid of everything but sets. (Some philosophers proposed that.) Furthermore, work was done on identity conditions for properties and this is still, today, a live topic. This is a better policy than throwing up our hands and trying to get along on Quine's prison diet of rice and cabbage soup (i.e. sets, first-order logic, sequences of sounds, truth-values, spatio-temporal points, maybe physical objects).[1]

Another reason for philosophers' good conscience in rejecting Quine's animadversions was the dramatic advances made by Saul Kripke in clarifying the nature of the competing systems of modal logic. Saul Kripke was a child genius – and is a grownup genius. He was born in 1940 in Omaha, Nebraska. While still in high school, he published significant technical papers on modal logic. He was an undergraduate at Harvard when he did further important work in logic. Later he taught at Harvard, then Rockefeller University, Princeton, and is now at City University of New York. Kripke has been

---

[1] Of course, some philosophers were willing to follow Quinean austerity at least part way. We saw in Chapter 5 that Davidson wanted to replace the intensional notion of meaning with extensional truth conditions. Davidson, however, as we also saw, had metaphysical tendencies. He and Quine disagreed about many issues.

the leading American philosopher since Quine and has contributed markedly to many areas of philosophy, as we will see.

In 1963 in *Acta Philosophica Fennica* (Finnish journal of philosophy) Kripke published his groundbreaking article "Semantical Considerations on Modal Logic" (Kripke 1971/1963). Since the publication of this article, modal logic has been based on Kripke's technical results. Kripke's methods were "in the air" in that several other logicians were independently suggesting similar ideas, but Kripke's were clear and decisive. The details need not detain us. (Those interested will find sources in the suggested further readings.) The intuitive idea, as we have seen, is that $\Box P$ means that P is true in all possible worlds. Kripke ingeniously showed that by rearranging the relations among the possible worlds in various ways one would get models for the various modal logics. He clarified the differences among S4, B, and S5, and also clarified the meanings of some troubling modal formulas. Kripke put modal logic on a firm formal footing. Kripke's methods were used by other logicians to formalize other intensional logics.

Thanks to Kripke, Quine and other extensionalists were not going to drive us out of our metaphysical heaven.

Possible Worlds

Possible worlds quickly became the "in" thing in analytic philosophy. Note well that a possible world is not a distant, or close by, planet. It is not part of our universe. A possible world is a total way that things could have been. A possible world includes all of time and all of space. The actual world from the beginning of time to the end and the entire actual universe is one possible world – the actual one.

Possible worlds and possible world talk was used to analyze the modal notions, of course, but also:

> The idea of possible worlds has both promised and, I believe, delivered understanding and insight in a wide range of topics. Pre-eminent here, I think, is the topic of broadly logical possibility, both *de dicto* and *de re*. But there are others: the nature of propositions, properties, and sets; the function of proper names and definite descriptions; the nature of counterfactuals; time and temporal relations; causal determinism; in philosophical theology, the ontological argument, theological determinism, and the problem of evil. (Plantinga 1979b, p. 253)

Here is one example. Quine claimed that we have no criteria of identity for properties, unlike sets. But with possible worlds, we do.

The problem with properties is that two different properties can be had by all and only the same things. How are we to differentiate them? Each possible world has a domain of objects that exist in that world. Treat a property as a function that associates each possible world with the set of things that exist in that world that have the property. Thus properties are functions from possible worlds to subsets of the domains of the worlds. Properties are distinct if in some possible world they pick out distinct sets of individuals. Thus two different properties that are had by all and only the same things in the actual world will differ in the things that have them in other possible worlds. In other words, properties are different if their extensions possibly differ.

Here is another. David Lewis and Robert Stalnaker, both pioneers along with Kripke and Plantinga, of the development and application of possible world semantics, used possible worlds to interpret counterfactual conditionals. A counterfactual conditional says what would have been the case if something else had or hadn't happened. For example, if Nader hadn't run for president in 2000, Gore would have won. This kind of statement is often meaningful and useful. Counterfactuals gave the logical positivists problems, because we do not seem able to verify them. Recall that Quine in a passage quoted above describes contrary-to-fact conditionals as a debatable device. But I believe that counterfactual about the 2000 election, and my belief affects my attitude to Ralph Nader, so I am not willing to dismiss it. How can we explain counterfactuals? According to Stalnaker:

> The concept of a *possible world* is just what we need ... The following ... is a first approximation to the account I shall propose: Consider a possible world in which A is true and otherwise differs minimally from the actual world. *"If A, then B" is true (false) just in case B is true (false) in that possible world.* (Stalnaker 1991/1968, pp. 33–4)

The idea is that we consider the possible world most like the actual world except in that world Nader does not run. If Gore wins in that world, then the counterfactual is true. Stalnaker's possible worlds analysis offers us a clear and concise way to conceptualize the truth conditions of counterfactual conditionals.

Lewis' analysis is similar to Stalnaker's. He begins his 1973 book *Counterfactuals* with an amusing conditional about kangaroos.

> *'If kangaroos had no tails, they would topple over'* seems to me to mean something like this: in any possible state of affairs in which kangaroos have no tails, and which resembles our actual state of affairs as much as

kangaroos having no tails permits it to, the kangaroos topple over. I shall
give a general analysis of counterfactual conditionals along these lines.

My methods are those of much recent work in possible-world semantics
for intensional logic. (Lewis 1973, p. 1)

Lewis prominently cites Kripke's semantics for modal logic in the
footnote to this passage.

Alvin Plantinga, the leading analytic philosopher of religion, mentions the applications of possible world semantics to theological
issues, and that has been his special focus. (We will visit his arguments
later in this chapter.) Possible worlds were initially introduced into philosophy by G. W. F. Leibniz in the seventeenth century for theological
reasons.[2] Leibniz notoriously claimed that the actual world is the best
of all possible worlds. God, before creation, considers all the possible
worlds. He knows all about each one from beginning to end and end to
end because He is omniscient. But which world would God choose to
actualize? Since God is perfectly good, He cannot choose less than the
best. Thus the actual world that we inhabit, the one that God chose to
actualize, is the best of all possible worlds. Modal logicians are more
embarrassed than enlightened by Leibniz' conclusion. Even Plantinga
rejects it. Fortunately, we do not have to settle the issue of whether
this is the best of all possible worlds in order to appreciate Leibniz'
contributions to metaphysics.

Plantinga calls the way I have been describing possible worlds, the
canonical conception of possible worlds. It is canonical because it is
the basic conception, in outline, that philosophers have been using.
To go over it again briefly: Possible worlds are total ways that things
could have been. Each world has a domain of individuals that exist
in that world. The domains need not be the same. In standard Kripke
semantics for possible worlds, they are not. Some things exist in some
other possible worlds but not in the actual world and vice versa.
Properties are functions from possible worlds to sets of individuals
in the domains of those worlds. A necessary proposition is true in
every possible world (and we can give a technical Tarski-style truth
definition for truth-in-a-world). A possible proposition is true in at
least one possible world; an impossible proposition is true in none.
A contingent proposition is true in some worlds but false in others.
Notice, the canonical conception involves no mention of analyticity.

---

[2] Perhaps their theological heritage is another unstated reason for Quine's rejection of
modal logic and possibilia.

This is not about language. Even though we speak of possible world semantics, it is metaphysics.

What about essentialism? An individual has a property essentially if and only if it has that property in every world in which it exists. It has a property accidentally if and only if it has it in at least one world and lacks it in another. Presumably, I have the property of being a human being in every world in which I exist. I have the property of living in Ithaca in some but not others. I am essentially human but contingently an Ithacan. (By the way, here is my answer to Quine's puzzle about the cycling mathematician: He is not necessarily a mathematician nor necessarily a cyclist. In some possible world he is neither a mathematician nor a cyclist. In fact, I would say, no human beings are necessarily mathematicians or necessarily cyclists. So our cycling mathematician is contingently a mathematician and contingently a cyclist. So he is neither necessarily rational nor necessarily two-legged. He has both properties accidently. He would be necessarily rational, if human beings are necessarily rational, but, alas, we know that's not true. Quine's puzzle can also be sorted out by using the distinction between *de dicto* and *de re*. All husbands are necessarily married. This is *de dicto* necessity. The necessity attaches to the linguistic description "husband." But I, a husband, am not necessarily married. *De re* I am contingently married as indeed is every other married individual.)

A necessary being exists in every possible world, a contingent being in some but not others. You and I are contingent beings. Some impoverished worlds lack us. If numbers exist, presumably they exist in every possible world. Quantifiers only apply within a given world. $\exists x$ (x is a zebra) is true because zebras are found in the actual world. $\diamond \exists x$ (x is a red lemon) is true if and only if $\exists x$ (x is a red lemon) is true in some possible world. $\exists x \diamond$ (x is a red lemon) is true if and only if some actual lemon is red in some possible world. Note also that when talking about other possible worlds we use our language with our meanings. Our symbols, those shapes, do mean other things in some other possible worlds, but that is no concern of ours.

So:

$$\exists x \Box (x > 7)$$

is true if and only if something in the domain of the actual world is greater than seven in every world. This would be the number nine (and infinitely many other numbers).

$$\Box \exists x (x > 7)$$

is true if and only if in every possible world something is greater than seven.

Here is an interesting modal formula, called the Barcan formula after Ruth Barcan Marcus, an early and influential advocate of quantified modal logic.

$$\forall x \square\, A\, x \supset\, \square\, \forall x A\, x$$

This turns out to be false in S5, allowing a few suppositions. Suppose every individual in the actual world is A in every world in which it exists. Then $\forall x \square A x$ is true. Now also suppose that the domain of some other world contains objects that do not exist in the actual world and are not A in that world. $\forall x\, A\, x$ is false in that world. So $\sim\square \forall x\, A\, x$. If all the domains of the possible worlds are the same, then the Barcan formula holds. All this was clarified by Kripke.

Since we are having so much fun, let's consider briefly another application of the canonical conception of possible worlds. You might be a determinist. That is, you believe that every event and action is causally pre-determined and we have no free choice. Ah, now that you've been infected with possible worlds, you think to represent your view by holding that there is only one possible world – the actual one. The canonical conception of possible worlds offers us a better, more flexible way to represent determinism. Possible worlds are temporally extended from the beginning of time to the end of time in each world. Determinism is the view that no two possible worlds have exactly the same initial segments of any length. In other words, determinism is the view that worlds cannot be the same up to a point and then diverge. In fact, they cannot overlap at all and then diverge. Isn't that neat?

The canonical conception is ingenious and helps to illuminate issues in philosophy and logic. We should take a moment to appreciate it, and to thank Leibniz, C. I. Lewis, Marcus, Carnap, David Lewis, Plantinga, Stalnaker, and other workers in the field (see suggested further readings), and especially Saul Kripke for it; and even Quine deserves a nod. His persistent challenges provoked advances in modal logic.

Problems with the Canonical Conception of Possible Worlds

Naturally, being a grand philosophical vision, the canonical conception of possible worlds suffers from numerous problems.

Number one is that it is supremely metaphysical. Claims about alternative possible worlds are not verifiable in the logical positivists' sense of verifiable. We cannot observe non-actual possible worlds. We cannot travel to them, and not because our rocket ships are too slow. So we have a meta-metaphysical epistemological issue: How do we decide metaphysical questions such as the ones that arise about possible worlds? The logical positivists said "You can't, so they're meaningless." That's not right. They are not meaningless. So what do we do? We proceed as best we can: by argument using our intuitions, our common sense, our shared linguistic abilities, our scientific and empirical knowledge, and our business sense. Yes, we use our business sense, in a sense. Philosophers proceed by a kind of intellectual cost/benefit analysis. We ask how intellectually costly a certain view, theory, or answer is, and what benefits does it offer. This harks back to Quine's pragmatic notions involving non-empirical virtues.

No doubt, the reader noticed that the canonical conception will not allow us to distinguish every pair of distinct properties. According to the canonical conception, properties are functions from worlds to sets within their domains. The properties triangularity and trilaterality will pick out the same objects in every possible world, so they would be deemed the same property. Propositions are functions from worlds to truth-values. Necessary propositions get the value T in every possible world, so they would all be the same proposition, the function that associates with each world the value T. Maybe we can shrug our shoulders and live with this. This is a cost we can bear for the benefits of the canonical conception.

Other problems are not so easy to shrug off. We have before us several interconnected metaphysical questions: Just what are possible worlds? We said "total ways that things could have been." But what is that? Are possible worlds real things or only imaginary or are they state descriptions as Carnap said? Do individuals in other possible worlds really exist? Aren't Quine's qualms about possible men in the doorway legitimate? We also have the vexed problems of trans-world identity and identification. If I say, for example, "If Aristotle had died in a plague that swept Stagira around the time of his birth, the West would not have developed the disciplines of logic and metaphysics," presumably my statement should be interpreted as saying that there is a possible world, very similar to the actual one up to 384 BC or 385 BC, except that Aristotle dies as an infant, and then different in ways following on that. But how do I know that baby Aristotle is in the domain of that world? Assuming he is, how do I identify Aristotle in that world? How do I know that I am talking about Aristotle instead of someone else? We do not have telescopes or metaphysiscopes that would enable us to peer into other worlds. And even if we did, how would we know what we were looking at?

Controversial answers to these questions were defended by the leading metaphysician of our times – David Lewis. We have already met Lewis' functionalism in the philosophy of mind (see p. 185) and noted above his theory of counterfactuals. Lewis is another Crimson philosopher. He got his Ph.D under Quine at Harvard in 1967; but obviously Lewis was no follower of Quine. He went in directions philosophically orthogonal to his teacher's. Lewis spent most of his career teaching at Princeton University. He died in 2001 at the age of 60 from complications of diabetes. Lewis made many notable contributions to many areas of philosophy – in fact, the definition of determinism in terms of possible worlds is due to him. But Lewis is best known for his modal realism.

Modal realism is the view that other possible worlds are just as real as the actual world. Individuals in those worlds are just as real and exist just as fully and concretely as actual individuals. The only difference is that we are actual and they are not. We inhabit this, our world, the actual world. Other people inhabit other worlds and for them their worlds are actual.

Other possible worlds are spatially discontinuous from our world, but they are almost like other planets, according to Lewis.

> Are there other worlds that are other ways? I say there are. I advocate a thesis of plurality of worlds, or *modal realism*, which holds that our world is but one world among many. There are countless other worlds, other very inclusive things. ... The worlds are something like remote planets; except that most of them are much bigger than mere planets, and they are not remote. Neither are they nearby. They are not at any spatial distance whatever from here. They are not far in the past or future, nor for that matter near; they are not at any temporal distance whatever from now. They are isolated: there are no spatiotemporal relations at all between things that belong to different worlds. Nor does anything that happens at one world cause anything to happen at another.
>
> ...
>
> Nor does this world differ from the others in its manner of existing .... Likewise some things exist here at our world, others exist at other worlds; again, I take this to be a difference between things that exist, not a difference in their existing. (Lewis 1986, pp. 2–3)

Lewis has no knockdown argument for his modal realism. Instead, he argues the benefits outweigh the costs.

> I begin the first chapter [of his book *On the Plurality of Worlds*] by reviewing the many ways in which systematic philosophy goes more easily if we may presuppose modal realism in our analyses. I take this to be a good reason to think that modal realism is true, just as the utility of set theory in mathematics is a good reason to believe there are sets. (Lewis 1986, p. vii)

According to Lewis the benefits of accepting the parallel existence of infinitely many other possible worlds and the things that exist in them is worth it. "The benefits are worth the ontological cost" (Lewis 1986, p. 4).

In *The Plurality of Worlds* (Lewis 1986), Lewis considers in detail all manner of objections to modal realism. The one objection he admits he cannot counter is the incredulous stare.

> The proper test, I suggest, is a simple maxim of honesty: never put forward a philosophical theory that you yourself cannot believe in your least philosophical and most commonsensical moments . . . .
>
> The incredulous stare is a gesture meant to say that modal realism fails the test. That is a matter of judgement and, with respect, I disagree. I acknowledge that my denial of common sense opinion is severe, and I think it is entirely right and proper to count that as a serious cost. How serious is serious enough to be decisive? – That is our central question, yet I don't see how anything can be said about it. *I* still think the price is right, high as it is. Modal realism ought to be accepted as true. The theoretical benefits are worth it. (Lewis 1986, p. 135)

In order to consider the costs and benefits of a view we must consider the alternatives. The alternative to modal realism is modal actualism. Modal actualism is the common sense view that only the actual world exists. The defining slogan of actualism is "Everything that exists is actual." According to modal actualists, then, other possible worlds and everything in their domains must consist of things found in the actual world.

Actualists do not want to give up any of the glories of possible world metaphysics. That would be too heavy a cost. So they have the burden of explaining how other possible worlds are to be constructed out of things found in our actual world. This is the philosophical analogue of explaining how to construct a short wave radio out of common items found around the house. Maybe you can do it, but it ain't gonna be easy.

The best-known and most vigorously defended version of actualism is Plantinga's. According to Plantinga, possible worlds are states of affairs, maximal states of affairs. This is like Carnap's state descriptions, except states of affairs are not sentences. A simple state of affairs is defined as an individual having a property. So Hilary Putnam's being a philosopher is a state of affairs. Complex and compound states of affairs include other states of affairs. Hilary Putnam's being a distinguished philosopher includes the state of affairs of his being a philosopher.

> A maximal state of affairs, then, is one that for every state of affairs *S*, it either includes *S*, or precludes *S*. And a possible world is a state of affairs that is both possible and maximal. As on the Canonical Conception, just one of these possible worlds – α – has the distinction of being such that every state of affairs it includes is actual. (Plantinga 1979b, p. 258)

Some possible states of affairs obtain, and thus are actual, but others do not obtain, such as Putnam's being a politician. Nevertheless, they exist and are part of the actual world. They are abstract objects, as are actual states of affairs.

> Of course it isn't my claim that this state of affairs [e.g., Putnam's being a politician] *does not exist*, or that there simply is no such state of affairs; indeed there is such a state of affairs and it exists just as serenely as your most solidly actual state of affairs. But it does not obtain; it isn't actual. It *could have been* actual, however, and had things been appropriately different, it *would* have been actual; it is a *possible* state of affairs. (Plantinga 1979b, p. 258)

So other possible worlds are non-actual total states of affairs that are abstract objects existing "serenely" in our actual world. An object has a property in a world if that world includes the state of affairs of that object having that property. [*Background 6.6* – Abstract versus concrete]

According to actualism, the domain of every possible world is contained in the domain of the actual world. Surely, however, we want to hold that some possible worlds contain individuals that are possible but not actual. How can an actualist handle this? With individual essences. An essence is a property or conjunction of properties that is necessary and sufficient for being a particular individual. According to Plantinga, essences exist necessarily but need not be exemplified.

> Socrates is a contingent being; his essence, however, is not. Properties, like propositions and possible worlds, are necessary beings. If Socrates had not existed, his essence would have been unexemplified, but not nonexistent. In worlds where Socrates exists, Socrateity is his essence; *exemplifying Socrateity* is essential to him. Socrateity, however, does not have essentially the property of being exemplified by Socrates; it is not

exemplified by him in worlds where he does not exist. In those worlds, of course, it is not exemplified at all .... (Plantinga 1979b, p. 268)

So this, then, is how it works for actualism: All the essences exist. They are abstract objects in the actual world and in every other possible world (which in turn all exist in the actual world). In some worlds, some essences are exemplified, and others are not. If the essence e is exemplified in world W, then it is true in W that the unique object that exemplifies e exists in W.

Existence in other possible worlds is different for actualists than it is for realists. According to Lewis, possible beings exist in other possible worlds just as concretely as we exist in ours. For Plantinga, to say that beings exist in other possible worlds means that if those worlds had been actual, those beings would have existed.

To say that an object x exists in a world W, is to say that if W had been actual, x would have existed; more exactly, x exists in W if it is impossible that W obtain and x fail to exist. ... To say that Socrates exists in W is not, of course, to say that Socrates exists, but only that he *would have*, had W been actual. (Plantinga 1974a, pp. 46–7)

So how can Plantinga capture the idea that there could have been objects that do not actually exist? For example, I might have had an older brother but do not. Plantinga would say that in some alternative possible world an individual essence of an older brother of mine is exemplified, but is not exemplified in the actual world. Some alternative possible world contains the state of affairs of that essence being exemplified. My older brother exists in that possible world but does not exist.

Actualism offers a dandy way with negative existentials – statements that something does not exist. Modal realism is going to have problems with negative existentials, because the statement that something does not exist will only be true in a world where the thing in question is not part of the domain, but then how can anything be true of it? For actualism, this is no problem at all. "o does not exist" is true in a world if and only if the essence of o is not exemplified in that world. "My older brother does not exist" means that no individual essence of an older brother of mine is exemplified.

Better hold the applause, however. Actualism is going to need a lot of individual essences – one for every possible person, and a lot more. It will need individual essences for every possible object, and maybe even for impossible objects. We might want to say that the round square does not exist in any possible world. The essence of round square is not exemplified in any possible world. All of these essences exist in the actual world, since everything that exists is actual. Isn't this just the sort of "metaphysical jungle" of essences that Quine claimed we'd be stuck with? Doesn't this merit an incredulous stare? Is actualism any more plausible than modal realism? Instead of existing alternative possible worlds and possible individuals, we have existing states of affairs and essences exemplified and unexemplified, all in the actual world. This seems just as distant from common sense and good reason as existing but nonactual worlds.

The actualist is likely to try regaining our credulity by pointing out that we accept all sorts of empires of abstract mathematical and geometrical objects. The set-theoretic levels of infinity quickly outstrip anything available to common sense or perception. (See *Background 5.3* – Infinite sets and the continuum hypothesis, p. 198.) For example, on the Euclidean line segment infinitely many points fit between any two points. Presumably, these Euclidean points exist in the actual world, if they exist at all. The cardinality of the set of points in a line segment is greater than the cardinality of the infinite integers, and so on. If we can accept such mathematical structures, why not abstract possible worlds including their contained essences, and so on?

Alas, unlike with possible worlds, we have methods of proof in mathematics, even if these do not answer every question. We can "see" more-or-less how mathematical objects are constructed and we have good intuitions much of the time, or at least we do if we spend the time to learn the systems. Furthermore, geometry and mathematics have indispensable practical applications. We have no such methods, intuitions, or applications, as Quine pointed out, regarding such objects as my possible older brother or brothers, or about any other individual essences exemplified or unexemplified. I, frankly, have no idea what property or properties *Socrateity* is or are.

Maybe it doesn't matter. Maybe all we need are vague ideas about these essences. Surely, I could have had an older brother; I can tell a plausible story. I might have good reasons for wanting to tell such a story. Maybe that is enough; and we should be grateful that Plantinga and other actualists have filled in the hairy details to make this metaphysically respectable. I am not willing to give up talking and thinking about what might have been, could have been, should have been, could not have been, and so on. One job of philosophers is to help us to comprehend the underlying logic, the commitments, and structure of such talk and thought. We have no reason to suppose that these are simple and commonsensical.

For me, Plantinga's version costs less than the modal realists' claim that my older brothers (and vastly many older brothers at that) exist concretely in some other space, but are not actual. I just can't buy that.

Transworld Identity and Identification

When we talk or think about Socrates or ourselves existing with different characteristics in other possible worlds how do we identify Socrates or ourselves there? I think to myself that I might have gone to business school instead of philosophy graduate school at Cornell. I might have become a stockbroker and made a bundle of money. I'd now be writing a book about how to avoid the coming market crash (for which I've been paid a huge advance) instead of a history of analytic philosophy. All of this is possible. In some possible world I am a wealthy retired stockbroker writing a bestseller about investing. How do I know this? Why do I believe it? More to the point here, since I certainly do believe it, how do I identify myself in those other possible worlds? I would have had a very different career, married a different woman, had different children (or maybe none), lived in a mansion in Scarsdale instead of a modest house in Ithaca, etc. etc. (Would I regret not having gone into teaching?) So different, yet me. Allowable possibilities are pretty extreme. I might have been an emperor of China or an arctic explorer. But the possibilities are limited. I could not, in any possible world, have been an emperor of China in 1500, or an arctic explorer in 1873. That would not have been me. Nor could I have been an alligator.

The problem of transworld identity becomes even more acute when we consider that in another possible world someone else has all of my obvious characteristics such as appearance, career, marriage, (but not children!), but is not me. What makes me me in those other possible worlds and makes him not me? How do we identify a very different me as me and identify another chap who looks and acts just like I actually look and act as not me?

One thing we know is that we do not identify individuals across worlds by any empirical method, since they are not observable. So one option we have is simply to avoid the problem by holding that no object exists in more than one world. Plantinga does not accept this option, but states the argument for it in order to dispute it.

(a)   (b)   (c)

Figure 6.1   (a) The author as a child in the mid-1940s. (b) The author as a young man in the late 1960s. (c) The author today.

> So, if it is intelligible to suppose that Socrates exists in more than one world, there must be some empirically manifest property that he and he alone has in each of the worlds in which he exists. Now obviously we do not know of any such property, or even that there is such a property. Indeed, it is hard to see how there *could* be such a property. But then the very idea of Transworld Identity is not really intelligible – in which case we must suppose that no object exists in more than one world. (Plantinga 1979a, p. 152)

In disputing this argument, Plantinga notes first that we also have the analogous problem of identifying individuals across time. Figures 6.1(a), (b), and (c) show pictures of me, the author: First as a tiny child in the mid-1940s, then as a grad student in the late 1960s, and now as a professor emeritus.

I could not recognize myself as an infant. We know no identifying empirical marks that a person carries throughout his life that we use for identification. (I have no idea about my DNA or even my fingerprints for that matter.) The actual identification or reidentification of a person can be highly contentious – Hitler, Elvis, etc. Yet we manage fine for the most part talking and thinking about the lives of people that span decades. We do the same in talking about alternative possibilities.

> Accordingly, the claim that I must be able somehow to identify Socrates in W – pick him out – is either trivial or based on a confusion. Of course, I must know which of the persons existing in W – the persons who would

have existed, had *W* been actual – I am talking about. But the answer, obviously, and trivially, is Socrates. To be able thus to answer, however, I need know nothing further about what Socrates would have been like had *W* been actual. (Plantinga 1979a, p. 154)

Individuals in other possible worlds must have the same individual essence as their actual selves. Whoever is me in other possible worlds must have my individual essence, whatever it is, and no other individual can have it in any world. We do not know, fully, the whole of an individual essence, but we can surmise a bit of it. This is why the possibilities are limited. I surmise that my essence, and yours, includes being human. Thus none of us is an alligator in any possible worlds. An alligator is, I also surmise, essentially an alligator. Thus in no possible world is your friendly pet alligator a human being. Further, I surmise that facts about DNA and parentage are essential to human beings (and alligators). Thus I could not have lived before my parents got together. When I say that in another possible world Aristotle dies as an infant, I am supposing that in that other possible world that very person – who actually was the founder of the discipline of logic and made many other monumental contributions to the founding of the Western tradition of science and philosophy and lived to be 62 years old – with his DNA, parentage, and birth facts, dies as an infant.

Of course, all of these metaphysical claims are disputable, as are claims about the temporal reidentification of individuals. The upshot, nevertheless, is that if individuals exist in alternative possible worlds, they must partake of their individual essence, known or unknown, and we can refer to them without knowing precisely what their essence is, and without being able to pick them out of a metaphysical lineup.

Kripke points out that we all learned about possible worlds in school when we did problems involving probabilities. We considered two dice and calculated the probability that two sixes would come up. "'Possible worlds' are little more than the miniworlds of school probability blown large" (Kripke 1980/1972, p. 18). Asking how we know that in that situation those dice would be the same objects as those in our hand would be crazy. In doing probability problems we stipulate the alternative possible situations and the objects in them.

'Possible worlds' are *stipulated*, not *discovered* by powerful telescopes. There is no reason why we cannot *stipulate* that, in talking about what would have happened to Nixon in a certain counterfactual situation, we are talking about what would have happened to *him*. (Kripke 1980/1972, p. 44)

Transworld identification is not a deep metaphysical puzzle.

> Don't ask: how can I identify this table in another possible world, except
> by its properties? I have the table in my hands, I can point to it, and
> when I ask whether *it* might have been in another room, I am talking,
> by definition, about *it*. I don't have to identify it after seeing it through a
> telescope. ... Some properties of an object may be essential to it, in that
> it could not have failed to have them. But these properties are not used
> to identify the object in another world, for such an identification is not
> needed. (Kripke 1980/1972, p. 53)

Thus Kripke and Plantinga, and many others, dismiss the problems
of transworld identity and identification as pseudo-problems. They rely
on our ability and willingness to stipulate alternative possible worlds.
When stipulating we do not need to, nor can we, stipulate the details
of entire worlds. We just describe the parts of them that we need for
our purposes and leave the rest unspecified. When I say that in an
alternative possible world I am a stockbroker, I assume that everything
else is pretty much the same as it is in the actual world except those
things connected with my being a stockbroker.

David Lewis, on the other hand, cannot take this relaxed way with
transworld issues. Indeed, the Lewisian modal realist is going to have
to accept the view, rejected by Plantinga and Kripke, that each concrete
object exists in only one possible world. (Leibniz also held that no
human being could exist in more than one possible world.) According
to Lewis, other possible worlds exist concretely and the ordinary spatial
objects in them also exist concretely. I cannot exist concretely in two
different worlds just as I cannot exist concretely at two separated places
at the same time. In any case, Lewis' view is that such a dual existence
is impossible if the objects are to differ in any way.

> If indeed Humphrey [Hubert Humphrey, Democratic presidential candi-
> date in 1968] – he himself, the whole of him – is to lead a double life as
> part of two different worlds, there is no intelligible way for his intrinsic
> properties [nonrelational properties such as size, shape, composition] to
> differ from one world to the other. (Lewis 1986, p. 201)

Instead of existing in other possible worlds, objects have counterparts
at other worlds, according to Lewis.

My counterpart at other worlds resembles me in certain crucial ways
but differs in various unessential features. To say that I could have
gone to business school instead of getting a PhD in philosophy means,

according to counterpart theory, that my counterpart (or counterparts) at another possible world goes to business school, etc. That other guy is not me but is very like me. Of course, he exists in only one possible world also. So I am likely to be his counterpart in this world.[3]

> Where some would say that you are in several worlds, in which you have somewhat different properties and somewhat different things happen to you, I prefer to say that you are in the actual world and no other, but you have counterparts in several other worlds. Your counterparts resemble you closely in content and context in important respects. They resemble you more closely than do the other things in their worlds. But they are not really you. For each of them is in his own world, and only you are here in the actual world. Indeed we might say, speaking casually, that your counterparts are you in other worlds, that they and you are the same; but this sameness is no more a literal identity than the sameness between you today and you tomorrow. It would be better to say that your counterparts are men you *would have been*, had the world been otherwise. (Lewis 1979/1968, pp. 111–12)

Thus, according to Lewis, when I ponder the 2000 election and think that if Nader had not run, Gore would have won, I am not precisely thinking about Nader and Gore. I am thinking about their counterparts in another world that is similar to the actual world except a person similar to actual Nader does not run, and no one like him does run, and a person similar to actual Gore wins.

Lewis' counterpart theory has several problems to face. Consider the thought that in some possible world Aristotle dies as an infant. This means that Aristotle's counterpart dies as an infant. Suppose in that world another fellow founds logic and does many of the things that Aristotle did, and even looks and acts like Aristotle, is Plato's pupil, etc. Which one is Aristotle's counterpart or are both his counterparts? The one who dies as an infant does not resemble the actual Aristotle very much, if we consider his entire lifespan. So the resemblance must consist merely in his counterpart DNA, birth facts, and parentage. When Lewis speaks of my counterpart resembling me more "closely than do the other things in their worlds," he has to explain how he construes resemblance. In order to accommodate all the differences from actuality that we think possible, no simple notion

---

[3] Not for sure, however. The counterpart relation is looser than identity. I have more than one counterpart in some other worlds and my other-worldly counterpart likewise has multiple counterparts in some worlds. The counterpart relation is also not symmetric, according to Lewis.

of resemblance is going to work. Lewis is going to have to appeal to unknown and unknowable essences just like the actualist. This is worse for Lewis, because he already has a much heavier ontological and plausibility burden. Perhaps Lewis can deal with this problem by bringing in multiple counterpart relations, but he has got a lot of explaining to do.

Another problem is that counterpart theory cannot explain the peculiar poignancy of counterfactual thought. I regret a few things that I could have done but didn't, and I'm sorry about or glad about things that I did do but might not have. These are thoughts about *me* in this and other possible worlds. Kripke asks why should I care about what someone else who resembles me does or doesn't do?

> The counterpart of something in another possible world is *never* identical with the thing itself. Thus if we say 'Humphrey might have won the election (if only he had done such-and-such)', we are not talking about something that might have happened to *Humphrey* but to someone else, a "counterpart". Probably, however, Humphrey could not care less whether someone *else*, no matter how much resembling him, would have been victorious in another possible world. Thus, Lewis's view seems to me even more bizarre than the usual notions of transworld identification that it replaces. (Kripke 1980/1972, p. 45)

Plantinga also takes this line against counterpart theory.

> Of course, the Counterpart Theorist will reply that Socrates – the Socrates of α [the actual world] – no doubt has unwise counterparts, which is sufficient for the truth that he could have been unwise. ... And how is that even relevant to the claim that Socrates himself – the Socrates of α – could have been unwise? There could have been a foolish person a lot like Socrates; how does this fact show that *Socrates* could have been unwise? ... No doubt there is a possible state of affairs including the existence of an unwise person who is similar to Socrates; but this fact is totally irrelevant to the truth that Socrates – Socrates himself – could have been unwise. (Plantinga 1974a, p. 116)

Lewis would reply that having an unwise counterpart is just what being possibly unwise means. Statements do not always wear their meanings on their faces, and that is certainly true of modal claims. Even so, the modal realist is still faced with the poignancy gap. The modal realist explanation of the meanings of modal thoughts and statements leaves facts about them unexplained.

Lewis is committed to counterpart theory, so any problems with it add to the already heavy costs of modal realism. Rejecting modal realism and its attendant counterpart theory has been the path that most analytic metaphysicians have taken.

The Modal Version of the Ontological Argument

The modal version of the ontological argument is a good example of an application of modal logic and possible worlds to a perennial philosophical issue. The ontological argument for the existence of God, originally formulated by Anselm about 1077, has been a battleground of philosophy ever since. [*Background 6.7* – The ontological argument] Those who embrace metaphysics and traditional rationalism tend to support the argument. Those who dismiss metaphysics and lean toward empiricism are keen to refute it. A lot is at stake. If the ontological argument is sound, it deductively proves the existence of God. The proof is a priori and would prove the existence of not just any old god, but the actual existence of God who is omnipotent, omniscient, perfectly benevolent, one, and so on. Many world-historical philosophers have offered updated versions – Descartes' and Spinoza's among the best known. Kant claimed to refute the argument.

According to Ryle, as we saw in Chapter 4, genuine metaphysics should have relevance to theological concerns. With the rebirth of metaphysics that occurred in analytic circles in the 1970s, we would expect a rebirth of that darling of metaphysics – the ontological argument. And indeed, it was dusted off, refurbished, and given a formal modal logical form by Plantinga.

Until recently, most analytic philosophers agreed that Kant's refutation was decisive. Kant argued that since existence is not a predicate, existence cannot be a great-making property or perfection. Existence is the ground of other properties but not itself a property. Modern logical theory supports this view. Existence is represented by quantifiers not predicates. To symbolize "Zebras exist" we would write "$\exists x Z x$." *Zebra* is the predicate, not *existence*. One of the virtues of symbolic logic, according to the logical positivists, is that it demystifies existence and thereby disposes of the ontological argument.

In an article published in 1965, Norman Malcolm claimed to descry a version of Anselm's argument that avoids Kant's refutation. Instead of predicating existence, this version of the ontological argument is based on predicating necessary existence of God. This is a modal version of the ontological argument that cannot be defused by first-order extensional quantificational logic.

> In other words, *necessary existence* is a perfection. His [Anselm's] first ontological proof uses the principle that a thing is greater if it exists than if it does not exist. His second proof employs the different principle that a thing is greater if it necessarily exists than if it does not necessarily exist. (Malcolm 1965, p. 142)

Malcolm notes, correctly, that if God exists necessarily, then God exists.

> The a priori proposition "God necessarily exists" entails the proposition "God exists," if and only if the latter also is understood as an a priori proposition: in which case the two propositions are equivalent. In this sense, Anselm's proof is a proof of God's existence. (Malcolm 1965, p. 147)

If we accept that necessary existence is a perfection or great-making property, and that God has all perfections or great-making properties to the maximum degree, then God exists necessarily. If God exists necessarily, then God exists. God is in the domain of the actual world. And thus God is actual, not merely possible.

Malcolm did not use formal modal logic or the possible worlds idiom – his article was a bit early for that – but Plantinga gives a formalized version. One problem with Malcolm's version is that if sound it proves that God exists in every possible world, but does not say anything about God's excellences in those worlds. God might, as far as Malcolm's version is concerned, be weak and stupid in the actual world. Plantinga is careful to make sure that his argument if sound establishes not just that God exists in every possible world, but that God has maximal perfections in every possible world.

According to Plantinga, and this is a stipulated definition, a being has maximal excellence in a world if and only if in that world the being is omnipotent, omniscient, and morally perfect. Here's another stipulated definition: A being has maximal greatness if and only if it has maximal excellence in every world. The argument can now be fully spelled out:

1. *There is a possible world W in which maximal greatness is instantiated.* (Basic premise.)
2. *Let G be the being who instantiates maximal greatness in W.* (Stipulation.)

3. *G has maximal excellence in every possible world.* (From 1, 2, and the definition of "maximal greatness.")
4. *G is omnipotent, omniscient, and perfectly good in every possible world.* (From 3 and the definition of "maximal excellence.")

Conclusion: *G is omnipotent, omniscient, and morally perfect in the actual world.* (From 4 and the fact that the actual world is a possible world.)

G's existence follows directly from the conclusion "for obviously a being can't be omnipotent (or for that matter omniscient or morally perfect) in a given world unless it *exists* in that world" (Plantinga 1974b, p. 108). Call G what you will, but G fits the job description of God.

Plantinga's modal version of the ontological argument depends on the uncontroversial S5 modal principle:

$$\Diamond \Box P \supset \Box P$$

And of course, $\Box P \supset P$.

In simpler terms, the modal version of the ontological argument is: If it is possible that God exists, then God exists. If it is possible that a necessary being who is omnipotent, etc. exists, then such a being exists. It is possible that God exists. Therefore, God exists.

Is this argument successful? Does it prove the existence of God? No. Not even Plantinga thinks it does. All that Plantinga claims for the argument is that it establishes the rational acceptability of belief in God – the rational acceptability of theism. Plantinga says that one might disbelieve (1), which is the crucial premise, but believing it is not irrational. So theism is not irrational.

Malcolm goes further in support of the argument, and I think he has got his finger on something that Plantinga missed.

> What Anselm has proved is that the notion of contingent existence or of contingent nonexistence cannot have any application to God. His existence must either be logically necessary or logically impossible. The only intelligible way of rejecting Anselm's claim that God's existence is necessary is to maintain that the concept of God, as a being greater than which cannot be conceived, is self-contradictory or nonsensical. (Malcolm 1965, p. 145)

The modal version of the ontological argument shifts the burden of proof. If the atheist wants to deny the existence of a being who has maximal greatness, he cannot simply claim that such a being happens not to exist. The atheist cannot claim that God is merely possible, but not actual. The atheist must demonstrate that maximal greatness cannot possibly be instantiated. The theist claims that God is at least possible. Then by modal logic and the definition of "God," God exists.

To my knowledge, no one has yet succeeded in demonstrating that the concept of God is impossible, self-contradictory, or nonsensical.

Background 6.1 – The modal system S5

The modal system S5 is the one most commonly in use. It includes the other S systems. In S5 all modal truths are necessary. Thus $\Diamond P \supset \Box \Diamond P$ is the characteristic principle of S5. Also $\Diamond \Box P \supset \Box P$ and $\Box P \supset \Diamond \Box P$ are principles of S5. In S5 iterated modalities are irrelevant. Only the innermost one matters. So e.g. $\Diamond \Diamond \Box \Diamond \Box P$ is equivalent to $\Box P$.

Background 6.2 – Material mode versus formal mode and semantic ascent

According to Carnap the material mode of speech is about things, properties, etc. whereas the formal mode of speech is about nouns, adjectives, etc. The material mode is confusing and has led to philosophical paralysis, whereas putting the questions into the formal mode enables us to make progress. Here is a famous example of Carnap's from his 1934 classic *The Logical Syntax of Language* in which he introduced the distinction between material mode and formal mode.

25a. A *thing* is a complex of sense-data. [Material mode of speech.]
25b. Every sentence in which a thing-designation occurs is equipollent to [has the same content as] a class of sentences in which no thing-designations but sense-data designations occur. [Formal mode.]

26a.   A thing is a complex of atoms.
26b.   Every sentence in which a thing-designation occurs is equipol-
       lent to a sentence in which space-time co-ordinates and certain
       descriptive functors (of physics) occur.

Suppose that a positivist maintains thesis 25a., and a realist thesis
26a. Then an endless dispute will arise over the pseudo-question
of what a thing actually is. If we transfer to the formal mode of
speech, it is in this case possible to reconcile the two theses. ...
For the various possibilities of translating a thing-sentence into
an equipollent sentence are obviously not incompatible with one
another. *The controversy between positivism and realism is an idle dispute
about pseudo-theses which owes its origin entirely to the use of the material
mode of speech.* (Carnap 1937, p. 301)

Quine approves of a similar move which he calls semantic ascent.

Yet we do recognize a shift from talk of objects to talk of words. ...
How can we account for this? Amply, I think, by proper account
of a useful and much used manoeuvre which I shall call *semantic
ascent*.

It is the shift from talk of miles to talk of 'mile'. It is what leads
from the material mode into the formal mode, to invoke an old
terminology of Carnap's. It is the shift from talking in certain terms
to talking about them. It is precisely the shift that Carnap thinks
of as divesting philosophical questions of a deceptive guise and
setting them forth in their true colors. But this tenet of Carnap's
is the part that I do not accept. Semantic ascent, as I speak of it,
applies anywhere. ... But it does happen that semantic ascent is
more useful in philosophical connections than in most. ... (Quine
1960, pp. 271–2)

An interesting exercise for the reader would be to go through this
book and count how often analytic philosophers have adopted the
formal mode in preference to the material mode in expounding
their views.

Background 6.3 – Essence versus accident

General essences or quiddities are essences of kinds. Individual essences or haecceities are essences of individuals. An essence of a kind is a property or conjunction of properties that an individual must have in order to be a member of the kind. Also nothing but members of the kind can have that general essence. The having of the general essence of a kind is what makes individuals be members of the kind. For some kinds we can state the essences. These are definitions of the corresponding general terms. For example, an individual is a grandmother if and only if she is the mother of a parent. For natural kinds, especially biological kinds, the essences are not always easy to state. Wittgenstein, with his notion of family resemblances, was denying that ordinary kinds have general essences.

Individual essences are properties or conjunctions of properties that an individual must have in order to be that individual. Nothing else can have that individual essence. An individual cannot fail to have its individual essence. The having of the individual essence of me makes me me. Each individual must have its essence in every world in which it exists. The nature of individual essences is controversial. I have no idea what my individual essence is nor do I have any idea what anybody else's is either. Kripke claimed that an individual's origins are essential to it. No qualitative properties could be essential to an individual, because these could all be different in different possible worlds, and for a qualitative property or set of properties that I have, there is a possible world in which some other individual has those properties. However, nobody else could have exactly my origin. Thus the sperm and egg from which an animal is formed are essential to it. The block of wood out of which a table is formed is essential to it. From this, it follows that for a biological organism, membership in its natural kind is essential to it. If this is right, then I am essentially a human being. My daughter's cat Pumpkin is essentially a cat, but only contingently or accidentally her pet. Pumpkin might have been someone else's pet, but he could not have been a rhinoceros.

Background 6.4 – Identity of indiscernibles, substitutivity, referential opacity, and more on extensional versus intensional

Two principles: If x = y, then every property of x is a property of y and vice versa. This is uncontroversial and is called the principle of the indiscernibility of identicals. Leibniz's Law or the identity of indiscernibles is if every property of x is a property of y and v.v. then x = y. Note that "=" here means identity. 2 = the only even prime number.

If x = y, then any name or description of x should be substitutable for any name or description of y without changing truth-value. In some contexts this does not hold. I might believe that the number of houses of Congress equals 2, but not believe that the number of the houses of Congress equals the only even prime number. Contexts in which equivalent terms are not substitutable without possibly affecting the truth-value are called intensional contexts, or non-extensional contexts. (There's a technical difference that need not delay us.) According to Quine, such contexts are referentially opaque. Terms do not have their standard reference in intensional contexts. Notions that set up intensional contexts are called intensional notions or entities. For example, meanings are intensional. The meaning of "2" is different from the meaning of "the only even prime number" but the reference is the same. Extensionalists such as Quine are suspicious of intensional contexts and entities, because they cannot be handled by first-order predicate logic. Extensionalists do not like meaning but are fond of reference.

To the chagrin of extensionalists, much work has been done by formal logicians in developing intensional logics. Modal contexts are intensional.

Background 6.5 – The ship of Theseus

The ship of Theseus is a famous philosophical puzzle. A ship's parts are replaced with similar parts, one by one, over several years until none of the original parts remains. Is the ship at the end, when every part has been replaced, the same ship or a different ship? If you say it is a different ship, then you are obligated to state at which exact point the old ship ceases to exist and the new one comes into existence. Presumably there is no nonarbitrary such point. If you say it is the same ship, wait a minute! I forgot to tell you that the all the pieces were saved in a warehouse after they were replaced. We now put all these pieces together and form a ship. Isn't this the original ship? But there cannot be two of them.

This puzzle is meant to show that criteria of identity are murky when parts are being continuously replaced.

Background 6.6 – Abstract versus concrete

These are technical terms in philosophy. A concrete object exists in time and space. It has spatial and temporal properties. An abstract object (if there are any) does not. For example, numbers are usually thought to be abstract, whereas tables and chairs are concrete. Perhaps, some objects exist only in time but not in space, e.g. thoughts. These are also usually considered to be abstract or semi-abstract.

Background 6.7 – The ontological argument (Note: There's another *Background* on the ontological argument at the end of Chapter 2)

There are many different versions of the ontological argument. (There is no special significance to the term "ontological" in this context. Arguments for the existence of God are divided by scholars into three different types – ontological, cosmological, and teleological.)

Anselm's original version of his ontological argument is an argument by contradiction.

(1) *God is that than which none greater can be conceived.* (By definition)
(2) *Suppose God exists in the understanding but not in reality.* (Assumption for the contradiction)
(3) *It is greater to exist in both the understanding and reality, than it is to exist in the understanding alone.* (Basic premise)
(4) *If God exists in the understanding alone but not in reality than we can conceive of a greater being than God, namely something that is like God in the understanding but also exists in reality.* (From 3)
(5) *Thus we could conceive of something that is greater than that which none greater can be conceived.* (From 4)
(6) *Thus the assumption that God exists in the understanding but not in reality leads to a contradiction.* (From 5)
    Conclusion: *Thus God does not exist in the understanding alone, but also exists in reality.* (From 6).

Controversy has swirled over what if anything this proves or was intended to prove. Does it, if sound, prove that God exists, or only that we cannot conceive of God not existing once we understand that God is a maximal being?

Descartes gave a simpler version:

(1) *God has all perfections.* (By definition.)
(2) *Existence is a perfection.* (Basic premise.)
    Conclusion: *God exists.* (From 1 and 2.)

Further Reading

There are several textbooks on modal logic and related intensional logics. The one that I found most useful is *An Introduction to Modal Logic* by G. E. Hughes and M. J. Cresswell (Methuen 1968).

A textbook devoted to possible worlds is *Possible Worlds: An Introduction to Logic and its Philosophy* by Raymond Bradley and Norman Swartz (Hackett 1979).

Michael Loux's introduction is an informative essay covering the topics of his anthology *The Possible and the Actual: Readings in the Metaphysics of Modality* (Cornell 1979). This anthology contains articles by Lewis, Plantinga, and Stalnaker cited in this chapter.

Reference and Modality (Oxford 1971) edited by Leonard Linsky is a very useful collection that contains classic articles on the topics of this chapter, including Kripke's seminal "Semantical Considerations on Modal Logic."

The Ontological Argument: From St. Anselm to Contemporary Philosophers (Doubleday 1965) edited by Plantinga contains many key historical and contemporary sources.

7

Naming, Necessity, and Natural Kinds: Kripke, Putnam, and Donnellan

An important class, philosophically as well as linguistically, is the class of general names associated with natural kinds – *that is, with classes of things that we regard as of explanatory importance; classes whose normal distinguishing characteristics are "held together" or even explained by deep-lying mechanisms. Gold, lemon, tiger, acid, are examples of such nouns. I want to begin this paper by suggesting that (1)* traditional *theories of meaning radically falsify the properties of such words; (2) logicians like Carnap do little more than formalize these traditional theories, inadequacies and all . . . In Austin's happy phrase, what we have been given by philosophers, logicians, and "semantic theorists" alike, is a "myth-eaten description." (Putnam 1977b/1970, pp. 102–3)*

Introduction

The developments in modal logic and the consequent interest in possible worlds metaphysics were reflected in the philosophy of language. And developments in the philosophy of language affected ideas in analytic metaphysics.

The most exciting advances were due to work by Saul Kripke, Hilary Putnam, and Keith Donnellan in the theory of reference. Their insights were truly revolutionary, because they rejected and replaced the old

A Brief History of Analytic Philosophy: From Russell to Rawls, First Edition. Stephen P. Schwartz.
© 2012 John Wiley & Sons, Inc. Published 2012 by John Wiley & Sons, Inc.

traditional theory of reference that had been assumed and accepted by all analytic philosophers from Frege on – until Kripke and Putnam and others dismantled it in the early 1970s. The new theory of reference is simple and compelling, and challenged many hitherto undisputed planks of the analytic program that had been inherited from traditional philosophy. Proponents of the new theory argued convincingly that names and many general terms refer without the mediation of descriptions, that identity statements such as "Tully is Cicero" are necessary, if true, but not analytic, and most astonishingly that many interesting scientific identities and general claims are synthetic but necessarily true and discovered a posteriori. The new theory thus gave support to the essentialism inherent in quantified modal logic and the possible worlds interpretation of modality, and in turn received support from it. This is an example of genuinely fruitful interaction between metaphysics and philosophy of language.

The most important influence in the emergence of the new theory of reference was Kripke's brilliant and seminal *Naming and Necessity* (Kripke 1980/1972). Other major contributions were Putnam's "The Meaning of 'Meaning'" (Putnam 1975c) and Donnellan's "Reference and Definite Descriptions" (Donnellan 1977/1966).

The Traditional Theory of Meaning and Reference

Before looking in more detail at the new theory of reference, we should review the main features of the traditional theory, many of which should be familiar.

Putnam describes the heart of the traditional theory:

> On the traditional view, the meaning of say, "lemon," is given by specifying a conjunction of *properties*. For each of these properties, the statement "lemons have the property P" is an analytic truth; and if $P_1, P_2, \ldots, P_n$ are all of the properties in the conjunction, then "anything with all of the properties $P_1, \ldots, P_n$ is a lemon" is likewise an analytic truth. (Putnam 1977a/1970, p. 103)

The conjunction of properties associated with a term such as "lemon" is the intension of the term "lemon." (See *Background 5.5* – Intension and extension and the problem of non-extensional contexts, p. 199.) This intension determines what it is to be a lemon. Thus according to traditional theories, intension determines extension. To understand a term such as "lemon" is to know the intension. This is the concept of lemon. The concept of lemon determines the necessary and sufficient conditions for being a lemon. "[T]he concept corresponding to a term was just a conjunction of predicates, and . . . the concept corresponding to a term must *always* provide a necessary and sufficient condition for falling into the extension of the term" (Putnam 1977b/1973, pp. 119–20). Carnap espoused a version of the traditional theory because for him "the concept corresponding to a term provided (in the ideal case, where the term had 'complete meaning') a *criterion* for belonging to the extension (not just in the sense of 'necessary and sufficient condition,' but in the strong sense of way of recognizing whether a given thing falls into the extension or not)" (Putnam 1977b/1973, p. 120).

Because of the difficulty of specifying necessary and sufficient conditions for many terms, according to more recent modifications of the traditional theory, a cluster of properties is associated with such terms rather than a strict conjunction. We cannot define "game" by a conjunction of properties such as having a winner and a loser, being entertaining, involving the gaining and losing of points, because some perfectly acceptable games lack some of these features. According to the cluster theory, something is a game because it has enough features from a cluster of properties like these. A cluster theorist would claim that there need not be any property in the cluster that is sufficient for the application of the term, but the cluster taken as a whole determines the extension of the term. Wittgenstein's position that there are only family resemblances among the individuals in the extensions of many ordinary terms is a version of the cluster theory.

The central features of the traditional theory of meaning, then, are the following: 1) Each meaningful term has some meaning, concept, intension, or cluster of features associated with it. This meaning is known or present to the mind when the term is understood. 2) The meaning determines the extension in the sense that something is in the extension of the term if and only if it has the characteristics included in the meaning, concept, intension, or, in the case of the cluster theory, enough of the features. 3) Analytic truths are based on the meanings of terms. Furthermore, beginning with David Hume and continuing to the logical positivists and beyond, all necessity was construed as analyticity or somehow based on linguistic conventions. *De re* modality was rejected, as was any sort of extra-linguistic necessity. The intension of a term was taken to be the essence of the kind of thing named. Since the conjunction of properties associated with "lemon" tells us what it is to be a lemon, and generates necessary truths about lemons, it is the essence of lemon. A cluster theorist would, of course, deny that there are essences of this sort, since there need be no property shared by all and only members of the extension of some term. Still, the cluster when taken together is a sort of essence. This is what Wittgenstein means when he states *"Essence* is expressed by grammar" (Wittgenstein 2009/1953, p. 123e).

Traditional theorists extended their treatment to ordinary proper names. Kripke focused on proper names first in order to undermine the traditional theory and then applied his results to general terms. The traditional theory is far less plausible when applied to proper names. Nevertheless it reigned unopposed, largely because no one could think of an alternative – until Kripke that is.

According to traditional conjunction theorists and cluster theorists, each meaningful proper name has associated with it a set of descriptions. The unique thing that satisfies the descriptions or, in the case of the cluster theorist, enough of the descriptions, is the referent of the name. When one uses a name, the intended referent is determined by the descriptions that are associated with the name being used. As examples of philosophers who embraced the traditional conjunction theory applied to proper names, Kripke cites Russell and Frege, whereas he mentions Wittgenstein and Searle as examples of cluster theorists. Here is Russell on proper names:

> The name 'Romulus' is not really a name but a sort of truncated description. It stands for a person who did such-and-such things, who killed Remus, and founded Rome, and so on. It is short for that description; if you like, it is short for 'the person who was called "Romulus"'. (Russell 1959b/ 1924, p. 243)

According to Russell, all of the so-called proper names of our common language are disguised descriptions.

Just as with general terms, the conjunction or cluster of identifying descriptions associated with a name generates necessary truths. If part of what we mean by "Aristotle" is "the teacher of Alexander," then "Aristotle is the teacher of Alexander" is a necessary truth. Although the cluster theorists reject the claim that any one description is necessary of Aristotle, Searle still holds that there are necessary truths about Aristotle generated by the cluster associated with the name "Aristotle."

> To put the same point differently, suppose we ask, "Why do we have proper names at all?" Obviously to refer to individuals. "Yes, but descriptions could do that for us." But only at the cost of specifying identity conditions every time reference is made: suppose we agree to drop "Aristotle" and use, say, "the teacher of Alexander", then it is a necessary truth that the man referred to is Alexander's teacher – but it is a contingent fact

that Aristotle ever went into pedagogy (though I am suggesting that it is a necessary fact that Aristotle has the logical sum, inclusive disjunction, of properties commonly attributed to him). (Searle 1963, p. 160)

Carnap, Searle, and Wittgenstein have held or expressed the traditional theory of reference. While they have differed about some of the details, they did not feel compelled to defend the foundations of the theory. Most have just taken for granted that some version of the conjunction or cluster theory is true. Most empiricists such as Berkeley, Hume, Mill, and the logical positivists have held the traditional theory, at least about common nouns. Among analytic philosophers of language, the traditional theory was still going through more elaborate and technical modifications when Kripke, Putnam, and Donnellan put all of that in doubt.

Kripke's and Donnellan's Criticism of the Traditional Theory: Names and Descriptions

The developments in modal logic and possible world semantics were already beginning to undermine the traditional analysis of necessity, since they indulged in *de re* modalities and needed real extra-linguistic essences. But more was to come.

The boldness of the new theory of reference is that it is no mere refinement. It is a complete rejection of the foundations and superstructure of the traditional theories of meaning and reference. In opposition to the traditional theory, Kripke and Donnellan demonstrated that proper names refer independently of identifying descriptions.

One of Donnellan's major contributions was to show that reference can take place not only in the absence of identifying descriptions but even when the identifying descriptions associated with the name do not correctly apply to the individual to whom the name refers. In "Reference and Definite Descriptions" he makes this point about certain uses of definite descriptions. Donnellan distinguishes between two kinds of use for definite descriptions – the attributive and the referential. When using a definite description attributively, the speaker intends to be saying something about whoever or whatever fits a certain description, without necessarily having any idea who or what fits the description. With the referential use, the speaker has independently a definite idea whom or what he means to be speaking about and uses the description to refer to that individual. A referential description is simply a tool for accomplishing the reference and may succeed in doing this even if the thing referred to fails to fit the description.

Consider the use of "Smith's Murderer" in the following two cases.

> Suppose first that we come upon poor Smith foully murdered. From the brutal manner of the killing and the fact that Smith was the most lovable person in the world, we might exclaim, "Smith's murderer is insane." I will assume, to make it a simpler case, that in a quite ordinary sense we do not know who murdered Smith ... This, I shall say, is an attributive use of the definite description.

On the other hand,

> Suppose that Jones has been charged with Smith's murder and has been placed on trial. Imagine that there is a discussion of Jones's odd behavior at his trial. We might sum up our impression of his behavior by saying, "Smith's murderer is insane." If someone asks to whom we are referring, by using this description, the answer here is "Jones." This, I shall say, is a referential use of the definite description. (Donnellan 1977/1966, pp. 46–7).

With the referential use of "Smith's Murderer" the speaker is referring to Jones even if it later turns out that he is innocent.[1]

Donnellan's point is vital, because it shows that descriptions do not always just refer to whoever or whatever happens to fit them. When we use a description referentially, we do not mean to be referring to whoever happens to fit it. Rather, we have a definite individual in mind. Likewise, when we use a name, we are not referring to whoever happens to fit some set of descriptions, although we may believe that the person, place, or thing named does fit the descriptions. When we use a name, we use it, like a referential description, to refer to some definite individual, independently of whether or not she fits some descriptions. Donnellan points out that if names are used attributively, that is, if they refer to whoever fits the identifying descriptions associated with them, then we get certain paradoxical results. For example, if a name such as "Thales" refers to whoever fits the identifying description "the philosopher who held that all is water," then if no one in fact held this view, we must say that Thales did not exist. But then, Donnellan asks, "to whom were Aristotle and Herodotus referring? Surely we cannot

---

[1] Donnellan notes that both Russell's and Strawson's theories of definite descriptions are incorrect if his distinction is valid. "I conclude, then, that neither Russell's nor Strawson's theory represents a correct account of the use of definite descriptions – Russell's because it ignores altogether the referential use, Strawson's because it fails to make the distinction between the referential and the attributive and mixes together truths about each (together with some things that are false)" (Donnellan 1977/1966, p. 58).

conclude 'to no one'. It seems to me to make sense that we should discover that Thales was after all a well-digger and that Aristotle and Herodotus were deceived about what he did" (Donnellan 1972, p. 374). Thus, we can refer to Thales by using the name "Thales" even though, perhaps, the only description we can supply is false of him.

Kripke makes the same point about names and in addition claims that they are rigid designators. "Rigid designator" is a term coined by Kripke to mean a designator, such as a name or description, that refers to the same individual with respect to every possible world in which that individual exists. If a name is a rigid designator, then it refers to the same individual when used to describe counterfactual situations as it does when used to describe the actual world. This means that a name will refer to the same individual whether or not she satisfies some list of commonly associated descriptions. In other possible worlds or possible counterfactual situations, an individual need have only those properties, if any, that are essential to her. As we have seen, the traditional theory of proper names entails that at least some combination of the things ordinarily believed of Aristotle are necessarily true of him. When considered carefully, however, this idea is doubtful. We cannot accept that, for example, Aristotle was necessarily a philosopher, necessarily a teacher of Alexander, necessarily a pupil of Plato, and so on. Contrary to Searle's account, not even a cluster or disjunction of common beliefs about Aristotle are necessary of him. Aristotle, that very man, might have died in a plague that swept his land when he was an infant. His dying thus would have been a great loss to humanity, but it is one of those things that given the proper conditions could have happened.

> There is a certain theory, perhaps popular in some views of the philosophy of history, which might both be deterministic and yet at the same time assign a great role to the individual in history. ... According to such a view it will be necessary, once a certain individual is born, that he is destined to perform various great tasks and so it will be part of the very nature of Aristotle that he should have produced ideas which had a great influence on the Western world. Whatever the merits of such a view may be as a view of history or the nature of great men, it does not seem that it should be trivially true on the basis of a theory of proper names. It would seem that it's a contingent fact that Aristotle ever did *any* of the things commonly attributed to him today, *any* of these great achievements that we so much admire. (Kripke 1980/1972, pp. 74–5)

Since it is not necessarily true of Aristotle, that is, it is not true of Aristotle in every world in which he exists, that he was a philosopher, taught Alexander, or did any, all, or any combination of things usually asserted of him, none of these properties are essential to Aristotle. Aristotle is Aristotle whether or not he satisfies some set of descriptions such as "is a philosopher," "taught Alexander," and so on. Thus, the name "Aristotle" if it is rigid refers to that man independently of his satisfying any of the descriptions commonly associated with "Aristotle."

Other evidence brought against the traditional theory of proper names is that we could discover about some individual that few or none of the things commonly believed about him are true in the actual world. For example, we could discover that Shakespeare was not the author of those plays attributed to him, was not even literate, as indeed some have claimed. We could discover of Gödel that he was not the one who discovered what is now called Gödel's proof, that he was not a mathematician, and that some huge fraud had been perpetrated. If the traditional theory were correct and names were not rigid designators, that is, if they referred to whoever or whatever fit certain descriptions commonly associated with them, then "Gödel" would refer to whoever discovered Gödel's proof, and "Shakespeare" to whoever was the author of *Hamlet, Othello*, etc., and thus it would be contradictory to suppose that we could discover that Shakespeare did not write those plays or that Gödel did not discover Gödel's proof. Of course, such a discovery is not likely given the evidence to the contrary, but it is not ruled out simply by the semantics of proper names.

Furthermore, I do not need to know any uniquely referring descriptions in order to use a name to refer to its bearer. What do I know about David Beckham? Not much. He's a soccer star, he's British, I believe, and plays for a team in Spain. These are not unique features of Beckham. He's probably the only soccer star named "Beckham," but maybe not. Nevertheless, I can refer to Beckham using his name. In fact, I just did. I could also discover that some or all of the things I believe about Beckham are in fact false. And is Russell even correct that Romulus was really called "Romulus"? Hasn't the name gone through an evolution of spelling and pronunciation, so that our name is a distant relative of the original, which was no doubt different?

If names are rigid, as Kripke claims, then identities in which both terms are names are necessarily true. Previous to Kripke, philosophers had held that such identities as "The Morning Star is the Evening Star" or "Hesperus is Phosphorus" and "Tully is Cicero" are contingent.[2] According to Kripke, if "Tully" and "Cicero" are rigid, and if the

---

[2] A notable exception is Ruth Barcan Marcus who held on the basis of her formal work in modal logic that such identities must be necessary if true. This predated Kripke's work.

identity "Tully is Cicero" is true, then it is necessarily true and not contingent. If "Tully" and "Cicero" are rigid and both refer to the same individual in the actual world, then since rigid designators refer to the same individual in all possible worlds, there will be no world in which "Tully" refers to an individual other then Cicero. This means that the identity "Tully is Cicero" is true in all worlds in which Tully exists, and thus it is necessarily true. According to Kripke, an identity statement that involves only rigid designators will be necessarily true, if it is true at all. Identity statements with nonrigid designators will generally be contingent. For example, the fact that the inventor of bifocals was the first postmaster general is contingent.

The reason that most philosophers have been led to believe that such identities as "Hesperus is Phosphorus" and "Tully is Cicero" are contingent is that they are not analytic. That Hesperus (the Morning Star) is Phosphorus (the Evening Star) was an empirical discovery. Surely, that these are the same celestial object is not a priori.

Kripke is willing to admit, and in fact insists, that the identities mentioned are not analytic or a priori. In spite of this, he holds that they are necessarily true. Kripke claims that most recent and contemporary philosophers have failed to distinguish the metaphysical notion of necessity from the epistemological notion of a prioricity and the linguistic notion of analyticity. If "necessarily true" means true in all possible worlds and a priori means knowable independently of experience, then we are talking about two different notions, and their extensions need not be the same. In fact, Kripke claims that "Hesperus is Phosphorus" is necessarily true but is neither a priori nor analytic. Of course, the claim that there can be synthetic necessary propositions was startling to most analytic philosophers at the time.

Kripke's distinguishing between necessity – a metaphysical notion – and a prioricity – an epistemological notion – and those two and analyticity – a linguistic notion – is one of the great landmarks of analytic philosophy. Not only did Kripke distinguish among the notions, but he also showed why some claims are necessary but neither a priori nor analytic. Kripke also argued convincingly that many scientific identities and generalizations are necessary and a posteriori. (Kripke also offered examples of claims that are a priori but contingent.)

Natural Kind Terms

In the controversy with the traditional theory of meaning, the second major feature of the new theory of reference is the extension of the insights about proper names to common nouns, and in particular to nouns standing for natural kinds like "gold," "water," and "tiger." According to Kripke, such nouns are like proper names in that they are rigid designators. If "gold" is a rigid designator, then it always refers to the same stuff independently of the stuff's superficial phenomenal properties. Furthermore, what gold is cannot be analytically specified by some list of properties, for no matter how much the properties of something resemble what we take to be the superficial properties of gold, the stuff would not be gold unless it was the same kind of substance that is rigidly designated by "gold." The reference of "gold" would be determined by an underlying trait, such as atomic number, that is discovered empirically. That gold is the element with atomic number 79 is an empirical hypothesis, but if this hypothesis is correct then "gold" rigidly designates the element with atomic number 79. Anything else is not gold no matter how much it resembles gold.

Being yellow is just the sort of property that a traditional theorist would include in the definition of "gold." Accordingly, "gold is yellow" would be analytic. Kripke argues, however, that such a statement is not analytic. We could discover that gold is not yellow in the actual world. In order to imagine such a discovery, we can suppose that we have all been victim of massive illusions, or some such thing. Such a supposition is outlandish, but the situation is not impossible. One well-known example, due to Putnam, to illustrate the fact that such statements about natural kinds are synthetic, is his example of the robot cats. We can imagine discovering that all the cats are robots sent from Mars to spy on us. Since this is conceivable, statements such as "cats are animals" are not analytic. A less outlandish example was the discovery that "whales are fish" is false, and thus not analytic. If such statements about natural kinds are not analytic, then we cannot specify the meaning of natural kind terms by conjunctions of properties. That examples of the kind in question have the properties that they do is a matter of nature, not language.

According to the traditional theory, the concept associated with a term functions like the set of identifying descriptions supposedly associated with an ordinary proper name. The new theory of reference holds that the descriptions, if any, associated with a natural kind term do not have a decisive role in deciding whether the term applies in a given case. At best, the descriptions associated with such a term are a handy guide in picking out things of the kind named, but the descriptions do not determine what it is to be of the kind. Its atomic structure determines whether some stuff is gold. Likewise, water is H_2O. Some stuff is water only if it has the right chemical structure. Biological kinds are determined by genetic structures or some other natural properties discovered by biologists, and other natural kinds are similarly determined by underlying traits.

Putnam has had the most important influence in the application of the new ideas on reference to natural kind terms. He holds that water, for example, is H_2O in all possible worlds. Thus, water is necessarily H_2O. This means that anything that is not H_2O is not water, even if it satisfies some list of superficial features that we think characterize water. Thus, a liquid could be clear, colorless, tasteless, etc., and still not be water, if it is not H_2O.

Putnam argues for this position by using his device of Twin Earth. Twin Earth is just like earth except that the lakes and rivers of Twin Earth are filled with some complicated chemical, XYZ, that exactly mimics the superficial properties of H_2O. Such a planet is certainly possible.[3]

> Suppose, now, that I discover the microstructure of water – that water is H_2O. At this point I will be able to say that the stuff on Twin Earth that I earlier *mistook* for water isn't really water. In the same way, if you describe, not another planet in the actual universe, but another possible universe in which there is stuff with the chemical formula XYZ which passes the "operational test" for *water*, we shall have to say that that stuff isn't water but merely XYZ. You will not have described a possible world in which "water is XYZ," but merely a possible world in which there are lakes of XYZ, people drink XYZ (and not water), or whatever. (Putnam 1977b/1973, p. 30)

Thus water is H_2O in all possible worlds, because nothing would count as a possible world in which some stuff that was not H_2O was water. An example offered by Kripke that reinforces Putnam's point is that of fool's gold. Iron pyrite looks and behaves in many ways like gold, but it is not gold, because it is not the element with atomic number 79. People think of natural kinds in this way. I want my wedding ring to be gold, not just something that looks like gold.[4] The ordinary language philosophers who claimed that the ordinary

---

[3]   If this seems too bizarre, I recall that years ago the product Sugar Twin was advertised as: "It looks like sugar, it tastes like sugar, it measures like sugar."

[4]   "Gold should mean gold. In fact, what these distributors and retailers were selling was nothing more than fool's gold. Without expert training or testing equipment, there is no way for consumers to know whether gold jewelry is real or not" Eliot Spitzer, Attorney General of New York State as quoted in *The Ithaca Journal* ("Rochester jeweler fined for 'fool's gold'") November 23, 2001.

uses and applications of a term determine the extension of a term had their ordinary language wrong. Kripke and Putnam have a better grip on our linguistic intuitions, at least about names and natural kind terms.

Satisfying some descriptions analytically associated with the natural kind terms does not make some liquid water or some metal gold. The having of a particular chemical nature makes water water or gold gold. We have seen that an imposter substance does not have a right to the name "water" just because it superficially resembles water; likewise, some stuff might still be water although it does not resemble other bodies of water, as long as it is H_2O.

> On the other hand if this substance [H_2O] can take another form such as the polywater allegedly discovered in the Soviet Union, with very different identifying marks from that of what we now call water – it is a form of water because it is the same substance, even though it doesn't have the appearances by which we originally identified water.[5] (Kripke 1980/1972, p. 323)

If Kripke's and Putnam's views are correct, the conjunction or cluster of descriptions associated with some natural kind term is neither necessary nor sufficient for the application of the term. What, then, is the role of the descriptions that are commonly associated with natural kind terms? Kripke distinguishes between fixing the reference of a term and giving its definition. When we fix the reference of a term, we give a description that helps the hearer pick out what we have in mind. Thus, for example, when teaching someone the meaning of color words, I may say: "By green we mean the color of that car over there." The description "the color of that car over there" is meant to fix the reference of "green," not give its meaning in the sense of supplying a synonym for "green." I did not mean that "green" is defined as whatever color that car over there happens to be. If I had meant this, then if someone painted that car a different color, say red, then "green" would refer to red, since that happened, then, to be the color of the car. When I fix the reference of a term, I give a description that is to be taken as giving the referent of the term, not the meaning in the traditional sense. I have a definite kind of thing in mind when I use the term, and now I want to help the audience pick it out. The descriptions associated with natural kind

---

[5] Polywater turned out to be a myth. There's no such stuff – but there might have been. In any case, we get Kripke's point. Tropical islanders might have been astonished to learn that ice is water.

terms function to fix the reference of the terms, not give their meanings. The traditional theorists assumed that descriptions given in connection with natural kind terms were defining the term, in the sense that anything satisfying the description falls in the extension of the term. According to Kripke, such descriptions are typically meant only to fix the reference.

We have seen that Kripke and Putnam hold that water is necessarily H_2O. H_2O is the nature of water. H_2O is the essence of water. "Water" rigidly designates H_2O, regardless of the superficial properties the H_2O may or may not have. The crucial point is "water is H_2O" is necessarily true, assuming it is true, but it is not analytic. Kripke and Putnam are not proposing to replace ordinary definitions with scientific ones so that instead of defining water as a clear, colorless liquid, we define it as H_2O. "Note that on the present view, scientific discoveries of species essence do not constitute a 'change of meaning'; the possibility of such discoveries was part of the original enterprise" (Kripke 1980/1972, p. 138). One would come closer to the position of Kripke and Putnam if one simply said that "water" has no definition at all, at least in the traditional sense, and is a proper name of a specific kind of substance.

"Water is H_2O" and "Gold is an element" are not analytic. For one thing, they could each turn out to be false. We could discover that there are certain fundamental errors in our chemical theories, or some such thing, and that water is some other complicated chemical compound. The same kind of thing could happen with gold. Since there is a possibility of such an error, the statements are not analytic. But now we seem to have a conundrum: How can a proposition be necessarily true and possibly false? It can't. If we are being most accurate, we must say that water is necessarily H_2O, if it is H_2O. If our theories are correct and there is no error and water is in fact H_2O, then it is necessarily H_2O. Our certainty that water is H_2O is the certainty of a well-established empirical theory, not the certainty that issues from knowledge of a definition; it is not analytic, but if it is true, it is necessary. This means that if water is H_2O, then we have an example of a necessary a posteriori synthetic proposition.

To help make this clear, we must distinguish between metaphysical modalities and epistemic modalities. Often modal terms such as "may," "might," "might not," "could," etc. are used to indicate the state of our knowledge or ignorance, rather than claims about metaphysical necessity or possibility. If I say, for example, that Goldbach's Conjecture might turn out to be false, I am expressing my ignorance of its truth-value.[6] In any newspaper or health website many statements are guarded with modal terms. "Yogurt may offer protection against cancer." We are all familiar with such statements. This does not mean that in some possible world yogurt offers protection against cancer. This metaphysical statement is true but irrelevant. The modal statement about yogurt expresses something about evidence. When I say that we could discover that water is not H_2O, I mean "could" in the epistemological sense that such a discovery is not absolutely ruled out by our present experiences, beliefs, and worldview. In the metaphysical sense of possibility, there is no possible world in which we discover that water is not H_2O, if it is H_2O in the actual world.

> [W]e can perfectly well imagine having experiences that would convince us (and that would make it rational to believe that) water *isn't* H_2O. In that sense, it is conceivable that water isn't H_2O. It is conceivable but it isn't possible! (Putnam 1977b/1973, p. 130)

"Water is H_2O" and other similar statements are not analytic, because they are matters of scientific discovery, not of definition. We discovered that water is H_2O. This means scientists are sometimes discovering necessary truths – not just contingencies as had been supposed. A scientific investigation into the atomic, chemical, or biological structure of some kind of thing is an investigation into the essence of that kind. And this is not some linguistic essence that Wittgenstein was writing about, but a natural or real essence that is in the things and determines the natural kinds independently of us, our languages, and concepts. Discovering essences of natural kinds is one of the tasks of science. "In general, science attempts, by investigating basic structural traits, to find the nature, and thus the essence (in the philosophical sense) of the kind" (Kripke 1980/1972, p. 138). Scientists seek to know the essences of things, and they are increasingly successful.

Here I must pause a moment to pay homage to Saul Kripke. I do not think that I am exaggerating too much if say that Kripke's *Naming and Necessity* is the apotheosis of analytic philosophy. Kripke's analysis involving his prying apart of analyticity, a prioricity, and necessity, including his demonstrating that such statements as "Water is H_2O," "Tigers are animals," and "Gold is the element with atomic number 79," are necessary, a posteriori, and synthetic is the dialectical synthesis of logical positivism and Quinean pragmatism. It respects Quine's insistence that such claims are revisable without admitting

---

[6] Goldbach's Conjecture is the claim that every even integer greater than two is the sum of two primes. It has not been proven, but is almost certainly true.

contingency. It respects the logical positivists' insistence that such claims are necessary while avoiding confusions about analyticity. Kripke's analysis is a fruitful application of modal logic, and a deep expression of our ordinary linguistic intuitions on which he relies. It honors Aristotelian essentialism and natural science. It is a melding of metaphysics and physics. His distinction between descriptions used as definitions and used to fix the reference is a masterpiece of philosophical insight. It clarifies all sorts of issues. I must pause to emphasize also that many others were involved in this apotheosis and had anticipated it in various ways: Putnam and Donnellan, of course; but also Carnap, Ruth Barcan Marcus, Alvin Plantinga, David Lewis and, of course, Quine as the spur. But no one else pulled it together, made it as cogent and compelling, and made as many connections as did Kripke.

Problems for the New Theory of Reference

The Causal Theory

If the reference of names and natural kind terms is not determined by descriptions, then how is it determined according to Kripke and Putnam? What determines that "water" designates H_2O and that "Aristotle" designates Aristotle?

According to Kripke, Putnam, and Donnellan, reference is determined by causal or historical chains. For example, one way in which a name might be connected to a referent is the following: a name is given to a person in a "baptism" or an initial use with the referent present. It is then handed on from speaker to speaker. As long as we have the right sort of causal chain, that is, as long as the later speakers in the chain intend to use the name with the same reference as the earlier, reference to the person "baptized" is accomplished by use of the name. In this way, reference to the initial referent of the name can be achieved even though the later user of the name knows no descriptions uniquely specifying the referent.

This pattern seems to fit our ability to use names to refer to well-known contemporary and historical figures. I may not know anything more about David Beckham than that he's a soccer star, he's British, and plays for a team in Spain. I can and do refer to him, because my uses of his name are connected by social, historical, and causal links to the very person himself. The same holds of my uses of "Aristotle." They are connected to that very man himself. This solves the puzzle, mentioned in the first chapter, about how we can refer to

George Washington with the use of his name even though he is no longer around.

The notion of causal chains also explains how a name that is shared by many people can be a rigid designator. Surely many thousands of people have been named "Aristotle." How does my use now pick out the famous Greek philosopher and not someone else? It does so because my use now is linked causally to that great philosopher and not to any of those other folks. My intentions can also play a role. The reference fixing descriptions that I attach to my use of the name "Aristotle" help to determine the reference, without being necessarily true of him (or anyone else).

Putnam and Kripke extend the causal theory to natural kind terms. Putnam suggests that we "baptize" items that we take to be good examples or paradigms of some substance such as water and then use "water" to refer to whatever has the same nature as the paradigms. When we introduce a term this way we need not already know the nature of the stuff we are naming. We hope that such knowledge will come with empirical scientific investigations. The term, once introduced, is handed on from person to person in the referential chain, maintaining its original reference at each link. Putnam calls a term introduced by means of a paradigm, and meant to refer to whatever has the same underlying nature as the paradigm, an indexical term. By "indexical" Putnam means to indicate the analogy of such terms to indexical words such as "I," "this," "here," and so on. A term that is indexical in Putnam's sense is a rigid designator in Kripke's sense.

If I am Adam defining terms and I point to a glass of clear, colorless liquid and say, "By 'water' I mean that stuff," then the liquid in the glass is serving as a paradigm in Putnam's sense. If, however, the stuff in the glass turns out to be hydrochloric acid, I withdraw my "baptism." I meant to point to some of the same stuff that fills the rivers, lakes, and oceans of earth.

When Putnam says that a natural kind term is indexical and is thus introduced by means of a paradigm, he does not mean paradigm in the sense of something that we would all concur in calling by the term in question and that is used as an example in teaching the use of the term. One of the more questionable moves of the ordinary language philosophers was the paradigm case argument. The idea is that if something is a paradigm in the sense of example used in teaching the use of a term, then it must necessarily be in the extension of the term. This sort of argument was used on occasion to defend freedom of the will. If I teach the use of the term free action by pointing to a particular case of someone's behavior, and that is considered to be a correct use of the term "free action," then that action must be correctly called free, and is thus free. Putnam denies that any paradigms can serve this sort of purpose. Even if some piece of metal served as a paradigm of "gold," and we all concurred in calling it "gold" and used that piece in teaching the use of the term, we could still discover that we were mistaken. It could turn out not to be gold, if it was not sufficiently like other pieces of gold. Likewise, we could discover that the behavior in question was not free, and that no behavior is free. Just because everybody agreed that someone is a witch, and pointed to him as a paradigm of "witch," does not entail that "witch" truly applies to anything.

The extension of the causal theory to natural kind terms is quite rough and leaves a lot of issue unresolved. Kripke says the following after an account bearing many similarities to Putnam's: "Obviously, there are also artificialities in this whole account. For example, it may be hard to say which items constitute the original sample. Gold may have been discovered independently by various people at various times. I do not feel that any such complications will radically alter the picture" (Kripke 1980/1972, p. 139).

The Reference of Natural Kind Terms

One issue still unresolved is how to interpret rigidity when applied to general and mass terms such as natural kind terms. A rigid singular term such as a name applies to the same thing in each possible world in which that thing exists. Formally, it is a constant function that associates with each possible world the same object, or none. "Aristotle" refers to the same man in every other possible world as it does in the actual world. We can speak of a proper name as referring to its extension. A rigid proper name has the same extension in every possible world. "Tiger" is supposed to be a rigid natural kind term. The extension of a natural kind term is the set of items to which it correctly applies. The extension of the term "tiger" is the set of tigers. Unfortunately, this varies from world to world, since some actual tigers do not exist in some other possible worlds, and some tigers in other possible worlds do not exist in the actual world. Thus, a supposedly rigid natural kind term cannot rigidly refer to its extension, since that varies from world to world. What then does it rigidly refer to? One suggestion is that it refers to the kind or species. In this way, "tiger" would refer to the same species in every possible world, "gold" to the same element, "water" to the same substance. The problem with this solution is that every general term would turn out to be rigid, even terms that are not natural kind terms and were not intended to be assimilated to proper names by Kripke. "Bachelor" would refer to the same marital status from world to world, "hunter" to the same occupation, "pencil" to the same sort of writing implement. This just seems to reflect the fact that our words keep their meanings when we talk about other possible worlds. If all general terms turn out to be rigid, then the distinction between rigid and nonrigid has lost its point. Natural kind terms are nothing special. Kripke and Putnam were hasty in extending the notion of rigidity beyond singular terms to general and kind terms, without supplying an answer to this problem.

The Puzzle about Belief

The problem of the meanings and denotations of terms in intensional contexts has plagued philosophers. If names have no descriptive meanings, but only denotations to which they are connected by causal chains, then we are faced with explaining why

Tully = Cicero

differs in cognitive content from

Tully = Tully.

The explanation must involve some sort of mode of presentation, connotation, or image – i.e. descriptive meaning. Likewise, someone might believe that Tully denounced Catiline but not believe that Cicero denounced Catiline. How can we explain this without using meanings? Names that rigidly denote the same thing behave differently in intensional contexts – they are not substitutable everywhere without changing truth-values. This seems to require meanings or some sort of cognitive content attached to the names that would explain the difference. They cannot be purely referring.

Kripke devoted a monograph to this puzzle about belief, which has been a serious problem for the new theory of reference. Kripke argues, with his usual ingenuity, that the problem is not specifically a problem for his theory of proper names, but is a general unsolved problem about belief which any theory must face.

The problems of explaining the rigidity of general terms and the puzzle about belief remain open questions today.

Applications of the New Theory of Reference to the Philosophy of Mind

Kripke against the Identity Theory and Putnam against Behaviorism

The standard type-type identity theory version of materialism holds that, for example, the proposition "Pain is brain state S" is contingent. (See Chapter 5, Part 2 for discussion of type-type identity theory.) As we have seen, Kripke argues that any identity statement in which both sides are rigid designators is not contingent. Since both "pain" and "brain state S" are rigid, according to Kripke, the identity "Pain is brain state S" must be necessary (if true) and not contingent. This means that if pain is brain state S in the actual world, then it is brain state S in every world in which it exists, just as if water is H_2O in the actual world then it is H_2O in every world in which it exists. The identity theorists were led into believing that "Pain is brain state S" is contingent, because it is not analytic; but this overlooks the possibility that a proposition could be both synthetic and necessary.

Why shouldn't the identity theorist just agree with Kripke by admitting his point that pain is necessarily brain state S, if it is brain state S? After all, the identity theorist wants to assert a scientific identity between pain and brain states like the scientific identity of water and H_2O or heat and molecular motion. Couldn't the identity theorist simply agree that the identity in question is necessary if true?

This move is not readily available to the identity theorist, however. Kripke gives reasons for supposing that the identity between pain and some brain state is not necessary. If his argument is correct, then type-type identity theory is refuted. Kripke's argument is different from, and independent of, the problems that we have seen the identity theorist has with multiple realizability.

Kripke points out that there is a disanalogy between the statement that water is H_2O and the statement that pain is a brain state, say, brain state S. In the case of water, there could be a water mimic that is not H_2O. In such a case, we could say that this water mimic is not water. It is a contingent fact, if it is a fact at all, that everything that looks and tastes like water is H_2O. With pain on the other hand, the situation is different, because nothing could be a pain mimic. If something feels like pain, then it is a pain. But couldn't someone have just this feeling of pain, and yet his brain not be in state S. At least, in some possible world this happens. Certainly it is metaphysically possible even if it is physically or physiologically impossible. [*Background* 7.1 – Physically possible, metaphysically possible, logically possible] We do not have an explanation for this apparent contingency as we do in the case of water and H_2O. We cannot say of the painful feeling that is occurring (in that possible world) without the brain state, that it seems superficially to be a pain but is not. On the other hand, a person could be in brain state S and yet feel nothing. Again, isn't there such a possible world? The identity theorist is in the uncomfortable position of having to say that although the person feels nothing, he is in pain, because being in brain state S is necessarily being in pain.

Speaking of the supposed analogy between the identification of sensations with brain states on the one hand and heat and molecular motion on the other, Kripke says the following:

> In the case of molecular motion and heat there is something, namely, the sensation of heat, which is an intermediary between the external phenomenon and the observer. In the mental-physical case no such inter-mediary is possible, since here the physical phenomenon is supposed to be identical with the internal phenomenon itself. ... To be in the same epistemic situation that would obtain if one had a pain *is* to have a pain; to be in the same epistemic situation that would obtain in the absence of pain *is* not to have a pain. The apparent contingency of the action between the mental state and the corresponding brain state thus cannot be explained by some sort of qualitative analogue as obtained in the case of heat. (Kripke 1980/1972, pp. 151–2)

Is Kripke right? Kripke's argument is couched in terms of the claim that "pain" is a rigid designator. But is he right about this? The argument works as long as the identity between pain and brain state S is presented as the sort of scientific identity that would be necessary if true and a posteriori. Since Kripke did not make entirely clear how the notion of rigidity is to be extended to general terms, it is not entirely clear that "pain" is a rigid designator.

Besides causing trouble for the identity theorist, the rigidity of mental terms has provided ammunition for those who argue against contemporary versions of philosophical behaviorism. For example, Putnam used the rigidity of psychological terms to attack criteriological analyses of terms like "pain" and "dreaming." If psychological terms are rigid designators of natural kinds, then they do not involve traditional concepts. Outer criteria of inner states will at best be good indicators of the inner states, not part of the concept of the inner state as behaviorists held. Scientists can and do discover better indicators of inner states than gross outward behavior. According to Putnam, the study of the ordinary use of such terms as "dreaming," "pain," or "thinking" will only indicate what the referents of these terms are, but nothing about the nature of those referents, nothing about dreaming, pain, or thinking. We must study the referents themselves of these terms, and this is an empirical investigation.

Externalism of Mental Content

One of Putnam's most famous remarks is "Cut the pie any way you like, 'meanings' just ain't in the *head!*" (Putnam 1977b/1973, p. 124). If Putnam is right, neither are beliefs in the *head!* Externalism about mental contents is the claim that certain sorts of mental states depend for their content on the external environment. Their nature does not depend entirely on the intrinsic character or functional role of the states. Externalism is inconsistent with most forms of functionalism. The mental states one is in are not determined by their functional roles, but by things external to one's mind.

Analytic philosophers have always been aware of certain examples of externalism. A person can only know that P, if P is true. So whether a state of mind is knowledge or mere belief depends on outside factors. The sorts of examples that the externalist points to are more philosophically interesting in that they are examples where the very content of the belief depends on outside circumstances. The arguments of the externalists are based on thought experiments such as Putnam's Twin Earth thought experiment. Recall that on Twin Earth everything is superficially the same as on earth except that the stuff that fills the lakes and oceans, comes out of the faucets, and quenches thirst, is XYZ, not H_2O. On earth "water" refers to H_2O. On Twin Earth "water" refers to XYZ. Presumably, Twin Earth has no water and earth has no XYZ.

Suppose someone on earth, who is ignorant of chemistry and Twin Earth, say, someone back in the 1800s, says "Water is the only drink for a wise man." No doubt, Thoreau was sincere when he uttered this. So Thoreau believed that water is the only drink for a wise man. Accordingly, the truth or falsity of his belief depends on whether or not H_2O is the only drink for a wise man. The wisdom of only drinking XYZ is irrelevant to Thoreau's belief. When Thoreau's twin on Twin Earth utters "Water is the only drink for a wise man," he is talking about water-twin, not water. The wisdom of only drinking H_2O is irrelevant to Thoreau-twin's belief. The two beliefs have differing truth-conditions and thus, one could say, content. Since by hypothesis Thoreau and Thoreau-twin are indistinguishable in terms of intrinsic properties (except Thoreau-twin's body contains XYZ instead of H_2O), the difference in their beliefs is dependent on things external to them. If we could get out the mental can opener and open up their heads and look into their minds, they would look exactly the same. All the images and internal contents would be exactly the same. The functional organization is the same. Thus, according to the externalist, the content of beliefs is not fully determined by internal mental contents or functional organization. This is a general feature of intensional mental states. It is not confined to beliefs. I hope for a glass of water, my Twin-Earthling does too. No. He can't, since he's never been around any water. He hopes for a glass of XYZ. We are hoping for different substances. The claim of the externalists is that externalism applies to any intensional mental states that involve natural kinds.

The Social, Cultural, and Institutional Basis of Meaning and Reference

The larger, and even more interesting, point here is that Kripke and Putnam although they never explicitly embraced externalism – that was left to other philosophers – emphasize the social, cultural, and institutional basis of meaning and reference. Externalism about mental contents is an extension of these ideas.

Putnam insists on what he calls the linguistic division of labor. He cannot distinguish between an elm tree and a beech. Most of us cannot distinguish between a fir and a spruce. Any mental images or ideas that I have connected to the terms "fir tree" and "spruce tree" are the same. Yet these certainly do not mean the same for me, nor do they have the same reference. We rely on experts to determine the references of many of our terms. We defer to experts to decide the reference of natural kind terms. I do not need to know the difference between firs and spruces for my words "fir" and "spruce" to have different and, I hope, correct reference. We have an institution of experts and science, and communities of users who intend to use the terms according to the accepted scientific account, even if we do not know what it is. I am a member of that community, and so I can use the terms accordingly.

> ... [E]veryone to whom gold is important for any reason has to *acquire* the word 'gold'; but he does not have to acquire the *method of recognizing* whether something is or is not gold. He can rely on a special subclass

of speakers. The features that are generally thought to be present in connection with a general name – necessary and sufficient conditions for membership in the extension, ways of recognizing whether something is in the extension, etc. – are all present in the linguistic community *considered as a collective body*; but that collective body divides the "labor" of knowing and employing these various parts of the "meaning" of 'gold'. (Putnam 1977b/1973, p. 125)

Putnam conceives of language as tool in way reminiscent of the later Wittgenstein. Putnam, like Wittgenstein, emphasizes that language is a social institution.

When a term is subject to the division of linguistic labor, the "average" speaker who acquires it does not acquire anything that fixes its extension. In particular, his individual psychological state *certainly* does not fix its extension; it is only the sociolinguistic state of the collective linguistic body to which the speaker belongs that fixes the extension.

We may summarize this discussion by pointing out that there are two sorts of tools in the world: there are tools like a hammer or a screwdriver which can be used by one person; and there are tools like a steamship which require the cooperative activity of a number of persons to use. Words have been thought of too much on the model of the first sort of tool. (Putnam 1977b/1973, pp. 126–7)

Kripke makes the same sort of point about our ability to use names to refer. He does not mention or even accept the division of linguistic labor, but he cleverly illustrates the essential role of communities for our successful use of names.

A speaker ... who has heard about, say Richard Feynman, in the market place or elsewhere, may be referring to Richard Feynman even though he can't remember from whom he first heard of Feynman or from whom he ever heard of Feynman. He knows that Feynman was a famous physicist. A certain passage of communication reaching ultimately to the man himself does reach the speaker. He then is referring to Feynman even though he can't identify him uniquely. He doesn't know what a Feynman diagram is, he doesn't know what the Feynman theory of pair production and annihilation is. Not only that: he'd have trouble distinguishing between Gell-Mann and Feynman. So he doesn't have to know these things, but, instead, a chain of communication going back to Feynman himself has been established, by virtue of his membership in a community which passed the name on from link to link, not by a ceremony that he makes in private in his study: 'By "Feynman" I shall mean the man who did such and such and such and such'. (Kripke 1980/1972, pp. 91–2)

Kripke describes this social aspect of the reference of terms.

> In general our reference depends not just on what we think ourselves, but on other people in the community, the history of how the name reached one, and things like that. It is by following such a history that one gets to the reference. (Kripke 1980/1972, p. 95)

I cannot imagine that Wittgenstein or Austin, Ryle or Strawson would disagree with the gist of these remarks. Thus even though the new theory of reference sharply breaks with traditional theories of meaning and reference, and is no mere refinement of them, in a sense it is also an extension, and improvement, and development of aspects of the ideas of the later Wittgenstein and Austin, Strawson, and Ryle. As I mentioned at the beginning of the chapter, the new theory is based on developments in formal semantics for modal logic. In its way, then, the new theory of reference is also a dialectical synthesis of formal philosophy and ordinary language philosophy.

Background 7.1 – Physically possible, metaphysically possible, logically possible

We can distinguish *physical* possibility and necessity, from *metaphysical* possibility and necessity, and both from *logical* possibility and necessity. Alternate physically possible worlds need to be the same as the actual world in terms of their natural structure. They must have the same natural laws. Metaphysically possible worlds include worlds that are physically impossible given actual natural laws. Much more is metaphysically possible than is physically possible. The only limit on metaphysical possibilities is that everything must have its essence in every metaphysically possible world. Logical possibility is the broadest category of possible worlds. The only limit on logical possibility is logical consistency.

We can think of the sets of physically, metaphysically, and logically possible worlds as nested in concentric circles. The innermost circle includes just the physically possible worlds, then the next circle includes the metaphysically possible worlds as well. The most inclusive circle is the logically possible worlds.

It is physically possible for me to have lived in San Francisco. This violates no natural laws. It is also metaphysically possible and logically possible.

It is metaphysically possible for me to swim across the Atlantic Ocean, but it is not physically possible. It is also logically possible.

It is logically possible for me to be an alligator (no logical contradiction), but it is not metaphysically possible (assuming that I am essentially human), and it is certainly not physically possible.

Metaphysics and analytic philosophy of language is mostly concerned with metaphysical possibility and necessity.

Further Reading

The anthology that I edited on this subject contains many classic articles including some cited in this chapter: *Naming, Necessity, and Natural Kinds* (Cornell 1977) edited by Stephen P. Schwartz.

"The Meaning of 'Meaning'" by Hilary Putnam is reprinted in *Language, Mind and Reality: Philosophical Papers, Vol. 2* (Cambridge University Press 1975). "Dreaming and 'Depth Grammar'" is an essay in which Putnam dissects Malcolm's ordinary language analysis of dreaming. That essay and many other important articles by him are included in that volume.

Nathan Salmon's *Reference and Essence* (Princeton University Press 1981) has received a lot of attention. It is a very detailed examination of the relation between Kripke's and Putnam's semantic theories and their essentialism.

Designation by Michael Devitt (Columbia University Press 1981) is a useful book-length treatment of semantics of natural language based on the work of Kripke, Putnam, and Donnellan.

Langauge and Reality: An Introduction to the Philosophy of Language (2nd edition) by Michael Devitt and Kim Sterelny (MIT Press 1999) is an ambitious survey of the entire area, that does a good job of situating the new theory of reference.

8

Ethics and Metaethics in the Analytic Tradition

It is not the business of the ethical philosopher to give personal advice or exhortation. (Moore 1960/1903, p. 3)

Introduction

Who are the greats of analytic philosophy that we have encountered so far? Frege is the precursor; Russell, Moore, and Wittgenstein, the founding fathers; Carnap, Quine, Davidson, Kripke, and Putnam, the giants of the middle period of analytic philosophy. The only one of this group recognized for his contributions to ethics is G. E. Moore. For decades his 1903 classic *Principia Ethica* was the only major work of analytic ethics. Early Wittgenstein, Carnap, and Quine dismissed ethics from the area of serious philosophical enquiry. The logical positivists "eliminated" normative ethics much as they had "eliminated" metaphysics. Even Russell, who wrote many popular works addressing moral issues, denied that moral valuations had cognitive content. This was the standard view.

> ... [Q]uestions as to "values" lie wholly outside the domain of knowledge. That is to say when we say that this or that has "value," we are giving expression to our own emotions, not to a fact which would still be true if our feelings were different. (Russell 1997/1935, pp. 230–1)

Thus ethics was shunted off to the side much like metaphysics. Analytic philosophers did not consider ethics to be worthy of serious

A Brief History of Analytic Philosophy: From Russell to Rawls, First Edition. Stephen P. Schwartz.
© 2012 John Wiley & Sons, Inc. Published 2012 by John Wiley & Sons, Inc.

philosophical endeavor. Unlike metaphysics, however, morality is not dispensable. One can live, I suppose, without any views about metaphysics. One cannot avoid having urgent views about what is right and wrong, morally good or evil.

Analytic philosophers could not forever ignore morality. People, all of us, will reason about what is right or wrong, just or unjust. We all have committed views about moral issues. Our moral views affect how we behave and treat other people. We are passionate about morality. This passion and reason can and ought to be guided by philosophical reflection. Moral issues cannot be answered by science, which is why the positivists rejected them as literally meaningless. A more mature view would be to realize that this leaves the field open to philosophy and religion. Moral issues will not be ignored. Analytic philosophers have indispensable tools for making contributions in this field.

Despite the moral imperative for analytic philosophers to engage in philosophical ethics, they were slow to do so. Symbolic logic and empiricism, which were at the center of early analytic philosophy, did not offer much to ethical philosophy. While logic and philosophy of language were revolutionized by early analytic philosophers, no revolutions were forthcoming in ethics. As long as analytic philosophers were focused on formal logic and natural science and mathematics, they had no enthusiasm for doing ethics. Only when the ordinary language philosophers began to break the grip of formalism and science-and-math-worship did ethics again become an area for analytic philosophers. They slowly dipped their toes in the waters, beginning with metaethics and coyly avoiding substantive ethics. [*Background 8.1* – The distinction between ethics and metaethics] Later they took courage and waded into the deeper waters. In the 1960s substantive ethics experienced a rebirth comparable to the rebirth of metaphysics in the 1970s and 1980s. Analytic philosophers took a long time to get around to normative ethics, but when they did, they did it with gusto. Ethics became a major philosophical industry with many branches. Nothing was out of bounds. In the later quarter of the twentieth century and the beginning of the twenty-first, analytically trained philosophers devoted attention to such applied areas as medical ethics, environmental ethics, and animal rights; political issues such as war and peace studies; and gender issues such as feminism and gay and lesbian philosophies.

Analytic ethicists bring the tools of analytic philosophy to bear on ethical issues: clarity of expression, sequential argumentation, clear and direct dialectical interchange with opponents. In other ways, analytic ethics is less reflective of the special character of the mainstream of analytic philosophy than are philosophy of language and logic.

Analytic philosophers doing ethics do not use much symbolic logic, nor has formal logic contributed much of note to the study of ethics. Ethicists are working within the traditions of older philosophies. Rather than to Frege, Russell, and Wittgenstein, analytic ethicists have looked to Aristotle, Kant, and Mill for their inspiration, issues, and positions when doing normative ethics.

The most distinctively analytic aspects of analytic ethics have been the dismissal of morality as non-cognitive[1] by the logical positivists and later ethical non-cognitivists; and the non-religious approach to ethics of all the major analytic ethicists. This is partly a remnant of the empiricist, pro-science, and anti-metaphysical orientations of earlier analytic philosophers, but is also rooted in Aristotle, Kant, and Mill who did not appeal to religion to ground morality.

G. E. Moore's *Principia Ethica*

Principia Ethica is primarily a work of metaethics. Moore describes his project as an attempt to clarify the nature of ethical reasoning rather than to determine what is good and evil. "... I have endeavored to discover what are the fundamental principles of ethical reasoning; and the establishment of these principles, rather than of any conclusions which may be attained by their use, may be regarded as my main object" (Moore 1960/1903, p. ix). His task is to define the predicate "good," since that is the primary subject of ethics. The question of the rightness and wrongness of conduct is secondary, and can only be answered when the nature of the good is determined. "This, then, is our first question: What is good? and What is bad? and to the discussion of this question (or these questions) I give the name Ethics" (Moore 1960/1903, p. 3).

" ... [T]his question, how 'good' is to be defined, is the most fundamental question in all Ethics" (Moore 1960/1903, p. 5). This is classical analytic philosophy: Focus on the language, the words, the meanings.

But Moore's next move is so startling as to almost make us lose our grip on his book. Here are Moore's famous lines:

> If I am asked 'What is good?' my answer is that good is good, and that is the end of the matter. Or if I am asked 'How is good to be defined?' my answer is that it cannot be defined, and that is all I have to say about it. (Moore 1960/1903, p. 6)

---

[1]   To say that morality is non-cognitive means that sentences expressing moral views "lie wholly outside the domain of knowledge" (Russell, quoted above). Moral views are neither true nor false. They are not "truth-apt."

This has the same flavor of triviality as Tarski's "'Snow is white' is true if and if only if snow is white." And like Tarski's truth definition, Moore's non-definition of "good" has profound implications. It is a rejection of all previous ethics.[2] Previous ethicists have attempted to define good as pleasure, or what we desire to desire, or self-realization, or whatever. Moore's way is a liberation from previous philosophy. "[I]f I am right, then nobody can foist upon us such an axiom as that 'Pleasure is the only good' or that 'The good is the desired' on the pretence that this is 'the very meaning of the word'" (Moore 1960/1903, p. 7). Moore devotes a hundred pages of his book to dismissing ethicists who have tried in vain to define "good": Among them are Herbert Spencer's Darwinian ethics which defined good as "more evolved," John Stuart Mill's utilitarianism, and Kant's ethics of duty. According to Moore, good is a simple property, like yellow, that cannot be defined. Unlike yellow, good is not a natural property and cannot be perceived by the senses, but is apprehended by moral intuition. The property denoted by the predicate "good" is not complex; it has no parts, and is not part of anything that has it, although it depends, partly, on the other aspects of things that are good.

Moore's argument for his claim that "good" is simple and indefinable is called the open question argument and has been influential and controversial. Suppose someone attempted to define "good" as "pleasure." The question "Is pleasure good?" is a substantive, open question. "Pleasure is good" is not a trivial tautology. Thus "good" cannot mean "pleasure." According to Moore, whatever anyone offers as a definition of "good" will admit of the open question whether it is good. If one were to try to define "good" as some complex property P, then we can sensibly ask "Is P good?" "P is good" is not a tautology as it would be if P were simply the meaning of "good."

> But whoever will attentively consider with himself what is actually before his mind when he asks the question 'Is pleasure (or whatever it may be) after all good?' can easily satisfy himself that he is not merely wondering whether pleasure is pleasant. And if he will try this experiment with each suggested definition in succession, he may become expert enough to recognise that in every case he has before his mind a unique object, with regard to the connection of which with any other object, a distinct question may be asked. (Moore 1960/1903, p. 16)

Okay, let's try the experiment. Conan the Barbarian, in an early scene in the eponymous movie of 1982, is in a class being taught by his

---

[2] With the exception of a few precursors who also claim that "good" is indefinable. In particular, Moore cites Henry Sidgwick and Franz Brentano.

warrior mentor.[3] The squatting warriors are asked to define "good." One benighted warrior says "Good is to dance, to sing, to be free, and be joyful." The teacher sadly shakes his head. Finally Conan speaks up: "Good is to defeat your enemies, to see them fleeing before you, and to hear the lamentations of their women." The teacher smiles, nods, and says "Yes, that is good." Moore's experiment seems to work. Surely, even if you agree in substance with Conan, you would not hold that Conan's proposed definition of "good" is a tautology and neither would he. The question "Is it good to defeat your enemies . . . ?" is an open question.

If Moore had been in the warrior school with Conan the Barbarian, he would have answered "Good is a simple, indefinable, non-natural property that is apprehended by moral intuition – and that's all I have to say about it." I wonder how Conan's teacher would have responded. Apparently Moore had abundant personal charm and persuasiveness. He might have taught the warriors a thing or two.

Moore would add that Conan and his mentor have committed the naturalistic fallacy. "The naturalist fallacy" is the name that Moore gave to the attempt to equate goodness with any complex natural (or non-natural) property.

> It may be true that all things which are good are also something else, just as it is true that all things which are yellow produce a certain kind of vibration in the light. And it is a fact, that Ethics aims at discovering what are those other properties belonging to all things which are good. But far too many philosophers have thought that when they named those other properties they were actually defining good; that these properties, in fact, were simply not 'other,' but absolutely and entirely the same with goodness. This view I propose to call the 'naturalistic fallacy' and of it I shall now endeavour to dispose. (Moore 1960/1903, p. 10)

The naturalistic fallacy has been one of the central topics in analytic moral philosophy. The questions are: "Is it really a fallacy?" "If so, what exactly is the fallacy?" "And if it is a fallacy, how do we avoid it?" Any philosopher who strives to define "good" as either a natural or non-natural complex property must have a response to these questions. Kant, Mill, Spencer, et al. in attempting to define "good" have all committed the naturalistic fallacy and thus vitiated their moral philosophies, according to Moore. Indeed, as I mentioned, the balance of his book is focused on exposing their failings.

---

[3] I have apparently reimagined this scene. In any case, that is irrelevant as it is still an illustrative experiment. Conan is superbly played by Arnold Schwarzenegger.

Moore, however, devotes the final two chapters to conduct, and to stating his views about intrinsic good and evil. "Right action" or "action we ought to do" can be scientifically defined according to Moore. It is the action that would result in the most good – in the best results. Of course, as a practical matter we often cannot know which action that is. The answer to the question what things are intrinsically good, Moore holds, is obvious and not worthy of dispute. "Indeed, once the meaning of the question is clearly understood, the answer to it, in its main outlines, appears to be so obvious, that it runs the risk of seeming to be a platitude" (Moore 1960/1903, p. 188). And what is the answer? (If it is so obvious, you must already know the answer.) Anyway, just for the record, here is Moore's answer:

> No one, probably, who has asked himself the question, has ever doubted that personal affection and the appreciation of what is beautiful in Art or Nature, are good in themselves; nor, if we consider strictly what things are worth having *purely for their own sakes*, does it appear probable that any one will think that anything else has *nearly* so great a value as the things which are included under these two heads. (Moore 1960/1903, pp. 188–9)

Whereas Moore's attack on traditional morality and his description of the naturalistic fallacy have been central issues in moral philosophy since 1903, his views about intrinsic value have had little influence on subsequent analytic philosophy. Moore's positive ethical claims enunciated in the final chapter of *Principia Ethica*, on the other hand, had a large following among his contemporaries. The Bloomsbury Group was a loose group of mostly modernist writers and artists that met in Bloomsbury in London. Among the "members" were Virginia Woolf, the modernist novelist, and John Maynard Keynes, one the world's leading economists. Moore's *Principia Ethica* served as the *de facto* philosophical bible of the group. As semi-bohemian modernists they liked Moore's rejection of traditional morality. They also especially embraced the final chapter with its emphasis on the intrinsic value of personal relations (with a beautiful, sensitive lover) and the intrinsic value of the artistic appreciation of beauty. This was just the thing for intellectual and arty Edwardians, 12 years before the Great War would shatter their cozy world.

The Non-Cognitivism of C. L. Stevenson

Moore's intuitionism has several problems. 1) How do we apprehend the supposed simple indefinable non-natural property – good? 2) Why should such a property, if we do apprehend it, motivate or interest us? Why is such a property any more valuable than, say, yellowness? 3) If intrinsic goodness is self-evident, what should we do when people disagree about it, as they are sure to do? Moore's views seem to cut off further ethical reasoning.

When arguing for the indefinability of "good," Moore states that we have three options: Either "good" stands for a simple property, or it stands for a complex property, or it is meaningless. Philosophers convinced by Moore's open question argument, but dismayed by the evident problems with his intuitionism, still have a fourth option to work with. Non-cognitivists reject the first two alternatives, but also would not say "good" is meaningless. They deny that it stands for a property, either simple or complex, and assert instead that it has non-cognitive or emotive meaning. In this way they elude the naturalistic fallacy and at the same time avoid committing themselves to moral intuition of indefinable properties.

The quote from Russell in the first paragraph of this chapter is a good example of emotivism. We saw in Chapter 2 that a similar view was defended by Ayer, and was part of the positivist program. The most sophisticated version of emotivism was developed by the American philosopher C. L. Stevenson in a series of articles and books from the 1930s to the 1960s, especially his classic book *Ethics and Language*, published in 1944. Stevenson viewed his project as advancing the non-cognitivism of Ayer and Carnap.

> Yet the present work [*Ethics and Language*] finds much more to defend in the analyses of Carnap, Ayer, and the others, than it finds to attack. It seeks only to qualify their views. ... It hopes to make clear that "emotive" need not itself have a derogatory emotive meaning. And in particular, it emphasizes the complex descriptive meaning that ethical judgments can have, in addition to their emotive meaning. (Stevenson 1944, p. 267)

According to Stevenson, the analysis of ethical statements involves a descriptive element and an imperative element. His preliminary version, which he calls a working model, is the following:

(1) "This is wrong" means *I disapprove of this; do so as well.*
(2) "He ought to do this" means *I disapprove of his leaving this undone; do so as well.*
(3) "This is good" means *I approve of this; do so as well.* (Stevenson 1944, p. 21)

This working model needs to be qualified for various reasons. Ethical claims are vague, context dependent, and so on. They also can contain more descriptive meaning than is here apparent.

Notice that the working model explains how people can disagree and reason about morality. I do not argue with your claim that you approve of something, but I can try to alter your attitude with reasons. We ask for reasons for imperatives. If told "Close the door!," asking for a reason to close it is not out of line. My asking "Why should I also approve of this?" makes sense, and can be the start of an interchange of ideas and reasons. Thus the non-cognitivist, according to Stevenson, is not reduced to cynicism about morality.

Reasoning can only go so far, however. Moral disagreements, according to Stevenson, are disagreements about facts, but also essentially involve differences in attitude.

> [E]thical arguments usually involve disagreements in belief; but they *also* involve disagreements in attitude. And the conspicuous role of disagreement in attitude is what we usually take, whether we realize it or not, as the distinguishing feature of ethical arguments. (Stevenson 1949, p. 589)

This means that ethical disputes cannot always be settled by cognitive methods. "But the purely intellectual methods of science, and, indeed *all* methods of reasoning, may be insufficient to settle disputes about values ..." (Stevenson 1949, p. 592).

The point of ethical discourse is to influence not describe.

> Doubtless there is always *some* element of description in ethical judgments, but this is by no means all. Their major use is not to indicate facts, but to *create an influence*. Instead of merely describing people's interests, they *change* or *intensify* them. They *recommend* an interest in an object, rather than state that the interest already exists. (Stevenson 1959/1937, p. 269)

Stevenson's treatment of moral statements in terms of their use to influence enables him to avoid the naturalistic fallacy.

> I may add that my analysis answers Moore's objection about the open question. Whatever scientifically knowable properties a thing may have, it *is* always open to question whether a thing having these (enumerated) qualities is good. For to ask whether it is good is to ask for *influence*. And whatever I may know about an object, I can still ask, quite pertinently, to be influenced with regard to my interest in it. (Stevenson 1959/1937, p. 280)

Cognitivists, of course, found much to criticize about non-cognitivism. One serious issue confronting non-cognitivists is the use of ethical terms in non-hortatory contexts. This problem is especially sharp when moral terms are embedded in complex assertions. For example, consider "If stealing is wrong, then tax evaders should be put in jail." Stevenson's analysis of moral terms is not able to handle the meaning of a sentence such as this. If we substitute his analysis of "Stealing is wrong" in the complex sentence, it makes no sense. "If I disapprove of stealing, do so as well, then ..." Or consider the sentence "I wonder if we ought to tax the rich." Does this plausibly mean "I wonder if we approve of taxing the rich, do so as well"? So at the very least, Stevenson's account of the meanings of moral terms is incomplete. Nor has any obvious way of extending it to embedding contexts been formulated.

The Universal Prescriptivism of R. M. Hare

The beginning of World War II caused Hare, an Englishman, a moral dilemma, as he was a pacifist. He did enlist, but spent most of the war in a Japanese prison camp. He returned to Oxford University at the end of the war and was made professor in 1966. Hare was an Oxford philosopher in the era of Austin and of Wittgenstein's influence. His ethical prescriptivism is a more sophisticated version of Ayer's and Stevenson's non-cognitivism, that has elements of speech act theory beholden to Austin. His 1952 book *The Language of Morals* is a classic of analytic metaethics, as is its 1963 sequel *Freedom and Reason*.

Although Hare was concerned, as a result of his war experiences, that ethics help people in difficult circumstances and his view is called prescriptivism, he did not view philosophical ethics as prescriptive. In a statement representative of Oxford ordinary language philosophy he states: "Ethics, as I conceive it, is the logical study of the language of morals" (Hare 1952, p. v) Such a statement, that now seems so limiting, was reflective of the view, inherited from the *Tractatus* and the positivists, that philosophers could not sensibly assert normative claims. Ethics as a branch of philosophy could only consist in the analysis of language.

Such an undertaking should be dispassionate and even arid. Not so. The most acrimonious and ugly philosophical interchange I have ever been present at was between Hare and a young commentator at a talk I attended in 1966 in Ithaca. It lasted almost two hours and was not friendly on either side. Hare may have been a pacifist of sorts but he was a fighter in philosophy. Later in life he joined the move in analytic philosophy toward normative ethics and contributed to issues in applied ethics. His most influential work remained his universal prescriptivism.

The non-cognitivists have gained a lot of mileage out of Moore's open question argument – a lot more than he did, as it turns out. Stevenson has a version of it up his sleeve: "If you say that 'good' means by definition some natural property, you cannot be correct, because that definition leaves out the peculiar emotive quality of 'good.'"[4] Moore was mistaken in thinking that since "good" cannot be defined naturalistically (or non-naturalistically), it denotes a simple, non-natural property – but he was on to something. No definition of "good" that equates it with a property can capture the emotive meaning of the term.

Hare approves of Moore's open question argument, but claims that it applies to all value terms. None can be defined naturalistically, because that would leave out their action-guiding purpose. Value terms are used, in a way that is central to their meanings, in speech acts that recommend or condemn. Thus, according to Hare, no value judgments are factual, nor are they derivable from factual premises alone. "[W]hat is wrong with naturalist theories is that they leave out the prescriptive or commendatory element in value-judgements, by seeking to make them derivable from statements of fact" (Hare 1952, p. 82).

> Value-terms have a special function in language, that of commending; and so they plainly cannot be defined in terms of other words which themselves do not perform this function; for if this is done, we are deprived of a means of performing the function. (Hare 1952, p. 91)

Hare's view is close to Stevenson's in that commending is not primarily descriptive. It is prescriptive, intended to be action-guiding:

> I have said that the primary function of the word 'good' is to commend. We have, therefore, to inquire what commending is. When we commend or condemn anything, it is always in order, at least indirectly, to guide choices, our own or other people's, now or in the future. (Hare 1952, p. 127)

Hare, unlike Ayer and Stevenson, would not emphasize the emotive aspect of moral terms. He would argue no definition of "good" that equates it with a property can capture the *prescriptive* (not emotive) meaning of the term.

Not all value judgments using the word "good" are moral. What is the difference between non-moral and moral value-judgments, according to Hare? In *Freedom and Reason*, Hare names the three most important points of his *The Language of Morals*: "two are that moral judgements are

---

[4]   This is my statement of his view, not his.

a kind of *prescriptive* judgements, and that they are distinguished from other judgements of this class by being *universalizable*" (Hare 1963, p. 4). (This is why Hare calls his ethical philosophy universal prescriptivism.) The third is "that it is possible for there to be logical relations between prescriptive judgements, including even imperatives ... " (Hare 1963, p. 4). Because of the latter two features, moral thought and discourse can be rational. Moral claims are not merely expressive.

Alas, Hare is not as clear as we would like about what he means by universalizability. Universalizability is the well-known, and ancient, moral principle that individuals or situations that are the same in all morally relevant respects must receive the same moral treatment. This principle, in turn, is based on the non-moral principle that we must treat similar cases similarly. If one dot is red and another dot is indistinguishable in color, then it also is red. So what then is unique about moral judgments? Hare seems to have in mind that moral prescriptions must be based on reasons that are universal in the sense that they do not depend on eccentricities of the situation. Hare illustrates his point by contrasting a moral claim such as "One ought not to smoke in the presence of children" with the command "No Smoking" posted in a railway compartment. The latter applies to just that particular space; the former to all spaces and times, and people. Moral rules or prescriptions would contrast with ones that are anchored in particularity, such as selfishness, romantic love, certain forms of patriotism and loyalty. Unfortunately, despite his examples and explanations, Hare left this key piece of his analysis of ethical language in a deficient state.

This is partly Hare's point, though. He insists that the logic of "good" is not essentially different in moral and non-moral contexts. Morality is an extension of the ordinary use of evaluative terms in non-moral contexts, as when, for example, we judge that that is a good car, or a good book, or a not very good movie.

> This special status [of moral judgments] does not require a special logic to back it up; it results from the fact that we are using the ordinary apparatus of value-language in order to commend or condemn the most intimate actions of ourselves and those like us. (Hare 1952, p. 143)

In a way that I suppose is salutary and that would appeal to empirically inclined philosophers, this is a demystification of morality and a demotion of it from the realm of the heavens. The process was started by Moore, but he still mystified with his simple indefinable property of intrinsic goodness. Hare's analysis returns morality to the mundane, without the excitement of emotivism. It is brilliant, actually, in its own subdued way.

The Return to Substantive Ethics

Many analytic philosophers did not approve of the evisceration of ethics that started with Moore and was fervently pursued by the logical positivists. Surely philosophers, even hard-nosed, empirically-minded, logic-chopping analytic philosophers, have more to contribute to ethics than the "logical study of the language of morals." The demise of the verifiability criterion of cognitive meaningfulness undercut much of the motivation for non-cognitivism. But would-be normative ethicists still had to confront the open question argument and worry about committing the naturalistic fallacy.

When subjected to philosophical scrutiny, however, the naturalistic fallacy turned out not to be a genuine fallacy. Conan the Barbarian may have had a barbaric idea of moral goodness but he did not commit a logical fallacy when he defined "good." Since the naturalistic "fallacy" is not a logical fallacy – there is no logical error in attempting to define an indefinable term – it looks like nothing but name-calling. Elizabeth Anscombe, in her groundbreaking article "Modern Moral Philosophy" (Anscombe 1968/1958), that helped to reintroduce normative ethics, dismisses the naturalistic fallacy without comment. "They [Bentham and Mill] are often said to have gone wrong through committing the 'naturalistic fallacy'; but this charge does not impress me, because I do not find accounts of it coherent" (Anscombe 1968/1958, p. 188). Moore claimed that "good" was analogous to "yellow" in being indefinable, because like "yellow" it named a simple, indefinable property. But if one attempted to define "yellow," she could not coherently be accused of committing a fallacy. "Fallacy" in the context of logic and philosophy does not mean just a false belief. It means a kind of invalid argument that is based on misrepresentation or trickery that is superficial and only persuasive to those who aren't thinking very clearly. A proffered definition of "yellow" could only be rejected on the basis of specific argumentation and analysis – not dismissed as committing a fallacy. Moore, of course, did not merely indulge in name-calling, he did suggest a blanket method of rejecting definitions of "good" – his open question argument.

But Moore's open question argument is doubtful as well. It would be too destructive. It would apply any time someone tries to define any term or give an equivalence. In any case, the fact that the definitions of "good" are not trivial seeming – leave an open question – does not show that they are not proper definitions. People who use a term may not be aware of the meaning they attribute to it. The meaning may require explication. Indeed, Conan the Barbarian's definition seems not to be right, even for him. It is not general enough. Perhaps he and his warrior mentor would come to realize that what they really mean by "good" is something like struggling with adversity (i.e. your enemy or whatever your "enemy" is) and achieving victory. Hearing the lamentations of your enemies' women may be delightful, but surely it is not part of the definition of "good" even for Conan, despite what he says. It is too specific. He would find it just as good if the women did not lament but rejoiced at the prospect of cavorting with the victors. Someone who defines "good" as successful struggle against adversity can be understood as attempting to explicate the term "good." The explication is still an open question even though it is proposed as an analytic definition, because the meaning of "good," or any term, may have to be unpacked – untangled – in surprising ways. The proposed unpacking may be mistaken, as any philosophical claim may be mistaken, but the mistake must be spelled out in detail. It cannot be dismissed via the open question argument or calling it a case of the naturalistic fallacy.

In fact, the supposed definition of "good" as struggling against adversity and achieving victory still cannot be correct. It is incomplete at best. Philippa Foot would argue that good cannot be defined as struggling against adversity and achieving victory. To be good, it would have to be struggle in a worthwhile cause.[5] The point is that admissible definitions of moral concepts are subject to limitations. Foot and Anscombe argued against non-cognitivism, in a series of influential articles, that "good" is not primarily emotive or prescriptive, or even if it is, the range of admissible prescriptions involves severe constraints. An utterance is not moral simply because it is a universal prescription. To be moral it must contain something about what is worthwhile, valuable, of benefit, and so on. And what is worthwhile, valuable, beneficial cannot be just anything. Someone could claim that, for example, collecting mud in a pail is morally obligatory, define "good" as collecting mud, but in order to be even minimally comprehensible, she would have to connect this in some way with something worthwhile. The mud has special magical powers to relieve human suffering; it is gold that will make us all rich and happy, or something to that effect. If she simply said "No, nothing like that … It is just that we are morally obligated to collect mud. I define that as 'good.' I approve of collecting mud, and you should do likewise," we would not understand her. She is not talking morality or goodness despite the words she is using,

---

[5] I do not want to suggest that Foot would have approved of such a definition of "good." I am merely using this as an example of a possible definition of "good."

no matter how emotive or prescriptive. Good cannot be to struggle to victory unless this struggle is connected somehow to something worthwhile, beneficial, or valuable, and not just to an individual but in a general way.

> How exactly the concepts of harm, advantage, benefit, importance, etc. are related to the different moral concepts, such as rightness, goodness, duty and virtue is something that needs the most patient investigation, but that they are so related seems undeniable, and it follows that a man cannot make his own personal decision about the considerations which are to count as evidence in morals. (Foot 1968/1958, p. 18)

Foot is right. Conan the Barbarian's definition of good is disturbing not just because of the violence and sexism implied, but because it is so self-centered and arbitrary. If he would connect the defeat of the enemy to something beneficial to humanity, contributing to human flourishing, and so on, it would begin to make more sense. Simply defeating your enemies because they are in your way may be part of the struggle for survival, but it is not part of morality. It is mere self-interest.

> One might compare this case to that of a man who in some discussion of common policy says "this will be the best thing to do," and announces afterwards that *he* meant best for himself. This is not what the word "best" does mean in the context of such discussion. (Foot 1968/1958, p. 18)

In the same vein, Conan's definition of "good" is not what "good" means in a moral context.

Foot's arguments are similar to Davidson's principle of charity (and antedate it). Recall that Davidson claimed that we could only interpret others as having beliefs and speaking a language if they agreed with us about most things. Unless we can interpret them as having mostly true beliefs, we cannot interpret them as speaking or thinking. We can only attribute mistakes and disagreement against a background of massive agreement. Foot similarly claims that a system that was too different from our moral system would not count as a moral system. To be a moral system it must be relevantly like ours.

> But the suggestion which has been put forward is that this could not be the right description [that it is a moral code] for rules of behaviour for which an entirely different defence is offered from that which we offer for our moral beliefs. If this suggestion is right, the difference between ourselves and the people who have these rules is not to be described as a difference of moral outlook, but rather as a difference between a moral and a non-moral point of view. (Foot 1968/1958, p. 19)

Foot has an insightful interpretation of Nietzsche to illustrate her point.

> The fact that Nietzsche was a moralist cannot, however, be quoted in favour of the private enterprise theory of moral criteria. Admittedly Nietzsche said "You want to decrease suffering; I want precisely to increase it" but he did not *just* say this. Nor did he offer as a justification the fact that suffering causes a tendency to absent mindedness, or lines on the human face. We recognize Nietzsche as a moralist because he tries to justify an increase in suffering by connecting it with strength as opposed to weakness, and individuality as opposed to conformity. ... That individuality is a good thing is something that has to be shown, but in a vague way we connect it with originality, and with courage, and hence there is no difficulty in conceiving Nietzsche as a moralist when he appeals to such a thing. (Foot 1968/1958, pp. 20–1)

Foot's articles are a manifesto for a return to normative ethics. The ethicist should now engage in "the most patient investigation" of how the concepts of harm, advantage, etc. are related to rightness, goodness, etc. Foot uses the term "concepts" here, but this is not a "logical study of the language of morals." It is substantive and normative. It is a philosophical investigation of moral right and wrong, good and bad, in the most general terms – and then applying those results to specific issues of practical concern.

Questioning the Fact/Value Divide

Both Foot and Anscombe worked on undermining the fact/value divide, and their work was successful. Undermining the fact/value divide was essential if analytic philosophers were to do normative ethics with a clear conscience.[6] Both Foot and Anscombe were at Oxford when they published works that overturned the non-cognitivism of Ayer, Stevenson, and Hare. Their philosophical outlook was more in tune with evolved views of Oxford ordinary language philosophers than were Hare's, which still had an aroma of positivism.

The real challenge for substantive ethics was not so much the threat of the naturalistic fallacy and Moore's open question argument. They

---

[6] We have seen in Chapter 4 that Putnam pursued this issue as well, as part of his pragmatism, but Putnam's point is different from, though related to, Foot's. Putnam denies the very terms of the distinction – facts are value-laden and values are fact-laden. For the most part, according to Putnam, one cannot pry them apart. The distinction is bogus. Foot seems to accept the validity of the distinction but argues that facts entail values.

had been defanged. The block to substantive ethics was the supposed fact/value distinction. If an unbridgeable gap exists between factual claims and value claims, then prospects for substantive ethics are dim. Values, if not factual, or based on facts, or derived from facts, will be seen as subjective, emotive, individual, and unconstrained – Foot calls it the "private enterprise theory of moral criteria." If values can be anything no matter what the facts, how can values be determined?

The fact/value distinction was fundamental to the logical positivist program derived from the *Tractatus*. Since all knowledge was embodied in natural science, and science could not establish values empirically, values were non-cognitive; value judgments did not represent knowledge, could not be true or false, were emotive, or prescriptive. This is Ayer, Stevenson, and Hare. Values are in a different "logical" dimension from facts. Facts by themselves cannot entail values.

> ... [A]ny statement of value always seems to go beyond any statement of fact, so that he might have a reason for accepting the factual premises but refusing to accept the evaluative conclusion. That this is so seems to those who argue in this way to follow from the practical implication of evaluation. When a man uses a word such as 'good' in an 'evaluative' and not an 'inverted comma' sense, he is supposed to commit his will. From this it has seemed to follow inevitably that there is a logical gap between fact and value; for is it not one thing to say that a thing is so, and another to have a particular attitude towards its being so; one thing to see that certain effects will follow from a given action, and another to care? Whatever account was offered of the essential feature of evaluation – whether in terms of feelings, attitudes, the acceptance of imperatives or what not – the fact remained that with an evaluation there was a committal in a new dimension, and that this was not guaranteed by any acceptance of facts.
>
> I shall argue that this view is mistaken; that the practical implication of the use of moral terms has been put in the wrong place, and that if it is described correctly the logical gap between factual premises and moral conclusion disappears. (Foot 1967/1958, p. 93)

Foot uses concepts such as injury, dangerousness, and rudeness, rather than full-blooded moral terms, to shake our confidence in the fact/value divide. "I think it will be agreed that in the wide sense in which philosophers speak of evaluation, 'rude' is an evaluative word" (Foot 1968/1958, p. 13). Yet not just anything counts as rude. Specific facts entail that someone has been rude. The fulfillment of specific criteria counts as rudeness – something like: causing offense by showing lack of respect. If someone claimed to hold some perfectly ordinary bit of behavior to be rude – say folding a piece of paper – we would not understand him. Of course, a story could be told about how the folding, given certain conventions, was an affront to dignity. But in order for the behavior to be rude it must meet those conditions, it must fit certain descriptions. To be rude, certain facts must hold about the behavior. These facts entail that the behavior in question was rude. Facts entail values.

> I conclude that whether a man is speaking of behavior as rude or not rude, he must use the same criteria as anyone else, and that since the criteria are satisfied if O [conditions of offense] is true, it is impossible for him to assert O while denying R [that a piece of behavior was rude]. It follows … that we have an example of a non-evaluative premise from which an evaluative conclusion can be deduced. (Foot 1968/1958, pp. 15–16)

The same sort of argument can be given for many terms that merge with strictly moral terms: "cruel," "courageous," "careful," "considerate," "thoughtless," "truthful," "honest," "inconsiderate," "fair," "just," "virtuous," and so on. They are each evaluative and at the same time applied on the basis of factual criteria.

You will notice that the terms "morally good," "morally evil," "morally ought," and "ought not" are missing from this list. Anscombe, based on considerations similar to Foot's, urges us not to focus on such terms that she claims are left over from an antiquated religious morality. Instead we should adopt the Aristotelian view of concentrating on moral virtues. Anscombe says of "morally ought":

> It would be most reasonable to drop it. … [Y]ou can do ethics without it, as is shown by the example of Aristotle. It would be a great improvement if, instead of "morally wrong," one always named a genus such as "untruthful," "unchaste," "unjust." We should no longer ask whether doing something was "wrong," passing directly from some description of an action to this notion; we should ask whether, e.g. it was unjust; and the answer would sometimes be clear at once. (Anscombe 1968/1958, p. 196)

Anscombe is scornful of what she calls the consequentialist moral philosophy of her analytic colleagues and British moralist predecessors. [*Background 8.2* – Consequentialist versus deontological moral theories] As an alternative, Foot and Anscombe founded a school of analytic ethics, based on Aristotle's ethics, called virtue ethics, which quickly became one of the major branches of normative ethics. They emphasize moral character rather than moral oughts and goodness. Virtue ethics is a genuine alternative to utilitarianism and Kantianism. Foot and other philosophers went on to develop detailed accounts of virtue ethics.

Breaking the hold of the fact/value distinction had the effect of releasing a huge outpouring of normative ethics. This era, beginning in the late 1950s, has been called "The Great Expansion."

> In the Great Expansion a sense of liberation came to ethics. Moral philosophers shed the obsessions of analytic metaethics, and saw – or thought they saw – ways of exploring normative morality as a cognitive domain, without a bad philosophical conscience. The result was an unprecedented pouring of philosophical effort and personnel into ethics, which in turn spread out into the most diverse issues and applications. (Darwall, Gibbard, and Railton 1992, p. 123)

The Great Expansion of normative ethics in turn generated renewed interest in metaethical issues such as the question of ethical realism versus anti-realism, which is an updated and more sophisticated version of the cognitivist/non-cognitivist debate. [*Background 8.3* – Ethical realism versus anti-realism]

Instead of attempting the impossible task of summarizing even the main lines of ethics and metaethics since the Great Expansion, I will focus on the two most famous, influential, and controversial ethical philosophers – Peter Singer and John Rawls. Both of them have had an influence and following that extend beyond academic philosophers. They have been major public figures – and analytic philosophers.

Peter Singer and Animal Liberation

Once the Great Expansion was underway many ethicists focused on specific areas of practical concern. Analytic philosophers realized that they had a lot to contribute to discussions of pressing social issues. This is applied ethics. Among the areas of applied ethics (with typical issues) are biomedical ethics – morality of abortion, medical testing, and access to medical care; environmental ethics – preservation of wildness, sustainability, obligations to nature; business and professional ethics – the status of corporations, the moral responsibilities of businesses, intellectual property rights; philosophy of war and peace – just war theory, rights and duties of combatants, morality of deterrence. Some philosophers also focused on sexual and gender issues – feminism, and gay and lesbian ethical and life issues.

Peter Singer is the most famous applied ethicist and the analytic philosopher best known to the public outside of philosophy. He has written and spoken on many issues, but he is best known (in some circles, notorious) for founding the animal liberation movement and advocating certain forms of euthanasia. Born in 1946 in Australia to parents who were refugees from the Nazi annexation of Austria, Singer lost three grandparents to the holocaust. He studied at Oxford University and wrote a thesis under the direction of Hare, who continues to be a major influence on Singer's thinking. Singer spent most of his career teaching at Monash University, but was appointed professor of bioethics at Princeton in 1999, setting off a flurry of protests. Singer has received many awards and honors. He has also been drowned out and driven off stages by protestors in Germany and Switzerland. Singer currently divides his time between Princeton and Australia, where he is laureate professor at the University of Melbourne.

By the use of the term "animal liberation" Singer wants to connect his views about the ethical treatment of animals,[7] to other liberation movements such as women's lib. He recognizes the oddity of this, but his point is that precisely the same arguments that are successful against racism and sexism are effective against what he calls speciesism.

> [T]he attitude that we may call "speciesism," by analogy with racism, must also be condemned. Speciesism ... is a prejudice or attitude of bias in favor of the interests of members of one's own species and against those of members of other species. It should be obvious that the fundamental objections to racism and sexism ... apply equally to speciesism. (Singer 1975, p. 6)

Of course, the species that Singer is accusing of indulging in speciesism is *homo sapiens*. We do things to animals that we would not do to human beings. Singer argues that we are morally bound to consider animals the same as our fellow human beings when it comes to causing suffering. In the first chapter of his revolutionary book *Animal Liberation* (Singer 1975), Singer starts by saying "the ethical principle on which human equality rests requires us to extend equal consideration to animals too" (Singer 1975, p. 1).

That animals lack language, are less intelligent, do not have a moral sense, lack religion, culture, and art is irrelevant. The only relevant fact is that animals are capable of suffering, and thereby have interests. Singer plausibly claims that higher animals' capacity for suffering is equal to normal humans.

> If a being suffers there can be no moral justification for refusing to take that suffering into consideration. No matter what the nature of the being,

---

[7] I use "animal," as does Singer, to mean "non-human animal." Most of Singer's remarks are concerned with higher non-human animals.

> the principle of equality requires that its suffering be counted equally with the like suffering – insofar as rough comparisons can be made – of any other being. (Singer 1975, p. 8)

Most human beings are speciesists in that we do not take into consideration the suffering of animals, or if we do, we do not give it equal weight with human suffering. This is as morally indefensible, according to Singer, as racism and sexism.

> Racists violate the principle of equality by giving greater weight to the interests of members of their own race when there is a clash between their interests and the interests of those of another race. Sexists violate the principle of equality by favoring the interests of their own sex. Similarly, speciesists allow the interests of their own species to override the greater interests of members of other species. The pattern is identical in each case. (Singer 1975, p. 9)

In *Animal Liberation*, Singer focuses on two major forms of abusive treatment of animals – animal experimentation and factory farming of animals for food. Singer's book is truly applied ethics in the sense that he documents the horrors of these practices. The animal liberation movement, since the publication of his book, has exposed particularly gruesome animal experiments. Often these are unnecessary for medical research. Thanks to Singer, many of these experiments have been stopped and people are now much more aware and disapproving of cruelty in using animals for testing.

Singer urges us to become vegetarians, because by eating meat we are participating in immoral practices and encouraging those who raise animals for food. Singer has been diligent in exposing the shocking ways in which animals raised for food are made to suffer. We do not need to eat meat; thus by continuing to be omnivores, we are indirectly and immorally causing suffering, merely to gratify our tastes, according to Singer. Many other forms of animal exploitation are morally wrong, according Singer; among them are hunting, circuses and rodeos, confining wild animals in zoos, trapping animals for fur, whale hunting, tuna fishing that drowns dolphins.

Singer does not base his argument for equal treatment of animals on animal rights. Singer is a utilitarian and does not recognize the existence of absolute rights – neither of human beings nor animals. This has put him at odds with those who believe in the absolute sanctity of human life – i.e., those who believe in the absolute right to life of every human being – and those in the animal liberation movement who argue for animals' rights to life. Killing animals is not the central problem with animal farming and eating animals, according to Singer. The biggest moral problem is the suffering that is inflicted by the practices of raising, confining, and bringing the animals to slaughter. "The case against using animals for food is at its strongest when animals are made to lead miserable lives so that their flesh can be made available to humans at the lowest possible cost" (Singer 1979, p. 55).

For utilitarians, killing is a more complex moral issue than causing suffering, since killing can be done quickly and painlessly.

> This means that in some circumstances – when animals lead pleasant lives, are killed painlessly, their deaths do not cause suffering to other animals, and the killing of one animal makes possible its replacement by another who would not otherwise have lived – the killing of non-self-conscious animals may not be wrong. (Singer 1979, p. 104)

Singer gives as a possible example the raising of free-roaming chickens for food. Naturally, Singer's views have not endeared him to the more radical members of the animal rights movement. His views on abortion and euthanasia have also generated heated controversy. If we accept utilitarian calculations of the sort that Singer urges as our moral determiners, then sometimes killing severely disabled infants and adult humans with no prospect in life except unmitigated suffering is morally obligatory.

Singer has applied his utilitarianism to many other ethical issues such as world poverty, abortion, human enhancement drugs, and the ethics of war. He argues that we who are well off should give at least 10 percent of our income to help relieve poverty in the Third World.

Philosophically, Singer is not just an applied ethicist. As well as giving many public interviews and speaking to general audiences, Singer has contributed to the ongoing discussions among analytic ethicists of issues in theoretical ethics and metaethics.

Singer is the most active analytic philosopher in the world today, outside the classroom. He is also the philosopher who has inspired and infuriated the most people. As writers and teachers working in the discipline founded by Socrates, this should be part of our job. Anscombe, in her article "Modern Moral Philosophy" that I quoted from earlier, attacks moral philosophers for supporting the status quo. She would be infuriated by Singer's consequentialism, but he certainly cannot be accused of supporting conventional morality.

John Rawls' Theory of Justice

Justice as Fairness versus Utilitarianism

Rawls' 1971 book, *A Theory of Justice*, is the greatest, most influential, and profound work of twentieth-century ethics. It is, as well, a classic of political theory that has influenced many areas outside of philosophy: economics, political science, legal theory, and public policy studies. Three hundred years from now *A Theory of Justice* will still be studied and admired. It goes on the shelf with the *Tractatus, Principia Mathematica, Principia Ethica, Sense and Sensibilia*, the *Aufbau*, "On Denoting," "Two Dogmas of Empiricism," *Naming and Necessity*, and a few other works of analytic philosophy that are contributions to world-historical philosophy. *A Theory of Justice*, and a series of articles by Rawls that preceded it and contained many of its main ideas, were a source of and inspiration for the Great Expansion in ethics.

John Rawls was born to a prominent family in Baltimore in 1921. Rawls got his BA and PhD degrees from Princeton University. In between, he served in the US Infantry in New Guinea and other areas in the western Pacific, including Japan right after the war. Rawls taught at Cornell, MIT, then at Harvard for almost 40 years. Rawls died in 2002. In addition to his monumental *A Theory of Justice*, Rawls made many other contributions to political theory including works on liberal political theory, international relations, and the history of ethics and political theory. *A Theory of Justice* and Rawls' other contributions to philosophy have generated an immense secondary literature. One collection of articles on Rawls runs to four volumes, another is five volumes, besides many single volume works. (See further readings for some less daunting suggestions.)

In the very first pages of the preface of *A Theory of Justice* Rawls sets out his purpose. His main concern is to offer an alternative to the classical utilitarianism of Hume, Adam Smith, Bentham, and J. S. Mill, which he correctly notes has been the dominant normative ethical theory. The alternative that Rawls formulates is a version of the social contract theory. [*Background 8.4* – Social contract theory]

> What I have attempted to do is to generalize and carry to a higher order of abstraction the traditional theory of the social contract as represented by Locke, Rousseau, and Kant. ... [T]his theory seems to offer an alternative systematic account of justice that is superior, or so I argue, to the dominant utilitarianism of the tradition. (Rawls 1971, p. viii)

Rawls' theory of justice is a version of Kantian ethics. "The theory that results is highly Kantian in nature" (Rawls 1971, p. viii).

Utilitarianism is subject to various well-known counterexamples and problems, among them is accounting for justice, rights, and liberty. "For example, it has sometimes been held that under some conditions the utility principle ... justifies, if not slavery or serfdom, at any rate serious infractions of liberty for the sake of greater social benefits" (Rawls 1971, p. 156). Rawls' theory of justice, that he calls justice as fairness, is an attempt to repair the problems with utilitarianism while retaining its appealing aspects. Justice as fairness is a dialectical synthesis of utilitarianism and Kantianism, where the dominant aspect is Kantian.

The brilliance of *A Theory of Justice* is not its originality. Indeed, Rawls claims none for his theory. Rather it is the methodical, detailed, and convincing way in which he sets out his theory and argues for it. Although Rawls says "I must disclaim any originality for the views I put forward," (Rawls 1971, p. viii) the methods and arguments that he uses and makes are strikingly original and fruitful. Among other deep ideas and methods, Rawls' work introduced the notions of reflective equilibrium, the veil of ignorance, the original position, and the difference principle. They have become staples of ethical and political reasoning.

Reflective Equilibrium

Reflective Equilibrium is the basic method of philosophical reasoning that Rawls employs. It is offered as an alternative to traditional ordinary language analysis of moral terms as well as to formal logical exposition. The idea is that we start with some moral principles that seem more-or-less right to us, and we test these against examples, imagined and real, and specific intuitive judgments such as that racial discrimination is wrong. Sometimes our reflective judgments and intuitions about examples will support our principles, and sometimes they will conflict with them. We adjust our initial principles to fit our intuitive judgments or change our minds about the judgments. In this way we should ultimately reach a balance where we've adjusted our principles to fit our firm intuitions, and given up some of our intuitions. In the end, our principles, judgments, and intuitions form a coherent moral system, or ideally should. In this process we learn how our principles are derived and why they are shaped the way they are. The method of reflective equilibrium has been adopted in areas beyond moral philosophy, such as in metaphysics, and has proved fruitful. Demonstrating the usefulness of and popularizing the method of reflective equilibrium has been one of Rawls' notable contributions to philosophy.

Rawls' notions about the nature of a moral theory and how it is to be constructed were influenced by his Harvard colleague W. V. Quine. (See Chapter 3 for discussion of Quine's philosophy.) Rawls' method is a version of Quinean holism applied to moral theory:

> There is a definite if limited class of facts against which conjectured principles can be checked, namely, our considered judgments in reflective equilibrium. A theory of justice is subject to the same rules of method as other theories. Definitions and analyses of meaning do not have a special place ... In any case, it is obviously impossible to develop a substantive theory of justice founded solely on truths of logic and definition. The analysis of moral concepts and the a priori, however traditionally understood, is too slender a basis. Moral philosophy must be free to use contingent assumptions and general facts as it pleases. (Rawls 1971, p. 51)
>
> ...
>
> A conception of justice cannot be deduced from self-evident premises or conditions on principles; instead, its justification is a matter of mutual support of many considerations, of everything fitting together into one coherent view. (Rawls 1971, p. 21)

Before we dig deeper into the details of Rawls' theory of justice, let us pause to compare Rawlsian moral holism based on reflective equilibrium to the ideas of another, earlier, influential social theorist – Karl Popper.

Karl Popper and Piecemeal Social Engineering

Among analytic philosophers Karl Popper was the clearest and most passionate exponent of moderation and limits. His 1945 two volume masterpiece *The Open Society and Its Enemies* (Popper 1971/1945) is his most extensive and influential expression of his political ideas. (See Chapter 2 for Popper's views about logical positivism.)

Popper, writing almost 30 years before Rawls, comes from a very different direction. The two hold similar views about some important issues, but differ strongly about others, reflecting differing orientations of analytic philosophy. Popper defends a form of modesty in social theory that he calls piecemeal social engineering. According to Popper, the most we can do is work to oppose palpable evils on a piecemeal basis. Our goals can only be to reduce bit by bit the misery around us. We cannot throw off our chains; we can only work to destroy them link by link.

> Such considerations lead us back to our plea for piecemeal, and against Utopian or holistic, methods of social engineering. And they lead us back to our demand that measures should be planned to fight concrete evils rather than to establish some ideal good. State intervention should be limited to what is really necessary for the protection of freedom. (Popper 1971/1945, p. 130)

This statement is opposed to justice as fairness. Rawls, for one thing, argues that the just state must intervene not just to fight concrete evils but to reduce social inequalities, as we will see shortly.

Popper's notion of piecemeal social engineering is a reflection of the philosophy of logical atomism, in the way that Rawls' justice as fairness is a reflection of Quinean holism. The method of the earlier analytic philosophers, under the influence of Russell, was to tackle problems individually and separately using logical analysis. Popper's piecemeal social engineering is a political philosophy that reflects the method of piecemeal analytical philosophizing.

> Modern analytical empiricism ... has the advantage, as compared with the philosophies of the system-builders, of being able to tackle its problems one at a time, instead of having to invent at one stroke a block theory of the whole universe. (Russell 1945, p. 834)

Popper's notion of the limited role of state power has found more recent expression in a book intended as a critique of Rawls. Robert Nozick, another Harvard philosopher, in his controversial book *Anarchy, State, and Utopia* (Nozick 1974) sets out his vision of the legitimate state.

> Our main conclusions about the state are that a minimal state, limited to the narrow functions of protection against force, theft, fraud, enforcement of contracts, and so on, is justified; that any more extensive state will violate persons' rights not to be forced to do certain things, and is unjustified; and that the minimal state is inspiring as well as right. Two noteworthy implications are that the state may not use its coercive apparatus for the purpose of getting some citizens to aid others, or in order to prohibit activities to people for their *own* good or protection. (Nozick 1974, p. ix)

Here is the basic issue that divides conservatives such as Popper and Nozick from liberals such as Rawls. Does the government have the right or moral duty as a requirement of justice to act to diminish social and economic inequalities by requiring the better off to give up some of their benefits to help those who are less well-off? Nozick says "No!" Rawls says "Yes!" Rawls has a particular ideal of justice that it behooves the society or government to institute. For Popper state power should not be used to institute a specific philosophical scheme. According to Nozick any state beyond the minimal state, any state that attempts to impose a scheme of distributive justice, immorally violates the rights of people that live under that state.

Despite their differences, Popper, Nozick, and Rawls agree that liberty – basic civil rights – cannot be violated for the purpose of achieving greater social benefits. Popper's orientation, unpopular at the time, was anti-Marxist. His piecemeal social engineering was an alternative to what he called utopian ideologies. The utopian has a vision of a future purified of all wrongs of history, in which mankind will find beatific peace and plenty. The utopian is willing to sacrifice the lives and freedom of contemporaries to move toward this goal. The utopian makes an epistemic error, according to Popper. No abstract theory can be so conclusively verified that it would justify tyranny and violence, no matter how noble the goals. Rawls would agree with Popper about this.

In epistemology, Popper adopted fallibilism. Fallibilism is the theory of moderation and limits applied to knowledge. We know that we are fallible – prone to error. We do not know precisely where our errors lie, although we often discover them. In the meantime, we must not be too confident in our claims to know. We must be especially wary of high-level, abstract, and very general or momentous beliefs. Popper applied his modest, pragmatic, and fallibilistic epistemology to politics. He was opposed to any absolute political scheme that was based on philosophy. Any such philosophy is dubious at best.

Rawls is a Popperian to the extent that he adopts fallibilism with regard to his own philosophy and moral philosophy in general.

> ... [O]ur present theories are primitive and have grave defects. We need to be tolerant of simplifications if they reveal and approximate the general outlines of our judgments. Objections by way of counterexamples are to be made with care, since these may tell us only what we know already, namely that our theory is wrong somewhere. The important thing is to find out how often and how far it is wrong. All theories are presumably mistaken in places. The real question at any given time is which of the views already proposed is the best approximation overall. (Rawls 1971, p. 52)

This is part of the point of reflective equilibrium. We are not discovering absolute, a priori, eternal truths about justice.

> More likely candidates for necessary moral truths are the conditions imposed on the adoption of principles; but actually it seems best to regard these conditions simply as reasonable stipulations to be assessed

eventually by the whole theory to which they belong. There is no set of conditions or first principles that can be plausibly claimed to be necessary or definitive of morality . . . .

Therefore, we do better, I think, to regard moral theory just as any other theory, making due allowances for its Socratic aspects. There is no reason to suppose that its first principles or assumptions need to be self-evident. . . . [J]ustification rests upon the entire conception and how it fits in with and organizes our considered judgments in reflective equilibrium. As we have noted before, justification is a matter of the mutual support of many considerations, of everything fitting together into one coherent view. (Rawls 1971, pp. 578–9)

The title of his book is indicative of this attitude – it is *A* theory of justice, not *THE* theory of justice.

The Two Principles of Justice as Fairness

The question or topic of social justice is about the basic structure of society: How to organize the major institutions of society that "distribute fundamental rights and duties and determine the division of advantages from social cooperation" (Rawls 1971, p. 7). Rawls is concerned to determine the structure of a just constitution for society as well as just economic and social arrangements.

Rawls' answer to this question is embodied in the two principles of justice as fairness. He gives several versions of the two principles that define justice, but the final version is this:

First Principle
Each person is to have an equal right to the most extensive total system of equal basic liberties compatible with a similar system of liberties for all.

Second Principle
Social and economic inequalities are to be arranged so that they are both:

(a) to the greatest benefit of the least advantaged, consistent with the just savings principle, and
(b) attached to offices and positions open to all under conditions of fair equality of opportunity. (Rawls 1971, p. 302)

The point of the first principle is that each person is to have the maximum amount of liberty consistent with an equal amount of liberty for everyone else. This is at odds with utilitarianism, which does not recognize absolute rights, but is otherwise not controversial and in this or another similar form would be accepted by Popper and Nozick.

Part (b) is equality of opportunity.[8] Part (a) of the second principle is Rawls' famous difference principle and is the heart of his theory. He states the general conception of his theory of justice:

General Conception
All social primary goods – liberty and opportunity, income and wealth, and the basis of self-respect – are to be distributed equally unless an unequal distribution of any or all of these good is to the advantage of the least favored. (Rawls 1971, p. 303)

The difference principle is highly controversial. Conservatives such as Popper and Nozick would balk at this. According to them, the state may not use its coercive power to force some people to help others who are less advantaged, nor is an unequal distribution unjust because it disadvantages the least favored. According to Nozick, the justice or injustice of unequal distribution depends on how it came about. The well-off may voluntarily aid the least favored, and be encouraged to, but the state has no moral right to force anybody to give up some of her properly obtained possessions to help those who are less well-off.

Rawls claims that the goods and benefits of society are a joint product of everyone who can work, working together. Our goods are a social product. Rawls argues that people can be expected to agree to a division of goods that is unequal only if everyone is better off because of the unequal distribution. Perhaps some people do harder work, or are motivated to achieve more, which is to everyone's benefit. The point is that we have no right to complain that some are better off than we are, if we are better off than we would be otherwise, especially if we have maximal liberty and equality of opportunity. Of course, Nozick would urge that the well-off would have a right to complain if "social and economic inequalities are to be arranged so that they are . . . to the greatest benefit of the least advantaged," especially if this arrangement meant that the well-off had to involuntarily give up some of their rightfully obtained personal goods.

Rawls has difficulties defining who are the least favored, but let's assume that we recognize that society consists of groups, families, or clans, some of which are better off in terms of having more of the primary goods than others. The difference principle asserts that when considering the unequal distribution of goods, we need only consider the representative individual of the least well-off group. To take a

---

[8] Nozick is dubious about fair equality of opportunity. He seems to regard it as impossible to achieve, not morally obligatory, nor particularly desirable.

hypothetical example, if a distribution of goods would raise the benefits of the best off group by 1000 units and the least well-off group by 10 units, and another would raise the benefits of the best off group by 150 units and the least well-off group by 20 units, justice requires that we choose the second arrangement even though total benefits are lower. This is a clear divergence from classical utilitarianism, since the first arrangement has greater overall benefits.

Finally, the phrase about the just savings principle in (a) is about allocating a reasonable amount of resources for future generations.

What happens when the principles conflict? The principles are lexically ordered. The principle of equal liberty comes first. Liberty cannot be bargained away for other benefits. "Liberty can be restricted only for the sake of liberty" (Rawls 1971, p. 302). Equal opportunity has priority over the difference principle.

The Original Position and the Veil of Ignorance

Rawls arrives at the two principles by creating a situation for people setting up a constitution or basic institutions of their society which is so structured that their decisions will be fair; thus – justice as fairness. The guiding idea is that the result of a fair decision procedure is fair. The problem then is to formulate a fair decision procedure. This problem is solved, according to Rawls, by the original position and the veil of ignorance.

The original position is a hypothetical version of people meeting to form a social contract that is a purely imaginary thought experiment.

> In justice as fairness the original position of equality corresponds to the state of nature in the traditional theory of the social contract. This original position is not, of course, thought of as an actual historical state of affairs, much less as a primitive condition of culture. It is understood as a purely hypothetical situation characterized so as to lead to a certain conception of justice. (Rawls 1971, p. 12)

The key feature of the original position is the veil of ignorance. The participants in the original position are ignorant of their economic and social status, race, gender, natural capacities, age, education level, and in general anything that would lead to inequalities. They do not know their conceptions of the good, in other words, what they want in life beyond the primary goods, which everyone wants no matter what their ends. Nor do they know these things about anybody else. They do know a lot about human psychology. They have common sense. They know we differ and compete for primary goods. They know that their society will have a moderate scarcity of goods. They understand that people have a desire to live in harmony under a just arrangement.

Given that the representatives of all the components of society are meeting to form the basic rules to govern their lives what rules will they choose? (Of course, no one knows which component she represents.) They will choose the two principles of justice as fairness. The fact that the participants will choose the two principles in the original position is the argument the two principles are fair and just, and the only fair and just principles.

> The principles of justice are chosen behind a veil of ignorance. This ensures that no one is advantaged or disadvantaged in the choice of principles by the outcome of natural chance or the contingency of social circumstances. Since all are similarly situated and no one is able to design principles to favor his particular condition, the principles of justice are the result of a fair agreement or bargain. For given the circumstances of the original position, the symmetry of everyone's relations to each other, this initial situation is fair between individuals as moral persons, that is, as rational beings with their own ends and capable, I shall assume, of a sense of justice. The original position is, one might say, the appropriate initial status quo, and thus the fundamental agreements reached in it are fair. This explains the propriety of the name "justice as fairness": it conveys the idea that the principles of justice are agreed to in an initial situation that is fair. (Rawls 1971, p. 12)

The Argument for the Two Principles – Maximin

In arguing that the participants in the original position would choose the two principles Rawls does not demonstrate that they would reject every other principle. Such would be impossible in any case. The only ones he treats with any detail are forms of utilitarianism. His reasoning is difficult and subtle.

Rawls argues that the participants would choose the two principles over the principle of average utility (the principle that says "maximize the average level of utility, benefits, pleasure, or satisfaction"). Under this form of utilitarianism someone could find themselves or their group in an unpleasant situation indeed. If a majority got satisfaction out of depriving a minority of the right to worship as it pleased, for example, such deprivation might raise the average utility. Under average utility no one is guaranteed that he would be better off than in a situation of absolute equality, and he might be worse off.

In the original position the rational policy is to use maximin reasoning. That is, one wants to maximize the minimum amount of liberty and other primary goods that one, or members of one's group, will get. Maximin reasoning is appropriate when one is reasoning under particular forms of uncertainty. According to Rawls, the original position fits the criteria for maximin reasoning. Maximin reasoning is indicated when one is not able to make rational assessments of probabilities of various outcomes, and some outcomes could be very bad. In such a case one wants to choose a safe minimum. Note, the participants are not able to gamble, and for example vote for a slave society in the hope that they would end up masters. Among other things, no one could rationally gamble with their entire life happiness without any sense of the probabilities of losing. Nor would the participants, under the veil of ignorance, know their own tolerance of risk-taking. Thus the most conservative approach is indicated.

> It is useful as a heuristic device to think of the two principles as the maximin solution to the problem of social justice. There is an analogy between the two principles and the maximin rule for choice under uncertainty. This is evident from the fact that the two principles are those a person would choose for the design of a society in which his enemy is to assign him his place. (Rawls 1971, p. 152)

In considering which form of society to adopt, the participants must also consider whether the two principles have various virtues. Would people willingly adhere to them? Would they lead to a stable society in which little disruption results from envy and resentment, and so on? Rawls argues at length that the two principles have these virtues.

In his massive book, Rawls takes up and deals profoundly with a vast number of other issues of moral and political philosophy. And of course every aspect of Rawls' theory and treatment has been dissected and criticized from various points of view in the voluminous literature on his ideas. Even outlining a few of the major lines of criticism would take us beyond what is possible in this context. (See further readings.)

Perhaps the most telling and easily understood attack is the claim that Rawls, despite his professed liberalism, is just supporting the status quo. It is all very measured, moderate, limited, and conservative. No revolutionary banners are hidden among Rawls' pages. To some, Rawls' justice as fairness may seem like nothing but drippy bourgeois liberal-democratic thinking, expostulated at achingly boring length. I suppose the notions of moderation and limits, maximin reasoning, and safe social minimums are not very inspiring to youths at the barricades. The implementation of any social system is subject to corruption as we have seen recently in the US where corporate and Wall Street greed have undermined reforms and controls on the economy. What is the chance of implementing anything like the difference principle, even if it isn't all that revolutionary? Marxists and others viciously criticized Popper as a gradualist and opportunist. And Rawls has come in for some of the same sort of abuse.

In view of the recent history of the twentieth and twenty-first centuries, I do not see how we can still be attracted to utopian or revolutionary thinking. We need moderation, limits, and modesty, and a vital dose of fallibilism in morality, political theory, and social policy. We need a lot less excitement and lot more careful reasoning, no matter how boring. And, I for one, would rather live in a society designed by Rawls, than one designed by Popper, or Nozick, or Marxists, or any other political philosophers that I am aware of. Now, I think that is the ultimate tribute! Rawls comes the closest to what Plato wanted: The Philosopher King.[9] He would, of course, have declined the office.

Unlike many earlier analytic philosophers, Rawls did not decline to do substantive, normative ethics. C. L. Stevenson, in his article "Persuasive Definitions" writes that:

> "Justice" can be defined in a great many ways, always without shocking the lexicographers. An eye for an eye, and a tooth for a tooth? The keeping of contracts, merely? The king's will? The distribution of social wealth in accordance with the amount of *labour* that each man does? We have a wide choice of meanings, and freedom, within wide conventional limits, to invent new ones. Which meaning we choose, however, is no trivial matter; for we shall dignify that meaning by a laudatory title. To choose a meaning is to take sides in a social struggle. (Stevenson 1938, p. 344)

Rawls took sides in a social struggle – not the revolutionary one that some would have liked, however. He argued for a liberal democratic vision of society in which the disadvantaged have the first claim on increasing benefits. His is not just an emotive definition or appeal, although it is appealing. In the finest tradition of philosophy, Rawls argued for his position with persistent reason, developed a method that anyone can understand, expounded his theory eloquently with very little jargon, considered fairly and decently every relevant objection of which he was aware. Always modest, careful, clear, precise, and thorough, Rawls is among the very best of analytic philosophy. No! Of philosophy, period.

---

[9] Plato would not have approved of Rawls, since Plato's political philosophy was anti-democratic.

Background 8.1 – The distinction between ethics and metaethics

Philosophical ethics is the study of moral right and wrong, good and evil, what we ought and ought not to do. Ethics is substantive and normative. Metaethics is an area of philosophy that emerged as a separate subject with the advent of analytic philosophy. Metaethics is the logical and analytical study of ethics. Questions that arise in metaethics are epistemological, logical, and metaphysical, not ethical. For example: Can we know the answers to ethical questions? If so, how? What is the meaning of ethical terms? Are ethical sentences true and false, like scientific propositions? Does "good" denote a property? Are ethical claims objective? If so, how are they verified? How are ethical disputes to be settled? The question of ethical realism versus anti-realism is an example of a metaethical dispute.

Generally, when philosophers speak of ethics as an area of philosophy, they include metaethics even though strictly speaking metaethical problems fall under the headings of epistemology, metaphysics, and logic. If the discussion is strictly about ethics, there is no harm in this. We also tend to use "ethics" and "morality" interchangeably. "What are your ethical views about x?" and "What are your moral views about x?" are, to my ear, the same question. "Ethics" is the name of one of the four main areas of philosophy, but it could also be called "moral philosophy."

Background 8.2 – Consequentialist versus deontological moral theories

"Consequentialism" is a general term for moral theories that assert that the moral rightness or wrongness of actions, policies, and institutions depends on the results, outcomes, or consequences of those actions, policies, or institutions. Deontological moral theories deny this. In one form or another, they claim that rightness or wrongness, goodness or badness depends on conformity to rules. For the deontologist the moral quality of an action depends on the type of action it is, not on its results or consequences.

For example, a deontologist might hold that lying is morally wrong and one is always morally wrong to lie, regardless of the consequences. A consequentialist might claim that lying is sometimes morally justified, even obligatory, when lying would save an innocent child's life.

The most common form of consequentialism is utilitarianism, which comes in many forms. The most simple and direct is act utilitarianism which asserts the principle of utility: "Always act in such a way as to produce the maximal amount of pleasure (benefits, happiness, satisfaction) for everyone concerned." Thus, one is to act for the greatest good for the greatest number. Clearly, the act utilitarian would morally condone lying in certain circumstances. Another term that is sometimes used for consequentialist moral theories is "teleological moral theories."

The most common deontological moral theory is Kantianism. Kantianism cannot be easily summarized. Kant held that an action is morally right if and only if it springs from certain sorts of motivation – in particular, if it is done purely out of moral concern. Deontologists proceed, in ethics, by finding a procedure or rule that is trusted. Moral actions are then defined as actions in accord with the rule. One must obey the rule no matter the consequences. Kant's famous rule is the categorical imperative: "Always act in such a way that you could will the maxim of your action to be a universal law of nature." No one could will that lying become universal. Therefore lying is never morally justified.

Background 8.3 – Ethical realism versus anti-realism

Realism about physical objects is the view that they exist independently of our thoughts and perceptions. The moon continues to exist even when it is not being perceived, and existed before human life appeared on earth. Ethical realism, similarly, is the view that ethical properties are genuine mind- and perception-independent properties. Ethical facts are objective and independent of people's beliefs or feelings. There is a fact of the matter whether abortion is morally wrong. We can try to discover this fact, but we do not create it.

Ethical anti-realism is the denial of ethical realism. Anti-realism comes in many versions, as does realism. The non-cognitivism of Ayer, Stevenson, and Hare is one form of anti-realism. Anti-realists recently have argued that moral systems are useful fictions created by human beings.

Background 8.4 – Social contract theory

Social contract theory arose as an alternative to the view that societies and governments are divinely inspired. The idea is that the state arises by the consent of those governed who enter into a contract with each other that sets up a government. Generally, the forming of the contract is not viewed as an actual historical event, but is a hypothetical reconstruction of how civil society arose. People come together and for their mutual benefit and protection, both from each other and outsiders, they agree to set a power over them to adjudicate disputes, make laws, set up bodies of armed men to protect them and enforce the laws, and so on. According to standard versions of contract theory, a legitimate government rules by the consent of the governed. Even though we have not been party to an original contract, we tacitly consent by participating in and benefitting from our civil society. The idea of the social contract was introduced by Thomas Hobbes in the 1600s and was developed in various ways by Locke, Rousseau, and Kant. Rawls is an example of a contemporary contract theorist.

Further Reading

Ethics by P. H. Nowell-Smith is a useful, mid-twentieth-century overview of analytic ethics (Penguin Books, 1956).
"Toward *Fin de Siècle* Ethics: Some Trends," by Stephen Darwall, Allan Gibbard, and Peter Railton is an excellent history of analytic ethics with emphasis on metaethics up to 1990. The authors are major contributors to metaethics (*The Philosophical Review*, vol. 101, no. 1, (January 1992), pp. 115–89).
Peter Singer's *Practical Ethics: Third Edition* (Cambridge University Press 2011) is still one of the best tours through the main issues of applied ethics.
Reading Rawls: Critical Studies on Rawls' "A Theory of Justice" (Stanford University Press 1989), edited by Norman Daniels, contains a number of important articles by leading philosophers.

9

Epilogue: Analytic Philosophy Today and Tomorrow

Any problem that enjoys a simultaneous vogue in ten of the hundred or so "analytic" philosophy departments in America is doing exceptionally well. The field these days is a jungle of competing research programs, programs which seem to have a shorter and shorter half-life as the years go by. (Rorty 1982, p. 216)

Analytic Philosophy since 1980

Scott Soames titled the epilogue of his monumental two-volume study of twentieth-century analytic philosophy "The Era of Specialization." Soames describes the current situation in academic philosophy.

> In my opinion, philosophy has changed substantially in the last thirty or so years. Gone are the days of large, central figures, whose work is accessible and relevant to, as well as read by, nearly all analytic philosophers. Philosophy has become a highly organized discipline, done by specialists primarily for other specialists. The number of philosophers has exploded, the volume of publication has swelled, and the subfields of serious philosophical investigation have multiplied. Not only is the broad field of philosophy today far too vast to be embraced by one mind, something similar is true even of many highly specialized subfields. (Soames 2003b, p. 463)

The only qualm I have about Soames' statement is his claim that "philosophy has become a highly organized discipline." I'm not sure

A Brief History of Analytic Philosophy: From Russell to Rawls, First Edition. Stephen P. Schwartz.
© 2012 John Wiley & Sons, Inc. Published 2012 by John Wiley & Sons, Inc.

what he means by that, but "highly *dis*organized discipline" would seem like a truer description given the rest of what he says. Since this is the situation with recent analytic philosophy, I cannot pretend to offer the sort of overviews and expositions that I have given of earlier analytic philosophy. In this section I will try to give brief indications of what seem to be some main lines of inquiry since about 1980 in the major areas of philosophy. I say "try" and "seem to be," because we are too close to the era to know what will have lasting value, and who will turn out to have been the central figures.

Any of the philosophers that I mention in the following could have been added to the list of leading analytic philosophers at the end of the introduction.

The material in the rest of this chapter relies on many of the distinctions, concepts, and expositions in the previous chapters. Refer back to them and the background snippets for explanations. Since I am covering so much ground here so quickly, I include a more extensive list of further readings at the end of this chapter.

Okay, then? Now for a whirlwind tour of some main themes of recent analytic philosophy.

Philosophy of Language

Almost all recent work in philosophy of language has been in the formalist tradition of Carnap. Ordinary language philosophy has been absorbed and surpassed by Kripke, Putnam, and Donnellan, and others. No one today would describe themselves or be correctly described as an ordinary language philosopher. Anti-formalism is obsolete.

When I say that ordinary language philosophy has been surpassed and that anti-formalism is obsolete, I mean that a certain negative and dismissive attitude to philosophy adopted by Wittgenstein, Austin, and their followers – and some American neo-pragmatists such as Rorty – is no longer fashionable. Rather, I get the sense that young analytic philosophers today have a "roll up our sleeves" and get-down-to-work attitude. They take philosophical problems seriously and believe they have something positive to offer to anyone who will listen. In every area, philosophers and logicians made progress, not by dismissing philosophical problems, but by bringing more sophisticated tools to bear.

For example, mathematical approaches to modeling language were (and are) promising. Richard Montague, a California logician, mathematician, and philosopher, who was a student of Tarski's, aggressively pursued the formalist program in the philosophy of language. The major collection of his essays is titled *Formal Philosophy* (Montague 1974). Montague's work generated a program in philosophy of language, semantics, and linguistics, which was the application of model theoretic methods to many areas of language and to some other philosophical issues. The main thrust of the project was to expand the use of set-theoretic methods that had been successful in formalizing the semantics of extensional logic to intensional, i.e., non-truth-functional, areas of language such as tenses, modalities, and indexical expressions such as pronouns. This project was a direct affront to ordinary language philosophers, since they had held that formal methods were inappropriate in the philosophy of language, because language is context dependent. They argued that formal methods could not capture the subtleties of linguistic contexts. Logicians working in the footsteps of Carnap and Montague showed that context dependence could be formally modeled mathematically. Montague proposed that a context of use replace possible worlds as the setting where a proposition is assessed as true or false. Then the possible worlds can be included as one feature of the context of use. The details of Montague's very technical approach were not entirely satisfactory, but that is less important than the stimulation and encouragement his work offered to semanticists. Semanticists set about representing and explicating complex pragmatic and contextual features of language using set theoretic models. They did, or so they claimed, what the anti-formalists said could not be done. Montague claimed that natural languages can be given the same formal treatment as formal languages such as computer programming languages and formal logics. His approach was influential in linguistics where the idea was to describe a Montague grammar for aspects of natural languages.

The work of philosophers of language, logicians, mathematicians, and linguists in pragmatics and intensional logic is technically sophisticated. Most of this work involves extending possible world semantics in various ways by adding further parameters of evaluation such as times, places, contexts. Another much admired California logician, David Kaplan, who taught at UCLA alongside Montague for many years, showed how formal semantics could account for such context dependent expressions as "I," "you," "here," "now," "actually," in ways that improved upon Montague's. Kaplan was a student of Carnap. Due to the work of Montague, Kaplan, and their students, inspired by Carnap and Tarski, philosophers speak of "California semantics," some grudgingly, others with awe.

Philosophers focused on several other problems in the philosophy of language. One of the most interesting is vagueness. Vagueness is the source of genuine philosophical puzzles such as the ancient sorites paradox – the paradox of the heap. [*Background 9.1* – The sorites paradox] The British philosopher Crispin Wright, one of the leading expositors of problems involving vagueness, pointed out that many of our ordinary predicates allow tolerance. For example, if someone is tall then someone else who is almost the same height is also tall. The application of the predicate "tall" allows small variations in height. Wright argued compellingly that many or most of our predicates could only operate if their meanings contained tolerance rules. For example, our application of the predicate "red" tolerates small variations in color. If "red" was not tolerant of small variations, then we could not tell by sight whether or not something was red. Two patches could be almost indistinguishable in color and one be red but not the other. We could not tell which was which. None of our ordinary vague predicates would be useful if they did not allow tolerance.

Unfortunately, Wright noted, such tolerance rules lead to problems and contradictions. Vague predicates will admit borderline cases that are not quite close enough to definite examples to fall under the predicate, nor far enough away to rule out the predicate. The tolerance rules are not strict. This means that some propositions will be neither true nor false. Some men are bald, and others are not bald. But some men are neither. The predicate "bald" neither truly applies nor fails to apply to such a man. This directly conflicts with classical logic in which the principle of bivalence[1] is fundamental. Vagueness leads to other annoying conflicts with classical logic, such as the sorites paradox.

Because of the conflicts with classical logic engendered by vagueness, philosophers and logicians explored many non-standard logics that would accommodate vagueness. Three valued logic, infinitely valued logic, and fuzzy logic were among the unsuccessful attempts to model vagueness. Problems of vagueness were tackled energetically by philosophers and logicians without much success, in my opinion.

Timothy Williamson is one of the boldest of recent analytic philosophers. Williamson is a British philosopher who has been the Wykeham Professor of Logic at Oxford University since 2000.[2] Although at Oxford, and Oxford educated, Williamson is not sympathetic to ordinary language philosophy or linguistic analysis. He does, and encourages other analytic philosophers to do, traditional speculative metaphysics. Williamson is also a traditionalist in logic. The last thing to give up is classical logic, according to Williamson. Williamson holds that the

---

[1] The principle of bivalence is that every statement is either true or false (and none are both). The law of excluded middle is closely related. Every instance of $P \vee \sim P$ is true.

[2] Previously held by A. J. Ayer and Michael Dummett.

way to accommodate vagueness is to acknowledge that all vagueness is epistemic. (His view is called epistemicism.) Vagueness is not in the world, but is only a reflection of our ignorance. The sharp lines are there. We just cannot know where they are.

Williamson has argued for his view with tenacity and ingenuity. His 1994 book on vagueness is a philosophical tour de force, and contains a full discussion of all the contemporary theories of vagueness. (See further readings.) Still, I do not think that most philosophers can believe that vague predicates are governed by unknowable, exquisitely sharp boundaries. I think that most of us agree with Wright that most ordinary predicates are tolerant. Vagueness is still an open problem for logicians and philosophers of language.

Williamson has also done influential work in many other areas of philosophy, especially epistemology and metaphysics. Lately he has been disparaging ordinary language philosophy and the idea that linguistic analysis is the primary method of philosophy. One of the favorite pastimes of the leading analytic philosophers of an era has been exposing and refuting all the "dogmas" of former dominant movements of analytic philosophy. This hasn't changed.

Philosophy of Mind

Jerry Fodor and Daniel Dennett have emerged as the leading and most influential philosophers of mind. Of course, they have different and opposed views. One characteristic that they share, though, is the extent to which their theories and arguments depend on, utilize, interact with, and have influenced work in empirical sciences such as cognitive science, evolutionary psychology, linguistics, neuroscience, and computer science. Unlike previous philosophy of mind, which was more a priori and purely philosophical in character, recent philosophy of mind, especially under the influence of Dennett and Fodor is interdisciplinary. In 1968, Fodor wrote:

> I think many philosophers secretly harbor the view that there is something deeply (i.e. conceptually) wrong with psychology, but that a philosopher with a little training in the techniques of linguistic analysis and a free afternoon could straighten it out. (Fodor 1968, p. vii)

Philosophers of mind these days no longer harbor such views, even secretly. Philosophy of mind needs to be informed by and work with the other disciplines that study the brain, the mind, and behavior.

Dennett and Fodor are both Americans, but Dennett studied at Oxford and wrote his dissertation under Ryle. Dennett is co-director of

The Center for Cognitive Studies and professor of philosophy at Tufts University. He is best known for his concept of the intentional stance.

Dennett's theory of the intentional stance is in some ways a sophisticated version of Rylean logical behaviorism. Dennett's view is called instrumentalism, instead of behaviorism, with which no one wants to be associated these days. We adopt the intentional stance when we attribute beliefs and desires to systems such as other people, but also when we attribute beliefs and desires to animals, machines, and even plants. The intentional stance is appropriate when it helps us to understand behavior as rational – that is, as appropriately accomplishing goals. The Rylean idea here is that in attributing beliefs and desires, we are not assuming anything about what goes on inside the system. For a system to have beliefs and desires is just for it to be usefully describable in those terms.

> The intentional stance is the strategy of prediction and explanation that attributes beliefs, desires, and other "intentional" states to systems – living and nonliving – and predicts future behavior from what it would be rational for an agent to do, given those beliefs and desires. Any system whose performance can be thus predicted and explained is an *intentional system*, whatever its innards. The strategy of treating parts of the world as intentional systems is the foundation of "folk psychology," but is also exploited (and is virtually unavoidable) in artificial intelligence and cognitive science more generally, as well as in evolutionary theory. (Dennett 1988, p. 495)

Surely lower animals, machines, and plants do not think even if we can usefully describe their actions in terms of desires and beliefs. According to Dennett, thinking only emerges when a system applies the intentional stance to itself. When I become self-aware as a rational system, and self-regulate, then I become self-conscious and think. Dennett holds that thinking is intimately connected to language acquisition. Thus animals, plants, and machines do not think, but they do have beliefs and desires (because they can be usefully described as having such intentional states).

My stating that Dennett's instrumentalism is in the spirit of Ryle's logical behaviorism is justified by Dennett's claim that his theory is based on linguistic analysis of our mental terms.

> Intentional systems theory is in the first place an analysis of the meanings of such everyday 'mentalistic' terms as 'believe,' 'desire,' 'expect,' 'decide,' and 'intend,' the terms of 'folk psychology' that we use to interpret, explain, and predict the behavior of other human beings, animals, some artifacts such as robots and computers, and indeed ourselves. (Dennett (no date), p. 1)

I doubt, though, that Ryle would approve of applying, non-metaphorically, the concepts of belief and desire to artifacts.

Dennett contrasts the intentional stance with two other stances that are also strategies for prediction and explanation. The design stance is based on a functional description of the system. When we adopt this stance, we treat systems as being engineered in certain ways to perform certain functions. The physical stance is the method of physical and chemical description. That is the most basic description of a system. The three stances reflect three different types of approaches to mentality and behavior. The physical stance would be adopted by neurophysiologists. They would explain mentality and behavior in terms of physical and chemical processes in nervous systems. Psychologists, cognitive scientists, and linguists would adopt the design stance. They would want to see how various parts interact to do particular jobs. For example, they would analyze language processing in terms of the operation of various sub-routines. At the level of folk psychology we adopt the intentional stance. [*Background 9.2* – Folk psychology and the philosophy of mind] No stance is ultimately the correct stance; none is eliminable. Each stance is appropriate in different settings, for different purposes.

One interesting note is that Dennett disagrees with Singer's claim that animals are capable of suffering. Suffering involves self-consciousness, according to Dennett. Animals cannot anticipate pain, cannot regret having undergone it, although they can learn to avoid it. Dennett, of course, acknowledges that animals experience pain, but it does not have the same quality as it would for a person, nor does pain have the same quality for human beings at different times. According to Dennett, we have no objective way of measuring animal pain compared to our own. In any case, pain seems to be a slimmer basis for ethical attitudes toward animals than would be the capacity for suffering, since pain is not always a bad thing. Such claims have not endeared Dennett to those in the animal liberation movement.

Jerry Fodor got his PhD at Princeton University under Putnam in 1960. He spent many years at MIT, where he was close to Chomsky and influenced by him. Although he has been very influential among analytic philosophers of mind, Fodor has strenuously resisted some of the basic leanings of analytic philosophers, such as empiricism. Unlike, for example Quine's critiques of empiricism, Fodor's have not been friendly; his attacks have more the flavor of Chomsky's rationalism. Lately Fodor has come in for scorn because, reminiscent of Popper, he has attacked Darwin's theory of natural selection for lacking explanatory power. Fodor was an early and adamant opponent of behaviorism. In his recent work, he claims that Darwin's theory is guilty of the same kinds of crude errors as Skinner's behaviorism. Fodor has long been troubled by evolutionary psychologists using and extending natural selection to mental operations in a way that he argued was unwarranted.

Fodor has been one of the most influential philosophers in the last 30 years and he has never been shy. In the philosophy of mind, Fodor has insisted on the centrality of mental representations. This is called Fodor's representational theory of the mind (as opposed to Dennett's instrumental theory of mind). This is the heart of cognitive science as opposed to behaviorism, which rejected appeal to anything "internal." The characteristic theme of cognitive science is that higher operations of our behavior and psychology can only be understood if we assume that our minds operate with internal representations that we manipulate according to computational procedures. Fodor rejects Dennett's claim that the attribution of beliefs and desires is merely instrumentally useful. Beliefs and desires according to Fodor are definite internal mental states with a particular character and role in interacting with other mental states and generating behavior. Fodor has been a leading defender of folk psychology. He claims that since it is so useful, even indispensable, it is almost certainly true. Although Fodor agrees with Dennett in honoring folk psychology, Fodor's interpretation is different. His is a realist, as opposed to an instrumentalist, theory of the intentional mental states of folk psychology.

Fodor is a prolific and controversial philosopher. His two most influential theories have been the language of thought hypothesis and the thesis of the modularity of mind. Two of Fodor's many books are titled *The Language of Thought* (Fodor 1979) and *The Modularity of Mind* (Fodor 1983).

To entertain a belief is to have a representation of that belief before your mind. The representation is formulated in the mental language of thought. The language of thought is structured like any shared human language. It has a syntax and semantics. It is compositional in the sense that complex items are built up out of simpler component items. The syntactical and semantical features of the sentences in the language give to beliefs and other thoughts their causal powers. Fodor bases his claims about the language of thought on the argument that once we abandon behaviorism the best theory of mind is that "cognitive processes are computational processes and hence presuppose a representational system ... " (Fodor 1979, p. 34).

The modularity of mind thesis has been especially influential among evolutionary psychologists. The idea is that various functions and parts of the mind are modularized in that they function more-or-less independently of each other and with set routines. The lower functions such as perception operate independently of the higher functions such as belief formation and reasoning. As evidence for modularity, Fodor points out that optical illusions do not go away when we understand them. Look again at the Checker Shadow Illusion (see p. 31). You know that areas A and B are precisely the same shade, but you still perceive them as different. This demonstrates that perception functions as a module somewhat independently of the cognitive belief system, according to Fodor. Fodor rejects the idea that our minds are modular all the way up. At the higher levels of, for example, belief formation our minds' operations are much more diffuse and general than at the level of perception. Our minds work like a computer, indeed are computers, with a big general processing unit, that takes input from several adjacent connected domain specific computers and operates on the inputs on the basis of the entire content of the system. The domain specific computers are the modularized parts of our minds and perceptual systems.

Evolutionary biologists have gone beyond Fodor, to his dismay, and argued that all mental systems are modularized and have evolved independently under adaptational pressure.

Beyond the details of Fodor's research programs, his contribution has been to help reorient the philosophy of mind.

> Fodor presented his view as an interpretation of work in psycho-linguistics and cognitive psychology. To many it gained plausibility because of its appeal to specific scientific practices. The picture and its relation to psychological theory are still very much in dispute. Fodor's work drew attention from linguists, psychologists, and computer scientists. It also benefited from and helped further a significant shift in the degree to which the details of scientific practice were seen to be relevant to philosophical problems about mind.
>
> Until the mid to late 1970s most philosophy in this area was carried on in a relatively a priori analytic spirit. (Burge 1992, pp. 42–3)

These notes on Dennett and Fodor only reflect some points on the surfaces of their contributions, which are deep, controversial, and cover a vast number of topics.

Metaphysics

Since the resurgence of metaphysics in the 1970s, analytic philosophers have been avidly devoted to that field. And this means substantive metaphysics, not faux-metaphysics such as Strawsonian linguistic analysis of our conceptual schemes, or swapping pragmatic answers to Carnapian external questions.

Substantive metaphysics is philosophical investigation into the fundamental nature of reality in its most general aspects. Analytic philosophers still agonize over how such an enquiry is possible, and some still doubt that it is. Meta-metaphysics has recently been just as much a central issue for analytic philosophers as it was at any point in the twentieth century. But meta-metaphysical doubts have not hindered analytic metaphysicians from pursuing traditional metaphysical issues and vehemently defending positions on them.

The main impetus for the rebirth of metaphysics was the development by Kripke and a few others of the semantics for modal logic and the subsequent widespread enthusiasm for the metaphysics of possible worlds. As we saw in Chapters 6 and 7, possible worlds are useful in illuminating all sorts of philosophical issues. Naturally, philosophers, all of whom were happy to avail themselves of possible world semantics, differed about the nature of possible worlds. David Lewis, who was the leading analytic metaphysician until his untimely death in 2001, argued that there really are other possible worlds that are just as real as the actual world. Alvin Plantinga, Stalnaker, and many others would not go that far. They opposed Lewis' modal realism, arguing that only the actual world is real. Other possible worlds are constructs from elements in the actual world. Such actualists as Plantinga and Stalnaker were sufficiently metaphysical, nevertheless, in that they countenanced abstract intensional objects that would have been rejected by anti-metaphysical positivists, Quineans, and neo-pragmatists.

The debate between the modal realists and modal actualists about the reality of non-actual possible worlds is paralleled in the metaphysics of time. Time in some ways is structured like the realm of possible worlds in that past and future times can be viewed analogously to non-actual possible worlds. The present time corresponds, then, to the actual world. The excitement about possible worlds led, in the last quarter of the twentieth century and the first decade of the twenty-first, to renewed interest in the philosophy of time. The irony is that British analytic philosophy began with Moore's and Russell's rejection of the metaphysical excesses of Bradley and McTaggart, as we saw in Chapter 1. Moore and Russell were especially scornful of McTaggart's denial of the reality of time. I do not think that contemporary analytic metaphysicians are combing the dusty texts of Bradley and McTaggart looking for insights, but much of the recent work in the philosophy of time would bring a smile to McTaggart's face if he could be aware of it. Analytic philosophers today are using some of the terminology and arguments introduced by McTaggart, and respectfully referring to him.

Presentism is the view in the philosophy of time that only the present time is real and only things now existing are real. Various versions of non-presentism have also been defended. The clearest and most extreme is eternalism. Eternalism is the view that all times, past and future, and their inhabitants are equally real. For the eternalist the present time is like a point in space that we occupy. The other parts of space are still there. "Now" is like "here." Presentism corresponds neatly to modal actualism, which denies the reality of non-actual possible worlds. Eternalism corresponds to modal realism, which holds that other possible worlds are just as real, and not unlike, the actual world.

Presentism seems commonsensical and to square best with out everyday temporal concepts. Surely Socrates and the World Trade Center are no more. They're gone forever, alas. Nevertheless, presentism is not without its problems and puzzles. Actualists must construct other possible worlds from things in the actual world. This turns out to be no easy task. Likewise, presentism must construct past and future objects from things present now. We presently have memories, pictures, videos, and records of the World Trade Center. The writings of Plato and a few other ancient Greeks supply everything we know about Socrates. When we talk about The World Trade Center or Socrates or future objects like the 2020 Olympic Games, we are not referring directly to those objects since they do not exist, according to presentists, but to some artificial construct out of memories, records, anticipations, and so on. Similarly, presentists need to have an artificial account of the truth-conditions of past- and future-tense statements. "Plato was the student of Socrates" is true or false depending on some complex and, again, artificial account in terms of presently existing records, memories, etc.

A form of eternalism has been defended by Williamson in a 2002 article titled "Necessary Existents." He argues that nothing comes into or goes out of existence. You and I (and our bodies as well) have always existed and always will. Basically, his argument is that there is no other way to make sense of propositions about Socrates, The World Trade Center, and other non-present objects. Do not take much solace from Williamson's views, however well-argued. He claims that Socrates exists but not concretely as a living person. Nor will you and I after we die, nor did we before we were born. We emerge from purely abstract existence into concrete living existence when we are born.

Socrates although he is no longer concrete is still there for us to talk about, but there only abstractly.

The traditional philosophical issue regarding the persistence of individuals over time is connected with the philosophy of time. One fundamental problem about persistence is that an individual's properties change over time. Anyway, that is the common sense view. Ten minutes ago this apple weighed 10 ounces. Now it weighs 8 ounces. (I took a bite or two out of it.) An apple cannot weigh both 10 ounces and 8 ounces. This problem is called the problem of temporary intrinsics by Lewis – how can an object temporarily have an intrinsic (i.e., non-relational) property? The presentist solves this problem by denying that the past 10-ounce apple exists. For the presentist every object exists only in the present with its present properties. It is entirely present in the present. The statement that that apple did weigh 10 ounces is true, if it is, because of some construction that does not involve an existing 10-ounce apple.

A different solution, favored by Lewis, to the problem of temporary intrinsics is that persisting objects have temporal parts. Thus, only one part of the apple is present now, and a different, wholly distinct, temporal part of the apple is/was present 10 minutes ago. Each temporal part of an object is equally real. One part weighed 10 ounces and another part weighed 8 ounces. Thus the apple's changing weight does not lead to a contradiction.

The view that an object has temporal parts is called perdurantism. Perdurantists say that a persisting object perdures. The opposing view, that an object is wholly present at each time that it exists, is called endurantism. Endurantists say that a persisting object endures. Lewis favors perdurantism, since it is the analogue of his counterpart theory. My 8-ounce apple, missing a bite or two, has a counterpart apple at the temporal point 10 minutes ago. (It's a bit longer ago now.) Indeed, it has a temporal counterpart at each previous moment of its existence. The perdurantist views objects as wormlike. The apple, and in fact every perduring object, is a four dimensional space-time object. These four-dimensional objects can be viewed as space-time worms or as a series of instantaneous stages. Each stage is a temporal part of the complete object that perdures.

Ted Sider, one of the leading younger analytic metaphysicians, has defended eternalism and four-dimensionalism with energy and sophistication. In his 2001 book *Four-Dimensionalism*, Sider argues that presentism cannot capture the notion of time on which physical theories are based. Special relativity requires a non-presentist theory of time. Eternalism and four-dimensionalism are more reflective of current scientific theories, according to Sider. His views are very influential and are moving philosophers away from presentism. These issues are very much alive in analytic metaphysics today.

Another area of traditional metaphysics where the theories and practice of natural science have influenced recent analytic metaphysics is the theory of universals. The question of universals, which is at the heart of metaphysics, goes back at least to Plato. What are properties and relations? A substance is a thing – the individual man or horse. The man or horse has properties. For example, the horse is white. Many other things are white as well. What is this whiteness that they share? The tendency of the anti-metaphysical analytic philosophers was to take a nominalist position on this question and deny that there is any such thing as whiteness itself. We have the predicate " . . . is white" which is truly applicable to some things and not others, and we may even have the set of white things. But that is all. Platonists view whiteness as a real, separate, non-physical thing that is shared by all white things. White things participate in or in some way fall under the form of whiteness. Another related view is that the universal whiteness is wholly present in all white things. Unlike an individual, according to this view, a universal is entirely present at different places.

The metaphysical notion that our physical world includes universals may seem spooky and connected to semi-religious mystifications. The leading Australian metaphysician and philosopher of science D. M. Armstrong argues that the theory of universals is not only scientifically respectable, but also necessary to make sense of scientific laws. Armstrong's arguments are not based on linguistic analysis. He is not claiming that we need to postulate universals to explain the meanings of predicates or any such thing. In fact, Armstrong rejects the idea that ontology can be derived from linguistic analysis and that ordinary predicates must stand for properties. Consider again my red apple. The following predicates apply to it. " . . . is red," " . . . is light red," " . . . is colored." We need not suppose that there are three distinct and independent properties. According to Armstrong, all contingent truths need truthmakers to explain their truth. The truthmaker is whatever it is that makes a true proposition true. "My apple is red," "My apple is light red," "My apple is colored" may each be made true by the one state of affairs of my apple having the property of being its specific shade of red. Which properties there are is not an issue that we can solve simply by looking at language, however. It must be settled by scientific investigation. Which properties, i.e., universals, there are and what are the truthmakers of true propositions are to be determined by empirical science. Chances are that the truthmaker for "My apple is red" will not contain the property redness, but rather a complex of properties recognized by physics and chemistry in which none is exactly a redness property. In any case, "My apple is red" must have a truthmaker, and such a truthmaker will involve universals but we cannot assume that there is universal that corresponds to the predicates " . . . is red," " . . . is colored," etc. according to Armstrong.

Unlike Davidson, who holds that laws of nature are linguistic items, Armstrong distinguishes between the statement of the law and the law itself. The law of nature is the truthmaker for the statement of the law. For Armstrong, a law of nature cannot just be based on a correspondence between the presence of two properties. Laws involve necessitation, and only universals could support lawlike necessitation. A law of nature is of the form "having property A (or universal A) necessitates having property B (universal B)." Unlike mere correspondences, natural laws support counterfactual conditionals. The law just stated would support the claim that if x were an A (contained universal A), then x would be a B (contain universal B). The laws of nature, and thus the universals, are determined by scientists. Only universals that are instantiated in natural laws exist.

Due to Armstrong, and several other Australians, Australia has been a major center of analytic philosophy since the latter third or so of the twentieth century. Australians have been particularly promiscuous in pursuing substantive metaphysics with characteristic Australian élan.

Epistemology

Despite Austin's and other ordinary language philosophers' attempts to dismiss it, epistemology has recently flourished, just like metaphysics. Philosophy cannot exist without epistemology, since epistemological questions lurk behind every philosophical issue. Assuming that an ethical claim is objectively true or false, how do we know which it is? The meta-metaphysical questions about how metaphysical knowledge is possible, or if it is, are epistemological.

One area that has recently received an immense amount of attention is characteristic of classical analytic philosophy. This is the problem generated by Gettier's short article that I mentioned earlier. Knowledge cannot simply be justified true belief, because the belief can be accidentally justified or justified in irrelevant ways. So the problem is to give necessary and sufficient conditions for knowledge that avoid Gettier-type problems of accidental justification. New suggestions are offered and other epistemologists find counterexamples to them. And so it goes. A great deal of ingenuity has been lavished on this project, but I do not think that anyone has actually succeeded in offering a widely accepted analysis of knowledge. This has not all been wasted effort, however, as the attempts and counter arguments have shed light on issues in the philosophy of language and mind. See further readings for overviews of the issues.

A troubling and to me far more interesting epistemological issue is the question of skepticism. Since Descartes, this has been the core issue of traditional epistemology. Descartes cast the problem in terms of a powerful evil demon that is fooling me into believing that I have a body, inhabit the earth among other people, and so on. More recently, skepticism has been sharpened by movies such as *Total Recall* and *The Matrix* in which characters experience a virtual reality. The skeptical challenge these days is "How do you know that the world you believe you inhabit is not a virtual reality?" "How do you know that you are not a brain in a vat?" How do you know that you are not a brain, right now, in a laboratory somewhere, being fed, electronically, all of your sensory experiences? After all, they are just electrical impulses going to your brain from your eyes, ears, etc. You do not know where your veil of perception is coming from. Maybe all of your beliefs about the external world, including your body, are false.

G. E. Moore famously attempted to defang the skeptic by claiming that he was more certain of various common facts, such as that he has two hands, then he ever could be of the steps in the skeptic's arguments. Later ordinary language philosophers tried to use the paradigm case argument to escape skepticism. I can correctly use "know" in certain situations in which I make statements about the external world. Sometimes it is correct usage for me to say, for example, "I know my keys are in the glove box." If so, then the skeptic is wrong to claim that I do not know these things. More recently Putnam created a flurry of controversy when he claimed by using technical results in set theory and the causal theory of reference to "prove" that I am not a brain in a vat, or at least if I say or think "I am a brain in a vat" what I say or think cannot be true, given what these words must mean (Figure 9.1).

To keep the story reasonably short, let me just say that none of these efforts have been successful, if by successful we mean have removed skeptical doubts. We still feel the pull of skepticism even after being steeped in Moore, Austin, and Putnam. On the other hand, we pay no attention to that pull when we are actively engaged. This would suggest a pragmatist answer. "Stay actively engaged; don't worry yourself about these philosophical conundrums. They are just the result of our minds idling, on a holiday." This response is appealing, but is also not satisfactory. The skeptic is touching something fundamental about

Figure 9.1 Cartoon from the participants' T-shirt at Putnam's NEH Summer Seminar 1986, in which I was honored to be included.

our understanding of ourselves. Skepticism is not just a figment of enlightenment, hyper-intellectual cogitating. Everybody understands it, in every culture, and feels its pull without a lot of lengthy tutoring. In almost 40 years of teaching, I've had many students who were confused about all sorts of concepts that I consider to be pretty basic to philosophy. I have never, to my knowledge, had a student who did not get the challenge of skepticism right away.

Recent epistemologists have focused less on refuting skepticism than on explaining the appeal of skepticism, and at the same time explaining how it is that we can have common sense knowledge. David Lewis, again, has been in the forefront here. In his brilliant article "Scorekeeping in a Language Game" (Lewis 1983) he notes that the boundaries of relevance and precision shift in various ways in conversations. In particular, it is easier to shift them toward more precision or to include more relevant possibilities, than is the reverse. If I say, for example, "Italy is boot shaped," you can challenge my claim in conversation by pointing out the differences. Automatically higher standards of precision will come into play. You cannot now say "France is hexagonal" and get away with it, even though in most contexts that is true enough.

314

For some reason, which Lewis does not feel able to explain, raising the level of precision or bringing in new possibilities is always easier and smoother than lowering it. The skeptic avails herself of this conversational feature.

> Take another example. The commonsensical epistemologist says: "I *know* the cat is in the carton – there he is before my eyes – I just *can't* be wrong about that!" The sceptic replies: "You might be the victim of a deceiving demon." Thereby he brings into consideration possibilities hitherto ignored, else what he says would be false. The boundary shifts outward so that what he says is true. Once the boundary is shifted, the commonsensical epistemologist must concede defeat. And yet he was not in any way wrong when he laid claim to infallible knowledge. What he said was true with respect to the score as it then was. (Lewis 1983, p. 247)

In his 1996 article "Elusive Knowledge" Lewis develops this idea in detail. Knowledge claims depend on context. This view has come to be called contextualism. A correct knowledge claim in one context may be incorrect if the context changes. When making ordinary knowledge claims we justifiably ignore untoward and bizarre possible scenarios in which we are mistaken. If I look around my study and see that Pumpkin the cat is sleeping in my chair, I can justifiably and correctly say that I know that Pumpkin is here in my study. I do not even consider the possibility that my wife has cleverly made a stuffed replica of Pumpkin and put it in my chair. I can justifiably ignore that possibility. Once the bizarre possibilities are brought to my attention, the context changes. Now if someone were to say to me "Maybe that's a replica of Pumpkin," I must have some way of eliminating that possibility or I have to withdraw my claim to knowledge. Lewis' point is that the skeptic switches the context by bringing up properly ignored possibilities. Once those possibilities (evil demon, brain in a vat, hallucination) are introduced, unless I can eliminate them, I must withdraw my claim to knowledge. I cannot eliminate the skeptic's possibilities because of the way they are formulated. Thus the skeptic wins by changing the context.

> Likewise in the sceptical argument the context switched midway, and the semantic value of the context-dependent word 'know' switched with it. The premise 'I know that I have hands' was true in its everyday context, where the possibility of deceiving demons was properly ignored. The mention of that very possibility switched the context midway. The conclusion 'I know that I am not handless and deceived' was false in *its* context, because that was a context in which the possibility of deceiving demons was being mentioned, hence was not being ignored, hence was not being properly ignored. (Lewis 1996, p. 564)

When we do epistemology, we are automatically in a context in which the possibilities of evil demons and virtual realities are relevant and not ignored. Thus, epistemologists cannot help being skepticism-enablers.

> Unless this investigation of ours was an altogether atypical sample of epistemology, it will be inevitable that epistemology must destroy knowledge. That is how knowledge is elusive. Examine it, and straightaway it vanishes. (Lewis 1996, p. 560)

But do not despair. We still know a lot of things, because epistemology is a special and rare context.

> That is how epistemology destroys knowledge. But it does so only temporarily. The pastime of epistemology does not plunge us forevermore into its special context. We can still do a lot of proper ignoring, a lot of knowing, and a lot of true ascribing of knowledge to ourselves and others, the rest of the time. (Lewis 1996, p. 559)

One possible objection to contextualism of the sort that Lewis is proposing is that it sounds dangerously like the paradigm case argument about knowledge. The skeptic could reply that Lewis is talking about correct and incorrect uses of the word "know," but skepticism has to do with knowledge or, rather, the lack of it, not language.

Philosophers in the last couple of decades have offered many different and ever more intricate versions of contextualism, and its opponent, invariantism. For example, some contextualists offer arguments to support the view that practical stakes affect knowledge attributions. If a lot is at stake, then we maintain much higher standards for knowledge. If we will lose the house to foreclosure if I cannot cash my check on Saturday, then my wife better have overwhelming evidence when she assures me that she knows that the bank is open until 1 p.m. this Saturday. If it's merely a matter of running a little short of cash, her knowledge claim can be correctly based on slimmer evidence. The topic of the effect of context on knowledge continues to be the focus of a great deal of attention.

One interesting, very recent, development has been experimental philosophy. Philosophers have actually gone out and conducted surveys testing non-philosophers' intuitions having to do with knowledge claims in various contexts. Initial results seem to conflict with contextualism, but not enough has yet been done in this area to make any firm judgments.

Ethics and Metaethics

One interesting and active form of ethical anti-realism that has recently been proposed is moral fictionalism. Moral fictionalism is an alternative to the non-cognitivism of Ayer, Stevenson, and Hare. Fictionalism about a sort of discourse is the view that the statements of that sort of discourse are to be understood on analogy with storytelling. They are not aimed at literal truth, but rather to create an effect or to portray a useful picture. Ethics is not the only area in which fictionalism is on the agenda. Fictionalism is an appealing way of avoiding difficulties in any area suffering from epistemological or ontological headaches. Mathematical fictionalists hold that mathematical discourse is fictional. Others have argued for fictionalism about ordinary objects; and still others, more plausibly, have adopted fictionalism about non-actual possible worlds. Eliminativists are fictionalists about intentional mental states. [*Background 9.2* – Folk psychology and the philosophy of mind]

Consider for a moment the appeal of mathematical fictionalism. We may have serious doubts about the actual existence of mathematical objects – eternal, perfect, abstract. They certainly are not part of the physical universe. How can we know about them, if we cannot perceive them? Rather than give up mathematics, we can choose to retain it as a useful story, or whole bunch of interrelated stories, with its own internal rules. Fictionalism is a way of retaining a realm of discourse in the face of ontological skepticism.

The main motivations for moral fictionalism are epistemological. Moral claims are not scientifically verifiable. They are not empirically checkable. Nor can they be derived by deduction from self-evident universally accepted premises. We do not have any clear, agreed upon sources of knowledge that would generate answers to ethical questions. This leaves ethical claims in an epistemological limbo. If moral claims are fictional, then they do not need to be verified except in the sense in which they fit in with a story. Thus the epistemological problems of explaining ethical knowledge go away. There isn't any ethical knowledge. Moral claims are literally false (or perhaps lack a truth-value, depending on your theory of truth and reference) just like the fictional claims in a novel.

Morality is a useful fiction, according to moral fictionalists. But how can a fiction be useful? Consider an analogy. Moral fictionalists invite us to consider that we might reasonably be color fictionalists. Color fictionalists hold that colors are not actual properties in the world out there, but just a way we have of perceiving things in certain conditions.

Do not worry about whether this theory of color is correct. We might be convinced that it is, but this would in no way diminish the usefulness of color talk. We get along with all sorts of fictions such as the notion of American society, or your conscience, or how much you're going to get done this weekend, and find them useful. If people came to agree to treat morality as fictional, this would not spell disaster. We find ourselves moved by and emotionally involved in fictions when we read novels, or view plays or movies. When engaged in the story, we forget that they are fictions. Morality could work in more-or-less the same way. We would share moral fictions in order to regulate our behavior and so that our relations with others and the natural world would go more smoothly. While at work or play, we would not focus on the fictionality of moral discourse. We could still let morality guide our behavior, at least to the extent that it ever does.

And moral fictionalism has advantages, according to moral fictionalists. If we are skeptical of the possibility of moral knowledge and objectivity, moral fictionalists argue that accepting fictionalism is better than throwing up our hands and giving up on morality or becoming moral relativists.

A metaethical alternative to moral fictionalism, that might satisfy the moral skeptic, would be Rawls' notion of reflective equilibrium. The method of reflective equilibrium will give us answers to moral questions and settle moral issues, but only given a generous amount of agreement at the beginning. Philippa Foot may be right that those who disagree too much with our basic moral notions are no longer talking morality, so we would have a substantive basis for objective moral judgments. Still, this approach has an air similar to Strawson's descriptive metaphysics. Moral philosophy would seem then to be a matter of exposing, analyzing, and clarifying our moral system or systems. Moral philosophers have work to do in ironing out conflicts within the systems, or between various competing aspects of the systems, adjusting our principles and intuitions by the method of reflective equilibrium, and so on. This seems to fall short of satisfying the moral skeptic, however. Our morality still seems to be open to something like epistemological skepticism. How do we know that our moral system or systems are not completely wrong? How do we know that our firm moral intuitions are true? For these and similar reasons, issues concerning moral realism and anti-realism continue to be the central concerns in metaethics.

One sort of last-ditch response that moral realists make is that skepticism is a problem for all areas where we suppose we have knowledge, not just ethics. How do we know that our logical or mathematical systems are correct? How do we know that our mathematical intuitions are correct? In the end, we have to trust something. Morality is no worse off than any other area. If morality is in the same boat with science and mathematics, then that is good enough. The point is that whatever the epistemological problems morality has, the same problems arise in other areas as well. The main difference, the moral skeptic might point out, is that there is a great deal more agreement in science and mathematics than there is in morality. And we have methods of settling disagreements in those areas, whereas we have no such agreed upon methods with moral disagreements. Perhaps something like Rawls' method of reflective equilibrium can be made to fill this gap.

Applied ethicists, however, cannot wait for these metaethical issues to be solved nor can we in our lives. We cannot dispense with justice. Whatever it is and whatever we know or do not know about it, justice is something we want for ourselves and others, and we want to live in a just society. Applied ethicists have recently worked closely with economists, anthropologists, cognitive scientists, and other social scientists, to determine what is feasible and morally relevant concerning justice. Rawls' theory of justice has been the starting point and foil of all recent analytical investigations of justice.

In the last 20 years or so, Martha Nussbaum has emerged as a leading political philosopher, feminist, ethicist, and public intellectual. Nussbaum has worked closely with Rawls, been influenced by him, and been critical of his contract theory of justice. She was born in 1946 in New York City and got her PhD in ancient philosophy from Harvard University. Nussbaum has taught at Harvard and Brown University and is currently professor of law and ethics at the University of Chicago. Originally she concentrated on ancient ethics, but since the early 1990s has contributed to many areas of philosophy, especially political philosophy.

Nussbaum's most influential work in ethics and political philosophy has been to challenge and expand upon Rawls' contract theory on the basis of the capabilities approach that she developed partly in collaboration with the economist and philosopher Amartya Sen,[3] and partly independently.

Nussbaum agrees with Rawls that utilitarianism has fatal problems, but she also finds flaws with Rawls' social contract approach. Rawls' theory of justice is concerned with basic equal rights and the just distribution of primary goods – liberty and opportunity, income and wealth, and the basis of self-respect – within a society of free and equal

---

[3] Sen won the Nobel Prize in economics in 1998 for his work in welfare economics.

individuals. One difficulty is that individuals are not free and equal. The initial problem is not the fair distribution of primary goods, but providing a minimum of entitlements to all people.

> Some theories, such as Rawls's begin with the design of a fair procedure. My capabilities approach begins with outcomes: with a list of entitlements that have to be secured to citizens if the society in question is a minimally just one. Particularly in the current world, where institutions and their relations are constantly in flux, I believe it is wise to begin with human entitlements as our goal. (Nussbaum 2004, p. 13)

Nussbaum using her capabilities approach questions whether the primary goods themselves are worthwhile, if people do not have the capacities to use them. This is her key point. Rawls' approach ignores morally relevant differences between individuals. An allotment of primary goods has to be sensitive to the different needs of people, such as pregnant women and the disabled, in order to be just. Women who have been kept out of the labor market in some countries would require more resources (e.g., educational opportunities) so that they could gainfully participate in the economy. Merely assessing resources – primary goods – may leave out essential features, such as a self-image that would enable one to take advantage of opportunities. Nussbaum says we need ways of measuring outcomes that go beyond distributions of primary goods. Thus Rawls' primary goods approach is insensitive to some vital issues concerning justice.

Nussbaum lists ten capabilities that should be guaranteed to all individuals. These ten capabilities are essential to a free and dignified human life. The following is a somewhat abbreviated list (lacking short explanations included with the list) of the ten essential human capabilities

1. *Life*. Being able to live to the end of a human life of normal length; ...
2. *Bodily health*. Being able to have good health, including reproductive health; ...
3. *Bodily integrity*. Being able to move freely from place to place; being able to be secure against violent assault, including sexual assault, marital rape, and domestic violence; having opportunities for sexual satisfaction and for choice in matters of reproduction.
4. *Senses, imagination, thought*. Being able to use the senses; being able to imagine, to think, and to reason – ... [This includes basic education, literacy, etc.]
5. *Emotions*. Being able to have attachments to things and persons outside ourselves; ...

6. *Practical reason.* Being able to form a conception of the good and to engage in critical reflection about planning one's own life.
7. *Affiliation.* (a) Being able to live for and in relation to others... (b) Having the social bases of self-respect and nonhumiliation; being able to be treated as a dignified being whose worth is equal to that of others...
8. *Other species.* Being able to live with concern for and in relation to animals, plants, and the world of nature.
9. *Play.* Being able to laugh, to play, to enjoy recreational activities.
10. *Control over one's environment.* [This involves the ability to participate in political decisions, and to own and use property, to work cooperatively, etc.]

The "capabilities approach," as I conceive it, claims that a life that lacks any one of these capabilities, no matter what else it has, will fall short of being a good human life. (Nussbaum 1999, pp. 41–2)

This list is from Nussbaum's book titled *Sex and Social Justice* (Nussbaum 1999). Clearly, these capabilities are directed at ways in which women have been deprived of a full and good life. Thus Nussbaum sees her capabilities approach as a needed form of feminism. It is also inherently tied in with economics. "Thus, all capabilities have an economic aspect: even the freedom of speech requires education, adequate nutrition, etc." (Nussbaum 2004, p. 13)

I suspect that Nussbaum would not be much in sympathy with Conan the Barbarian's idea of the good human life (see p. 268). Conan's warrior conception of good shows something about Nussbaum's capabilities approach, however. Conan the Barbarian probably has all ten of the capabilities Nussbaum lists, except perhaps the first one, but would we say that his life is a good human life? (I know. Conan is a fictional character, but work with me on this one. As the moral fictionalists remind us, fictions can be useful.) If not, this shows that Nussbaum's list is at best a specification of the necessary conditions for a good human life. It is not sufficient. So what more would be needed? I leave the reader to ponder this question.

What is the Future of Analytic Philosophy?

I hope that the previous sections of this chapter have indicated in which direction I think analytic philosophy is going. Analytic philosophers are working with natural scientists, mathematicians, linguists, psycholinguists, cognitive scientists, sociologists, economists, and with the information, theories, and insights of those disciplines. The leading analytic philosophers are pursuing their occupation with the cooperation and results of the sciences. Philosophers can no longer expect to make significant contributions to philosophy of language and philosophy of mind without a firm background in the relevant areas of the social or natural sciences. They are expected to integrate the results and methods of the sciences with their own philosophizing. Also scientists are integrating philosophy into their own undertakings. (Alas, not as much of that as we might wish.) Even in philosophical areas that seem remote from science, such as metaethics, ethics, aesthetics, and philosophy of religion, analytic philosophers are becoming more sensitive to the empirical and social setting of their subject matters. I predict that the philosophical scene will continue to become more interdisciplinary.

Distinguishing between philosophy per se and the sciences will get more difficult. Philosophy of language is merging with linguistics, cognitive science, evolutionary psychology, and mathematics. Logic has already been largely absorbed by mathematics. Philosophy of mind is merging with psychology, cognitive science, neuroscience, and biology; epistemology with the same disciplines. Ethics, at least applied ethics, is connecting with economics, social psychology, law, politics, and political science, and will continue to critically examine the practice of science and technology. Moral psychology is emerging as a major area of current research. Metaphysics is interpenetrating with cosmology, physics, and the other natural sciences. Ted Sider, echoing Quine, says "I think of metaphysics as being continuous with science" (from a talk given by Sider in February 2008). His remark applies as well to other areas of philosophy.

The notion that philosophy is or ought to be continuous with science is not new. Russell and the logical positivists wanted philosophy to be scientific. The Marxists insisted that philosophy was the most abstract or general branch of natural science. Quine, certainly no Marxist, urged that epistemology be naturalized and he viewed metaphysics as continuous with physics. The difference today is that analytic philosophers are not just talking about it. It's happening for real. Philosophy and science are absorbing each other, at least in philosophy of mind, philosophy of language, metaphysics, and logic.

My prediction is that soon few separate a priori analytic philosophy research programs will exist in those areas. The analytic philosophers' old preoccupations with linguistic analysis; a priori reasoning about language, metaphysics, or mind; conceptual analysis of our conceptual schemes will no longer find many, or even any, practitioners. To the extent that philosophers do focus on ordinary language and our conceptual schemes, research will be done empirically in the way of the growing field of experimental philosophy, which I think must be considered to be continuous with social science. The jungle that Rorty notes in the introductory quote, and the era of specialization that Soames describes are reflections of this absorption of analytic philosophy into other, scientific and social scientific, disciplines. Analytic philosophy will not be so much dispersed into multifarious, tiny philosophical research groups whose members understand and appreciate only each other. Rather, analytic philosophers will be coordinating with the vast and multifarious web of scientific research.

Does this mean that philosophy will or ought to disappear as a separate discipline or department within the academic community? Absolutely not! For one thing, philosophy has a glorious and distinct literature that goes back to Plato. This indispensable tradition must be preserved and interpreted. This is no mean, subsidiary task, despite Quine's scorn for the history of philosophy. Historical philosophers have played a role in shaping our culture and formulating ways that we conceive ourselves and the world. Furthermore, historical philosophers serve as sources and inspiration for people working on research programs today. Consider, for example, the way in which Aristotle has inspired virtue ethics. Nussbaum also appeals to Aristotle in support of her capabilities approach. Metaphysicians currently embrace (or reject) Aristotelian essentialism. Leibniz introduced possible worlds metaphysics. For another, there are areas of philosophy that resist absorption in science – areas such as ethics, aesthetics, and philosophy of religion – although even in these areas many analytic philosophers are becoming more sensitive to social and empirical aspects of their subject matters.

As Western philosophers we trace our heritage back to Socrates, the founder of our discipline. Philosophers have a distinct and invaluable dialectical approach that is different from the methods of the empirical sciences. As analytic philosophers we do not simply cooperate in the various research programs of the sciences with which we are allied. We are distanced, critical, skeptical, creative, and eclectic. We work at the edges and the frontiers of science. We pursue global questions regarding the scientific enterprise, such as how can the scientific image be reconciled with our common sense notions of ourselves.

Will science with the help, and goading, of analytic philosophers solve the riddles of the ages that have given life to philosophy and, despite the attempts of early analytic philosophers to eliminate them, will not go away? Why is there something rather than nothing? What is the nature of consciousness and how can it be explained? How can we respond to the epistemological skeptic? What is best in life? Does God exist? I do not think that analytic philosophers have given up on these and similarly profound questions. I think they see their work, no matter how specialized, as connected to the quest for understanding of these fundamental philosophical questions. I do not know, obviously, if these questions will be answered, but I believe that analytic philosophy informed by and working with science has the best chance of making progress.

Background 9.1 – The sorites paradox

The word "sorites" comes from "*soros*" the word for "heap" in Greek. Suppose we have a nice big heap of sand in front of us. If we gently remove a single grain of sand from the heap, we will still have a heap of sand in front of us. We can generalize. The gentle removal of a single grain of sand from a heap will leave a heap. By iteration this leads to the paradox that no matter how many grains of sand we remove from a heap, we will still have a heap left.

We can present this as an argument.

1. n grains of sand properly arranged make a heap. (Choose some sufficiently large n.)
2. If n grains of sand properly arranged make a heap, then n-1 grains make a heap.
3. If n-1 grains of sand make a heap, then n-2 grains make a heap.

Etc.

We can derive the conclusion that $n - n$ grains of sand make a heap.

The puzzle is that the premises seem to be true and the argument is deductively valid. Indeed no single premise is deniable. Nor can we just deny a bunch of the premises. And if any premise is false, then its immediate neighbors are automatically true. (Brief explanation: If one of the conditional premises is false, then its antecedent is true, but its consequent is false. Its antecedent is the consequent of the previous conditional premise, thus that premise is true. Its consequent is the antecedent of the next conditional premise, so that premise is also true. Recall that a conditional is true if its antecedent is false or its consequent is true.) But the conclusion is false. Thus we have an unsound argument that is valid and all the premises are true. This cannot be.

This paradox can be run with any vague term. And it can take many different forms. No successful resolution has yet been proposed.

Background 9.2 – Folk psychology and the philosophy of mind

The topic of folk psychology has been the subject of a great mass of articles and books in the philosophy of mind. Folk psychology is not strictly defined and is used in different senses by different philosophers. The basic idea, though, is that we attribute mental states to ourselves and others, use these attributions to explain and predict behavior, and have views about the relations of mental states. All of this adds up to a theory about the mind and its functioning. This theory is not a scientific theory that is derived from controlled experiments and other scientific methods. It is a common sense theory of the mind. It is folk psychology.

Philosophers of mind have been keen to deny various features of folk psychology. Behaviorists denied that sensation words and talk of beliefs and desires referred to anything inner. Type-type identity theorists claimed that mental states are identical to neurophysiological states of the nervous system. Eliminativists want to chuck the whole thing and deny that there are any such things as beliefs and desires or other intentional states. The mental states of folk psychology are no more real than phlogiston or elves or fairies. All explanation of behavior will eventually be done in terms of physical-chemical processes in the nervous system, but none of these processes are identical with desires, beliefs, etc.

The issues in the philosophy of mind regarding folk psychology are: What is it? How much of it is correct? What parts of it are dispensable? What can replace it, if anything?

Further Reading

A good place to start on any of the topics in this chapter is *The Routledge Companion to Twentieth Century Philosophy* (Routledge 2008). Here you will find articles on the main areas of philosophy that cover the era from 1900 to 2000. This book also contains articles on Continental philosophy.

Vagueness by Timothy Williamson (Routledge 1994) covers the entire topic, including all the paradoxes generated by vagueness.

A good introduction to Dennett's philosophy of mind is his *The Intentional Stance* (MIT Press 1987).

For Fodor, a good source is his *Psychosemantics* (MIT Press 1988).

For current philosophy of time there is Ted Sider's *Four Dimensionalism: An Ontology of Persistence and Time* (Oxford University Press 2001).

D. M. Armstrong, *Universals: An Opinionated Introduction* (Westview 1989).

D. M. Armstrong's *Truth and Truth-Makers* (Cambridge University Press 2004) is a thorough investigation of that topic.

Fictionalism in Metaphysics (Oxford University Press 2005) is an anthology of articles by eminent philosophers on all sorts of fictionalism. The article on moral fictionalism is by Richard Joyce.

A good place to start for those interested in moral realism versus moral anti-realism is the anthology *Essays on Moral Realism* (Cornell University Press 1988). This is divided into two sections. One on realism, the other on anti-realism. The articles are by leading philosophers.

One of Martha Nussbaum's most recent books is *Creating Capabilities: The Human Development Approach* (Harvard University Press 2011).

For a view of the present and future of analytic philosophy that is different from mine, see his essay "Philosophy in America Today" in Rorty's *Consequences of Pragmatism* (University of Minnesota Press 1982).

References

Anscombe, G. E. M. 1968. "Modern Moral Philosophy." Reprinted in *Ethics*, edited by Judith J. Thomson and Gerald Dworkin, New York: Harper & Row, pp. 186–210. (Originally published in 1958.)

Anscombe, G. E. M. 1969. *Intention*. Ithaca: Cornell University Press. (Originally published in 1957.)

Austin, J. L. 1961a. "A Plea for Excuses." Reprinted in *Philosophical Papers*, Oxford: Clarendon Press, pp. 121–52. (Originally published in1956–7.)

Austin, J. L. 1961b. "Performative Utterances." Reprinted in *Philosophical Papers*, Oxford: Clarendon Press, pp. 121–52. (Originally published in 1956–7.)

Austin, J. L. 1961c. "Other Minds." Reprinted in *Philosophical Papers*, Oxford: Clarendon Press, pp. 44–84. (Originally published in 1946.)

Austin, J. L. 1962. *How to do Things with Words*. Cambridge, MA: Harvard University Press.

Austin, J. L. 1964. *Sense and Sensibilia*. New York: Oxford University Press. (Based on lectures Austin gave from 1947 to 1959.)

Ayer, A. J. 1946. *Language, Truth and Logic*. New York: Dover Publications. (Originally published in 1936.)

Ayer, A. J. 1959. *Logical Positivism*. New York: The Free Press.

Ayer, A. J. 1969. "Has Austin Refuted Sense-Data?" In *Symposium on J. L. Austin*, edited by K. T. Fann, London: Routledge & Kegan Paul, pp. 284–308.

Block, Ned and Fodor, Jerry A. 1980. "What Psychological States are Not." Reprinted in *Readings in Philosophical Psychology Volume 1*, edited by Ned Block, Cambridge, MA: Harvard University Press, pp. 237–50. (Originally published in 1972.)

Bloom, Harold. http://prelectur.stanford.edu/lecturers/bloom/interviews.html [accessed 2 January 2012].

Born, Max. 1955a. "Statistical Interpretation of Quantum Mechanics." *Science*, Oct. Available online: http://nobelprize.org/nobel_prizes/physics/laureates/1954/born-lecture.pdf [accessed 2 January 2012].

A Brief History of Analytic Philosophy: From Russell to Rawls, First Edition. Stephen P. Schwartz.
© 2012 John Wiley & Sons, Inc. Published 2012 by John Wiley & Sons, Inc.

References

Born, Max. 1955b. "Continuity, Determinism, and Reality," Danish Academy of Science, Mathematics and Physics, section 30, no. 2.

Bridgman, Percy Williams. 1927. *Logic of Modern Physics*. New York: Macmillan.

Burge, Tyler. 1992. "Philosophy of Language and Mind: 1950–1990." *The Philosophical Review*,vol. 101, no. 1, Philosophy in Review: Essays on Contemporary Philosophy Jan., pp. 3–51

Carnap, Rudolf. 1937. *The Logical Syntax of Language*. London: Routledge & Kegan Paul.

Carnap, Rudolf. 1956a. *Meaning and Necessity: A Study in Semantics and Modal Logic*. Chicago: University of Chicago Press. (Originally published in 1947.)

Carnap, Rudolf. 1956b. "Empiricism, Semantics, and Ontology." Reprinted in *Meaning and Necessity: A Study in Semantics and Modal Logic*, Chicago: University of Chicago Press, pp. 205–21. (Originally published in 1950.)

Carnap, Rudolf. 1959a. "The Elimination of Metaphysics through Logical Analysis of Language." Reprinted in Ayer 1959, pp. 60–81. (Originally published in 1932.)

Carnap, Rudolf. 1959b. "The Old and the New Logic." Reprinted in Ayer 1959. pp. 133–46. (Originally published in 1930.)

Carnap, Rudolf. 1963. *The Philosophy of Rudolf Carnap*, vol. XI of the *Library of Living Philosophers*,edited by P. A. Schlipp, LaSalle, IL: Open Court Publishing Co.

Carnap, Rudolf. 1967. *The Logical Structure of the World and Pseudoproblems in Philosophy*, translated by Rolf A. George, Berkeley: University of California Press. (Originally published in 1925.)

Cavell, Stanley. 1964. "Must We Mean What We Say?" Reprinted in *Ordinary Language: Essays in Philosophical Method*, edited by V. C. Chappell, Englewood Cliffs, NJ: Prentice-Hall, pp. 75–112. (Originally published in 1958.)

Chisholm, Roderick. 1950. "The Theory of Appearing." In *Philosophical Analysis: A Collection of Essays*, edited by Max Black, Ithaca: Cornell University Press, pp. 97–112.

Chisholm, Roderick. 1957. *Perceiving: A Philosophical Study*. Ithaca: Cornell University Press.

Chomsky, Noam. 1966. *Cartesian Linguistics: A Chapter in the History of Rationalist Thought*. New York: Harper & Row.

Chomsky, Noam. 1977. *Language and Responsibility*. New York: Pantheon Books.

Chomsky, Noam. 1980. "A Review of B. F. Skinner's *Verbal Behavior*." Reprinted in *Readings in Philosophy of Psychology, Vol. 1*, edited by Ned Block, Cambridge, MA: Harvard University Press, pp. 48–63. (Originally published in 1959.)

Courant, Richard and Robbins, Herbert. 1941. *What is Mathematics? An Elementary Approach to Ideas and Methods*. Oxford: Oxford University Press.

Darwall, Stephen, Gibbard, Allan, and Railton, Peter. 1992. "Toward *Fin de Siècle* Ethics: Some Trends," *The Philosophical Review*,vol. 101, no. 1, Jan., pp. 115–89.

Davidson, Donald. 1980. "Mental Events." Reprinted in *Readings in Philosophical Psychology Vol. 1*, edited by Ned Block, Cambridge, MA: Harvard University Press, pp. 107–19. (Originally published in 1970.)

Davidson, Donald. 1985a. "Truth and Meaning." Reprinted in *Inquiries into Truth and Interpretation*, Oxford: Oxford University Press, pp. 3–36. (Originally published in 1967.)

Davidson, Donald. 1985b. "Semantics for Natural Languages." Reprinted in *Inquiries into Truth and Interpretation*, Oxford: Oxford University Press, pp. 55–64. (Originally published in 1968.)

Davidson, Donald. 1985c. "Radical Interpretation." Reprinted in *Inquiries into Truth and Interpretation*, Oxford: Oxford University Press, pp. 125–39. (Originally published in 1973.)

Davidson, Donald. 1985d. "Belief and the Basis of Meaning." Reprinted in *Inquiries into Truth and Interpretation*, Oxford: Oxford University Press, pp. 141–54. (Originally published in 1974.)

Davidson, Donald. 1985e. "On the Very Idea of a Conceptual Scheme." Reprinted in *Inquiries into Truth and Interpretation*, Oxford: Oxford University Press, pp. 183–98. (Originally published in 1974.)

Davidson, Donald. 1985f. "Thought and Talk." Reprinted in *Inquiries into Truth and Interpretation*, Oxford: Oxford University Press, pp. 155–70. (Originally published in 1975.)

Davidson, Donald. 1985g. "The Method of Truth in Metaphysics." Reprinted in *Inquiries into Truth and Interpretation*, Oxford: Oxford University Press, pp. 199–214. (Originally published in 1977.)

Davidson, Donald. 1999. "Intellectual Autobiography." In *The Philosophy of Donald Davidson*, Vol. XXVII of *The Library of Living Philosophers*, LaSalle, IL: Open Court Publishing Co., pp. 3–70.

Dennett, Daniel. 1988. "Précis of *The Intentional Stance*." *Behavioral and Brain Sciences* vol. 11, pp. 495–505.

Dennett, Daniel. n.d. "Intentional Systems Theory." Available online (no date): http://files.meetup.com/12763/intentionalsystems.pdf [accessed 2 January 2012].

Dewey, John. 1973. "The Development of American Pragmatism." Reprinted in *The Philosophy of John Dewey: vol. I, The Structure of Experience*, edited by John J. McDermott, New York: G. P. Putnam's Sons, pp. 41–58. (Originally published in 1922.)

Donnellan, Keith. 1972. "Proper Names and Identifying Descriptions." In *Semantics of Natural Language*, edited by Donald Davidson and Gilbert Harman, Boston: D. Reidel Publishing Co., pp. 356–79.

Donnellan, Keith. 1977. "Reference and Definite Descriptions." Reprinted in *Naming, Necessity, and Natural Kinds*, edited by Stephen P. Schwartz, Ithaca: Cornell University Press, pp. 42–65. (Originally published in 1966.)

Dummett, Michael. 1975. "What is a Theory of Meaning?" In *Mind and Language: Wolfson College Lectures 1974*, edited by Samuel Guttenplan, Oxford: Oxford University Press, pp. 97–138.

References

Dummett, Michael. 1978. "Can Analytical Philosophy be Systematic, and Ought it to Be?" Reprinted in *Truth and Other Enigmas*, Cambridge, MA: Harvard University Press, pp. 437–58.

Fodor, Jerry A. 1968. *Psychological Explanation*. New York: Random House.

Fodor, Jerry A. 1979. *The Language of Thought*. Cambridge, MA: Harvard University Press.

Fodor, Jerry A. 1983. *The Modularity of Mind*. Cambridge, MA: MIT Press.

Foot, Philippa. 1967. "Moral Beliefs." Reprinted in *Theories of Ethics*, edited by Philippa Foot, London: Oxford University Press, pp. 83–100. (Originally published in 1958.)

Foot, Philippa. 1968. "Moral Arguments." Reprinted in *Ethics*, edited by Judith J. Thomson and Gerald Dworkin, New York: Harper & Row, pp. 7–21. (Originally published in 1958.)

Gettier, Edmund. 1963. "Is Justified True Belief Knowledge?" *Analysis*, vol. 23, pp. 121–3.

Goodman, Nelson. 1965. *Fact, Fiction, and Forecast*. Indianapolis: The Bobbs-Merrill Company, Inc. (Originally published in 1955.)

Goodman, Nelson. 1978. *Ways of Worldmaking*. Indianapolis: Hackett Publishing Co.

Grice, Paul. 1989a. "Logic and Conversation." In *Studies in the Way of Words*, Cambridge, MA: Harvard University Press, pp. 22–85. (Originally given as lectures in 1967.)

Grice, Paul. 1989b. "Postwar Oxford Philosophy." In *Studies in the Way of Words*, Cambridge, MA: Harvard University Press, pp. 171–80.

Grice, Paul. 1989c. "Presupposition and Conversational Implicature." In *Studies in the Way of Words*, Cambridge, MA: Harvard University Press, pp. 269–82.

Hahn, Hans. 1959. "Logic, Mathematics and Knowledge." Reprinted in Ayer 1959, pp. 147–64. (Originally published in 1933.)

Hall, A. Rupert and Hall, Marie Boas. 1964. *A Brief History of Science*. New York: New American Library.

Hare, R. M. 1952. *The Language of Morals*. Oxford: Oxford University Press.

Hare, R. M. 1963. *Freedom and Reason*. Oxford: Oxford University Press.

Hempel, Carl. 1950. "Problems and Changes in the Empiricist Criterion of Meaning." *Revue Internationale de Philosophie*, vol. 11, pp. 41–63.

Hempel, Carl. 1965. "Empiricist Criteria of Cognitive Significance: Problems and Changes." In *Aspects of Scientific Explanation*, New York: The Free Press, pp. 101–22.

James, William. 1955. *Pragmatism and Four Essays from The Meaning of Truth*. Cleveland: The World Publishing Co. (Originally published in 1907.)

Kim, Jaegwon. 1989. "The Myth of Nonreductive Materialism." In *Proceedings and Addresses of the American Philosophical Association*, vol. 63, no. 3, Newark, DE: The American Philosophical Association, Nov., pp. 31–47.

Kripke, Saul. 1971. "Semantical Considerations on Modal Logic." Reprinted in *Reference and Modality*, edited by Leonard Linsky, London: Oxford University Press, pp. 63–72. (Originally published in 1963.)

Kripke, Saul. 1976. "Is There a Problem about Substitutional Quantification?" In *Truth and Meaning: Essays in Semantics*, edited by Gareth Evans and John McDowell, Oxford: Oxford University Press, pp. 325–419.

Kripke, Saul. 1980. *Naming and Necessity*. Cambridge, MA: Harvard University Press. (Originally published in 1972.)

Kuhn, Thomas. 1970. *The Structure of Scientific Revolutions*. Chicago, University of Chicago Press. (Originally published in 1962.)

Lewis, David. 1973. *Counterfactuals*. Cambridge, MA: Harvard University Press.

Lewis, David. 1979. "Counterpart Theory and Quantified Modal Logic." Reprinted in *The Possible and the Actual: Readings in the Metaphysics of Modality*, edited by Michael J. Loux, Ithaca: Cornell University Press, pp. 110–28. (Originally published in 1968.)

Lewis, David. 1983. "Scorekeeping in a Language Game." Reprinted in *Philosophical Papers, vol. I*, New York: Oxford University Press, pp. 233–49.

Lewis, David. 1986. *On the Plurality of Worlds*. Oxford: Basil Blackwell.

Lewis, David. 1996. "Elusive Knowledge." *Australasian Journal of Philosophy*, vol. 74, no. 4, Dec., pp. 549–67.

Malcolm, Norman. 1951. "Philosophy for Philosophers." *The Philosophical Review*, vol. 60, no. 3, July, pp. 329–40.

Malcolm, Norman. 1965. "Anselm's Ontological Arguments." Reprinted in *The Ontological Argument: From St. Anselm to Contemporary Philosophers*, edited by Alvin Plantinga, Garden City, NY: Doubleday & Co., pp. 136–59.

Monk, Ray. 1990. *Ludwig Wittgenstein: The Duty of Genius*. New York: The Free Press.

Montague, Richard. 1974. *Formal Philosophy*. New Haven, CT: Yale University Press.

Moore, G. E. 1959. "The Refutation of Idealism." Reprinted in *Philosophical Studies*. Patterson, NJ: Littlefield Adams & Co. (Originally published in 1903.)

Moore, G. E. 1960. *Principia Ethica*. Cambridge: Cambridge University Press. (Originally published in 1903.)

Moore, G. E. 1993. "A Defence of Common Sense." Reprinted in *G. E. Moore: Selected Writings*, edited by Thomas Baldwin, London: Routledge. (Originally published in 1925.)

Nagel, Thomas. 1980. "What Is It Like to Be a Bat?" Reprinted in *Readings in Philosophical Psychology, vol. 1*, edited by Ned Block, Cambridge, MA: Harvard University Press, pp. 159–68. (Originally published in 1974.)

Neurath, Otto. 1959. "Sociology and Physicalism." Reprinted in Ayer 1959. (Originally published in 1931.)

Nozick, Robert. 1974. *Anarchy, State, and Utopia*. New York: Basic Books, Inc.

Nussbaum, Martha C. 1999. *Sex and Social Justice*. Oxford: Oxford University Press.

Nussbaum, Martha C. 2004. "Beyond the Social Contract: Capabilities and Social Justice," *Oxford Development Studies*, vol. 32, no.1, March, pp. 3–18.

Plantinga, Alvin. 1974a. *The Nature of Necessity*. Oxford: Oxford University Press.

References

Plantinga, Alvin. 1974b. *God, Freedom, and Evil*. New York: Harper & Row.

Plantinga, Alvin. 1979a. "Transworld Identity or Worldbound Individuals?" Reprinted in *The Possible and the Actual: Readings in the Metaphysics of Modality*, edited by Michael J. Loux, Ithaca: Cornell University Press, pp. 146–65.

Plantinga, Alvin. 1979b. "Actualism and Possible Worlds." Reprinted in *The Possible and the Actual: Readings in the Metaphysics of Modality*, edited by Michael J. Loux, Ithaca: Cornell University Press, pp. 253–73.

Popper, Karl. 1963. *Conjectures and Refutations: The Growth of Scientific Knowledge*. New York: Harper & Row.

Popper, Karl. 1971. *The Open Society and Its Enemies*. Princeton: Princeton University Press. (Orginally published in 1945.)

Putnam, Hilary. 1975a. "The Nature of Mental States." Reprinted in *Mind, Language and Reality: Philosophical Papers, vol. 2*, Cambridge: Cambridge University Press, pp. 429–40. (Originally published in 1967.)

Putnam, Hilary. 1975b. "Philosophy and Our Mental Life." Reprinted in *Mind, Language and Reality: Philosophical Papers, vol. 2*, Cambridge: Cambridge University Press, pp. 291–303.

Putnam, Hilary. 1975c. "The Meaning of 'Meaning'." In *Minnesota Studies in the Philosophy of Science, Vol. VII: Language, Mind, and Knowledge*, edited by Keith Gunderson, Minneapolis: University of Minnesota Press, pp. 131–93.

Putnam, Hilary. 1977a. "Is Semantics Possible?" Reprinted in *Naming, Necessity, and Natural Kinds*, edited by Stephen P. Schwartz, Ithaca: Cornell University Press, pp. 102–18. (Originally published in 1970.)

Putnam, Hilary. 1977b. "Meaning and Reference." Reprinted in *Naming, Necessity, and Natural Kinds*, edited by Stephen P. Schwartz, Ithaca: Cornell University Press, pp. 119–32. (Originally published in 1973.)

Putnam, Hilary. 1978. *Meaning and the Moral Sciences*. Boston: Routledge & Kegan Paul.

Putnam, Hilary. 1981. *Reason, Truth and History*. Cambridge: Cambridge University Press.

Putnam, Hilary. 1994. "Why Functionalism Didn't Work." In *Words and Life*, edited by James Conant, Cambridge, MA: Harvard University Press, pp. 441–59.

Quine, Willard Van Orman. 1960. *Word and Object*. Cambridge, MA: MIT Press.

Quine, Willard Van Orman. 1961a. "On What There Is." Reprinted in *From a Logical Point of View: Logico-Philosophical Essays*, New York: Harper & Row, pp. 1–19. (This is a revised version of an article that was originally published in 1948.)

Quine, Willard Van Orman. 1961b. "Two Dogmas of Empiricism." Reprinted in *From a Logical Point of View: Logico-Philosophical Essays*, New York: Harper & Row, pp. 20–46. (Originally published in 1951.)

Quine, Willard Van Orman. 1961c. "Reference and Modality." Reprinted in *From a Logical Point of View: Logico-Philosophical Essays*, New York: Harper & Row, pp. 139–59.

Quine, Willard Van Orman. 1966a. "Mr Strawson on Logical Theory." Reprinted in *The Ways of Paradox and Other Essays*, New York: Random House, pp. 135–55. (Originally published in 1953.)

Quine, Willard Van Orman. 1966b. "On Carnap's Views on Ontology." Reprinted in *The Ways of Paradox and Other Essays*, New York: Random House, pp. 126–34. (Originally published in 1951.)

Quine, Willard Van Orman. 1966c. "Three Grades of Modal Involvement." Reprinted in *The Ways of Paradox and Other Essays*, New York: Random House, pp. 156–74. (Originally published in 1953.)

Quine, Willard Van Orman. 1966d. "Reply to Professor Marcus." Reprinted in *The Ways of Paradox and Other Essays*, New York: Random House, pp. 175–82.

Quine, Willard Van Orman. 1969. "Epistemology Naturalized." In *Ontological Relativity and Other Essays*, New York: Columbia University Press, pp. 69–90.

Quine, Willard Van Orman. 1974. *The Roots of Reference*. LaSalle, IL: Open Court Publishing Co.

Quine, Willard Van Orman. 1981a. "On the Very Idea of a Third Dogma." Reprinted in *Theories and Things*, Cambridge, MA: Harvard University Press, pp. 38–42.

Quine, Willard Van Orman. 1981b. "On the Individuation of Attributes." Reprinted in *Theories and Things*, Cambridge, MA: Harvard University Press, pp. 100–12. (Originally published in 1975.)

Rawls, John. 1971. *A Theory of Justice*. Cambridge, MA: Belknap Press.

Rorty, Richard. 1979. *Philosophy and the Mirror of Nature*. Princeton: Princeton University Press.

Rorty, Richard. 1982. *Consequences of Pragmatism: Essays: 1972–1980*. Minneapolis: University of Minnesota Press.

Russell, Bertrand. 1897. *An Essay on the Foundations of Geometry*. Cambridge: Cambridge University Press.

Russell, Bertrand. 1913. "The Philosophical Implications of Mathematical Logic." *Monist*, Oct., pp. 481–93.

Russell, Bertrand. 1914. "The Relation of Sense Data to Physics." Reprinted in *Mysticism and Logic and Other Essays*, London: Longmans, Green & Co., 1919, pp. 145–79.

Russell, Bertrand. 1919. *Introduction to Mathematical Philosophy*. London: George Allen & Unwin, Ltd.

Russell, Bertrand. 1933. (Personal essay with no title.) In *Living Philosophies: A Series of Intimate Credos* (no editor), New York: Simon & Schuster, pp. 9–19.

Russell, Bertrand. 1945. *A History of Western Philosophy*. New York: Simon & Schuster.

Russell, Bertrand. 1957. "Mr Strawson on Referring." *Mind*, vol. 66, no. 263, July, pp. 385–89.

Russell, Bertrand. 1959a. *The Problems of Philosophy*. London: Oxford University Press. (Originally published in 1912.)

References

Russell, Bertrand. 1959b. "Logical Atomism." Reprinted in Ayer 1959, pp. 31–50. (Originally published in 1924.)

Russell, Bertrand. 1963. "My Mental Development." In *The Philosophy of Bertrand Russell*, edited by Paul Schlipp, New York: Harper & Row, pp. 3–20. (Originally published in 1944.)

Russell, Bertrand. 1968. *The Autobiography of Bertrand Russell: vol. 1, 1872 – 1914.* New York: Bantam.

Russell, Bertrand. 1971. "The Philosophy of Logical Atomism." In *Logic and Knowledge: Essays 1901–1950*, edited by Robert Charles Marsh, New York: Capricorn Books, pp. 175–281. (Originally delivered as lectures in 1918.)

Russell, Bertrand. 1973. *Essays in Analysis.* Edited by Douglas Lackey. New York: George Braziller, Inc.

Russell, Bertrand. 1997. *Science and Religion.* Oxford: Oxford University Press. (Originally published in 1935.)

Ryle, Gilbert. 1949a. "Discussion: *Meaning and Necessity.*" *Philosophy*, vol. 24, no. 88, Jan., pp. 69–76.

Ryle, Gilbert. 1949b. *The Concept of Mind.* New York: Barnes & Noble.

Ryle, Gilbert. 1957. "Final Discussion." In *The Nature of Metaphysics*, edited by D. F. Pears, London: Macmillan, 1957, pp. 144–5.

Ryle, Gilbert. 1962. *Dilemmas.* Cambridge: Cambridge University Press.

Ryle, Gilbert. 1968. "Systematically Misleading Expressions." Reprinted in *Logic and Language* (First Series), edited by Antony Flew, Oxford: Basil Blackwell, pp. 11–36. (Originally published in 1931.)

Ryle, Gilbert. 1971. *Collected Essays: 1929–1968.* London: Routledge.

Schlick, Moritz. 1962. *Problems of Ethics.* Translated from the German by David Rynin. New York: Dover Publications. (Originally published in 1930.)

Searle, John R. 1963. "Proper Names." Reprinted in *Philosophy and Ordinary Language*, edited by Charles E. Caton, Urbana, IL: University of Illinois Press, pp. 154–61.

Searle, John R. 1969. *Speech Acts: An Essay in the Philosophy of Language.* Cambridge: Cambridge University Press.

Searle, John R. 1981. "Minds, Brains, and Programs." Reprinted in *The Mind's I: Fantasies and Reflections on Self and Soul*, edited by Douglas R. Hofstadter and Daniel C. Dennett, New York: Basic Books, pp. 351–73.

Sellars, Wilfrid. 1973. "Empiricism and the Philosophy of Mind." Reprinted in *Empirical Knowledge: Readings from Contemporary Sources*, edited by Roderick M. Chisholm and Robert J. Swartz, Englewood Cliffs, NJ: Prentice-Hall, pp. 471–541. (Originally published in 1956.)

Sider, Theodore. 2001. *Four-Dimensionalism.* Oxford: Clarendon Press.

Singer, Peter. 1975. *Animal Liberation.* New York: The New York Review of Books.

Singer, Peter. 1979. *Practical Ethics.* Cambridge: Cambridge University Press.

Soames, Scott. 2003a. *Philosophical Analysis in the Twentieth Century, vol. 1: The Dawn of Analysis.* Princeton: Princeton University Press.

Soames, Scott. 2003b. *Philosophical Analysis in the Twentieth Century, vol. 2: The Age of Meaning*. Princeton: Princeton University Press.

Stalnaker, Robert. 1979. "Possible Worlds." Reprinted in *The Possible and the Actual*, edited by Michael J. Loux, Ithaca: Cornell University Press, pp. 225–34.

Stalnaker, Robert. 1991. "A Theory of Conditionals." Reprinted in *Conditionals*, edited by Frank Jackson, Oxford: Oxford University Press, pp. 28–45. (Originally published in 1968.)

Stevenson, Charles L. 1938. "Persuasive Definitions." *Mind*, vol. 47, no. 187, July, pp. 331–50.

Stevenson, Charles L. 1944. *Ethics and Language*. New Haven: Yale University Press.

Stevenson, Charles L. 1949. "The Nature of Ethical Disagreement." Reprinted in *Readings in Philosophical Analysis*, edited by Herbert Feigl and Wilfrid Sellars, New York: Appleton-Century-Crofts, pp. 587–93.

Stevenson, Charles L. 1959. "The Emotive Meaning of Ethical Terms." Reprinted in Ayer 1959, pp. 264–281. (Originally published in 1937.)

Strawson, Peter. 1963. *Individuals: An Essay in Descriptive Metaphysics*. Garden City, NY: Doubleday & Co. (Originally published in 1959.)

Strawson, Peter. 1971. "On Referring." Reprinted in *Readings in the Philosophy of Language*, edited by Jay F. Rosenberg and Charles Travis, Englewood Cliffs, NJ: Prentice-Hall, pp. 175–95. (Originally published in 1950.)

Stroll, Avrum. 2000. *Twentieth-Century Analytic Philosophy*. New York: Columbia University Press.

Tarski, Alfred. 1949. "The Semantic Conception of Truth." Reprinted in *Readings in Philosophical Analysis*, edited by Herbert Feigl and Wilfrid Sellars, New York: Appleton-Century-Crofts, Inc. (Originally published in 1944.)

Urmson, J. O. 1956. *Philosophical Analysis: Its Development Between the Two World Wars*. Oxford: Clarendon Press.

Warnock, G. J. 1958. *English Philosophy since 1990*. London: Oxford University Press.

Warnock, G. J. 1969. "John Langshaw Austin, a Biographical Sketch." In *Symposium on J. L. Austin*, edited by K. T. Fann, London: Routledge & Kegan Paul.

Weitz, Morris. 1953. "Oxford Philosophy." *The Philosophical Review*, vol. 26, no. 2, April, pp. 187–233.

Williamson, Timothy. 2002. "Necessary Existents." *Royal Institute of Philosophy Supplement*, no. 51: pp. 233–52.

Wittgenstein, Ludwig. 1961a. *Notebooks 1914–1916*. Edited by G. H. von Wright and G. E. M. Anscombe, translated by G. E. M. Anscombe. Oxford: Basil Blackwell.

Wittgenstein, Ludwig. 1961b. *Tractatus Logico-Philosophicus: The German Text of Ludwig Wittgenstein's Logisch-philosophische Abhandlung, with a translation by D. F. Pears and B. F. McGuiness and with the introduction by Bertrand*

References

Russell, FRS. London: Routledge & Kegan Paul. (Originally published in 1921.)

Wittgenstein, Ludwig. 1969. *On Certainty*. Edited by G. E. M. Anscombe and G. H. von Wright, translated by Denis Paul and G. E. M. Anscombe. New York: J. & J. Harper Editions. (Originally written in 1951.)

Wittgenstein, Ludwig. 2009. *Philosophische Untersuchungen / Philosophical Investigations*. Revised 4th Edition by P. M. S. Hacker and Joachim Schulte, translated by G. E. M. Anscombe, P. M. S. Hacker, and Joachim Schulte. Chichester, UK: Blackwell Publishing. (Originally published in 1953.)

Index

A Brief History of Analytic Philosophy: From Russell to Rawls, First Edition. Stephen P. Schwartz.
© 2012 John Wiley & Sons, Inc. Published 2012 by John Wiley & Sons, Inc.

epistemology (*continued*)
 naturalized, 99–101, 113, 322
 Oxford philosophers on, 99,
  152–3, 155
 recent, 312–16, 322
 see also empiricism, fallibilism,
  Gettier, pragmatism,
  rationalism, skepticism
essence, 228, 243, 262
 vs accident, 208, 209, 234
 actualism and, 220–2, 228
 general, 234, 241
 individual, 214, 220–2, 224–5,
  234
 Kripke on, 251–2
 of a natural kind, 251–2
 of philosophy, 5, 19
 Quine on, 208–9, 221
 Wittgenstein on, 121, 129, 133,
  241–2, 252
essentialism, 214, 240
 Aristotelian, 207–8, 210, 253,
  323
 Quine on, 207–10
eternalism, 309–10
ethics, 3, 15, 16, 21, 148, 206, 281,
  264–298
 Anscombe on, 155, 275–6, 280
 applied, 265, 272, 281, 283, 284,
  319, 322
 Ayer on, 67–8, 270, 272–3, 278–9,
  298, 317
 consequentialist vs deontological,
  280, 296–7
 current, 317–21
 ethical intuitionism, 269–70
 Foot on, 276–80, 318
 Hare on, 155, 272–5, 278, 279, 298,
  317
 Kantian, 266–8, 280, 285–6, 297,
  298
 logical positivists' views on, 57–8,
  60–1, 67–8, 78, 83, 110–11,
  155, 264–6, 270, 272, 275,
  278, 279
 metaethics, 155, 265, 296, 318

Moore on, 29n, 264, 266–8, 275,
  278
moral fictionalism, 317–18, 321
moral psychology, 322
non-cognitivism, 67–8, 264, 266,
  269–76, 278–9, 281, 298, 317
Nozick on, 288–9, 291
Nussbaum on, 320–1
ordinary language philosophers'
  views about, 154–5
Popper on, 287–8, 291
prescriptivism, 272–5
Putnam on, 104, 110
Rawls on, 285–87, 290–6,
  318–20
realism vs anti-realism, 297–8,
  318
Singer on, 281–4
Stevenson on, 269–72, 279, 295,
  298
substantive and normative, 265,
  266
in the *Tractatus*, 56–8
utilitarianism, 68, 267, 280, 284,
  285–6, 290, 292–3, 297, 319
virtue ethics, 155, 280, 323
see also fact/value distinction,
  naturalistic fallacy, open
  question argument
excluded middle, 34, 55, 89, 302n
experimental philosophy, 316, 323
extension, *see* intension and
  extension
extensionalism, 209, 212, 235
externalism, 107–8
 of mental contents, 259–60

fact/value distinction, 104, 109–10,
  264, 273, 278–81
fallibilism, 115, 289, 295
falsifiability criterion, 81–2, 87–9
Feigl, Herbert, 58, 68n
Fichte, Johann Gottlieb, 27, 43–4,
  47n
Fodor, Jerry, 303, 305–7
folk psychology, *see* psychology/folk